Nathanael West: The Art of His Life

BOOKS BY JAY MARTIN

NATHANAEL WEST:
  THE ART OF HIS LIFE

HARVESTS OF CHANGE:
  AMERICAN LITERATURE 1865–1914

CONRAD AIKEN: A LIFE OF HIS ART

Nathanael West
The Art of His Life
by Jay Martin

CARROLL & GRAF PUBLISHERS, INC.
New York

To my dear wife, Helen,
and to my children—
Helen Elizabeth, Laura Ann, Jay Herbert
—who taught me how to follow,
with love, the lives of others.

Preface

This biography of Nathanael West could not have been written without the cooperation of many people; the acknowledgments which I make here can go merely part way in indicating the indebtedness I feel.

First and last, my chief debt is to Laura and S. J. Perelman, West's sister and brother-in-law, who have done everything possible to aid me in this work. They have submitted to taped interviews, answered letters, turned West's manuscripts over to me, given me introductions to West's friends, been patient with my progress, found photographs of West for me, and counseled me at every stage. No acknowledgment to them could be adequate. Only the book, if it is good enough, could repay them for their generosity.

A number of people read this book in various drafts. Roy Harvey Pearce, who labored through my first version, pointed out the lines for future revision. The late Josephine Herbst read a second version and modified my views about the political and intellectual life of the twenties and thirties. At a crucial stage, several other critics read the third draft: A. Dwight Culler, Maynard Mack, Louis L. Martz, Norman Holmes Pearson, and Robert Penn Warren. Dr. Albert Rothenberg advised me on the psychoanalytic aspects of West's life. The fourth draft was read by Alfred Kazin, who graciously encouraged me to be satisfied, and then gently encouraged me to go further. Hannah and Matthew Josephson read the same version and gave me the benefit of their expert knowledge about the construction of biographies. Finally, the Perelmans read the book and aided me in the preparation of the version now published.

My account of West's life is derived from documents, interviews, and correspondence.

Laura and S. J. Perelman loaned me the papers of Nathanael West remaining in their possession. These constitute nearly 700 separate pieces, consisting mostly of correspondence, but including short stories, poems, sketches, clippings, and personal items. These papers provided the crucial starting point for a life of West.

During my research I collected a number of additional documents. For these I wish to thank: M. K. Abernethy (for files of *Contempo*), Shana Alexander (for aid in searching Time-Life files), Garnet McCoy of the Archives of American Art (for letters of Hilaire Hiler referring to Nathanael West), the Cedars of Lebanon Hospital, Los Angeles (for letting me inspect West's medical records), Bennett Cerf (for allowing me access to the Random House files and for Xeroxes of several West letters), the City Soviets of Vilna, U.S.S.R. (for a copy of the birth certificate of Anna Wallenstein Weinstein), Robert M. Coates (for letting me copy West's inscription to him in *The Day of the Locust*), Gerald Ayres of Columbia Pictures (for copies of West's scripts and original stories at Columbia), William T. Conklin, New York Senator (for obtaining a copy of West's birth certificate), Josephine Conway (for several letters written to her by West), Malcolm Cowley (for a West letter), Walter J. Degnan, Principal of De Witt Clinton High School (for the academic transcripts of West and his cousins), Alice Dougall (for letting me see West's inscription to her in *The Dream Life of Balso Snell* [copy number 1] and for photographs of West), Professor Victor Erlich (for a translation of a Russian document), John Erwin (for a translation of an Italian document), James T. Farrell (for allowing me to read an unpublished essay and his manuscript notes on West), Donald Gallup (for a copy of *Il Mare*), Richard Gehman (for giving me copies of letters written to him by Josephine Herbst, I. J. Kapstein, James T. Farrell, and others, as well as for letting me copy an unpublished essay by him on West and a sheaf of notes taken after interviews concerning West), Gordon N. Ray (for giving me a copy of West's application to the John Simon Guggenheim Foundation, including letters of recommendation by F. Scott Fitzgerald, Malcolm Cowley, Edmund Wilson, and George S. Kaufman), the management of Harcourt, Brace (for allowing me to inspect their business files concerning *Miss Lonelyhearts*), Josephine Herbst (for letting me see letters written to her by West), Louise M. Houseman (for allowing me to Xerox West's grammar-school records), Herbert Hughes, (for giving me a copy of the inquisition concerning West's death), Rabbi Richard Israel (for the translation of a Hebrew document), Dr. Saul Jarcho (for a genealogy of the Wallenstein family and for Russian documents concerning the Wallensteins), Matthew Josephson (for a letter written by Ruth McKenney to Hannah Josephson), I. J. Kapstein (for an advertisement of *The Dream Life of Balso Snell* and for getting me access to a transcript of West's undergraduate record at Brown University), the Library of Congress Photoduplication Service (for a Xerox of *Gentlemen, the War!*), James F. Light (for allowing me to inspect the materials which he gathered during his research on West), Edith Tolkin of Metro-Goldwyn-Mayer (for sending me a copy of West's *Flight South*), Jerrold Moore (for getting me sheet music to "Miss Lonely Hearts"), the Motion Picture Academy (for reviews of West's films), James Laughlin and Robert MacGregor (for giving me access to the West files at New Directions), Charles A. Pearce (for letting me see correspondence concerning Eileen McKenney), Norman Holmes Pearson (for allowing me to copy letters by Hilaire Hiler and Robert McAlmon concerning West), Richard Pratt (for allowing me to use the inscription in his copy of *A Cool Million*), Alexander P. Clark, Curator of Manuscripts in Princeton University (for sending me copies of West–Fitzgerald letters), Vernon Harbin of R.K.O. Radio Pictures (for letting me read West's scripts, treatments, and business files at R.K.O.), Dr. Brae Rafferty (for a photograph of a drawing of him by West), Daniel J. Bloomberg, Vice President of Republic Corporation (for allowing me to read the scripts and business files concerning West at Republic Studios), Hinda Rhodes, West's sister (for a West letter and photographs), Beatrice Mathieu Roos (for several letters and telegrams sent to her by West), Wells Root (for the original of notes on West), Gerald Roselle of Camp Paradox (for copies of the camp magazine during West's years there), William P. Saldini (for aid in obtaining a West document), John Sanford (for West photographs and copies of letters, journal entries by Ruth Shapiro, a newspaper article, and letters by S. J. Perelman and Philip D. Shapiro about West and his family), Joseph Schrank (for a copy of the final version of *Good Hunting*), Budd Schulberg (for giving me a copy of West's inscription to him in *The Day of the Locust*), Douglas H. Shepard (for sending me a Xerox of his unpublished work on the sources of *A Cool Million*), Edwin A. Sy, Curator of Special Collections at the State University of New York at Buffalo (for a copy of a letter by West to W. C. Williams), Caroline Lee Sturak (for a bibliography on the Hollywood novel), Erwin Swann (for letting me inspect copies of several books once owned by West), Sherwood A. Barrow, Recorder, and Frank A. Tredinnick, Jr., Vice President, of Tufts University (for giving me access to West's record at Tufts), the United States Department of State, Barbara Hartman authentication officer (for a Xerox of West's passport file and photographs), Vera Culwell and Michael Ludmer of Universal Pictures (for access to West's scripts and business files there), Brooke Whiting, Literary Manuscripts Librarian at the University of California at Los Angeles (for letting me inspect the manuscript of *A Cool Million*), James L. Wallenstein (for West photographs), and Edmund Wilson (for a copy of an entry in his journal concerning West).

The following people allowed me to make tape recordings of our conversation—sometimes several conversations—concerning Nathanael West: Leo Ars, Herbert Biberman, John Bright, George Brounoff, Lester Cole, Josephine Conway, James T. Farrell, Leonard Fields, Sheridan Gibney, Jesse L. Greenstein, Jeanne Cole Haber, Josephine Herbst, Ann Honeycutt, Boris Ingster, Sidney Jarcho, Matthew Josephson, I. J. Kapstein, Charles Katz, Burt Kelly, Robert W. Kenny, Arthur Kober, Ring Lardner, Jr., John Howard Lawson, Darrell McGowan, Jeremiah P. Mahoney, Henriette Martin, George Milburn, Dorothy Parker, Laura and S. J. Perelman, Richard Pratt, Wells Root, John Sanford, Budd Schulberg, Dalton Trumbo, James L. Wallenstein, and Elizabeth Wilson, comprising forty-six tapes.

I interviewed the following people without the use of a tape recorder: M. K. Abernethy, Cecelia Ager, Sy Bartlett, Claude Binyon, Michael Blankfort, Peter Blume, Kay Boyle, Lazlo Bush-Fekete, Robert B. Campbell, Bertha Case, Bennett Cerf, Robert

M. Coates, Malcolm Cowley, Edward Dahlberg, Tillman Daley, Frank Davis, Alice Dougall, Guy Endore, John Fante, Leonard S. Field, Richard Gehman, Michael Gold, Sheilah Graham, Albert and Frances Goodrich Hackett, Raymond Healy, Lillian Hellman, Stanley Edgar Hyman, Dan and Lilith James, Dr. Saul Jarcho, Martin Kamin, Aben Kandel, John Kazanjian, Alfred Kazin, Louis Kronenberger, Richard Lehan, Melvin Levy, Allan Lewis, James F. Light, Milton Lubovitsky, Philip Lukin, St. Clair McKelway, Ruth McKenney, Benjamin Medford, Edwin A. Meyer, Yetive Moss, Robert Newman, Charles Norman, Jo Pagano, Charles A. Pearce, Laura and S. J. Perelman, Dr. Brae Rafferty, Leane Zugsmith Randau, Hinda Rhodes, Harry Riegel, Stanley Roberts, Beatrice Mathieu Roos, Wells Root, Dr. Albert Rothenberg, Ernest E. Schaible, Joseph Schrank, Gilbert Seldes, Sol D. Seldin, George Sklar, Milton Sperling, Sylvia Sullivan, Erwin Swann, Mary Tankenson, Shepard Traube, Nathan Weinstein, Lester Wells, Samuel W. West, John Wexley, Professor William White, Tiba Garlin Willner, and Edmund Wilson.

A still larger part of my research was conducted through extensive correspondence with the following people who responded to my queries: Daniel Aaron, Cyrilly Abels, M. K. Abernethy, Conrad Aiken, Nelson Algren, Richard D. Altick, Harry J. Alderman of the American Jewish Committee, Garnet McCoy of the Archives of American Art, Boris Aronson, Leo Ars, Peggy Bacon, Carlos Baker, Djuna Barnes, Sylvan Barnett, Sy Bartlett, Cedric Belfrage, Alvah Bessie, A. I. Bezzerides, Edward Biberman, Herbert Biberman, Claude Binyon, Michael Blankfort, Harold Block, Louise Bogan, Kay Boyle, Harry Bridges, John Bright, Dr. Burton K. Brock, George Brounoff, Earl Browder, Felix E. Browder, Milton E. Noble, Registrar of Brown University, Virginia H. Bourne of the Brown University Alumni Association, Christine D. Hathaway of the Brown University Library, Sidney Buchman, Kenneth Burke, William H. Butler, Erskine Caldwell, The State of California Department of the Highway Patrol, Angus Cameron, Victor Candell, Robert Cantwell, Harry Carlisle, Morris Carnovsky, Robert Carson, Bertha Case, Vera Caspary, Bennett Cerf, John R. Chamberlain, John Cheever, Jerome Chodorov, LeRoy Clayfield, Ben C. Clough, Robert M. Coates, John Cogley, Lester Cole, Gerald Ayres and David Dworski of Columbia Pictures, Wesley

First of the Columbia University Alumni Records Center and Office of University Relations, Dorothy B. Commins, Marc Connelly, Jack Conroy, Josephine Conway, Dorothy Covici, Pascal Covici, Jr., Malcolm Cowley, Mrs. E. E. Cummings, Edward Dahlberg, Tillman Daley, David C. DeJong, Frank Di Gioia, the Directors Guild of America, John Dos Passos, Alice and Bernard Dougall, Melvyn Douglas, the Dramatists Guild, Marcel Duchamp, F. W. Dupee, Doris Post of the Dwight School, Max Eastman, Edward Eliscu, Guy Endore, Max Ernst, Clifton Fadiman, William Fadiman, John Fante, Howard Fast, Janet Flanner, Deborah Jarcho Fishman, Angel Flores, James T. Farrell, Leonard S. Field, Waldo Frank, Eleanor Friede, Melvin Friedman, Daniel Fuchs, Lewis Galantière, Erle Stanley Gardner, Richard Gehman, Renne W. Geller, Martha Gellhorn, Ira Gershwin, Sheridan Gibney, Ann Girsdansky, William Goetz, William Goldhurst, Jay Gorney, Jesse L. Greenstein, Horace Gregory, Albert and Frances Goodrich Hackett, Alma Hallenborg, Albert Halper, Walter Pilkington, librarian of Hamilton College, Maurice Hanline, E. Y. Harburg, Henry Hart, William T. Hastings, John Hawkes, Helen Hayes, Leland Hayward, Lillian Hellman, Josephine Herbst, Granville Hicks, Hilaire Hiler, Jr., Doris Holmes, Albert Hirschfeld, Frederick Hoffman, Ann Honeycutt, John Houseman, Sonora Babb Howe, Langston Hughes, Rolfe Humphries, Ian Hunter, Boris Ingster, Sam Jaffe, Sidney Jarcho, Dan and Lilith James, Dr. Saul Jarcho, Barbara Kahn, Leonard Kalisch, I. J. Kapstein, Elia Kazan, Alfred Kazin, Matthew Keating, the Kenmore Hotel, Nettie King, Alfred Knopf, H. S. Kraft, Norman Krasna, Louis Kronenberger, Frances Scott Lanahan, John Howard Lawson, Max Lerner, Julian Levi, Meyer Levin, Melvin Levy, Anne Finsthwait of *Life*, Maxim Lieber, Harold Loeb, Susanne W. Loeb, Walter Lowenfels, Marvin Lowenthal, Philip Lukin, Mary McCall, Jr., Stuart McGowan, St. Clair McKelway, Ruth McKenney, Archibald MacLeish, Carey McWilliams, Jeremiah P. Mahoney, Albert Maltz, Joseph L. Mankiewicz, Fletcher Martin, Groucho Marx, Sam Marx, Edwin A. Meyer, George Milburn, Henry Miller, Joseph Mitchell, Arthur Mizener, John J. Monk, Harry T. Moore, Marianne Moore, Yetive Moss, Mount Sinai Hospital, Hadley R. Mowrer, Lewis Mumford, Gorham B. Munson, Robert Nathan, Marie Naylor, Jacques

Nevard, Deputy Police Commissioner for Press Relations in the New York City Police Department, Robert MacGregor of New Directions, Truda T. Weil, Assistant Superintendent, New York City Board of Education, New York University Alumni Office, Edward Newhouse, Robert Newman, Mrs. Dudley Nichols, Charles Norman, Joseph North, Maxwell Nurnberg, Georgia O'Keeffe, Arthur Ornitz, Herbert Ortman, Paul Osborn, Frederick Packard, Jo Pagano, Dorothy Parker, Russell Patterson, Charles A. Pearce, Laura and S. J. Perelman, Leo D. Harris, Executive Vice President of Pierce Brothers Mortuaries, Henry Dan Piper, C. Wilson Porrier, Richard Pratt, the Producers Guild, Dr. Brae Rafferty, Leane Zugsmith Randau, Charles Reznikoff, Hinda Rhodes, Ira S. Robbins, Melvin C. Robbins, Stanley Roberts, Edward G. Robinson, Richard Rodgers, Frederick H. Rohlfs, Harold Rome, Beatrice Mathieu Roos, Lin Root, Wells Root, Gerald Roselle, Grace Ross, Leo Rosten, Muriel Rukeyser, Allen Saalburg, George Samter, John Sanford, William Saroyan, Ernest E. Schaible, Dore Schary, Joseph Schrank, Budd Schulberg, the Screen Actors Guild, George Seldes, Gilbert Seldes, Irwin Shaw, Irving Shulman, Belle Becker Sideman, Sol C. Siegel, Albert O. Silverman, George Sklar, Gene Solo, Nina Spark, Leonard Spigelgass, William Steig, John Steinbeck, Irving Stone, Harold Strauss, Arthur Strawn, the Hotel Sutton, Allen Tate, Roy V. Titus, George Tobias, Leo Townsend, William R. Trask, Shepard Traube, Frank A. Tredinnick Jr., Lionel Trilling, Dalton Trumbo, Andrew Turnbull, Twentieth-Century United Artists, Parker Tyler, United States Department of Immigration and Naturalization (James E. Smith, District Director), United States Department of the Navy, United States Department of State, University of North Carolina Alumni Association, Dr. Michael Uris, the Rare Book Collection in the Charles Patterson Van Pelt Library of the University of Pennsylvania, Mark Van Doren, Peter Viertel, James L. Wallenstein, K. M. Sieling, Personnel Director of Walt Disney Productions, Lynd Ward, Robert Penn Warren, Dr. Nathan Weinstein, Lester Wells, M. R. Werner, Glenway Wescott, Samuel W. West, Neda M. Westlake, John Wexley, E. B. White, William White, Patricia C. F. Mandell, Research Curator of the Whitney Museum, George Wickes, the William Morris Agency,

Florence Williams, Edmund Wilson, Elizabeth Wilson, Edwin Wintermute, Yvor Winters, the Writers Guild of America (West), Philip Wylie, YIVO Institute for Jewish Research, Yale University Library, and Louis Zukofsky.

My account of West's life is derived entirely from these sources; West's papers are held by Laura and S. J. Perelman and the additional papers, notes, and interview records by me. In the text I have generally identified quotations that come from these sources. References to published sources relating to the history and background of West's time are documented, through catch phrases, at the end of the book.

By his special kindnesses and steady confidence, Robert Giroux made work on this book a pleasure and a responsibility. I am also grateful to Michael di Capua, Carmen Gomezplata, Peter Deane, and Dorris J. Huth, all of whom helped in important ways to bring it to print. James J. Flink and Malcolm Cowley helped me correct the book in galleys.

Support for my research and preparation of my materials was given to me by the Johnson Fund of the American Philosophical Society, the James Morris Whiton Fund of Yale University, and by the University of California, Irvine. I am especially indebted to Gordon N. Ray and to the John Simon Guggenheim Foundation for support during 1966–7 which freed me from my teaching duties and allowed me to devote my time wholly to research.

Contents

Illustrations

West photographed against a process shot on a Hollywood set
With his sister Hinda; in Hollywood, *c.* 1933
The photograph of West used on the jacket of *Miss Lonelyhearts*
West fishing in California
West on a hunting trip made with William Faulkner
West, with a guide, on a fishing trip in Oregon
Eileen West
Eileen at the station wagon in which she and West were killed
Eileen and West on a hunting trip (*two photographs*)
A newspaper photograph of the wreck
Nathanael West; Mexico, 1937

Suppose he had the Horatio Alger slant and was a guy who was trying to get one foot on the ladder of success and they were always moving the ladder on him, but they couldn't touch the dream.

—Nathanael West to S. J. Perelman
OCTOBER 1939

He was like a large, amiable lion wandering around with a thorn in his paw. Most of the time it didn't hurt. . . . But when he sat down to write, the paw that picked up the pen was the one with the thorn in it.

—Wells Root, "Notes on Nathanael West"
(1947)

Nathanael West: The Art of His Life

1 / *December 22, 1940*

West may not be an Isaiah to us, but his tropes are often as fresh & as apt as those of the old prophet: let the floods of our unhappiness clasp their hands over his memory.

—William Carlos Williams to James Laughlin,
August 20, 1950

Eileen's watch stopped at 2:55 on the afternoon of December 22, 1940. A moment earlier, she and her husband, Nathanael West, had been driving north, toward Los Angeles, after a weekend of hunting below the Mexican border. In the back of their Ford station wagon lay their liver-colored pointer bitch, Julie.

It had been a good weekend, though as late as Friday afternoon West had still seemed undecided about going. It was near Christmas, he had some shopping yet to do, and the weather had been bad. Even this Sunday afternoon, rain puddles from a morning shower lay on the road. Yet, the hunting season was nearly over, and so he had called Jimmy Alvarez in Mexicali and let himself be convinced that the hunting was superb. Hesitating briefly, he told his secretary, "I don't know—you can't believe him, he just wants you to come down and spend money." But it was clear all along that he was determined to go, and he and Eileen left late Friday.

The hunting *was* good. Alvarez, the owner of the only good bar and restaurant in Mexicali, the Leon d'Oro, had arranged for West, as usual, to have as his guide a Yaqui Indian named Jesús who had once been a professional hunter for the Los Angeles markets and knew the country intimately. After a full day of duck and quail hunting on Saturday, they ate at the Leon d'Oro and then crossed back to Calexico to the De Anza Hotel, where they stayed overnight. On Sunday morning, they again shot duck, and afterwards stopped in at Jimmy's for a beer. They were joking and laughing: it had been a fine time. Now they were returning with a car packed to the legal limit with game.

The newspapers for that day showed the nation preoccupied with the Christmas season and local news, even while the international reports foreshadowed the approaching world war. The Los Angeles *Times*, declaring, "Christmas to Be Gay Here Despite Conflict," announced the opening of such plays as Maxwell Anderson's *Knickerbocker Holiday*, a "bright New York hit play" titled *This Thing Called Love*, and an adaptation of Dickens's *Christmas Carol*. It described the Christmas decorations of Los Angeles as "one of the most beautiful sights to be seen in the Southland (or in the world, for that matter)." Bob Crosby, star of West's most recently released picture, *Let's Make Music*, was announced to play in San Diego, while in the United Artists' theater at El Centro the double bill was *The Marx Brothers Go West* and *Angels Over Broadway*. *The Grapes of Wrath* was voted the best picture of the year by the National Board of Review, while not one of the several films on which West had worked was listed among the year's ten best.

Also apparent in the California papers was a decided concern over increasing traffic fatalities. In 1940, even the cheapest automobiles—$25 a month on the installment plan—were capable of speeds over ninety miles an hour; licensing laws were lax; and drivers were too often ill-trained, while the archaic roads were dangerous at high speeds. The papers for December 22 announced the death of the popular bandleader Hal Kemp, from injuries sustained in a head-on collision on the Golden State Highway. The Central Business District Association of Los Angeles told the press that traffic reforms were imperative, even while the mayor was proposing a "New Four-Point Traffic Safety Plan" for the city. On that same day four sailors were killed in San Diego in a head-on collision with a bus, and Lucille Mulhall, known as "the original cowgirl of vaudeville" was killed in an auto crash in Oklahoma. In the Imperial Valley there had been twenty-seven auto fatalities for the year, and residents were idly hoping that no more would occur in the few days remaining.

West had hunted across the border since 1936, and the road was familiar, particularly the short stretch from Calexico to El Centro, where, on a Sunday afternoon, one might not see another car. He would drive north on route 111 until it intersected with 80, make the boulevard stop, then turn west on 80, two and a half miles to El Centro, and continue home.

That day he failed to make the stop and never completed the turn. At the same time, Christine and Joseph Dowless and their two-year-old daughter, Ann, were returning to El Centro from a job in Yuma, Arizona, driving west along route 80 at about forty-five miles per hour in a 1937 Pontiac sedan. Dowless, who followed the produce business, was known in local parlance as a "fruit tramp." There, in flat country, a driver could see for about a mile, and Dowless was aware of the station wagon approaching from the south, but "it was a long ways from the highway 80 when I saw it first," he said. "I naturally know of the intersection there because I am accustomed to the roads around here, as I have lived around here for several years. I looked up this side road and saw the car coming. It was, or seemed to be, moving pretty fast. However, I didn't pay much attention to that because I know there is a boulevard stop. As I drew nearer the cross roads I looked to the right more than to the left because the cars coming over the railroad there, it is a little more dangerous as I always figured there was more danger than the ones coming from the left; therefore I didn't look back to the left in time to see this fellow until it was too late to do anything about it. The wife says, 'He didn't stop,' and as she says 'Stop' the two cars collided."

West saw the Pontiac an instant earlier, braking his car four feet before entering the intersection, but then skidding, in a straight line, with all four brakes working, fourteen feet more across the south lane of route 80, and into the front of Dowless's car. The force of the impact spun the two cars around in a kind of whiplash, springing the doors open and throwing Eileen between the colliding machines and into a ditch north of 80. West, too, was thrown from the car to the highway. In the sedan, virtually demolished and knocked into a ditch, Dowless had an artery in his arm severed, and his wife a broken leg and pelvis; his infant daughter was "crying terribly."

Several accidents had already occurred at this intersection, and, as usual, a person in a nearby house phoned a report of this one into the sheriff's office.

West's body lay on the road for twenty-five minutes while a patrol car made its way up the Calexico road to the intersection. Julie, "cut with glass in a number of places," was "running around attempting to get into the station wagon." It was more than another half hour before an ambulance arrived to bring West and Eileen the three miles to the Imperial County Hospital. "There was a very unfortunate situation in Imperial County at that time," the first patrolman who reached the scene of the accident writes. "There was only one ambulance to take care of the south half of the County and it was not sent out on a call unless there was assurance that it was needed. . . . The County authorities would not send it out without verification of its need." No doctor came with the ambulance to provide immediate treatment. But, ironically, a doctor who was driving by did stop at the scene of the accident before the ambulance arrived. However, he satisfied himself from a distance that there was nothing he could (or should) do and so neither examined nor treated the unconscious couple. He chatted with the patrolmen until the ambulance came.

Considerably smaller than the El Centro Hospital and with barely adequate medical facilities, the Imperial County Hospital was designed chiefly to provide care for the migratory farm workers or indigents who lived in camps throughout the valley. Eileen died on the way to the hospital, apparently from a skull fracture, nearly an hour after the accident. Neither she nor West regained consciousness, but West was still alive when the ambulance arrived at the hospital and a doctor finally examined them. "Routine resuscitative measures then in current use—e.g., oxygen and intravenous fluids—would have been started, assuming that the survivor lived longer than fifteen to twenty minutes, but," the doctor who treated West writes, "it is my impression that [West] lived approximately that length of time. It would not have been possible to use blood as there was no blood bank. . . ." The doctor contented himself with smelling West's "breath to see if there was alcohol on it." There was none.* Then, at 4:10, Nathanael West, thirty-seven years old, died from a skull fracture and cerebral contusions.

Perhaps West was hurrying back from Mexicali—he did not

---

* There was a rumor that West had been drinking, based on a report that the odor of alcohol was discernible at the scene of the accident. But this, as the inquest makes clear, was due to the breaking, on impact, of some Mexicali Beer bottles which were still unopened.

usually leave so early—preoccupied with the news of the death of his friend F. Scott Fitzgerald, who had died on December 21 at 5:30 of a heart attack, leaving behind 37,000 words of a first draft of a book he was calling, tentatively, *The Last Tycoon*; his death was made known on the twenty-second. Perhaps West and Eileen wanted to get back before Tommy, her three-and-a-half-year-old son from an earlier marriage, went to bed. West may simply have failed to notice the stop sign, since he was color-blind to dark shades of red and green. It is likely, and would be characteristic, that West either was talking excitedly or was absorbed in his streaming thoughts; for, as West's friend Gordon Kahn remarked, his "absorption in driving was never great." Perhaps, as Edmund Wilson concluded, his "accident was due to his desire to do all the exciting things that people were doing at that time"—even those, like hunting and driving fast, which were not naturally congenial to him.

Few people were surprised, though many were shocked, at the news of his accident. His friends were stunned by the tragic waste, but they nodded their heads over the kind of lapse in driving which they had seen many times before. It is obvious that West drove badly chiefly because he was quickly bored by the mechanical routine of driving and either shifted his attention to conversation or loosened his imagination to drift and daydream. Under very difficult motoring circumstances he proved himself to be an exceptionally skillful driver, but under normal circumstances, on familiar roads, and particularly with close friends or with Eileen, he talked animatedly, "looking over at you as he talked . . . just as if he were sitting in a bar having a conversation"; or he easily gave himself up to fantasy.

In 1931, West drove from New York City to Connecticut with George Brounoff, and as they started down a long hill going into New Haven, Brounoff saw that there were school children crossing at the bottom of the hill, and "for a moment thought [West] was never going to stop. . . . The carnage would have been something awful." On the way home from that trip, in a foggy and misty night, West (inevitably) ran out of gas. Later, in the mid-thirties in Bucks County, West frequently had to be towed out of ditches beside the narrow roads. An Erwinna neighbor, Joseph Schrank, called him "the world's worst driver," and once, when West, driving with him, "shot out of a side road like a bat out of hell," Schrank cried out to him: "This is the last time I ride with you— some day you're going to get killed driving like that!" West himself told Schrank's wife that he had been driving since he was thirteen and had had innumerable minor accidents. "And," he added with amusement, "I've no doubt that's the way I'm going to go."

Characteristically, West drove over the speed limit; he drove on the inside of mountain curves; he once made a U-turn across six lanes of rush-hour traffic on Ventura Boulevard; before dawn, at Los Banos, in central California, West crossed over the center line on a curve, broke the car axle on a 4 × 4 guard post, and ran it down into a shallow irrigation ditch—the tales are numerous.

His most spectacular motoring episode occurred in 1937 when he and Leonard Fields, his producer at Republic, were driving home after hunting at Los Banos. "We were coming home late [Fields says] . . . in a light rain, and we had to cross a main irrigation ditch. It was about 40 or 50 feet deep, with sullen, black, cold water, and it was about 50 feet wide and had no regular bridge, only a series of pine planks laid across—no guardrail, no nothing. In this sleety rain we could hardly see, and suddenly he realized he's passing the so-called bridge—so he swings the car abruptly onto the bridge . . . and the momentum . . . tips the car and with the slippery wood we tilted over on our side and started to fall . . . and then stopped . . . at a slight angle. Now, I'm sitting in Nate's lap . . . and we're both sitting there looking down into this jet-black water . . . scared to death. We're afraid that the car is going to topple at any moment, and we don't know what the devil is holding us up.

"Now, Nate had great physical and personal courage . . . and he sat there very quietly. *I* was so scared I *couldn't* talk, frankly, I had no muscular reaction at all, and I was afraid to move out of his lap. Then Nate says: 'Well, now what do we do?—let's think about it.' He steadied me because he was so cool and unhurried. *This* was a West gesture: the world's worst driver, when he got into a jam, he thought coolly and properly. He finally said: 'Look, Lennie, *slowly* try to crawl over your way, and maybe your weight will counterbalance the car. If *not*, and we go over, try to throw that door open. . . . When you start moving, think of only one thing: if the car starts to fall, you reach for that door handle and throw

it—get it open no matter what else you do . . . because we can
get out of the car through that door, even if we go into the drink.'
So I started to inch my way over. And in those days we had the
gear shift between us; that was a problem because in some weird
manner I had vaulted over it completely. . . . Now it stood in my
way. Nate said, 'Take your time, don't rush it. It'll be all right—so
we'll get wet.'

"I slowly crawled over that way. For some reason the car trem-
bled but didn't fall. I got more and more courage the further I got
because finally I was in reach of that door. So I slowly opened the
door—I didn't push it open very far, but just enough to get one leg
out of the car—and then slowly wormed my body out of it. Then
. . . I opened it more and held onto the car and said, 'You try
the same thing.' . . . For an apparently ungainly man, he's pretty
agile—well built and in good condition. He gets out of the car and
nothing happens. So we back up a way from the car and look. In
constructing this pine bridge, they left a beam extending up about
six to eight inches . . . the door handle had caught on this 2 × 2
and the car was joggling and teetering on it. *That's* Nate West."

All the sad legends, all the gloomy prophecies, were fulfilled.
When another writer at Republic "bluntly warned [West] that
some day he would be killed if he didn't keep his eyes on the road
ahead, his answer was always the same scornful laughter." Perhaps,
after all, only such laughter, mocking but mirthful, was appropriate. West held—one of his closest friends, Robert M. Coates, has
said—a "metaphysics of the accidentalness of doom." It was a
chance world, to be regarded seriously but taken (or even lost)
lightly. With Leonard Fields at Los Banos he had been doomed to
live; and with Eileen at El Centro, doomed to die.

With his death, the West myth took on new life. Eventually, as
his novels commanded more and more attention and respect, the
myth threatened to replace the man. The subject, during his lifetime, of only one newspaper feature article, and that one in 1931,
West had attracted little personal attention outside the circle of
his friends. He had not brawled with critics or returned dispatches
from Spain; he published no book which veiled thinly the scandals
of the famous; he neither traveled to nor lived in exotic places; he
did not speak at ladies' teas and was never taken up by a book club;
nor did he seem to have spoken for his age: he had not been popu-

lar with either conservatives or radicals. But he had died in a spectacular fashion and had left four novels which more and more seemed not only to have accurately characterized his time but to be permanent and true explorations into the Siberia of the human spirit. And so the West legend flourished after the man had perished.

The newspaper accounts of his death, hastily gathered, encouraged confusion. West's age was usually given as forty, though sometimes as thirty-four (he was thirty-seven), while Eileen's age ranged, in various accounts, from twenty-seven (her actual age) to thirty-five. Either he was said to have written such books as *The Day of Locusts* and *Miss Lovely Hearts*, or he was characterized as "a Hollywood scenarist." In many accounts, Eileen played the leading role, as the model for the heroine "in Ruth McKenney's popular book, *My Sister Eileen*." The caption beneath a photograph of the scene of the accident gave this information: "Nathaniel West, 36, a Hollywood scenarist, and his wife, Ruth McKenney West, 30, were killed."

Indeed, Eileen was soon to become even more famous, through the stage adaptation of Ruth McKenney's book. The play was first performed, to understandably favorable notices, four days after the accident, on December 26, after a "tossup between a sentimental gesture and the cold business of postponing a Broadway opening" had resulted in a decision to open on schedule.

This was only one of the absurd circumstances following the accident. In El Centro there were curious questions about the money found on West. Although he had cashed a check for $25 on Saturday and paid his hotel bill by check on Sunday, only $1.46 in loose change was in his pockets when a lawyer went through his effects on Tuesday. In West's North Hollywood house, too, acquaintances moved in and divided West's books and Eileen's wardrobe among them; one person laid claim to the furniture in the bedroom. "What went on at Pep's house," his secretary says, "was unbelievable"; the locusts were swarming.

After West's friend and brother-in-law, S. J. Perelman, arrived to restore order and West's friends gathered at his house, they found cartons of china and dishes, household appliances, blankets and linen—all recently bought—still unopened or unpacked. Married for just eight months, West and Eileen had only recently moved into this large house. They had had a good time buying things, and they had bought a great deal. What parties were anticipated by the dozen highball glasses and what outings were promised by the picnic basket, both still sealed in cartons from Brooks Brothers? When his friends found their Christmas presents wrapped and waiting, the tragedy became not only absurd but inexpressible.

None of the newspaper accounts of the accident had mentioned Julie, and it was not until several days later that the dog, survivor of the crash, was found. Thrown from the car, she had limped away and disappeared when the ambulance approached with its siren screaming. So West's life ended like *The Day of the Locust*, his last novel. A native of the area found the dog, shot through with glass splinters, and brought her to a veterinarian. Later he refused to give her up until a court order forced the dog's return, and she was brought by the Perelmans to the Bucks County house which West had loved and shared with them. Danny, his earliest hunting dog, old now and trained for hunting in the East, was sent finally to Robert M. Coates's house in Connecticut, where he had been brought to hunt by West many times.

Eileen's young son, bewildered and deeply disturbed, was brought to Westport, legally adopted and renamed Patrick Bransten in early 1941 by Ruth McKenney and her husband, the journalist Richard Bransten. Their daughter, born sometime later, they named Eileen.

The bodies of both West and Fitzgerald were cared for at Pierce Brothers Mortuaries. While Fitzgerald's body was sent to Baltimore, Maryland, S. J. Perelman brought West's body to New York on the Santa Fe Super Chief, which left Los Angeles at 8:00 p.m. on Friday, December 26, the same train on which Sheilah Graham was going East after Scott's death. After simple services at Riverside Chapel in New York City, where ceremonies for his father had also been held, West's casket, containing Eileen's ashes, was interred in Mount Zion Cemetery in Maspeth, Queens.

During that same winter and early in the spring, along with West and Fitzgerald, an extraordinary company of writers died— Sherwood Anderson, Virginia Woolf, and James Joyce. What lived, of course, were their books. Shortly after West's death, Edmund Wilson wrote that West "left two books more finished and complete as works of art than almost anything else produced by his generation." And shortly thereafter, during the war, when the public chaos at last obviously matched the chaotic America which West had foreseen and depicted, the artistic finish and essential truth of his books began to be recognized. Critics began to suggest that West had been the most talented American novelist of the thirties, and virtually the only one whose fiction had not been victimized or softened in that decade either by the dogmatism, the clichés, and the romanticism of radicalism, or by the hysteria and utopianism of conservativism. "Had he gone on," William Carlos Williams declared, "there would have unfolded . . . the finest prose talent of our age." That conviction now became general, as West's work was praised by Malcolm Cowley, Daniel Aaron, Leslie Fiedler, the French surrealist Philippe Soupault, and W. H. Auden.* Stanley Edgar Hyman declared *Miss Lonelyhearts* to be "one of the three finest novels of our century." Soon after the publication of his *Complete Works* in 1957, it became apparent that West was not only attracting advanced-degree candidates in literature and bibliographers but also influencing younger novelists like James Purdy, Joseph Heller, Thomas Pynchon, John Hawkes, and Flannery O'Connor. He was known not only to college students or what had once been called "a discriminating minority," but to a wide public: his books have sold, in all editions, over a million copies, and have been translated into nearly a dozen languages.

The West myth thrived on the combination of increased interest in West's works along with inadequate or misleading knowledge about his life. His myth has become part of our modern history. But his true history began with his family's, much earlier, in Russia during the last years of the nineteenth century.

* It is also an appropriate and essential part of the West legend that the first long article published on him should have been plagiarized from an unpublished Master's thesis; that the first West bibliography was riddled with errors; and that the publishers of the first book dealing with his work should have failed to copyright it.

2 / The Birth of Nathaniel von Wallenstein Weinstein

"We've got nothing to look back to.
It's up to us to be ancestors."
—Samuel Ornitz, *Haunch, Paunch and Jowl* (1923)

During the last twenty years of the nineteenth century, at the end of which West's family immigrated to America, the Russian empire still lay in the shadow of the fifteenth century. Its tsar, Alexander III, was "less a contemporary of Queen Victoria than of Isabella of Castile." Numbered among its 29 million inhabitants were more than eighty nationalities or ethnic groups, whose languages were as different as the peoples; their religions were also diverse. Scorned as an unwelcome inheritance from Old Poland, as early as 1791 several million Jews were loosely confined by Catherine II within a Pale of Settlement in western Russia, chiefly to forward the policy of Russification which the government began at this time vigorously to pursue. This policy did not imply and did not immediately lead to religious intolerance or persecution; indeed, as part of the same program by which he had granted freedom to the serfs in 1861, Alexander II later issued a rescript allowing Jewish artisans and members of professions to settle outside the Pale, and encouraging the education of Jewish youths. Only in the spring of 1881, after the coronation of Alexander III, did violent pogroms break out, followed later by the so-called "May Laws."

These enactments drastically restricted Jewish rights throughout the empire, excluding Jews from self-government and forcing many professional people and members of trade guilds back into the Pale. Even there, restrictions were imposed which prevented Jews "from obtaining landed property of any kind in any part of the

Baltic governments," and pressing them into the already over-crowded cities or ghettos. Despite the immediate and continuing protests of Russian intellectuals—Tolstoy and Andreyev among others—the government extended and intensified the laws in the winter of 1889–90. Jews whose families had lived in ease only a few years earlier were now threatened with poverty; already beggars were everywhere, and in the district of Kovno, where West's family lived, many Jewish families, a traveler reported, "only break their fast at eventide, and then, only if the father, having found employment during the day, has been paid his wage."

The province of Lithuania, where Kovno is located, was subject to special historical circumstances which affected West's family and ultimately West himself. As early as the seventeenth century, when Kovno was the district customs and excise center for the Teutonic Hanseatic League, the influence of Germany there was strong, and Germans—in particular, ambitious tradesmen and artisans, West's ancestors among them—began to extend East Prussia into Vilna, Suvalki, Dünaburg, and Kovno, as well as parts of Grodno and Minsk. The desires of the Germans for territorial expansion, their sense of a high mission to be Kulturträgers, and the terms of the Treaty of Nystad (1721), happily coincided with the policy, set during the tsarship of Peter I, of establishing inlets for Western culture. Thus the German barons who were extending their concept of Alldeutschland to Lithuania Major, whence they would carry culture into the vast "Asiatic empire" of Russia, were welcomed, and occupied high positions in the empire, even in the imperial palace of St. Petersburg. By the early nineteenth century the whole region was flourishing. Cities like Kovno, Dünaburg, Tartu, and Vilna, where Germans constituted seven-tenths of the population, were centers of commerce, industry, and learning. A railroad line, which West's grandfather had a part in building, ran directly east from Hamburg to Königsberg on the German frontier, through Kovno to St. Petersburg. After Bismarck's Prussian ideal became a powerful factor in the Berlin government, the Germanization of the area was intensified. Compulsory primary education was conducted in German. By 1876 German was decreed the official language; both the legal Russian rulers of the province and the native Lithuanians were scorned as culturally inferior. Germany had dispatched its merchants, tradesmen, and educators to this cultural outpost, and in this alien land, declaring "Russen werden wir nimmer werden," * they set about to redeem it for civilization.

Moreover, there was a good deal of cultural interchange with the homeland. The sons of Livonian Germans returned to Königsberg, Leipzig, or Berlin, and traveled to Paris for their educations. Well-known Germans visited this Vorposten of their culture; they controlled industry, trade, the professions, and the intellectual life of the area. Both Immanuel Kant and J. G. Von Herder were born in this area. Emma Goldman was born in Kovno in 1869.

Under German Home Rule, free from the pressures exerted in other parts of Russia, the Jewish population prospered. It is essential to realize that not only national, social, and political, but also religious patterns in this area differed markedly from those of the rest of Russia. Here the predominant religion was Roman Catholicism; the Jewish faith, held by nineteen percent of the population, was second in importance, while the creeds of Greek-Russian Orthodoxy and of the Old Believers followed behind Lutheranism. Under these conditions, the intolerance common in the rest of Russia was almost wholly absent. There were no educational quotas for Jews—and a professional degree would allow a Jew free movement in Russia. Jews held positions of political and economic importance.

Of particular relevance to West's family was the fact that Jews were eminent in the crafts: "Many Jewish artisans were superb craftsmen and the gentry relied on them almost exclusively." Invariably, stone houses were built by Jewish craftsmen, like West's father, who monopolized the building and carpentry trades. It was acknowledged even by the Russian government that Jews "were more competent to do the work," and building was the only trade in which the government itself regularly continued to employ Jewish workmen in all parts of the empire. Jews, moreover, practiced their religion with little interference. A contemporary observer well named the Lithuanian Jews the "Scotchmen of . . . Jewry": "They exhibit the same hardiness and energy, the same push, the same 'canniness,' the same predilection for philosophical

---

* "We will never become Russians." So, at least, the rector of the University of Tartu, Karl Ch. Ulmann, informed S. S. Uvarov, minister of Russian education, in 1839, when Uvarov moved to Russify the educational system of Livonia.

and religious speculation." Indeed, Vilna, "the Jerusalem of Lithuania," became a renowned European center of Talmudic study,
and gave a focus to the enlightenment (Haskalah) movement
which introduced modern ideology into traditional Jewish thought.

West's ancestors, under these circumstances, regarded themselves as Germans until they were taught by Russia that they were
Jews. The style of their names as recorded on Russian documents
provides a significant clue to their family ethos in being completely
un-Russified and unassimilated in form. Around 1881, however,
Alexander III revoked German Home Rule in Lithuania and issued imperial edicts which forced Russification into the western
departments of the empire. German officials were replaced at once
and Russian was declared the official language in 1888; the right of
free movement for Jewish artisans, granted in 1865 by Alexander
II, was revoked, and educational quotas were established even
within the Pale. These changes abruptly taught the unhappy Livonian Jews that the laws of the Russian Pale applied to them.

The Wallensteins and Weinsteins, West's ancestors, were in
fact living at this time outside the Pale, in Dünaburg, although
several of the Wallensteins had been born in Kovno and some still
lived there. West's mother had herself been born in Kovno on the
first of March 1878. Her birth certificate, still on file in the Republic Archives of the City Soviets of Vilna, shows that she was originally named Chana-Mindel Leizerovna; it was natural that this distinctly Jewish form should later be Americanized to Anna. Hers was
a family of some importance. West's maternal grandfather, Lazar
(or Eleazer) Samuelovitch Leibick Vollenstein, "a bourgeoise of
Jewish religion," or simply "a bourgeoise of Kovno," as he was
styled in Russian documents, had achieved a secure position. It is
significant that, in violation of even imperial edicts concerning
Jews, he had enough power to prevent the indication of nationality
on his children's birth certificates. He had made his fortune during
the seventies in the building boom that accompanied the early in-
dustrialization of the area. In particular, Lazar Wallenstein was
well known as the builder of railroad stations within and beyond
the Pale, all along the Hamburg–St. Petersburg line and its
branches. His contracting and construction firm was large and its
business regular, and he employed many workers. Among these
were West's father, Max Weinstein, and his brothers. Along with

the three sons of Lazar Wallenstein, Max and his four brothers learned and pursued the trade of builder; essentially carpenters and stone masons, they hewed timbers by hand with adzes, burned limestone for mortar, and became thorough artisans. The sons of Lazar Wallenstein and Nachman Weinstein worked together and learned the skills that would eventually help to make for their quick success in the building trades of New York City, where they again worked together. But in Russia the Wallensteins were wealthier, employing the Weinsteins, and held hopes of distinguished futures for their children.

Lazar Samuelovitch was especially interested in education for his family of nine children, born (in this order) beginning around 1870: Marie, Pauline, Sophia, Saul, Samuel, Anna, Susanna, Sidney, and Fanny. He sent his daughters, among them West's mother, Anna, to the Girls' Gymnasium in Dünaburg, where they pursued the regular courses of study in the German and Russian languages, history, religion, arithmetic, geography, and "handiwork." His children were unusually intelligent. His second oldest daughter, Pauline, for instance, had special facility with language and mastered Latin, French, and English in addition to Polish, German, and Russian. She was known as a skilled writer and diarist.

The older sons of Lazar and his wife, Chaja-Rochel Raphelovna Wallenstein, were skilled with their hands and early showed abilities in the arts which were encouraged, probably, by the emphasis on handiwork and ornamental architecture in their father's establishment. Both Saul and Samuel attended art schools. At first, they were educated privately at Vilna, where Lazar Samuelovitch's brother, their uncle, held the important position of attorney-general for the province. Here Saul met Maurice Sterne, another young Jewish art student, who was born at Libau and would become a famous painter, later courting West's mother in America. Lazar Wallenstein possessed considerable influence, extending far beyond his power to educate his children. He was able to send Samuel to the Crimea for his health and subsequently arranged for Saul to be legally adopted by a Russian general who lived nearby, so that he might travel freely to St. Petersburg and there enroll in the art conservatory.

But all their influence, their apparently secure position, and their wealth could not protect West's family from history. For after 1881 the position of the Wallensteins and Weinsteins, as Germans but especially as Jews, was seriously threatened. The forces that would flow together explosively in the 1904–5 revolution were beginning, in the eighties, to take shape separately. West's family would be caught between them and eventually forced out of their country, by the nineties a strange land. Not simply the Jews, but the Germans as well, were under attack by developing rival national ideologies in Lithuania. From the German establishment, with which the Wallensteins were associated, flowed the idea of a pan-Germany and the concept of the "German-Balts"; from imperial Russia, which had substituted the phrase "Western Provinces" for Lithuania, the idea of a unified empire; and from the native Lithuanian peasant class, stirrings of nationalism and reassertions of hatred against invaders from both East and West. The poems of Adam Mickiewicz, who had lived in Kovno, still sang in the blood of the natives. Socialist agitators like Felix Dzerzhinsky made great organizational headway in the district and boldly predicted the end of both German and Russian rule in such poems as "And After the Bloody Dawn, the Sun of Truth Will Rise." Caught in these currents, the Jews of Lithuania, West's parents among them, turned their eyes and hopes elsewhere—to Germany, England, South Africa, Argentina, and, of course, to what they hopefully called the "New World." Whatever their destination, they knew, as the scholarly Rabbi of Dresden, Zacharias Frankel, counseled them, that "for the Russian Jews there is one way out; namely, to emigrate and settle under a sky where human rights are recognized by law."

For both the Wallensteins and the Weinsteins, as for many other families, departure was precipitated by the approach of military service. To Jews, bonded by law to three years of active duty and twenty-five years of reserve service, yet unable to rise above the rank of noncommissioned officer, conscription was particularly odious. For a Jew military service amounted to "actual if not formal de-Judaization"; and for affluent families like the Wallensteins, it led to a drastic loss of position and privilege. Yet, unless a male were registered in his recruiting district, he could not obtain a work permit. If he failed to appear for the annual drawing of recruits, his family could be fined 300 rubles. For this reason, many young men

took the dangerous chance of accepting the conscript and then fleeing the country.

By Russian law, the oldest son was exempted from service, although after 1890 even he, if Jewish, was threatened with impress-
ment in substitution for absentees. The Weinstein family consisted of five sons and one daughter: Jacob (born around 1868),
Julius, Charles, Max, Abraham, and Rose. It was in 1887 that the
first son of either family, Julius, was drawn in the annual recruit-
ment. It was clear that one by one the whole family was now to be
threatened. What should they do? At that time, as Mary Antin
said of Plotzk, a town not far removed from Dünaburg, " 'America'
was in everybody's mouth. Businessmen talked of it over their accounts; the market women made up their quarrels that they might
discuss it from stall to stall; . . . children played at emigrating; old
folks shook their sage heads over the evening fire." Emigration also
occurred to West's ancestors. It was natural that in their position it
should: most of the early emigrants came from the province of
Kovno, where a Hebrew Emigrant Aid Society was early established. The route from Kovno or Dünaburg through Königsberg,
and eventually to Hamburg, was not at all unfamiliar to the
Wallensteins or the Weinsteins. Moreover, passports to cross the
border would have been easy to obtain, either by influence or by
bribery.

When Julius was conscripted, then, he removed at once to
America. In the next year, during the great blizzard of 1888,
Charles Weinstein followed his brother to New York. Both began
work in the building trades on the lower East Side. At that time,
lower New York was being so rapidly built up with light industry
and housing that by 1890 the East Side, with an average of 290,000
persons per square mile, would be, as Jacob Riis observed, "the
most densely populated district in the world, China not excluded."
As builders, the Weinsteins found their skills at once in demand.
Politics had expelled them from Russia; now, in America, the economics of the rapid influx of an émigré population would ensure
their prosperity. They planned carefully for success. Supported by
capital from the members of the family still remaining in Russia,
Julius and Charles securely established themselves in the building
trade. Now the Westward migration of the families was fixed, and
others followed at regular intervals. West's father, Max, then Abe

and Jacob, joined their brothers and founded a contracting firm which grew rapidly. Max Weinstein, a contemporary of his says, "branched out in the real estate and construction business, where he became well-known and successful."

An important factor in American prosperity from 1900 through the Presidency of Coolidge was the boom in building construction. Particularly in New York, with building going on feverishly to keep pace with the housing demands of immigrants in the East Side, Harlem, Washington Heights, and the Bronx, there was a likelihood of success for a fairly large but unified group like the Weinsteins and the Wallensteins who began with some capital and could combine to support each other in times of individual distress. Mortgage credit, moreover, remained fairly loose throughout this period: with only blueprints, a builder could borrow money to construct cheap houses with fast turnover; with a mere $10,000 in cash, he could finance the erection of a $500,000 apartment house. West's father rode the tide of prosperity to considerable affluence. The builder, at first, of lower East Side walk-up tenement houses, he soon began to erect a whole series of six-story elevator houses above Central Park in Harlem and large luxury apartments as far north as 157 Street and west to Riverside Drive. He anticipated the uptown movement of the population and made good use of his earlier training, for his buildings can still be recognized by their ornamental work in limestone.

The way his family followed in the wake of his construction, ever moving into his newest or best house, was a gauge of their increasing affluence as well as their personal family style. Largely due to their earlier identification with the German establishment, the Weinsteins and Wallensteins never accorded the shtetl community the same respect that Russian Jews did. Like the German Jews who were already established in New York, they attempted at once to become Americanized. They delighted in the free, open American culture, and they moved freely in it. They refused to speak Yiddish or Russian; instead, they taught German to their children and learned English themselves. Max indulged his own delight in elegant American names and American history in calling his buildings the Arizona, the Colorado, or the Colonnade. He even delighted in the American past. The Hudson and the Fulton, buildings completed in 1909, he named for that year's centenary of

Fulton's *Clermont* and tercentenary of the discovery of the Hudson River.

The two families were closely united by ties of affection. Apparently there had been an understanding concerning marriage between several couples. In the nineties, Pauline Wallenstein, accompanied by her brother Saul, left Dünaburg to join and marry Charles Weinstein. Though it was determined that Saul's responsibility to see his sister safely to America overrode his plans for attending art classes at St. Petersburg, he was provided with sufficient funds to allow him and his sister to tour the galleries of Paris and London before sailing for the United States. Their younger brother, Samuel, now in danger of conscription, followed soon after. Celebrations for the regular arrivals of new members of the family were mixed with an equally regular series of marriages. When Pauline and Charles Weinstein moved into a private house which Charles had recently built on East 70 Street, Pauline made a place in it for her sister, Anna.

On May 25, 1902, at a small private orthodox ceremony, signing their names in Hebrew, Mordecai, the son of Nachman Weinstein, and Chana, the daughter of Eleazer Wallenstein, were married in a hall on the lower East Side of New York City. The bride, as was the custom, wore a floor-length dress with a flowing veil, and the groom a formal black coat and silk hat. On separate sides the men and women members of the closely knit families gathered around the couple. Shortly after the wedding, Max moved his bride into a house he had recently completed at 151 East 81 Street.

On October 17, 1903, a son was born to Max and Anna Weinstein, delivered by Dr. I. Levin, at their 81 Street home. This child, who would later call himself Nathanael West, would also reflect in many, sometimes strange, ways his past and the history of his parents.

He was their first child. His birth certificate gives his father's occupation as builder; his parents' ages as thirty and twenty-eight and their birthplace as Russia. He was named, after Max's father, Nathan, which in Hebrew means "gift." In that year, when hundreds of Jews were killed or injured in the violent pogroms which broke out at Kishinev, was not a son a gift? Was it not a gift to be prospering in America, in a time of peace, and for the families to have been safely united? So, at least, the families thought, and two of West's cousins, born within a year, were also named Nathan.

A studio portrait of Anna Wallenstein taken before her marriage shows an attractive and rather elegantly dressed young woman looking wistfully beyond the camera. In the style of that period she would have been considered not only beautiful but "interesting." After the birth of her children she was absorbed in them; she appeared to one of West's close friends to be a "born mother," and cherished hopes for her son, in particular. She was interested in the home, in cooking, in comforts. It seems likely that one of the things that gave West the quality of boyish innocence which he always retained was his ability to maintain a wholly sympathetic relation with his mother, even though all she may truly have wished for him was the kind of success whose futility and hollowness he soon recognized and repudiated.

Max Weinstein was a hard worker. A family portrait of 1904, which shows Anna settled firmly into domestic pleasures, confirms the character attributed to Max: he was energetic, wiry, and aggressive, but also quiet and gentle; somewhat sad, yet with a quizzical sense of humor; of slight build, with a firm carpenter's hand. In the portrait he is wearing the kind of mustache which his son would later adopt when it was no longer quite fashionable. Indeed, in many ways, his son would be remarkably like him, and there is no doubt that West talked about his father frequently and affectionately after his death: he was one of the two men—the other was S. J. Perelman—about whom West always spoke with deep affection. A contemporary of Max's described him as "short in stature, about 5 feet 7 or 8 inches in height and about 140–150 pounds. . . . Max was a quiet, retiring, and soft-spoken individual and any conflicts or controversies in his business dealings were left to his associates for adjustment. . . . Of the qualities which endeared him to me and which I admired, [one] was in greeting you: he always had a broad smile and hearty handshake, and left you in good spirits. [He] was not what is usually known as a 'sporting' or 'man about town' but preferred to spend his evenings at home with family or friends and ponder over his next day's affairs." Yet he also shared something of the spendthrift qualities of his family and of his time; and he was, necessarily in speculative construction, a tough-minded man, willing to gamble for big profits with largely

unsupported loans and mortgages. Whatever his natural inclinations, after his marriage Max was absolutely possessed, it seems,
by three aspirations: to live fashionably; to send his family to the
country during the summer; and to educate his children.

In 1908, shortly after his completion of the Kortright and
DePeyster apartments, occupying the entire block front on Seventh
Avenue between 119 and 120 Streets, Max moved his family over
to the now more fashionable West Side, into the DePeyster. Later,
during the First World War, when there was a general exodus of
the upper middle class from Harlem, Max moved them to Hamilton Terrace, a short street on Washington Heights just north of
City College and overlooking Harlem. Afterwards, Max and
Charles's families were neighbors on Mount Morris Park West.
Still later, as the West Side of Central Park became a center
for fashion and gentility, he built and occupied houses on 110
Street, directly across from Central Park. The Weinsteins liked a
view. They liked to live in what a friend of West's, John Sanford,
bitterly called "The Gilded Ghetto."

They also liked the country. West's mother had, as a child, been
brought to the Baltic coast during the summers. In America, when
summer arrived, the women packed trunkfuls of new clothes and
took their children off to resorts. Between 1905 and 1915, Anna
took her children first to a farm in Colchester, Connecticut, then
to a hotel in Hunter, New York, and later to the Lorraine Hotel
in Deal or the Hollywood Hotel in Bradley Beach, New Jersey.
Especially in Colchester, where the roads were not yet suited to
the automobile and the fathers arrived for weekends by horse and
carriage, something of the primitive mystery of the American land
opened to them. Released here from city restraints, West began
early to give this wilder country an important place in his fantasy
life. In Colchester, he and the other boys stole vegetables from the
garden, got poison ivy, fished, and shot at woodchucks, rabbits, and
raccoons with the .22 caliber rifle that West owned. Here, or in
the Catskill and Adirondack camps, like Zelenka or Paradox, to
which the boys subsequently were sent, West learned not simply
to love the outdoors but to regard the wilderness as powerfully
curative of city ills. In contrast to the confusing city, where commerce and conformity pressed upon him, the country seemed to

provide a place of simple order. In part, of course, such a belief was characteristically American, but West's early experience gave it deep personal immediacy.

Friends of Max Weinstein noticed that he "was unusually proud of his ability to give his children the education he himself had been deprived of. He spoke of this often . . . and must have gotten pleasure from it beyond the ordinary." By family tradition, the Wallensteins respected education, even above religion, as their attendance at secular schools in Dünaburg and their unwillingness to send their children to Hebrew schools in America proved. One of the few legal avenues by which Jews in Russia could escape the imperial Pale was through education. And in America, it was through education, they believed, that their children would have opened to them the avenues of democratic success. Here, the assumptions at the heart of American life told them, they might escape from the pale of Jewishness through the equality of the informed mind and economic achievement. "Success" was a concept which dazzled immigrant parents, as much for their children's sake as for their own. Absorbed in their children, both of West's parents regarded themselves as sacrifices, justified by the success of their offspring. Matthew Josephson has remarked of his own childhood during this same period in New York: "We might be of mixed English, German, Irish or French ancestry, or, as in my own case, Jewish, yet the prevailing 'Protestant Ethic' of middle-class America seemed to possess all our parents alike. They were anxious and mainly preoccupied with all that was material and useful in 'getting ahead.'" Their hopes, of course, admirably coincided with the American dream of success. It is not surprising that before West was ten, his parents gave him presents of Horatio Alger's books. The Weinsteins would live close to schools, where they could consult with the teachers; they would point their girls toward private schools and their boys toward De Witt Clinton, the best academic high school in New York; and eventually toward Columbia or a New England college. They would hold up for their sons' admiration doctors, lawyers, or successful businessmen. They would give them what they liked to call "advantages." Surely, success would follow.

In the moves which they made around New York, in the summers they spent in the country, and in the way they conceived of their children's education and future, the Weinsteins showed a quick and easy—perhaps a too sudden—adjustment to the established patterns of American life. In an important sense they shed, at once, traditions, histories, and recollections which their children might have needed. They refused to have a past, and their children's futures would reflect this loss despite the goodhearted indulgence which they were abundantly given. No doubt their rapid assimilation to American ways was facilitated by the way they had earlier regarded themselves as aliens—as Russians but not Russians; as Jews but not Jews. Essentially, the Weinsteins gave up their Judaism with their emigration. The two families had refused to become Russian, but now they would be Americans. They no doubt agreed with the voice of the German intelligentsia, *The Hebrew Standard*, when it declared that "the thoroughly acclimated American Jew . . . has no religious, social, or intellectual sympathies with [Russian Jews]. He is closer to the Christian sentiment around him than to the Judaism of these miserable darkened Hebrews." They would not be part of what Emma Lazarus called "the wretched refuse of [the] teeming shore." Instead, they would cry, with David, the hero of Israel Zangwill's *The Melting Pot* (1908): "Germans and Frenchmen, Irishmen and Englishmen, Jews and Russians—into the Crucible with you all! God is making the American."

The Wallensteins, in particular, had regarded themselves as Germans in Russia. In New York, Anna, her daughter Hinda remembers, "retained a cook and governess who spoke only German," and other German-speaking servants, from the time of her marriage until West was about thirteen years old. Her three children—Nathan, Hinda, born a year after him, and Laura, born in 1911—all learned German. In their personal and business associations the two families tended to form a kind of clan; and socially they tended to associate with other Litvak Jews. With intellectual organizations, musicians, and painters on the upper West Side and in Yorkville—with Platon Brounoff, and the young Maurice Sterne, who was studying at Cooper Union around this time—they had some association. As a matter of course, they went regularly to the Metropolitan Opera, in full dress, jeweled and elegant. They were prosperous and charitable. If they went to the Temple—as they did twice a year, on the high holidays—it was to the German Temple Israel, where Rabbi Robert Harris, the author of several books, had been called from England to preach the learned message of Judaism in an impeccably correct and rhetorically distinguished English accent. They had been Kulturträgers in Russia, and in some part now they regarded even the culture of America as inferior and condescended to it. As one of West's cousins remarks, they wished to be assimilated into American life, but only at a distinguished, high level. "We were not going to be American peasants," he says, "we were going to be American gentlemen." There is no doubt that the conflicting desires to shed the past and be assimilated into American ways, but to remain essentially superior to that life, produced, in part, some of the personality tensions and perhaps some of the creativity shown by West and his cousins. Theirs was not an uncommon response: indeed, conflict in Jewish immigrants between their respect for European culture and their desire to be assimilated into commercial society in America provided the subject for Sholem Asch's earliest novels. It would be in the background of West's novels, as well; for all are built on the dramatic irony that the hero is drawn into the society which he scorns, while ever forced to remain alien from the ideal society, the impossible society, which he envisions.

It is not surprising, in any event, to see that as late as 1926, when West applied for a passport, he gave his father's birthplace as "Danenberg, Germany." Up to that time, he gave his friends "to understand that [his parents] came from Germany, considered among Jews at that time as being second in desirability to Portugal." The sense of status which they carried with them to America was part of West's heritage, and was derived largely from the Wallenstein side of his family. Of higher social standing in Russia, better educated, and more interested in the arts than the Weinsteins, the Wallensteins cultivated a sense of superiority, while the Weinsteins were more practical, earthier, and less romantic. Inevitably, their children would regard their Wallenstein heritage romantically, even while being drawn into the world of American commerce, where the Weinsteins flourished.

One of the most significant ways in which this attitude was expressed over a long period was the great interest the whole family showed in Schiller's play *Wallenstein*. The drama and its historical background were known intimately and discussed intensely and often. For Schiller, of course, Wallenstein was a heroic figure, the tragic hero, the outsider, hated by the German princes whom he saved and ultimately murdered by them. Perhaps in compensation for feelings of insecurity common in second-generation immigrants, West and his cousins saw personal meaning in the story and felt that they were somehow related to the actual Wallenstein, Duke of Friedland and Mecklenburg. This tradition persisted in the family: the Wallenstein crest was adopted by some of its members, and several of the boys whose mothers were Wallensteins took that as their middle name. West himself would confide to his roommate at Brown that his ancestors were of gentle birth, and he cultivated the role which Lillian Hellman saw him play, of a Polish or Czechoslovakian baron, "certainly not delicate and not quite aristocratic, but . . . both distinguished and casual."

Finally, when his first published writings appeared in the Brown literary magazine, *Casements,* West would give this family myth a unique twist by signing a poem and an essay Nathaniel von Wallenstein Weinstein. "Nathaniel von Wallenstein Weinstein, Nathaniel von Wallenstein Weinstein, Nathaniel von Wallenstein Weinstein," West wrote over and over again in his notebook during lectures at Brown. From the history of his family he would make a myth for himself. Imaginatively, he brooded upon his distant nobility. Like Yeats, West was shaping a legend. Imagination and myth, both writers believed, were their true ancestors. "Nathaniel von Wallenstein Weinstein"—through this myth, West would give birth to his own romantic, heroic version of himself.

3 / The Paradoxes of the Pepper King

> It was not Brooklyn that I hated; it was rather the way of life that Brooklyn represented for me. There were my parents saying repeatedly: "Poetry? But how *will* you ever earn your living?" In reality, my father, who certainly thought me an odd one, was a sensitive man and showed far more tolerance toward me than I possessed for him. "Oh, he will get over his dreams in time; they all do," he would say good-humoredly.
>
> —Matthew Josephson, *Life Among the Surrealists* (1962)

Nathaniel von Wallenstein Weinstein was not by any means the first name he assumed. Name changing could hardly be questioned in a family almost all of whose names had been Americanized, on entering the country, by immigration registrars—Serge to Saul, Chana to Anna, Sara to Susan, and Sophia to Sophy, among others. Being Americanized, it was thus early hinted, had some connection with a facility to change names easily. (They knew at once, too, that it was necessary to alter their foreign appearance; all the early photographs of members of the family show the same concern for the proprieties and graces of genteel fashion that would mark West's own style of dress.) Moreover, three Weinstein boys, born around the same time, were called Nathan: in addition to West, the sons of Julius and of Charles Weinstein; and Saul Wallenstein's son was also named Nathan. All these were double cousins. Such childish nicknames as Ninny (Charles's son), Nissy (Max's), Nutsy (Julius's), and Wally (Saul's) naturally followed, used particularly when the boys, who were fast friends, were together. At other times, West was called Ned. To the end of his life, he would be affectionately called Natchie by his mother and sisters, and he would usually sign his letters to them with that diminutive.

Due doubtless to his obvious interest in the outdoors, he also acquired early the nickname "Trapper." The image of the sportsman would provide one of his earliest romantic identities. While it is true that for the son of an Eastern European Jew the figure of the hunter would have been traditionally associated with oppressive authority, of Cossacks and pogroms, peasant and lord, still West's personal sense of his past varied sufficiently from the usual pattern that he could regard the role of hunter as forming part of his image of the gentleman, heir of Wallenstein.

West drew his cousin, Nathan Wallenstein, two days older than he, into this interest, and the two boys pored over sports magazines like *Field and Stream*, intensely discussing the technical aspects of fishing and hunting. With liberal allowances, they happily occupied a good deal of time sending for special equipment. In part, the lore with which West would later amuse and fascinate his friends—of bees, of guns, birds, of the names of trees and plants, the peculiarities of certain water fowl or fish, and of famous wilderness areas—was gathered chiefly in this simple way. West's mind was encyclopedic; and when he focused his fantasies upon his knowledge, he invested it with interest by bringing up what had lodged in his brain in new, fictive combinations. From childhood on, living mostly in the city, he substituted imagination for action: the accumulation of information thus led directly to the discovery of the powers of fancy. By the time he reached Hollywood, for instance, he could make from magazine stories a heroic tale of a mythical, epic float trip which, he told his friends, "he had taken as a younger man with an uncle, down the Salmon River in the Idaho wilderness, one of the first trips of its kind."

West's fantasy self-image as the hunter and explorer reached its youthful climax in 1918. When an older cousin was called into the naval reserve, West and Wally became so excited over the romantic possibilities of military service that one day they raided all the depositories of small change in their houses and set out to travel as far West as possible. Both were tall for fifteen and in the West, they believed, might be accepted into service. With them they carried fishing equipment and a rifle; and after they had been intercepted (with train tickets to Buffalo) at Grand Central Station by Max and Saul and safely returned to their homes, they talked bravely and often about their adventurous notion of living off the land (and waters) until they could enlist.

For most Americans during this period the simple and heroic life included organized sports, especially baseball. For the immigrant, in particular, an essential part of Americanization consisted in a technical acquaintance with the baffling rules of play. As early as 1909, Abraham Cahan's Yiddish newspaper, *The Forward*, published an article, "The Fundamentals of Baseball Explained to Non-Sports," which unraveled the national pastime with the aid of a three-column diagram of the Polo Grounds. But for West, sports became a crucial focus for his ambivalences toward American life. Quick and flexible in every aspect of acculturation, West's family had not been "non-sports" for long. Two of West's older cousins, Samuel and Nathan Weinstein, both made records in baseball which amazed and delighted their families. Ned was signed by a farm team of the New York Giants, and Sam was regarded as one of the best athletes who had ever attended Columbia. Not surprisingly, then, baseball too became a natural area of action for West's fantasy to play upon (as it would, much later, for another son of Jewish immigrants, Bernard Malamud, whose novel *The Natural* draws on the myths and magic of baseball). In one part of his fantasy life, West's dream of success was to be a baseball hero. He told his Brown classmates that he had been an expert sandlot player, while later he confided to Hollywood friends that he had played on the Brown team. But he really had little success at the game. Characteristically, he adopted a curious stance which gave him at least a certain distinctive appearance at bat. "When the ball was thrown," a teammate of West's at Camp Paradox vividly recalls, West "placed all of his weight on his right foot, leaning backwards at the same time, and thus had a terrific leverage when he swung at the ball. It was not that he was an unusually good hitter but, when he did hit the ball, it was likely to go out of the park." He didn't connect very often; but in a time when the home run was regarded with awe, it was typical of West to put his efforts wholly into that. In consequence, though with more than a little irony (and in imitation of a current baseball hero), he was accorded another nickname, "Home Run Weinstein."

To both the wilderness and sports, with little real experience in either, West responded deeply, and at last with deep suspicion. In retrospect, it is clear that both were basically vehicles for the play of his imaginative life: they gave him superficial ways of investing his life with heroic and romantic qualities.

Of course, his chief way of opening this life of the imagination was, predictably, through reading. That he was able to retain the details of his early reading even many years later shows how intensely he pored over his books, how much he was in love with the magic of words, striking phrases, or unique characters, and how responsive and sympathetic he was to the writing of others. Moreover, his reading was, as his sister Laura says, "enormous": he would often be reading several books at the same time and was ever recommending books to friends and family. Yet he also fiercely protected his solitude for the sake of his fantasies. Until his toy bulldog bit Laura in the cheek, West kept it in his room, trained to threaten anyone who disturbed him while he was reading.

Of the two concepts basic to the Jewish personal ideal, Landan (learning) and Chassid (piety), West's family had almost exclusively emphasized the first. It is true that West briefly took religious lessons and memorized parts of the Torah by rote in preparation for his bar mitzvah; but he looked forward enthusiastically only to the presents the occasion would bring: for he could be confident of receiving leather-bound sets of "standard authors." At one time or another, West received volumes or sets of the classic Russian and English authors, of Tolstoy, Turgenev, Pushkin, Dostoevsky, and Chekhov, as well as of Thackeray, Dickens, Shakespeare, and Hardy. Balzac and Maupassant stood beside them. His family liked to give books to the children as presents; and in all their parlors long rows of morocco-bound books stood at attention, like lines of soldiers, row upon row. By the age of ten, West was reading Tolstoy; subsequently, he would haunt used-book stores when he should have been in school, and alternate *Field and Stream* with the catalogues of English booksellers, collecting books with the same enthusiasm as sports equipment. By accident and design, then, he would find his way to a vast number of books. Doubtless, he was indiscriminate in much of his reading and was attracted to the bizarre and exotic qualities in books far more than to their qualities of excellence.

During his teens, West tended to emphasize the bizarre or unusual aspects of any subject. To some extent this was surely a pose. "We pretended," Josephson says of his friends at this time, "to be interested chiefly in the abnormal, the morbid, and the neurotic, posing as frightful cynics and even as decadents." But the truly strong and personal bent of West's activities suggests that he responded genuinely to the bizarre, to the grotesque, wherever he found it. A younger brother of Nathan Wallenstein, who was often with West and Wally, recalls the excitement of West's extraordinary conversation. West collected and told strange tales, almost always dealing with the odd or unpleasant aspects of his current interests. He delighted particularly in stories about strange weapons and exotic methods of torture and would describe both in considerable detail. He early thought, as a friend would say, "in violent terms and in terms of violence." He was interested in cruelty and its limits. He had not, at this time, read Sade; but like him, West spoke of cruelty as "something special and distinguishing." Nor did he know Breton, and he certainly had none of Breton's metaphysical interest in surréalité; but, like Breton and *fin de siècle* writers, he was fascinated by witchcraft, occultism, and mysticism. He showed, too, a striking preoccupation with the human body, particularly with its odors, its orifices, its corruptibility and diseases, with parasites that feed on the human body. Such interests led him to question another cousin, a medical student, closely about the dissection of a cadaver. West had, Saul Jarcho recalls, "some fantastic and poetic conception . . . about the colors of various viscera." He related fantasy stories to his cousins as convincingly as if they had been his own experiences, even when the listeners would know them to be untrue. He was, in short, as one cousin says, "the master of the convincing lie," a compulsive role-player.

II

In West's preoccupations with the outdoors and sports, in his reading, and in his delight in the bizarre, he was clearly shifting the basis of his identity to his imagination—what "special or distinguished" identity he could give himself rather than what ordinary identity he must accept. His need for status as a young man was so intense, he later told Lester Cole, that he had to find some activity in which he could be distinguished. Very early, he found in his fantasy life kinds of distinction which he failed to find in social life and separated the life of his imagination from his outer activities. His was a not uncommon response. Arthur Kober, another writer who was born of immigrant parents around the same time as West and lived not far from him, has said: "When I lived in Harlem, in the Jewish community there . . . I was so busy hating [it] it wasn't until I grew up and thought back that I discovered in retrospect how rich it was, and like a fool I hadn't explored it deeply enough." West, too, hated his community life because he needed so intensely to find some simple, separate value for his selfhood. Since his society was not strong or stable enough to give him status in it, he would seek status outside it. If he was not different, he feared, he would be (like his community) nothing. Thus he early made the dangerous experiment of separating his personality from his family, community, and culture. West was in danger of losing his self in searching for a self.

Certainly, he reacted violently against the aspirations for a conventional life which his family held for him. His father assumed that West would probably enter a profession or succeed him in the construction business, in which the future, like the past, seemed to promise only prosperity; the industry was recording one large gain after another and by the mid-twenties nearly equaled agriculture and transportation in importance. Or, might he not, like other members of the family, begin to think about medicine, law, or banking? The Weinsteins valued culture and wanted it abundantly for their children. But who could afford to be a writer, they would ask in wonderment and dismay.

Although West worked for his father, held an apprentice bricklayer's union card, and did gain a certain skill in plumbing, construction or commercial business evoked no imaginative response from him. Quite the contrary. He resisted, by indifference, all of his family's efforts to enlist him in work or to encourage him to enter a profession. Generally speaking, in his youth this meant simply that West set himself strongly against conventional goals. All those professions which his family valued, he ignored; all that his father hoped for him, he rejected. In particular, West focused his opposition to the principles of conventional authority and achievement by opposing school. It was not simply that in his classes he was usually found to be reading novels instead of paying attention, as his sister Hinda remembers, but that he seldom attended classes at all.

Located around the corner from his house, West's first school, P.S. 81, was called the "Model School" because it was the first teachers' in-class training school in New York City. On its lower floors were the grammar-school classes, while on the upper floors teachers' training classes were held. Part of this training consisted of sitting in with the tenured teachers down below and observing their methods in practice. The establishment of this school shortly before 1908, when West entered it, had marked a crucial and signal change in the concept and pattern of education in New York. Accepting progressive concepts and methods, the schools of education began to break away from the formal, classical tradition by emphasizing experimentation, individual creativity, and participation by the children in workshops, laboratories, and other activities adapted to the group itself. West's school was a model for this movement; full of hopes, West's father deliberately built his newest house on a lot near this school so that his son could begin his education there.

From the beginning, West's parents were called into the school for frequent consultations. Nathan's teachers would be patient; there would inevitably be presents for them—"you know, you could sort of bribe in those days," West's sister Laura says—and after school they would stop at West's house for coffee and sympathy or more consultation with Mrs. Weinstein. But West hardly cooperated with these efforts of his parents. For his part, he continued to find other diversions more interesting. During his seven years at the Model School, he was absent as many as thirty times in a single term; living a block from the school, he was late as many as thirteen times in a term; he failed to achieve any grade, either for work or for conduct, higher than a B, and indeed began to be given C's; he was never skipped, in a period when the prevalent theory was that academically competent students would advance rapidly (one of his cousins was skipped four times); and, even more distressingly, he was dropped, in the sixth grade, from the bright to the average class.

In the fall of 1915 West was registered at P.S. 10 but never went to a class there and was soon switched to P.S. 186, where he finished the seventh and eighth grades in the second scholastic division of his class, and with a fair record of attendance. In June 1917 he was graduated and registered for De Witt Clinton High School, a strong academic high school, where, at the same time as West, Mortimer Adler, Countee Cullen, Ernest Nagel, and Lionel Trilling were enrolled. Here, however, the haphazard character of his grammar-school attendance and interest would no longer suffice.

With Julius's son Nathan, and more often with Nathan Wallenstein, West had been investigating the resources of New York. Although Wally was a far quicker student, most of the imaginative elements in their play originated with West. There were, of course, the used-book stores, and there were books to read and adventures in them to contemplate and play out. Along Tenth Avenue were several lunch rooms where the boys could sit and order, experimentally, whatever foods they were not allowed at home. Of course there were baseball or football games to go to—especially when Columbia was playing at home and Sam was at shortstop or end. There was the American Museum of Natural History. For a time West lived right off Central Park, where he explored the interesting, hidden spots off the main paths. In an unpublished, unfinished story of the early thirties, West attempted to make fictive use of his adventures in Central Park and so revealed the character of some of his childhood activities there. Because the park was originally landscaped in the "natural style," he explains, it is full of "little secret nests":

Some are merely holes in the brush, just large enough to sit in without being seen and from which nothing can be seen. Others are located near spots used by lovers and from these the whole progress of an affair can be watched, usually with envy by the lonely spy. A few are larger, almost like a hut, and the occupant can lie down at full length and play at being in the forest. . . .

I first learned about these places when I was a child and used to play Indian scout in the park with a little gang of other boys. We fished for goldfish in the lake with a bent pin for a hook and balls of dough for bait. We also had a trap line of mice traps, a few rat traps, and several badly made snares after a design in the boyscout manual. We caught squirrels and an occasional rabbit. We skinned everything with old razor blades, stretched and salted the skins, also according to the instructions in the manual, and tried to cook and eat the carcasses. . . .

As we grew older, the trapping and fishing became less exciting. We started to go to the park at night. We used the trails then to spy on the grown people who hid in the brush. We would sit by the hour watching two men kiss or a woman masturbate. We would wait until they were at the height of their excitement, then suddenly shout foul names and run, yelling wildly.

It is a strange thing, but we were untouched in any serious way by the things we saw. We were playing a game that involved certain virtues (also found in the Scout Manual) such as knowing the signs and habits of our quarry, stalking, trailing, observing carefully, remaining absolutely still and so forth. We would no more think of imitating the people we hunted than Daniel Boone would imitate a bear he had seen grubbing in a rotten tree. The climax of our hunt was savagely cruel and yet it was the only climax we could manage.

Beside those in the park, most adventures paled. But of almost equal lushness was the rich jungle of the theater's fantasy world. 125 Street was lined with theaters which ranged in quality all the way from those where successful Broadway shows made their first stop as they began to tour the country, to vaudeville and burlesque houses. West's interest in the theater, on all levels, began early and was lifelong. He claimed that before he came to Brown he saw "every worthwhile production on Broadway and . . . a great many that were not." In Providence he regularly attended performances of touring companies. By the twenties he had a wide acquaintance with the conventions of burlesque comedy. He was an accomplished aficionado of the standard routines. And, of course, there were movies beckoning from all over town. By 1915, feature pictures were developed and "stars" came to be an integral part of movie publicity and the expectations raised by movies. West responded with enthusiasm. Here was the actual transformation of reality with which he had been fascinated from the first. Had not the familiar Bethesda Fountain in Central Park been made to serve as an Italian setting for *Romeo and Juliet* (1908)? Were not Edison's studios to be seen in the Bronx, and the swamps around Bayonne, New Jersey, made to serve as vast Western prairies?

All these activities, it is clear, strongly indicate the development in West of an observational imagination. Separating his person

from his society, he defined the self by what he could observe yet
remain untouched by. He would be (as he declares in his story) a
"lonely spy," watching but never participating. He was interested
in society only as a foundation for fantasy, hardly at all as an area
for action. With such excitement abounding in New York, West
spent even less time, in high school, on his work or in attendance.
He regarded education as social behavior and so, inevitably, he rejected school. In a time when success in society was conventionally
measured by the acquisition of money, he refused to be convicted
to success. During the fall term of 1918–19 he recorded a new high
of thirty-eight absences. This was no grammar school. He was not
missed or so well treated at De Witt Clinton, the oldest high
school in New York, with 6,000 students in attendance. Although
Sam Weinstein was still remembered there as an athletic hero, and
Nathan Wallenstein appeared in class often enough to skip a grade
and become associate editor of the *Clintonian*, the class yearbook,
West did not participate in any of the activities of the school, not
even on the newspaper or on the staff of *The Magpie*, the literary
magazine. He belonged to no clubs and did nothing sufficiently
notable to cause his name to appear in the *Clinton News*. Quite
simply, he attended classes only occasionally during 1917–20.
Neither John Sanford nor Lionel Trilling, both students there at
that time, remember ever seeing West; and Sanford, who had
known him earlier, would recognize him immediately in 1924.

At the end of his fall term at De Witt Clinton, on his first report
card, West received a 70 in English, 60 in Latin, 75 in drawing, 70
in music, 60 in physical training, 75 in biology, 40 in algebra, and
70 in elocution. So far, he had struggled through; but in the spring
semester of that year his grades fell. English, 50; Latin, 40; biology,
60; algebra, 60; elocution, 60—not quite enough passing grades to
send him forward to the sophomore class. At the end of a year he
was still a freshman. In the following two years, before he left
without graduating, he showed ability in only two subjects—in
drawing, where, amazingly, he received a 90 and 95, then in an advanced course an 81; and in elocution, where he achieved an 85.
For the rest, he apparently stopped going at all to music, physical
training, hygiene, and, finally, elocution; during 1919–20 he received zeros in all these; he failed English 2 twice consecutively,
barely passed and then failed courses in Spanish; managed, in his

last year, 80 and 65 in history; successfully completed a year of chemistry after first failing a term; and passed a year of algebra, but failed plane geometry twice. Not until he had spent three years at the school did he finish the requirements for advancement into the junior class.

There had been a good many tears at home and anxious talks with teachers, who remembered Sam and Wally and were helping Julius's son (also Nathan Weinstein) to get through. West's parents encouraged and counseled him endlessly. All during high school he was subjected to regular tutoring. And he was undoubtedly often told, as a "Clintorial" in *The Magpie* reminded the students, "It is the fellow who has earnestly done his work, and, when he is sure of his ground, comes steadily into the limelight, whom we all admire. *Character, Service, Scholarship,* this be your motto, and success is yours."

But just outside De Witt Clinton, situated at Tenth Avenue and 59 Street, in the notorious San Juan Hill section of Manhattan, there was a rank and grotesque mass life that exposed the pretense in that motto. Around his school, West saw in full bloom frustration, compensation, perversion, and pain. "After a home neighborhood place like the Model School," John Sanford says, "De Witt was like a Bowery flophouse after the St. Regis." More and more, West was to become aware of that Bowery underworld of American life. Like most satirists, including Swift and Pope, he was not a good student: like theirs, his way of adjusting to society would be through satire rather than knowledge. Perhaps like Henry Adams's, West's education had failed him; but perhaps too by that failure he was to be released, shocked, into a modern education more essential in the twentieth century for his peculiar talent, his vision of the truly monstrous in modern life.

West was thus unwittingly learning his vocation as a satirist at a time when the contradictions of American life were deep and obvious. It was no accident that the sophisticated wit of the time flourished on paradox, since paradox was everywhere. A guest speaker at Clinton praised advertising as the "Salesman of Today"; but advertising was ill-regulated and shot through with deception. He spoke of honesty as the "best policy in the business world," but investigating committees would soon show how widely the best policy had been ignored, in war profiteering and stock manipulation. America was fighting, while West was at Clinton, to make the world "safe for democracy," but at home, immediately after the war, there were numerous manifestations of bigotry and organized campaigns against Jews, Catholics, and "Reds," ending in federal legislation to limit immigration. In a dramatic move, while West was in high school, Americans voted in Prohibition as one of the evangels of progressive thought; but instead of purity, it brought bootleggers; instead of purging politics, it deepened corruption. What kind of peace had been won, moreover, when by November 1919 two million workers were on strike, and four million workers were involved in strikes during the year?

In May 1920, Warren Gamaliel Harding would sum up the period of West's adolescence, naming its paradoxes as if they did not really exist or as if there were a choice between them. What the country needs, he said, "is not heroism but healing, not nostrums but normalcy, not revolution but restoration, not agitation but adjustment, not surgery but serenity, not the dramatic but the dispassionate, not experiment but equipoise, not submergence in internationality but sustainment in triumphant nationality." He assured his constituents that all they needed to do was relax and blow off steam—he himself liked nothing better than "to go out into the country and bloviate," and his various bloviations were, as H. L. Mencken said, like "a string of wet sponges." But the country in the next fifteen years, as West came to maturity, would have all that Harding had eschewed for it—revolution, agitation, surgery, experiment, and international involvement. It was true, as McAdoo quipped and time would show, that Harding's speeches were "an army of pompous phrases moving across the landscape in search of an idea." But this was the style of the age, one that West and his creative contemporaries would all analyze as pitiable or laugh to scorn.

Such were the paradoxes of the era in which West's earliest education occurred. He was seeking out his identity in an era deeply perplexed about its own character; and he was trying to envision a future in a time when thought of the future, like that of the present, was virtually inconceivable. As he would prove both in his books and in his life, West was almost unbearably sensitive to the paradoxes of his time. Perhaps, as he showed by his rebellion against the business and academic ethic, he was in danger of being destroyed by his resistance to the nostrum of normalcy; he would make his novels all that was inimical to easy solutions. He was part of the Lost Generation, the youngest and last of that generation. And surely his work would be the more savagely true in that the whole of his mature life coincided with the sense that this generation had of betrayal and irredeemable loss.

III

Fittingly, the paradoxes in West's time and life were summed up in his own activities at a summer camp located on a lake where the currents ran in two opposite directions—Camp Paradox. West spent his summers in this Adirondack camp from the time he was thirteen until he was seventeen, during the same period that he was sporadically going to Clinton. No less than his failure to succeed in high school, his varied and ambivalent responses to the highly conventional, formalized middle-class Jewish camp life suggest how he could himself early learn to face society paradoxically.

In many ways, the camp became a focus for West's interest in the outdoors and in sports; for the activities of the camp were virtually restricted to these. The counselors led the boys on difficult hikes and the baseball team often traveled more than forty miles away in the Adirondacks to play the teams of other camps. Surviving issues of the camp magazine, *The Paradoxian*, document both these activities and West's part in them. It is clear, as one of his contemporaries at Paradox writes, that he "tried hard to conform to the standards of a boys' summer camp where the main theme was athletic prowess." But at last it is even more clear that he could not do so.

The Paradoxian, devoted chiefly to sporting news, gives full reports of each baseball game. West, these show, played for the baseball team in 1918 and 1919 and was regarded as a weak batter and fielder, batting eighth or ninth and playing right field (while Sam played shortstop and led off and Charles's son Nathan was a pitcher and batted third or fourth). Altogether there are records of five games, in which West compiled a record of five hits in twenty times at bat and one error while making twelve putouts. During the four years he spent at Paradox he won ignominious awards in "rowing and canoeing" (second place) and a bronze medal for "batting and fielding," while his cousins swept the major athletic awards. His failure to "measure up," as the other campers (and even he) were bound to see it, West would need to justify to himself. It so haunted his imagination that eventually, a decade later, he would attempt to free himself from the bitterness it left by writing a story called "Western Union Boy," in which he makes his protagonist fail even more dramatically. Drunk, F. Winslow, "known simply as F," attempts to analyze himself:

"I am a sun field player," he said; "I'm always in right field."
. . . If you have ever played ball, you'll know what he meant. In the big league the right fielder is usually as good as the other fielders, but not in the lots. There he is the last man chosen; no one wants him on his side. A right fielder always has the sun in his eyes; he always gets a bad bounce; it is the short field and he is always running into the fence.
The liquor made F poetic, but I'll try to give you what he said as best I can. It seems that he suffers from nightmares, or rather one recurring nightmare. It is about a ball game he once played in.
He has a cousin who had been captain of baseball at Princeton. Every summer, this cousin, as was usual in those days, organized a semi-pro team to play for some town or other. One season his team was to represent Mineville in the Adirondack League. He gave F a job as right fielder. F showed up pretty good in practice, but then the first game came along. It was Mineville vs. Pottersville on the Pottersville fair grounds. To show that they were real pros, all the players took a chew of tobacco before the game started. F had never chewed before, but he took one too because he was anxious to make good.
The sun was very hot in right field as it always is. What with the heat and the tobacco, F felt like going home. So far he had been lucky; he had gotten to the fifth inning without having a ball hit to him. But in the fifth, with a man on second and third, a pop fly was hit to right field. F didn't move except to swallow the plug of tobacco. The ball hit him in the chest. He fell to his [knees] and fumbled for it in the grass, but his eyes were closed and he couldn't find it. The first baseman had to come out and field it for him. When he opened his eyes, he saw his cousin running towards him with a bat in his hands. F ran off the field and hid in the woods behind third base. His cousin thrashed around in the bushes looking for him until the umpire called play ball.
When the game was over, F came out of the woods and went to the bus that was getting ready to take the team back to Mineville. But his cousin picked up a bat and wouldn't let him get near the bus. He had

to hitch hike back in his spiked shoes. That night he packed up and went home.

F still dreams of that fifth inning and of his cousin with the bat. He has this dream regularly about once a week.

For West, F stood for Failure. In their success, his cousins were monstrous, threatening creatures of his imagination. To preserve his own ego, he would need to deny the standards of their success. Yet he was haunted by the appearance of his own failure.

Outdoor activity at Paradox was as highly valued as a measure of success as baseball. Campers regularly canoed or hiked to distant parts of the Adirondacks. *The Paradoxian* reported, for instance, in July of 1918, that fourteen boys left camp for a "three-day paddle," which began with "a heated discussion carried on by Milt Silverman and Pep Weinstein regarding each other's ability with the paddle." By the summer of 1920 West was leading the campers on a similar ten-mile trip. "With Brant Lake as our goal," *The Paradoxian* account begins, "Pep Weinstein as our line, our end in view . . . it is little wonder that the four days of 'roughing it' and plowing through the water were so heartily enjoyed by the six boys. . . ."

It was on one such trip that West got his nickname, although he would later foster many alternate romantic tales concerning the origin of this name. " 'Pep' did not," a contemporary has said, "acquire his nickname by an abundance of energy. Quite the contrary. . . . He was party to an extremely arduous and difficult hike and climb of Mount Marcy and returned to the camp so thoroughly exhausted that he literally slept for over twenty-four hours and then dragged himself around camp for the next few days. It was at this point that he was dubbed 'Pep.' " Due also to his reticence in speech, the name stuck. *The Paradoxian* for July 1918 hinted at this in reporting that "Nat Weinstein, the Pepper King," and another camper "are visiting Irv Wallach, but altho' they sit at the table with him . . . Irv says, 'Did you ever hear such a quiet bunch?' " Moreover, the other campers were gently mocking West for his absurd slowness in all things. Even his cousin Sam was struck by the fact that he seemed to have "few ambitions." He even seemed, of all things, "to have no interest in schooling."

At a time when push and drive were the qualities most admired,

West moved slowly; when a gift of tongues, the magic of salesmanship, and "personal magnetism" obsessed the American business
mind, West was reticent; and at the camp, where pep on the
baseball field—pepper, snappiness, zip—was particularly emphasized, "Pep" was an ironical (though not necessarily an unkind)
assessment of all he lacked. In recognition of his laziness, he was
even, in his last year at Paradox, presented with a comic award, "a
box marked 'Ingersoll Alarm,'" that "... contained a trained
chipmunk, which would hereafter wake Pep in time for breakfast.
Lucky boy, Pep." Paradox, clearly, was allied with conventional
values, and encouraged not only sports and hearty outdoorsman-
ship but business success, respectability, perseverance, loyalty and
sentiment for the camp, and a belief in the goodness of work, all
combined with a prevailing spirit of good fun. The campers delighted in the screening of such snappy films as Mack Sennett's
The Sleuths, John Barrymore in *On the Quiet*, Jack Pickford in
Mile-a-Minute Kendall, Fatty Arbuckle's *The Bell-Boy*, Wallace
Reid in "a wonderful story of the Western lumber camp regions,"
and William S. Hart's *Branding Broadway*. The camp's style is
expressed perhaps best of all in a song called "A Paradox Day,"
written by two of its counselors, both soon to be famous, Herbert
Fields and Richard C. Rodgers:

> When summer has come with its heat and its rain,
> And there's always vacation from school;
> Every boy who loves fun knows it only begun
> At our camp where it's sunny and cool.
> He knows that our lake is a real paradise,
> And it offers him all sorts of joy;
> Each hour supplies some new pleasant surprise
> For the fortunate Paradox boy.

In his own paradoxical way, West went against this current at
Paradox, but more subtly than he had at De Witt Clinton. At
Camp Paradox, West became an artist and satirist in compensation for his inability to conform and succeed along conventional paths. He discovered this early that he could remain in society while defending himself against social demands through art, by
satirically caricaturing camp values in cartoons shrewdly juxtaposed
to the conventional affirmations in the rest of the camp magazine.

By 1919 he was an assistant on the art staff, and in the summer of 1920 "Nathan 'Pep' Weinstein" was listed as Art Editor on the *Paradoxian* masthead. Through his art he satirized the values and conventions of his camp and the society it could symbolize. A study of his cartoons shows a variety of techniques and targets for his satire. In the first number of 1920 he sandwiched an idealized portrait of a hiker between two other drawings of a comic-grotesque group of Arabian figures who are laboring absurdly, carrying water jars and baskets in the heat of the blazing sun. One has fallen awkwardly against a tree, but he smiles happily, while the others, terribly misshapen, labor on. This cleverly expresses West's view of the idealized camper whose activity is of no greater value than that of the grotesques who frame him. Later in the same issue, West published a full-page comic strip mocking various activities at the camp, including a "Brooks Brothers Revue" of the cheap school sweaters hanging on a clothesline. (In the middle, colored darkly, is one with the De Witt Clinton letters.) The "comic strip" ends with a blank square, entitled "What the Faculty Thinks About." Two pages later, another West cartoon shows two motion-picture cameramen photographing the sentimental gesticulations of a ham actor. In his final contribution to this issue, placed beside an idealized picture of sports activities drawn by the previous art editor and reprinted from an earlier issue, he again drew a full-page cartoon series, this time ridiculing baseball. Doubtless influenced by Ring Lardner, whom he had read, he satirized the baseball lingo so popular with Americans (a man making a "shoe-string" catch trips over his laces, and a pitcher who has "wound up" is tied in knots), and showed a series of stupid mistakes in fielding and base running (e.g., "The Hero of the Game Steals 2nd with the Bases Full").

In the next number of *The Paradoxian*, similarly, he published a picture of two knights jousting before tournament flags which spell Paradox, followed by a picture of a baseball player finishing a swing with his bat. In another full-page cartoon strip, he shows a counselor lying back in a soft chair sucking a lollypop ("An Ideal Faculty"), jokes about the food, and again ridicules the clothes of the campers. In short, all his drawings are critical of the camp and its values—he shows the campers as grotesques and their activities as absurd. One of his contemporaries at Paradox described him as having "a helluva sense of humor . . . a sense of the ludicrous." But West's humor was bitter and potentially savage. Through it, certainly this early, and to some extent always, he gave himself assurances that he was no less manly or strong than his fellows; indeed, he placed them on the defensive, for all their conventional superiority, by virtue of his power to ridicule them. Through his art he would assert his superiority. The lessons he learned at Camp Paradox were crucial in his development. Though he was to be a novelist, not an artist, art would provide models for his narratives. Cartoons, silent-comedy films, surrealist dream photographs, etchings, collages, romantic canvases, movie sets—all gave him hints about how to create a new style appropriate to his observational sensibility and as fluid and surprising as the world he saw. His work on *The Paradoxian* started him toward this discovery.

Indeed, at the camp he was already generalizing his satire through visual caricature. In mockery of the naïve enjoyment which the other campers found in their movies of adventure, West took part in live entertainment satirizing the typical Hollywood product. Spotlighted against the movie screen, *The Paradoxian* declared, he "scored a distinct hit as the fiendish villain." Finally, at the very end of his camp career, on "Camper's Day," he went on stage with a caricature of a speech by the owner of the camp, Mr. Goldwater, and was a "scream." Behind the current cliché was literal truth; for West managed to satirize, in all, every aspect of the camp.

Paradoxically, he had learned to defend himself against convention by means of art. That was not much, a gesture of defiance, but it was a beginning.

It was, in any event, what he had needed to learn. When De Witt Clinton reopened in the fall of 1920, he did not return. The first phase of his education was ended.

4 / West's Providence

> On the one hand we have a tottering world, wedded to the
> Glockenspiel of Hell; on the other the new men, rough,
> hard-riding. . . . Let each man proclaim: there is a great
> negative work of destruction to be accomplished. We must
> sweep everything away and sweep clean. . . .
>
> —Tristan Tzara, in a Dada manifesto, *c.* 1918

The 1920's in America were suffused with possibilities for what the
French prophet of surrealism, Guillaume Apollinaire, called the
"new laughter." 1920, when West was beginning to rebel seriously
against current conventions, was a pivotal year in American history,
when the failure of Wilson's New Freedom disillusioned and dis-
affected the young. The malaise which produced dadaism in Europe in 1916 bloomed in America to give West, in New York,
Boston, and Providence, the same evidence of modern absurdity
that Malcolm Cowley, E. E. Cummings, and Robert M. Coates
found in Paris. West, a few years younger than they, watched the
spirit of Dada spring from native soil. He did not need to read
descriptions of the Paris scene published in *Broom* by Matthew
Josephson or in *Vanity Fair* by Edmund Wilson; he by no means
formulated dadaist principles himself. But he made, on his own,
the same decisive rejection of society as his contemporaries. "You
all stand accused here," Picabia had said in his *Manifeste Canni-
bale* while West was in high school; but West was already accusing
his society by refusing to enter it.

Fully awake to the absurdity of his age, West would make literature from it. While some of his contemporaries, as Bliss Perry remarked, had their "capacity for emotional and moral reaction to
events" exhausted by the war and the grotesque period which it
ushered in, West remained vividly alive to the civilization of the

twenties. In general, in America, there were two responses of the sensibility to this condition—genteel, ascetic withdrawal or rebellion against the genteel tradition. Of these two, of course, the creative power of the twenties would rise from the ethics of rebellion, the urge to affront the bourgeois, commitment to the irrational, and an attitude of contempt—in short, the urge to destroy.

The absurd was everywhere. One had only to have his eyes opened to see it. While others went to Paris to give full expression to their estrangement, West was an exile in America. For his slightly older contemporaries, dadaism was a form of protest, but West needed neither Dada manifestoes nor economic crises to know that irrationality prevailed in America and that he hated its commercial life. All aspects of American life, as he saw it, touched on the grotesque and the absurd.

Anyone who stood aghast at American conventions was, as the slang of the day had it, "a knocker," when the ideal was to be "a booster." West was really neither, since his pessimism reached deep. He was not alone in this. Mencken, Ring Lardner, Sherwood Anderson, and Theodore Dreiser were all unmasking American optimism. West admired all these writers except Dreiser and he would follow in their tradition.

During 1920-1, not yet an artist but already a rebel, West worked out a bizarre personal model of rebellion against bourgeois conventions. The new values which gained importance in the twenties included the virtue credited to a college education. Whereas Americans in the nineteenth century had been suspicious of higher education, and both businessmen like Commodore Vanderbilt and intellectuals like Henry Adams mocked its medievalisms, now the postwar generation and their parents were convinced that college would provide a path to the good life. College became a kind of "social necessity," one historian has observed, ranking "with having a bathroom and keeping a car." Increasing affluence, advertising campaigns conducted (chiefly through football) by colleges, a weakening of social barriers leading to the belief that a degree would guarantee social mobility—these American circumstances coincided in the twenties with the emphasis which the Wallensteins had learned to place on education in Russia and the pride which Max had in being able to educate his son in America.

His society and his parents wanted West to go to college? Very well, he would do so. He was attracted personally, it seems clear, by the myth of College Life. By 1920 the college campus had replaced the plantation and the ranch as a symbol of the free, expansive life; and on one level of his consciousness and emotional responsiveness, West could unquestioningly be as fascinated by college values and rituals as Scott Fitzgerald had been at Princeton. College truly appealed to West's desire for admiration and his need for status, as well as to his commitment to the distinguished ideals of the gentleman.

On the other hand, he was far from accepting without suspicion the conforming values of college life. He scorned college codes, yet desired to experience college life. Here was another affair in which he could be a lonely spy, at once having the pleasures of society and mocking them. Certainly, his attitude toward college was always to be ambiguous. He would, in time, satirize college life by being, as it were, an insider in it: by caricaturing it in his complete adoption of its conventions. He too could don a thirty-skin raccoon coat, slip a flask in the pocket of his bell-bottoms, and, blessed by Brooks, streak in a Stutz for an ivy tower. That would be the measure of his scorn for college. He would be an outsider exactly to the extent that he could imitate the absurd insider.

First, however, he had to become an insider—no easy job, since he had not graduated from high school. For a man of West's proved ingenuity and imagination, this was no insuperable bar, of course. In the spring of 1921, with the help of Wally, ink, and ink eradicator, West took his own transcript from De Witt Clinton and added to it passing grades in one term of Spanish; a year each of English, history, and plane geometry; five terms of Latin; and two terms of physics. Except for Latin, these were all subjects West would conceivably have been able to pass if he had stayed on for another year at Clinton. He passed them, in any event, in a genuine act of imaginative improvisation: he created his successful, conventional self, making out a transcript as if he were still at Clinton, and passing all his courses. All told, he awarded himself 6 credits in a transcript showing 15½. Since college usually required but 15 credits for admission, West— with half a credit in freehand drawing—ironically got a bonus which he had, in fact, earned. As an added flourish of elegance in preparing the transcript for a school in New England, he added a few letters to his given name (on the transcript his last name was first, leaving space for this) and at last sent the transcript of one "Nathaniel Weinstein" to Tufts College, in Medford, Massachusetts. This, as Malcolm Cowley remarks, "was the ethics of Dada." It would have been "exactly what Faulkner would have done if *he* had wanted to go to college."

In due course, and probably without lengthy consideration, he was admitted to the College of Letters at Tufts and matriculated for a Bachelor of Science degree beginning in September 1921. His college course plan differed from that for the B.A. only in not requiring the study of ancient languages. Infused by the spirit of the modern, and in full revolt against the massive past, West saw in the languages of antiquity the summation of all that was most sterile and dead in American life. Indeed, his first published piece of satirical prose and his first novel would both be wastelands made of the inert fragments of ancient works and days.

Tufts, a private school, had been founded under Universalist leadership and auspices, yet it was nondenominational in character and had easy rules concerning attendance at chapel. The *College Catalogue: 1921–22*, which West received when he entered in the fall of 1921 as a freshman, declared: "The college is fortunate in its location. Student life at 'The Hill' is substantially like that of the smaller colleges in New England. The students and the faculty form a community. . . ." Everything about his choice of Tufts was average and typical. It was West's representative college. The fees were average for the early twenties: $100 each semester, plus room, board, and personal expenses. Its athletic teams were supported with the same hysteria as at other colleges. The architecture and faculty were both indistinguishable from those of similar colleges.

Like other colleges, too, Tufts was infested with fraternities. Since the college drew its students largely from the Boston area and New York, a Jewish fraternity had already been established on campus, and not long after West arrived, with a friendly personality and an ample allowance, he was pledged to Phi Epsilon Pi, and moved into the House at 19 University Avenue. He registered for the basic freshman program—English, math, biology, history, physical education, French, and hygiene.

An annual ceremony at Tufts was the Russell lecture, usually given by a well-known speaker, at which attendance was compulsory. On October 29, 1921, this lecture was delivered by a frequent contributor to the genteel *Atlantic*, the essayist Samuel McChord Crothers, who was introduced as "the Emerson of this generation." Dealing, as the terms of the lectureship stated, "with the sufficiency of the promises of the Gospel to meet the reasonable wants of man in time and eternity," his talk did not seem to promise much of interest. It would not have suited Emerson. But if West was paying attention, Crothers's talk might have struck something in him. He concluded that "the tendency of all forms of Protestantism is toward atrophy of thought through fear of going too far." But, he asked, "Have you ever been struck by the boldness of thought of many of the leaders of the Catholic Church? . . . The infallibility of the Church has something of the function of the net back of the tennis players—without it, the players would lose time chasing lost balls, and the game would slow up."

This problem of the loss of firm standards of value—of the disintegration of values into convention and of convention into illusion —was to become the problem central to West's view of life. He had found no absolute standards of value in the beliefs of his parents or family. They wanted nothing but to be Americanized as rapidly as possible. Nor did he find sources of value in the rituals or traditions of Judaism. His parents left their religion in Russia. They, and his whole community, had thrown over the traditional ideals of religion and culture. And since by heritage West was empty of ideals, he was able to see how few of them society in general could truly claim. Thus, he rejected too the only values, of success, which his family offered him. He was opposed to orthodoxy in culture no less than to orthodoxy in religion. He had scorned intellectual orthodoxy at school. Yet, ambivalently, he yearned for orthodoxy of some kind. In the strange combinations of his reading both in the moderns and in traditional literature, from the Church Fathers and the mystics to Flaubert, West was instinctively working his way to a secular absolutism of self and art. In 1921 this had its form chiefly in the ethics of scorn which he held for college.

He experimented with it. In his later story "The Adventurer" he characterized his own values as concentrating in observation. His virtue would be the accurate and pitiless observation of others'

values, "knowing the signs and habits of our quarry, stalking, trailing, observing carefully. . . . " Now he stalked the tracks of college life. There were football games to go to, life in the fraternity
to be sampled, plays in Boston to be seen (like Eugene O'Neill's
Beyond the Horizon: An American Tragedy in Three Acts),
dances to find dates for, and a new city to explore. West was leading the conventional life of a freshman. He is remembered by a
fraternity brother as a "snappy" dresser who had plenty of money
to spend. Well dressed and well featured, his hair parted slightly
off center, West followed the collegiate high life in the fall of 1921.

He neglected only to go to classes. On November 30, 1921, an
editorial in the college newspaper drew a conventional moral:
"The meeting of the Promotions Committee last week calls to attention, sadly to some, the primary reason for going to college—to
do one's best scholastically. There were a few who had overlooked
this important fact in the first two months of the college year, and
of necessity they had to withdraw." West was one of the chosen
few. After the meeting of the Promotions Committee on November 25, 1921, the day following Thanksgiving, West was advised to
withdraw. His first grades had been turned in a week earlier and
he had achieved failing marks in every course, including a double F
in French; in physical education he was marked "Not Attending"
and failed. A joke could go only so far.

Well, Wally had been expelled from Columbia and Haverford
and now he was at Tulane. Pep too might transfer, on his Tufts
record, to another school. He had not been at Tufts for a full term
and so had not had a single official mark recorded—only the 15½
entrance credits. He too might easily be admitted to another college. At this point the absurdity of chance matched the absurdity
of West's very presence at Tufts. Dada bloomed on the campus.
By bizarre coincidence, there was another Nathan Weinstein registered at Tufts. He was born in 1899, attended the English High
School in Boston, lived in Dorchester, Mass., and had entered the
Harvard Dental School during World War I, where he pursued
the regular scientific course and, in addition, enrolled in a military-
drill course in the Student Army Training Corps. In February 1920
he had transferred to Tufts for a B.S. degree. Apparently his credits
from Harvard had been conditionally accepted, since after he successfully completed one term at Tufts, he had 9 previous credits

recorded. During the year 1920–1 he earned 35 credits in scientific subjects and German at Tufts. In good standing, with a straight C average, and with half of his college credit requirements completed, he transferred into Tufts Medical School beginning in the fall of 1921, at the same time that West entered the college. Previous credits for chemistry and drill were credited to his record soon after, giving him, in all, a total of 57 college credits.

West and this Nathan Weinstein never met; yet there is no doubt that West had heard from one of his fraternity brothers—two of whom also lived in Dorchester—about his namesake. The absurd had conspired to put another Weinstein in reach. Whether accident or design next prevailed is not clear. One story has it that a girl in the registrar's office had a crush on West and helped him to combine his record with the elder Nathan Weinstein's for transmission to Brown University. It is certainly true that, in the fall of 1922, West drove from Providence back to Tufts with a friend, Brae Rafferty, explaining to him that he had to see a girl in the office to have his credits straightened out. It is also possible, of course, that quite by chance the two transcripts were confused and the 57 credits awarded to West by error. (Confusion already existed, since in 1920–1 the Tufts general grade list gives to both L. Weinstein and A. Weinstein credits that had been earned by Nathan Weinstein.) West himself may unwittingly have aided this confusion by forgetting that he had registered as Nathaniel and asking for his transcript under his given name, Nathan Weinstein, to be sent to Brown as part of his application for admission.

Whether the ultimate chances were arranged by fortune or calculation, West was admitted, for the spring term of 1922, to Brown University. Having failed to graduate from high school or to pass any courses at Tufts, he would arrive in Providence with a year and a half advanced standing. There, with 57 credits in scientific subjects, German, and economics, West became a second-term sophomore candidate for the Bachelor of Philosophy degree, one that did not require courses in Greek or Latin.

West mysteriously told his new classmates, one of them recalls, "that he had burst on the Brown campus full-blown out of the United States Navy"—a tale compounded of his earlier plan to enlist, the nearby naval base, and the fact that there were several World War I veterans on the Brown campus who were regarded with great respect. Their kind of special distinction was part of West's dream, and he was learning better and better to make convincing roles of his fantasies. He succeeded in convincing even the army veterans, such as the future novelist Frank O. Hough, that he was one of them. Like a Huck Finn who could not give up his disguises, West now began to create himself anew out of his own conception of himself. At least to give the appearance of having been in college for two years, he gave his birthdate as 1902 on a Brown registration card.

In the two and a half years following, West would involve himself enthusiastically in two quite opposed worlds. The one he would suggestively name the Bacchanalians. This consisted, of course, of the pleasure seekers at Brown—chiefly those in the athletic and fraternity groups. West could be wholly what Quentin Reynolds called "a completely normal product of his times; he liked football, drinking, and hell raising." He saw himself, to some extent, in the sensualist tradition of Rabelais and Villon, and cultivated capacious views toward food, alcohol, and women. Moreover, he was tall and wished to be distinguished in appearance, and so dressed with great care.

Certainly, his clothes were splendid. His roommate, Philip Lukin, described him as "a typical college type of the sophisticated variety." West wore "Brooks Brothers suits, argyle socks, Whitehouse and Hardy brogues, Brooks shirts and ties and Herbert Johnson or Lock and Co. hats." He was even, as S. J. Perelman summed up his appearance, "a dandy," an exquisite. In some part his style was a rebellion against the low tastes which he found around him. As early as 1919, he had been laughed at in *The Paradoxian* as "Joe Brooks"; but that too, he probably told himself, could be regarded as merely a proof of his superior taste. He kept his image distinctive by wearing certain clothes which simultaneously stressed his taste and his refusal to be merely fashionable. Fifteen years later, in Hollywood, where the styles were much more garish and improbable, he would still insist on wearing Brooks Brothers clothes, and thus differentiate himself from his Hollywood cronies. In part, his concern with dressing in the Brooks mode derived from his reading in stylish, sophisticated British authors, from Wilde to Michael Arlen and Huxley. Indeed, as the novelist Nathan Asch said of West's appearance in the early thirties, he "looked as I suppose Michael Arlen would have liked to look." His cousin Sam, who was entering in 1921 upon a career in investment banking with L. F. Rothschild, had already developed a style of dress in the English pattern and wore a clipped military mustache. Sam was "correct and quiet," John Sanford says, and his success was pointed to as a model for emulation. It may be, too, as West's roommate believed, that he felt that he was not handsome and substituted approved fashion for approved features.

It is hardly unusual for clothes to be used as a symbol of taste or distinction. If Mark Twain joined the Christian Sons of Temperance so that he could wear their gaudy red sash and later not only affected white suits but also wore his scarlet Oxford gown at his daughter's wedding, West's use of Brooks Brothers clothes as an expression of his own breeding was not remarkable. Then too, West, easily adapting, could fall into ostensible acquiescence to almost any condition or situation. He was in an Ivy League school when a certain style began to be *de rigueur*, and instinctively wanting to do things in good fashion or cleverly, he dressed in a heightened conventional mode. He was decidedly a Bacchanalian in his clothes, although he also showed a certain curious scorn even of these by treating them carelessly and with disregard, and by insisting with self-mockery that he even got his shoelaces in Brooks.

His Bacchanalianism was not limited to clothes. In other ways Brown gave his ego certain conventional satisfactions. He made a moderately successful attempt to play the banjo. He believed, too, that he was a good dancer, and he faithfully appeared at the tea dances at Churchill House, in company with a certain willowy Pembroke student. From New York he once brought back a new dance to the college and bent all his efforts on teaching it to his friends. Moreover, he went often to Providence's Arcadia Ballroom, where Al Mitchell, formerly a sideman of Paul Whiteman, led his orchestra through dances satisfactory to both town and gown, the camel walk for the collegiates and the grapevine for the "sharpies." Here, the dancers wore green Norfolk suits with white polo shirts and red ties while they spun around the floor with local girls or college widows. West, his roommate recalls, "cut in frequently." One night West and his friend Brae Rafferty were attacked when their elegant clothes and elaborate affectations provoked the town sharpies.

An itching desire to define his identity through success in sports still lingered from his Camp Paradox days. He told his friends that he had played outfield at De Witt Clinton, and he would inform later acquaintances that he had played on the Brown team. One comic tale which Wells Root heard him tell "a half dozen times" in the late thirties very closely parallels his short story "Western Union Boy":

"In his college days he played on the Brown University baseball team. He was an outfielder, and in the summer used to play semi-pro ball with resort teams. . . . N. was playing for some summer team in New England which had won most of its games, and was battling an arch rival. They were playing on the home grounds, and everybody in the hotel had bet his last penny. Came the ninth inning with the score tied and the enemies at bat. They got a man on base with two out and the next batter hit a long fly to N. Normally, it would have been an easy out, so N. ambled over to the point where the ball was due and relaxed. He put up his hands to catch it and for some inexplicable reason didn't hold them close together. The ball tore through, hit him in the forehead, and bounced into some brush. There was a roar from the crowd and N. took one look and turned tail. To a man, the crowd had risen, gathered bats, sticks, stones, and anything they could lay hands on and were in hot pursuit. He vanished into some woods and didn't emerge until nightfall. In telling the story he was convinced that if they had caught him they would have killed him."

At Brown, interest in sports was as intense as at Camp Paradox. (Even the librarian, in listing the world's best books in the *Brown Daily Herald*, gave them as the All-American, All-British, and All-Continental "teams.") By the age of nineteen West had reached his full height and decided to report for the basketball team in November 1922. By January, however, he was cut from the squad. At Camp Paradox he had taken revenge in cartoons for his lack of success. Now, turning to literature, he named the ludicrous hero of the book he soon began, after the basketball coach, Walter Snell.

At football games West cheered with his athletic friends and apparently showed as much enthusiasm as anyone in the lively discussions of the sport of the day. In the fall of 1923, indeed, he and Lukin traveled as far as western Pennsylvania to cheer the team on against Washington and Jefferson. This trip provided the source of a fantasy tale, about his part in one of the violent coal-mine strikes of the twenties, that West told as autobiography in the thirties. The truth was that his red Stutz Bearcat broke down near a coal town on the way back from the game and while waiting for it to be repaired he and Lukin briefly eyed the idle miners, then bought hunting clothes, boots, and buffalo plaid shirts in the local general store. The fashion they thus began at Brown was interest not in labor problems but in clothes, for the whole college began to imitate them and the rural fashion held brief sway in the Ivy League.

West, it seems clear, was also attracted to life in the fraternities, even while he scorned fraternity values. The Brown fraternities at that time, as Quentin Reynolds remembers, sought "freshmen who were impeccably Nordic and of distinguished ancestry." West was not pledged. A contemporary says that he was often with the DKE's, the fraternity most noted for being typically extroverted, the essential Bacchanalians. There was no Jewish fraternity at Brown, as there had been at Tufts, and so it was the one activity from which West was excluded not by his own choice. He was close friends with some of the Catholics who belonged to the one non-Protestant fraternity, particularly with Brae Rafferty and Quentin Reynolds. But although one Jewish boy—a football quarterback, Reynolds's roommate—was pledged, West was excluded here as well, and he was irritated by being refused admission; even years later he confided to Lester Cole that he had wanted not to belong to a fraternity so much as to be pledged. He refused to accept rejection by the fraternities which he rejected, and he suffered considerably over his social exclusion.

But he could never be wholly a Bacchanalian. He was also a self-styled member of what he named the Hanseatic League. The Hanseatic League, like the figure of Wallenstein, had a personal meaning for West, associated with aristocratic, romantic, distinguished qualities. West devised the title for a small group of his friends, one says, "as something special." The name, of course, meant to confer distinction and was drawn from his Baltic ancestry. The confederation of free north German towns formed in the thirteenth century for protection and promotion of commerce had included the Baltic provinces, where Kovno was a district center.

West regarded himself and his friends as similar to the free towns, centers of enlightenment and modernism set in the midst of the medieval barbarism of the Bacchanalian sensualists. In the one he was Pep Weinstein; in the other, Nathaniel von Wallenstein Weinstein. In the one he rebelled against the college type which he imitated in the other. His roommate has remarked that "the West of later years is a mystery to me in terms of the Pep Weinstein of college years." But the division already existed.

A key to the relations between the two groups is given by one of the Hanseatic League, Jeremiah Mahoney. The principle of the League, he declares, was its mockery of "what the common man was relishing [in] those days. [We were] a kind of intellectual elite, perhaps, descending from our ivory tower to sample and reject the cloying sweets of the public fare." The key symbol of this attitude is certainly the bookplate which his college friend S. J. Perelman designed for West in 1923. (Friendship not withstanding, Perelman had a difficult time collecting his fee for the design.) It shows a figure with his arm affectionately thrown around the neck of an ass, above a motto from Goethe, "Do I love what others love?" and the signature, "N. von Wallenstein Weinstein." West was inclined to satirize his own inclinations. "One of his most . . . disarming characteristics," as a classmate said of West, "was his readiness to laugh at himself."

Doubtless he took his Hanseatic League activities comically as well. They were simply the absurd reversal of all that life among the Bacchanalians implied. The most sensational experiments of West's Hanseatic League were with magic. Interested at once in J. K. Huysmans's description of a Black Mass, West withdrew several books on magic and occultism from the library, among them Eliphas Levi's *Dogmes et rituel de haute magie* and Montagu Summers's *History of Witchcraft*. Then, gathering with his friends around a table and using fresh eggs and chalking elaborate yellow circles on the floor, he attempted to summon up the dead. He was skeptical of the chances for success, but professed a hope that he might accidentally hit upon the true magic formula.

At Brown he was content with the same simple exoticism that interested the aesthetes of the 1890's. Once, another student brought opium into West's room at 28 University Hall (West owned De Quincey's *Confessions of an English Opium Eater*), but their experiments with it failed decisively since no one could discover precisely how to use it. Each night in the room, West and his friends resumed, too, a game of imaginary conversations and so developed a serial fantasy life. His more permanent interest in the Catholic Church was still largely concentrated in its mysticism and ritual. "On the subject of Catholicism," a friend of the thirties, Wells Root, would say, "he could talk for hours. He had an incredible array of facts, from earliest Church history to the present." With Rafferty and Mahoney or Reynolds, he went to High Mass in the Providence cathedral, pretending to be impressed by its perfumed ceremony. In *Miss Lonelyhearts* and the funeral scene of *The Day of the Locust*, he would turn this interest to fictive use, making religious tradition symbolize the kind of values which had been lost in modern times. In the meantime, he bought and read such books as Bennett's *Handbook of the Early Christian Fathers* and De Labrialle's *History and Literature of Christianity*, as well as Pater's *Greek Studies*, Jesse Weston's *From Ritual to Romance*, Nicholson's *Mysteries of Islam*, and Abelson's *Jewish Mysticism*.

Toward the forms of American collective fantasy on the stage or in the movies, the Hanseatic League held ambivalent attitudes. Interest in theater was lively at Brown: the college daily ran a regular drama column. West and Rafferty, with passes from the drama critic of the *Providence Journal*, saw all the plays on tour, as well as those staged by Jessie Bonstelle's excellent local company. West also went often to see the Fays Theatre vaudeville acts. And, of course, in the fashion of the time, they were, as S. J. Perelman has said, "inveterate movie-goers." Here they fell in with collective fancy. In 1922 the weekly attendance at movie houses was estimated at 40,000,000: West and his friends helped to keep up the national average by going to the movies at least one evening (and usually two) each week, as well as supporting the bargain 30¢ Monday matinees at the B. F. Keith house. But they also mocked their entertainments by crying at Chaplin comedies and laughing at melodramas like *Ramona*. In 1922, *that* was a sufficiently Dada response.

West also had a rich fund of esoteric references (some of them invented) which he could bring startlingly and impressively into conversation. His mind was quick, and he desired to stand out, to be distinguished, and thus he was as quick to create as to recall special knowledge. Already inclined toward the literary hoax, he spoke knowingly of writers who never existed, as if he alone were especially intimate with their work, but he was genuinely an encyclopedist of the decadent and exotic, through which he satirized established values. Moreover, he would carry into action, Rafferty recalls, "any idea that appealed to him, particularly if it were novel." Once, for instance, he signed for the purchase of a Norfolk jacket from a traveling clothing salesman. "They'll never be able to read *that* writing," he said later, as he donned the jacket. On several occasions—this was during Prohibition—he took Brae Rafferty to the synagogue and, introducing him as Mr. Fisher, purchased port wine, which they consumed with quantities of pistachio nuts. The climax of his dadaist willingness to experiment with the absurd came one night when he became so impressed with the symbolism of a Chinese medallion printed on the cover of a book of Oriental philosophy that he carried the book to a tattoo parlor, whose clientele usually came from the naval base nearby, and had it copied on his arm.

Many of these adventures came during his junior and senior years. In West's first term on College Hill, however, although he scored his first academic success by passing the required swimming test, he continued, as at Tufts, to follow his own interests and failed to complete any of his courses. In May 1922, due to excessive cuts, he was advised to withdraw for discipline, without penalty. Now, one would have supposed that the following fall would find West at still a third college. Yet, upon consideration, he was credited by the Brown University registrar with all 57 college credits earned by Nathan Weinstein, including the modern-language, science, and economics credits required for graduation. Even though he had not yet completed a single course for credit either at Tufts or at Brown, his entrance credits now gave him two years' advance standing. Thus, the Brown authorities allowed him to reapply and he was readmitted in the fall as a junior, with no grades recorded for the previous year.

The courses that he had failed to complete in his first term, he repeated in his junior year, with the additions of basic art history and social science. Indeed, during his entire two-and-a-half-year college career, West was obliged to spend most of his time fulfilling the requirements for the Ph.B., in philosophy, classical civilization, and history. Even in the courses required for the English major, he showed little inclination to pursue a rigorous plan of study. Among literature courses, he carefully avoided all those in the novel, which left him ample time to read prose of his own choosing—the substance, as he regarded it, of his true education. With literary interests devoted largely, though not exclusively, to contemporary writing, particularly that of Joyce, Pound, Eliot, and Proust, he did not even take the one course in the English department devoted to "modern" literature, where the main authors studied were Hewlett, Bennett, De Morgan, Wells, Galsworthy, and Edith Wharton. The literature courses he selected were the following: English Literature from 1700 to 1900, a required basic survey course; Types and Models of Literature, also required; two terms of Public Speaking, devoted to the purification of diction and oral interpretation; two terms of Modern English Drama, from Wycherley and Congreve to Pinero and Shaw; English Romantic Literature from 1798 to 1832: Poetry; Browning; and Lyric Poetry. In these he earned no grade higher than a gentlemanly C, and in more than one course he barely passed, with a D. (Indeed, he failed two courses in his junior year, Philosophical Systems, and the European-history survey.) His two electives in philosophy, in the retrospective light of *Miss Lonelyhearts* and West's concern with the problem of value, have some interest. One was the Philosophy of Religion, described as "a constructive study of the nature of the religious consciousness and of the ultimate problems of religious belief." And the other, "Ethics: an introductory course dealing in a concrete way with the moral values of everyday experience."

His outstanding grades came in three courses. All touch upon particularly interesting areas of West's imagination and aspirations. He received a B in a French course conducted in English ("French literature and civilization: an interpretation of French culture as seen in its history, literature, religion and philosophy"); he was already looking away from America to France, like all other good Americans, as Harold Stearns had recently, in 1921, advised young men to do. He earned an A in an advanced course in music appreciation of the symphony. His other A was in a course on the Greek drama in English, in which the "poetical dramas of Aeschylus, Sophocles, Euripides, Aristophanes, and Menander, both tragedy and comedy," were "read in translation and discussed in relation to later drama." His grade in this lecture course was based on an erudite term paper which he had written and which subsequently was published, along with poems by Robert Hillyer and James Gould Cozzens, in the first issue of the Brown literary magazine, *Casements*, dated July 1923. West titled his essay "Euripides—A Playwright," and signed it "Nathaniel v. W. Weinstein."

The essay, like the signature, is a form of hoax. In a clear sense, it is the literary equivalent at Brown of his cartoons at Camp Paradox: as those had jibed against facile athletics, so this essay is a mockery of his professors, college education, and scholarship. He begins by speaking wittily and freely of the art of Euripides as made from elements similar to: "The tawdry melodrama of 'Uncle Tom's Cabin.' The dirt of a Restoration play by Wycherley. The sex alarums by the propagandist Brieux. The bloody sensationalism of the Old Testament. The box office symbolisms of Carl Čapek. The waving of his country's flag as George M. Cohan never waved it. The stretching of the long arm of coincidence as Thomas Hardy never dared to stretch it." In this fashion, he proceeds to make his essay a compendium and anatomy of all knowledge and attitudes; his allusions are esoteric and his scholarship apparently universal. Even while he speaks of the "wholesale borrowing and rewriting" of Euripides, he is borrowing widely from critics, history, and the visual arts and literature. But it is a compendium of nonsense, a profoundly ridiculous pedantry. He characterizes a dialogue in *The Bacchae* as "a vaudeville act" starring the "team" of Tiresias and Cadmus.* He moves from the urbane sophistication of his opening paragraph to flip comparisons; to whole paragraphs which are merely solemn quotations strung together; all the way, in tone, to appreciative school-girlish remarks like, "This scene . . . belongs among the greatest things in drama"; and at last, to satires of critical commentary, through juxtaposition of several critics. He concludes his essay in the tone of mock abasement before a master: "In summing up, I feel the desire to express the inexpressible praise, but I realize that I am incapable. The most I can accomplish is to throw a few soiled flowers on a Parnassus of laurel and bay, heaped up by his more capable admirers." His essay has dis-

---

* In *The Dream Life of Balso Snell*, his first novel, West would satirize his own parody by quoting a line ("Bromius! Bacchus! Son of Zeus!") from *The Bacchae*.

posed of that mountain of laurel by piling it up and thus exposing the stupidity of pedantic scholarship and the vacancy of hollow praise. Sometimes Euripides seems to be, West says, now speaking almost of himself, "a charlatan"; but all one can say ultimately is, "He was a great playwright." West was himself being, if not a charlatan, at least a satirist, in both his essay and his signature. By his hoax he asserted, satirically, his own sense of his superior vision of the nature of Euripides's art. It was, in part, the kind of comic art that he himself would practice.

West handed in a term paper which satirized his professor's idea of the nature of literary study, yet his satire was so skillfully conceived and concealed that he received an A. But he was a skilled hand at the hoax. Nor was he content with this one. At least once, in another course, he submitted a paper written by his cousin, Nathan Wallenstein. In Percy Marks's course in romantic poetry, he copied his examination answers, including the errors, from Philip Lukin, and Lukin was induced to confess to cheating.

In general, as at Tufts, he was all the while playing a hoax on the systems and demands of the course of study at Brown. He could not be entirely successful in this. Even though he conspired to select only courses meeting after lunch, he often overslept and was registered in February 1923 on probation. He spent a great many afternoons, nevertheless, on Federal Hill, consuming beer and red wine. Again, he was allowed to return for his senior year under warning. He was hired in the dining hall, but quickly fired, since he seldom appeared for work. These were all ways by which the leader of the Hanseatic League expressed his contempt for the Bacchanalians.

Another such expression was the production of a play, written by West, Reynolds, and others. The annual St. Patrick's Day musical, this dramatic extravagance was called *The Plastered Duchess*—satirizing the titles and substance of Percy Marks's 1924 novel *The Plastic Age* (supposed to be a sensational exposé of undergraduate mores at Brown) and Oscar Wilde's *The Duchess of Padua*, a play produced at Brown in March of that year. *The Plastered Duchess* was a bawdy, drunken farce in which the students satirized the college, its faculty, and themselves. West took a leading part in it, playing a dandified villain called Macaroni. At the climax Macaroni poisons the Duchess (majestically played by Quentin Reynolds) and calls:

> What ho! The guard. Bring in some booze.
> GUIDO
> Nay, this seemeth like wood alcohol to me.
> I'll drink no further.
> MACARONI
> They swore to me it was distilled in Olneyville.
> [*the Duchess falls*] . . .
> Quick! Catch her, she beginneth to pass out!
> This is worse than the prom I do believe.

For a moment, the spirit of the absurd stalked College Hill.

Finally, in the last month of his senior year, disgusted at Professor Thomas Crosby's treatment of "modern drama"—in which he did not reach the twentieth century—West refused to do any of the final work in the course and flunked it. West had spent the term writing "Nathaniel von Wallenstein Weinstein" in his composition book (while Perelman, nearby, amused himself by drawing caricatures of the dramatists they were studying), instead of taking notes. This failure might, at the last moment, prevent his graduation. His anarchy, it seemed, had reached its limit. But his role playing had not. His professor he regarded as a frustrated actor who occasionally performed in eighteenth- and nineteenth-century comedies with Bonstelle's company, and in class did little else than read from the plays. But West could act too. He would try one more hoax. After his E was recorded, West ostensibly broke down in Crosby's office over the failure. His parents were counting on him, he himself was heartbroken and contrite. Crosby was touched. The grade was changed to a D.

In June 1924, West's proud parents arrived in Providence for the commencement ceremonies and took their son and his friends to dinner at the Biltmore after he had been awarded his Ph.B. Their son, they were satisfied, was an educated man.

II

They were right. For the most part, West's knowledge at Brown had been generated less by his classes than by his curiosity. Still, in the early twenties certain fruitful and suggestive channels opened at Brown for curiosity to pursue.

When West entered Brown, he apparently still regarded himself as an artist. As Quentin Reynolds acknowledges, West "was not considered primarily a writer at college." The period of West's youth witnessed a truly amazing growth in America of a popular interest in painting and sculpture, following after the World's Columbian Exposition of 1893, which attracted many young men to careers as artists. Interest went in two directions—to the relatively new form of the witty, nonpolitical cartoon; and to avant-garde experiment. West's interests were similarly divided. He drew cartoons for *The Paradoxian* on the one hand. On the other, he designed the cover for the first *Casements*, a simple, draftsman's rendering of a casement window, illustrating a line of Keats. There is abundant evidence that he was keenly interested in new modes of art, at a time when avant-garde art was often no less comic than cartoons and sometimes was separated from them—as in the drawings of Benchley and Picasso—by only a thin line. Among other recent artists, he particularly admired Charles Meryon, Max Beerbohm, and Aubrey Beardsley, and he owned expensive books by all. Of the older artists, not surprisingly, his favorite was Hogarth. He had taken, necessarily, a positive and evident dislike for the art-history survey course at Brown, and had failed it even though possessing a fair acquaintance with the history of art. But his contemporaries at Brown regarded him as an artist and noticed his drawings. The description of West in his senior yearbook, the *Liber Brunensis* (1924), for instance, declared that "he passes his time in drawing exotic pictures, quoting strange and fanciful poetry, and endeavoring to uplift *Casements*."

His "exotic pictures" were of several kinds. Anyone who knew him at all well had seen him drawing them. One kind consisted of what may be called religious doodles—improvisational, rapidly done sketches of suffering saints, martyrs, or Christs. These resembled, at their best, the drawings of Georges Rouault and depicted, mostly, enormous heads set on emaciated bodies, with thick noses, heavy lips, and fiercely staring eyes sunken into darkly shaded sockets. The suffering of the figures was emphasized by the exaggeration of their features, especially the elongation of the face and eyes, aided by the heavy use of a soft pencil. He repeated the same figure again and again, with endless variations on what was one basic style and convention, and continued to sketch this figure into the thirties, at least as late as the publication of *Balso Snell* (1931), when he drew it into some of the copies of the book presented to his friends. He left a trail of this suffering man—it was in some measure his symbol for himself—in the margins of his books, on scraps of paper, and on restaurant napkins.

His roommate at Brown also saw him do numerous sketches in the styles of Beardsley and Beerbohm. Indeed, he had a drawing in the Beardsley manner published in the December 1922 issue of *The Brown Jug,* the college humor magazine. Here, he employed the heavy penciling characteristic of his pictures of martyrs to suggest a concentrated stare of lamia-like evil. The wit of the picture consists in the school-girlish sun visor which the woman wears, on which is drawn a galloping half-horse, half-female archeress, a symbol of lasciviousness.

He also drew mythological figures in the exotic styles of Puvis de Chavannes and Elihu Vedder—strange or haunting, mysterious creatures whose symbolic meanings were as unclear as they were suggestive. As one classmate has described them: "Whatever they *were,* they looked like some particularly evil gargoyles. They were quite horrifying and I was very much impressed." But he could also draw fairly accurate representations of his friends, as a portrait he did of Brae Rafferty proves. Later, in Hollywood, he told his secretary that he had studied art before literature and he drew dozens of accurate sketches of her. "He seemed to know a great deal about [art] when I . . . met him" in 1924, John Sanford says; and it is clear that, as an aspirant in art, he was attempting to find his own style in trying out the styles of others.

His own style, of course, would lead him not to art but to literature. At Brown, he began to move in this direction under certain local influences. West had drawn cartoons to preserve his self-esteem through attacking conventional categories of success. But with little training in art and only a minor talent for it, he found in the more complex atmosphere at Brown that his satirical drawings did not measure up to the standards being set by his peers. S. J. Perelman, in particular, became famous among college humorists for his cartoons while still an undergraduate. Having established prestige through one art, West inevitably turned to another. Because he had read so widely and was so naturally responsive to fantasy, he soon found his way to the art of fiction. West had the kind of absorptive mind which immediately made other people's best knowledge his own, and in the twenties on the Brown campus the focus of imaginative power lay chiefly in the study of literature. During the war, when the prominent critic and editor of the complete works of Stephen Crane, Wilson Follett, was in the English department, a sense of excitement over literature had begun to predominate at Brown. Even after Follett's departure, this spirit was sustained by a few younger members of the English department, notably Ben C. Clough and Percy Marks, who were near to the undergraduates in age and easily formed friendly associations with the literary aspirants on campus. Clough, with wide interests in contemporary literature, including "popular" writers like Heywood Broun and Alexander Woollcott, was the more popular teacher; but when Marks published *The Plastic Age*, he stood before his excited students a full-blown novelist, the image of the distinguished man of letters. S. J. Perelman well remembers the sensation which Marks made when he returned to the campus from a conference with his New York publishers and met his undergraduates "wearing a bright blue Langrock jacket, and carrying a stick, which was absolutely stupefying, since no one carried a stick at Brown but doddering old professors."

Marks may have served as a kind of *beau idéal*, but the substance of education could hardly come from his books, whose success the undergraduates admired but whose art West and Perelman scorned, even though one of the friends of the novel's hero was said to be a portrait of West himself. Between 1922 and 1924 Brown was genuinely invaded by modern ideas, as Harvard had been a decade earlier. "At the time that Pep and I were at Brown," a classmate says, "there was a . . . literary renaissance . . . and Pep, together with many of us, majored in English. Included were such people as Quent Reynolds, Sid Perelman, George Potter, Frank Hough, John McClain, and Duncan Taylor. Prior to this particular period any undergraduate who read more than a book a month was regarded as longhaired and admired as a man of considerable literary stature. Pep was right in the midst of all this."

Perhaps the most important factor in the literary awakening was the opening in 1922 of the Booke Shop, at 4 Market Square in

Providence, the first shop in the area specializing in modern literature. Whereas the offerings of the college bookstore ranged from
textbooks to sweatshirts, this shop, Ben C. Clough recalls vividly,
"had a large and choice selection of the newest books—and a wood-
fire in cool weather—and talks by writers of the day (poets especially); it was a focus." Here, both the American and English little
magazines and the newest books of European and English writers
could be perused, and West, with a more than ample allowance of
$22 each week, could buy contemporary writing even faster than he
could read it.

In 1931, constructing a myth by which a reader might understand the intellectual background of *The Dream Life of Balso
Snell*, West would tell an interviewer for the New York *Telegram*
that the Brown campus in his day had been split between Catholic
mysticism and French surrealism. To some extent, of course, that
split existed wholly in his own sensibility. But it was also true that
during West's junior and senior years several distinguished writers
lectured on the Brown campus. Among these were some connected
with the Celtic literary movement—the fact behind his remarks on
Catholic mysticism—including James Stephens, AE, and Padraic
Colum. Stephens's *Crock of Gold*, especially, aroused considerable
interest at Brown. What West referred to as French surrealism was
actually symbolism, and knowledge of it was probably confined to
West and another undergraduate, I. J. Kapstein, who translated
Corbière and Laforgue for *Casements*.

The lasting and important friendship which West made at
Brown was with S. J. Perelman, whose parents, like West's, had
immigrated from Russia. Born in Brooklyn and moved by his parents to Rhode Island, Sidney Joseph Perelman early showed distinction of mind. At the Classical High School in Providence he
was chairman of the debating society. At Brown, even though a
day student, he was active in the intellectual life of the campus
and was soon writing for both *Casements* and *The Brown Jug*,
where he became the leading spirit. As his work on these very different magazines suggests, he was both serious-minded and witty,
learned and humorous, sensitive and satirical.

Perelman entered Brown in 1921, five months before West arrived from Tufts, and they did not meet until 1922–3, when they
were enrolled in a class together. Both had read widely, admir-

ing Joyce and the dadaists as comic writers and experimentalists, and both cultivated ironical views toward the scene around them, romantic fantasy, and fashionable poses. Perelman, indeed, was at first ironical toward West, whom he regarded as a dandy, a campus aesthete. "But when I got to know him," Perelman says, "he had a warm and fanciful humor and great erudition that made the rest of us feel sort of juvenile." On his side, West, who worked very hard over his own writing, admired Perelman's finish as a writer as well as his satirical skill in cartooning. Both valued skepticism and good taste as distinguishing the elite from the mass, as well as professional competence and an artistic integrity based on a genuine striving after excellence. Years later West gave Lillian Hellman the impression that he regarded his college acquaintance with Perelman as crucial in his development.

Finally, there were vehicles on campus which gave expression, both in discussion and by publication, to literary interests. The Brown *Daily Herald* occasionally issued literary supplements; *The Brown Jug* accommodated a wide range of satirical writing; and *Casements*, founded in 1922 on the pattern of other small magazines, published the exotic and esoteric. Perhaps Malcolm Cowley is right in saying that the universities in the first and second decades were the "seedbeds of Humanism" in America—with their emphasis on the middle-class virtues of good taste, manliness, and restraint. They also, for this very reason, provided a plain example of the genteel codes against which young men could rebel, and in magazines and literary clubs give that rebellion a ready (and sanctioned) outlet.

But, above all, it was West's omnivorous reading which made for his education. During his high-school years, he purchased a set of Bell's *English Theatre* and eventually made his way from the Elizabethan to the Restoration playwrights. He read, with fascination, about the Church Fathers, and by the time he reached college could quote with apparent learning (even in a fragment of accurate Latin) from Bishop Odo of Cluny; but he also read Rabelais and Donne and looked into French symbolists like Laforgue, whose names he found mentioned in *Poetry*, where he followed with growing interest the work of Eliot, Pound, Yeats, and others. Around the time that he reached Brown, he knew the stories of Max Beerbohm, the novels of James Branch Cabell, and the precious dream tales of Arthur Machen, as well as the writers of *The Yellow Book*; but he also had dipped into (or at least could refer to) such classics as Petronius, Suetonius, and Apuleius. He decidedly preferred the strange and exquisite to the accomplished and achieved. Paris and London, not New York, were the centers of publishing to which he looked. Clearly, there were few Americans among the authors he read. But if he felt—as he commented in the twenties in the margin of his *Madame Bovary*—that there were "no good Americans," and professed to find little of value in the American literary scene, he was *being* characteristically American in his interest on the one hand in the great tradition and on the other in the avant-garde. He was drawn to the past, but also, as his Brown contemporary, I. J. Kapstein says, "strongly touched by the modern spirit." On these extremes he exclusively concentrated.

Literature, at first his talisman against the philistinism of family and school, a kind of black magic by which he kept conventional society at a distance, was more and more a serious necessity of his imagination. In this he was, of course, hardly unique; for as Josephine Herbst remarks, "Nearly every literary young person of the time . . . devoured everything he could lay his hands on."

Like most of his contemporaries, he ignored such precious American writers as Elinor Wylie, Joseph Hergesheimer, and Frances Newman. He was certainly unsympathetic to the (as he called it) "muddle-class" realism of Sinclair Lewis and Theodore Dreiser. Apparently, too, under the influence of Eliot and Pound, he lost his taste for the Russian writers, whose interest for him—since he could not read Russian—had been in content rather than style. He liked, rather, the aesthetes in the tradition of the nineties or avant-garde writers. Machen, Wilde, Edgar Saltus, Pater, Norman Douglas, James Branch Cabell, and Aldous Huxley, on the one hand, and Joyce and Wyndham Lewis and their American counterparts, Eliot and Pound, on the other—*The Yellow Book* or *The Egoist* and *The Criterion*—produced the writing for which West showed special enthusiasm. In both groups, what he was responding to was the emphasis on style, the perfection of form, the gem-like flame of verbal exactitude—in essence, the symbolist hope, which bridged the nineties and the twenties, for "pure" poetry, exact craftsmanship, and literature largely separated from ideas. This notion would perhaps be best crystallized in the axiom of *transition*, that "the writer expresses; he does not communicate." Cubism, imagism, vorticism, pointillism, unanimism—these movements and their manifestoes West followed closely and pondered carefully.

Similarly, in his more intense interest in French literature, he naturally preferred poets to prose writers, and symbolists to realists. Here, perhaps, his hesitancy in reading French was an asset which forced him to attend more closely to style and thus to duplicate, in a sense, the search for "the exact word," a concern which contemporary French literature inherited from Flaubert. Probably learning of it from Eliot, he read Arthur Symons's book on the French symbolists, then Amy Lowell's and Ezra Pound's essays on French writers. There is no doubt that he read Baudelaire, Verlaine, Rimbaud, and Villiers de l'Isle-Adam in French, and almost certainly made efforts at Laforgue and *Du côté de chez Swann*, while he was at Brown. He bought such current French periodicals as the *Mercure de France* and the *Nouvelle Revue Française* and could repeat from them vivid and scandalous anecdotes about French artists and writers, among them Jarry and Huysmans. He expressed continuing affection for several French works of fiction—for Lautréamont's *Les Chants de Maldoror*, Stendhal's *Le Rouge et le Noir*, the madeleine scene in Proust, and Raymond Radiguet's *Le Bal du Comte d'Orgel*. All, he felt, were true expressions of the modern spirit; but he also read (in translation) Daudet, the Goncourts, Jules Romains, Anatole France, St.-Jean Perse, and Flaubert. To the end of his life, he ranked Flaubert above the great Russian novelists by virtue of his greater perfection of style, and he regarded *Madame Bovary* as the masterpiece of the craft of fiction. His commitment to emphasis on style in French literature is best shown by the fact that when he arrived in Paris one of the first purchases he made was of the complete works of Flaubert in French; this, in part, was what he had come to Paris to learn.

He alternated, this is to say, between the French and English symbolists—a line which Edmund Wilson would later chart in *Axel's Castle* as the main current of modern literary history. Better than most of his contemporaries, who generally scorned the English if they praised the French, and so failed to see the connection between the two, West followed the implications of the one into the other. Beginning as the "campus aesthete," he would thus become a serious novelist drawing some of his imaginative energy from the main sources of modern literature.

Like his contemporaries, of course, he wished to follow the line of literary geography through, from England and France, back to the situation and possibilities of the American writer. His earliest model for this task seems to have been James Gibbons Huneker; West owned a half dozen of his books, including *Iconoclasts* (1905), *Egoists* (1909), *Ivory, Apes and Peacocks* (1915), and *Bedouins* (1920). But more recent models were at hand and West tried these. Robert McAlmon's Contact Editions—including experimental work by Hemingway, Ezra Pound, Djuna Barnes, John Herrmann, Gertrude Stein, and William Carlos Williams—all stressed the primacy of literary experiment, the hope for a discriminating audience, the respect for bookmaking, and the idealization of "style" in the largest sense, which West shared with his contemporaries. He was reading the newest writers with enthusiasm. He borrowed Stevens's *Harmonium* (1923) from Kapstein, and he also admired the poetry of Hart Crane and E. E. Cummings (had *he* not made an original adaptation of Apollinaire's *Calligrammes* into the American spirit?). Perhaps more than any other, F. Scott Fitzgerald, the spirit of whose fiction pervaded the campus, provided for West a model of the kind of fiction he aspired to write.

West learned from all these men what it could mean for him to be a writer. By the time he received his Ph.B. in 1924, his parents beaming like suns upon him, he had educated himself to the meaning, though he was not far into the methods, of their accomplishment. He had rebelled against conventions, but now he had literary conventions to learn. He had scorned and mocked contemporary values, but now value would become his central concern. He had delighted to go, with Huysmans, against the grain; but now he would need to learn to go as well, with William Carlos Williams, *in* the American grain.

In short, he was preparing to begin his education anew. And to begin in Paris.

5 / *All Good Americans*

Otherwise everything is about the same. Dull. . . . I guess
that's what's the matter with our generation, eh? For us
Life has lost its savour.

—Nathanael West to Beatrice Mathieu, April 12, 1930

In the spring of 1924, when Quentin Reynolds was threatened
with expulsion from Brown for making and selling bootleg liquor,
it was to West, "the idea man and quick thinker," that he turned
in gloomy desperation. "Pep said, 'Here—take some notes.' Hand-
ing me a pad and pencil, he began pacing. 'You will start by telling
[Dean] Randall of the stroke your father had which has kept you
from working for two years. Your sister is still in the hospital recov-
ering from a serious operation. . . .'" West continued for an hour
to spell out Reynolds's story—one probably resembling in essence
the kind of story he would give to his professor of drama—ending
at last with what he called "a nice touch": "Tell him that only
yesterday you went to confession and told the priest all about this.
He made you promise to give it up and you agreed." On the following evening, the tale successful, Reynolds raised a beaker of his
contraband liquor to West: "Here's to the greatest literary talent
that I know—Pep Weinstein." West's collegiate hoaxes would
share one quality with his later fiction—in them he was able to create instinctively the kind of fantasy which would be believable in a
certain situation or by a particular person.

It was only natural that in June 1924, with this recent hoax in
mind, Reynolds should turn again to West for aid. Called upon to
give a Class Day speech, by tradition both learned and humorous
(Reynolds was neither), he was stumped. West agreed to write it
for him. The result was a sensation. "It was such a speech," Reynolds said, "that the author of *Ulysses* might have sprung on a select

gathering of like-minded wits. . . . Obscurely off-color anecdotes succeeded one another, and a barrage of cockeyed classical allusions and educated puns clothed the central theme—if there was any." However baroquely decorated, the central story of West's speech was clear enough, if strange: it drew upon one of West's preoccupations, the notion of an insect feeding on one's body, and concerned the adventures of a flea named St. Puce, who had been born in the armpit of Christ, and died of pneumonia at the instant of Christ's death. Reynolds called it "a true literary hoax." That June, with this speech, West's college career was over. He ended it with a hoax reversing the one by which he began it, with another man using his materials. He had dabbled in education and literature at Brown. Now he was ready to begin the education of a writer. The Class Day speech is the bridge between these two careers. For its central story, the Tale of St. Puce, was to be one of the most striking episodes in West's first novel, *The Dream Life of Balso Snell*. In June 1924, he was already writing sketches for this book. That summer, when he met John Sanford on an Asbury Park golf course, he declared that he was hoping to be a writer. Sanford says that as early as 1924 "he told me almost all that finally appeared as *The Dream Life of Balso Snell*."

The fact is that West had been writing during his last two years at Brown—though rather casually, regarding himself primarily as a dilettante, a gentleman of letters. Perhaps at first he wanted more to be regarded as a literary man than to write literature. Alternately he read and loafed and read and wrote. To achieve any finished work, he labored with great difficulty and care (*Balso Snell* would take six years to complete), but he much preferred to give the appearance of improvisational genius. Occasionally his friends would watch him dash off a poem or a sketch facilely and then, with a casual air, crumple it and toss it toward the fireplace. Those that were saved were often well regarded by them. Occasionally he would read a piece aloud and dismiss it. Often these pieces were demonstrations that incidents of real life—his own or his friends' experiences, for example—could be regarded as material for absurd literature when viewed from a certain curious angle. These were, as *Balso* is, essentially exhibitions of wit, and his conversation crackled with verbal irony. His friends regarded his wit well enough to preserve some of it in their letters, much of the same material later appearing in *Balso Snell*. He possessed, as one of his creative sources, and in common with Joyce and Max Ernst, a murderous intellectual humor. He regarded all experience—even suffering—as material for the artist. Like his tale of St. Puce, of course, his actual writing of this period was exotic, either in the manner of the nineties or of more contemporary experimental writing.

Jeremiah Mahoney remembers that West was accused by a classmate of having made a poem by amalgamating two or three dadaist pieces. But that itself was in the tradition of Dada. Occasionally, too, he attempted poems in the style of Baudelaire or Villon. The poem which he published beneath his lamia sketch in *The Brown Jug* is much in the manner of Ernest Dowson and Licnel Johnson and imitates their use of archaic language, old French verse forms, and their characteristic weary sophistication. He entitled it "Rondeau":

> My lady's eyes appear to be
> Like brimming pools of ecstasy,
> Deep wells, from which the twinkles flow
> Unceasingly, as on they go
> To charm me with their witchery;
> Mayhap an easy prey they see,
> Enmeshed by their dexterity;
> I can't protest; they thrill me so—
> My lady's eyes.

His poem "Death," published in *Casements* (1924), also has strong echoes of the poets of *The Yellow Book*. "Where can we find the Paters and Beardsleys of this day and generation?" S. J. Perelman inquired in a piece called "The Exquisites: A Divagation," published in the same issue, skillfully satirizing such postures and attitudes, and with a mischievous eye winking at his fellow contributor.

West had seen his cartoons printed in *The Paradoxian*; he had published two poems, an essay, and a drawing in college magazines; he had begun a novel; and he had been certified by an Ivy League university as a gentleman of letters. All at once he had taken on shapes in society, at the same time that he had been mocking it.

He had assumed earlier that eventually he would be forced to enter his father's construction business, and to some extent this was what he had been rebelling against since high school. His father's business—not his father—stood for much that he feared in society. At this time, he told Lillian Hellman, he had been deeply afraid of being drawn into business. Certainly his family kept trying to interest and enlist him in a business career. But he insisted, "when he talked about what he wanted to do, that he would never go into the real-estate business and suffer the way his father had— he couldn't think of any worse suffering." In an age when almost every writer seemed to rebel against his father—when the young Fitzgerald went so far as to tell the neighbors that he had been adopted—West was at odds not so much with his family as with the life they would impose upon him just when he had begun to discover his own identity and aspirations. During his summer vacations he had been obliged to work on apartment houses being built by his father in the Bronx, occasionally as bricklayer but more often as timekeeper, while he was presumably learning the business of construction and contracting. He worked on the erection of a cooperative apartment building on Allerton Avenue sponsored by the Amalgamated Clothing Makers Union. In part, he found the work engaging. He had learned the decorative methods and the art styles of brick courses and molding. On such jobs, too, he had immensely admired the teamwork of the bricklayers; he told a later acquaintance that "he liked them—particularly the Italians—and he made friends with them." Moreover, as Quentin Reynolds, who worked as a hod carrier with West in the summer of 1923, recalls, "It used to amaze me to see how Pep endeared himself to these ignorant and rather rough characters. They never knew that he was the boss's son; they just liked him. He had a knack for drawing them out . . . and when he talked, he talked their language—the language of the Bronx, where he too had grown up." Perhaps, when he told Rafferty that there was a Wallenstein who had been a distinguished architect in Germany and that he too had thought of becoming an architect, he was making an unconscious attempt to reconcile, for himself, business with art.

But by 1924 the possibility of becoming a writer grew upon him, and he fitfully resisted a career in business, certain that this would be inimical to the talents and career of any writer. Uneasily, and on a loose leash, he agreed to begin work in the fall of 1924, after a summer spent in New Jersey, as construction superintendent for his father. But he also spent a great deal of time at home on 79 Street near Central Park West, visiting museums and otherwise entertaining himself, reading and, above all, laboriously trying to write. His father, he reasoned, had plenty of money, and he could postpone work—that he had been three years at college seemed adequate proof of this. Now, not simply rebelling against his future, he was perplexed about what it would be. "Solid bourgeois," as S. J. Perelman says, West's family—like Americans in general—had made a dangerous attempt to separate culture and imagination from society; and West, who had scorned society, now was uncertain how to commit himself to art.

West's revulsion against business was so extreme and his desire to escape a commercial career so intense that his fears became, characteristically, a part of his fantasies. In the summer of 1925, half-seriously revealing a plan of escape to Brae Rafferty, he showed how far, and in what direction, his daydreams had gone. Since his father ordinarily built large apartment houses and had established his credit for considerable sums, West told his friend, he had devised a scheme to use his father's name to receive a large loan, then to abscond to Paris with the money and there live on the income from its investment. His father, he suggested, could not be held responsible for him. What he meant was that he could not be responsible for the expectations of his father. Clearly, this plan was fantasy—an expression of desperation. But at the same time he began to talk seriously about another daydream—that his family support him in Paris while he made an attempt to write fiction.

For his own good reasons, Max opposed these hopes. Late 1925 was a period of economic contraction in the building business—not an unfamiliar occurrence for Max Weinstein, who had built his fortune on expansions and contractions in the population growth of New York. He was as accustomed to the decrease in demand for housing, when New York seemed to be overbuilt, as he was to the increase in demand, when the most rapid building seemed insufficient. In 1925, buildings were again not selling or renting and Max's credit was dangerously extended; he needed, most of all, liquid capital in order to hold his assets. Business was bad, and his health was bad—he had not yet recovered from an automobile accident in which the steering wheel of his car had been driven into his chest. Always slight, he now looked sickly and emaciated. He was not able to get around to his building sites so well and for this reason he may have put additional pressure upon his son to give himself up entirely to the business. It would be difficult to send his son to Paris. But Anna took her son's side and insisted that he should have a chance to go. Business, she reasonably and persistently argued, was down but was bound to increase. Prospects always appeared good. Why should he not have at least a brief visit to Europe before settling down to business? Max, who took pride in indulging his wife and family, could not resist this argument and at last made the arrangements. As usual, the family agreed to work together. They would support West in Paris.

Business would never improve, though in 1926 no one would have believed that New York was so overbuilt that when the Depression struck, apartments, hotels, and even business and loft space, the most reliable of properties, would not be fully used for nearly a decade and that the assets of contractors would dissolve into nothing, unable to return even operating expenses. In 1926, when West was resisting a career in real estate, he was dealing with ghosts of the future, since the contraction of credit which Max was feeling would be permanent, one of the first signs of the coming Depression, and would wipe out any hopes that the most conventional of sons could have had for success in the construction trade. History proved society no less deceptive than West had believed it to be. Perhaps it is true, as Joseph Freeman suggests, that "bohemianism requires a certain amount of social stability. The bohemian wishes to 'shock' the bourgeois. For this purpose, the bourgeois must be well entrenched, secure financially . . . and the bohemian himself must feel that the road back to the world he is 'shocking' is not entirely closed." West, thinking of going to Paris, had been reading novels about bohemian life by Murger and Francis Carco; supported from home, he too could be a bohemian there. But in 1926 speculative fortunes such as that of West's family were already flitting shades; and for West there was to be no way back, no way home to a spectral world.

Still, in 1926, prosperity seemed bound to revive; as yet, only the building business was slow. West would be able to go to Paris, it was decided. The expense would be borne by Max's brother Charles and Saul Wallenstein, who were not yet feeling the pinch of reduced construction. Saul had himself gone to Paris in his youth, and Charles perhaps regarded his part of the financial aid as what he would have given his own son, Nathan, who had recently died. By September of 1926, it was all arranged.

II

Paris proved to hold a particular fascination for West. On the one hand, it was the source of rich, fantastic tales; on the other, it constituted and symbolized for him a decisive break with the world of business. In filling out his De Witt Clinton transcript, publishing his first prose and poetry, signing his first printed drawings or cartoons—on each crucial occasion of self-expression, West had invented a new name whereby to express the new identity he had invented. Clearly he saw himself as complex, a maelstrom of identities. Thus, in 1926, showing again the same facility for self-naming, West conceived for himself a new name as an expression of this decisive new beginning. He would not go to Paris, would not take out a passport even, as Nathan Weinstein, for he was leaving Nathan Weinstein behind. He would be made a new man by an act of his own will. As he understood it, his role as an artist concerned only a particular aspect of his self and constituted a freeing of his personality in the shearing off of its commercial peripheries. Since pseudonyms were taken for similar reasons by Voltaire, Anatole France, Lewis Carroll, Orwell, Swift, Mark Twain, Dickens, and Molière, it is not surprising that West too should have felt the need for a new name. At the City Court of New York, on August 16, 1926, Nathan Weinstein legally changed his name to Nathanael West. It was to be his true name, the distinctive one for the serious artist.

Concerning his choice of this particular name he told many tales. It too gave him a fertile field for comic invention. He remarked to his secretary in Hollywood, for instance, that he had chosen "Nathanael" in 1931 because the publisher of *Balso Snell*, Martin Kamin, told him that there was a Nathaniel in the Bible who was good, but a Nathanael who was evil—and that *his* should be the evil (and so the much more exotic) name. (This was an interesting tale; but, of course, there is only one form of the name in the Bible. Nathanael was one of the twelve apostles, "an Israelite in whom is no guile" [John 1:49]. "Nathaniel" is a New England corruption.)

The truth is that one of his cousins named Nathan, Charles's son, had called himself Nathaniel long before and that West had added that ending to his name even before he entered Tufts. In New England, of course, this name had various associations with the colonial and Revolutionary past—there had, indeed, been a famous mariner named Nathaniel West—and so the name had a romantic, slightly archaic American appeal. Later, when he was advising Julian Shapiro (John Sanford) about a change of name, West suggested a similarly romantic, historic (and nautical) American name—"Starbuck." After leaving Brown and experimenting with the altogether new name "West," he decided that the "ael" ending for Nathan suited "West" and was the more distinguished and aristocratic in being the less usual in America, but the more traditional. Concerning his choice of "West," he told witty tales, answering William Carlos Williams's question "How did you get that name?" with "Horace Greeley said, 'Go West, young man.' So I did." In fact, it is clear that he adopted "West" from his older cousin Sam, who had been using it for some time in Wall Street.

Decidedly, however, West was symbolizing in this name change his rejection of commercial values and, to this extent, of his family. It is significant, but not surprising, that until the time he severed all business dealings with his family, six years later in 1932, he continued to use the name N. W. Weinstein for business correspondence—subordinating the artist into a middle initial; thereafter, he usually signed his name Nathanael W. West, a similar burying of the middle-class man.

Of course, there were other but more superficial reasons for his change of name. It is true that West identified Judaism with the orthodox religion to which he was wholly indifferent, and thus resented the prejudices exercised against him. Certainly he was far from indifferent to anti-Semitism. "He knew more about it historically than any man I have ever met," Wells Root would later say. "He seemed to regard the present wave principally as history repeating itself. He denied emphatically that such a thing as a Jew really exists. He held, and underwrote his opinion with facts and figures, that the original Jewish people had wandered so far and blended so deeply into the blood of the countries they found that it was senseless to identify them as a blood strain. He did not regard himself as a Jew at all, but as an American." His new name change allowed him a way of avoiding the more ordinary daily occasions of annoying prejudice. Being a Jew at this time in America meant being automatically classified into a certain segment of society, and neither by training nor by inclination would West put himself in the ghetto. He was a man living so close to contemporary life and so sensitive to it, that he attempted so far as possible to minimize tensions in his life in order to preserve them powerfully for his art. West rejected Judaism, moreover, insofar as he associated it with the dominance of the commercial spirit in life, and for much the same reason he disliked the Jewish stage humor of Potash and Perlmutter, Fanny Brice, and others.

But he had no shame about his Semitic heritage. He could joke about it along with Perelman or Arthur Kober, and give as bad imitations of a Yiddish accent as he did of other American dialects. Indeed, West's particular humor was deeply affected by Jewish tradition: in particular, his tender treatment of the underdog figure in his fiction may be seen as his own perfection of a well-defined folk mode of Jewish humor. Certainly he had, as Edmund Wilson describes him, "a kind of eastern European" suffering and sense of the grotesque, "in common with Gogol and Chagall," and also, "a sad, quick Jewish humor," a "quality of imagination which was . . . both Russian and Jewish."

In a cultural sense, too, the name changing of Jewish immigrants was compelled by more than the mere attempt to avoid discrimination. It was a part of coming to a consciousness, as West did, of what it means to be modern, of the separation between old Russia and America, past and present. At Brown, West had spoken of himself as a "Jewish outsider," a "Jew and a not-Jew at the same time." In tracing the consequences of the delayed history of Jewish adjustment to modern life, Stuart E. Rosenberg has concluded: "Those Jews who accepted modernism did so most radically." This was particularly the case with Jews who possessed, markedly, a "high degree of intellectualism," and who, the historian of Jewish immigration says, "brought with them the intellectual vitality, the moral perplexity, the religious optimism, the sound and fury of a great awakening . . . [and therefore] attained a cultural and intellectual richness in New York greater than any in Eastern Europe." West was a part and a product of this awakening. His birth was separated from his father's by four centuries and unnumbered changes. He would be modern. As an American, variously responding to the urban delights of New York, the secular world; as an intellectual; and at last as a writer, dedicated to French symbolism and American experimentation, he had made modernism his creed. His feelings about his minority status as a Jew had long since been translated into a sense of his superior status as part of the elite minority of well-dressed men, of the gentleman and the author. He had become Nathanael West.

As the witness to his Oath of Allegiance to the United States— and to the modernism which it implied—he took Julian Shapiro to the Sub-Treasury Building in downtown Manhattan to apply for his passport in September 1926. He described himself as exactly six feet tall, with brown hair and brown eyes, no distinguishing features, and gave his occupation as "student." He declared that he would return within one year, during which he would "study" in "Italy, Switzerland, France, Belgium." Appearing, in a picture taken just before his ship sailed, confident and sophisticated, and elegantly dressed, he departed for Paris on October 13, 1926.

Other Americans went with him on the same ship; all good Americans were setting sail for Paris. For not only was foreign travel, always popular with Americans, made widely possible now by apparently increasing wealth, but also there was obvious discontent among young Americans. West, like his fellow travelers, could not swear allegiance to all aspects of the American creed. While Henry Ford declared his belief that "ninety percent of the people are satisfied" it was obviously more true, as Will Rogers quipped, "that ninety percent of the people in this country don't give a damn." Still, Rogers viewed the Americans who were in a mortal haste to depart the country as "half-wits who think that a summer not spent among the decay and mortification of the Old World is a summer squandered."

But expatriation, even for only a summer, had become fashionable; Americans collectively were restless, and the more sensitive among them, like West, sensed that at home their energy was consumed wholly in rebellion, since American society in which they should have been active seemed to hold no place or respect for their creative accomplishments. "The American literary scene," as

T. S. Eliot described it, "didn't offer . . . much encouragement. That was a very dull period. In Europe there was a desire to aid other people. Pound introduced me to Yeats. I got to know Virginia Woolf. People were interested in my poetry. I had never experienced such interest at home." It may be that most of the American tourists who arrived knew only enough geography to take them from Napoleon's Tomb to the Gare de Lyon, with stops at the Bastille and the Folies Bergères, and only enough French to find their way to an American café. But they were not so much exploring Europe as escaping America, and visiting themselves. How much deeper, then, was the response to Paris of the young writers who had all read French literature and for whom France was an imaginative home.

For West, of course, there was the attraction of the Paris literary and artistic scene about which he had read so many vivid reports. The *Manifeste du Surréalisme* had been issued by Breton in December 1924, just at the time that West himself was similarly moving from the high jinks of his college activities to serious preoccupation with the craft and nature of fiction. West's own surrealist fiction—if it can be called that—was surely, as his whole career shows, partly the result of his response, in the American tradition, to the same absurdity which the French were feeling more widely, but no more intensely. The French influence upon West can easily be overemphasized, however. He had been a surrealist at home. Then, too, the German expressionists are no less important than the French as perspectives on and parallels to his native vision. Kafka and Brecht bear as much resemblance to West as the French do. He read Kafka in 1930, when Knopf published a translation of *The Castle*, and he probably heard Josephine Herbst talk about Brecht. He admired Gottfried Benn. But since he was unable to read German at all well, he attended the more closely to German art, responding with greater enthusiasm to Max Ernst, George Grosz, and Otto Dix than to either German writers or to French writers or painters. The expressionists' awareness of the grotesque was closer to his own vision than the more comic French expression of the absurd; and the savage and bitter treatment of dreams by the Germans resembled his own vision more than the French idealization of dreams as intimations of the surreal. But the truth is that both parallels are inexact: the *humeur noir* about which Breton wrote in Paris, West was practicing personally in Providence and New York. The feeling for myth and archetypal experience which Jung was emphasizing in Berlin, West was experiencing on his own. West had issued no manifestoes, he simply acted out with immediacy his sense of absurdity in rebellion. Having hardly experienced the chaos of Europe, he knew intuitively that Dada reigned in America.

Still, he was coming to Paris to touch, however lightly, the literary scene, to watch surrealist performances; to reenact the café scenes of Hemingway's *The Sun Also Rises*, just published and a great success; to meet some of the people around the burgeoning little magazines; perhaps to see Hemingway and Joyce—and certainly Philippe Soupault, Paul Éluard, Aragon, and the others whose work he read in the now defunct *Littérature*; and to see a literary burlesque by Cocteau and listen to a Satie concert.

He would have some of these experiences in time, of course, but for the moment there was very little chance of his participating freely in French or even American literary life. He was hesitant in forming friendships and as yet he had published only two poems in college magazines and had completed only a few pages of a prospective novel. He was, by position and desire, a spectator of French life. Again, he was content, ambivalently, to be a lonely spy: Paris was the artistic Central Park of his need to see. Then too, by 1926 most French writers had moved to the Right Bank or the Saint-Germain quarter, leaving Montparnasse to a motion-picture colony, scores of would-be American writers, and tired habitués of such American bars as the Coupole. The French were simply not interested in them. As Henry James had said much earlier of Flaubert's circle, French writers were surprisingly provincial and had no interest at all in Americans or their literature. When William Carlos Williams asked McAlmon to introduce him to French poets in 1924, McAlmon told him that "he didn't know any of them, and understood they had no talent anyway." Those who arrived at the floodtide of American travel in 1926—like Guy Endore, Charles Norman, and Walter Lowenfels*—associated almost entirely with

---

* Walter Lowenfels remembers that "someone I knew said West was in town," but they never met there.

other Americans. Hemingway had hit exactly the right note, writing a novel about a Paris from which Frenchmen seemed absolutely absent.

Like Hemingway's characters, West certainly visited the cafés. He lived first on the fringe of Montparnasse, at 43 boulevard Raspail, at the rather expensive Hotel Lutétia, and then close by at 9 rue de la Grande Chaumière, in the Hotel Libéria, both hotels on streets intersecting the boulevard du Montparnasse. He made the obligatory rounds of the nearby Dôme and Rotonde, as well as the Coupole, Deux Magots, and the Sélect. Part of the café scene made its way into the only section of *Balso Snell* which was written in Paris. The Café Carcas, on the rue de la Grande Chaumière, as well as the two academies farther down the street, appear when Janey Davenport contemplates suicide after a love affair with Beagle Darwin. Much later West would write that this section, influenced by "the ideas of Spengler and Valéry," was "an exercise in rhetoric." And still later—characteristically—he would parody himself in the speech of Chief Israel Satinpenny of *A Cool Million*: "The day of vengeance is here. The star of the paleface is sinking and he knows it. Spengler has said so; Valéry has said so. . . ." But for now his use of the philosophy of decline provided for one of his stylistic experiments in attitude and emotion.

Generally, in Paris, West was making personal rather than literary experiments. He bought many books—including several copies of *Ulysses*—at Sylvia Beach's Shakespeare and Co., and there met some of the people who were putting together the first issue of *transition*, to appear in April 1927. He had glimpses of Cocteau and Gide. He observed Hemingway, and told friends, when he returned to Brown (wearing yellow gloves and an elegant new Homburg) that Hemingway in person was much like the poses he adopted in his fiction. He apparently saw Eliot, who was visiting Paris. While he had no more success than his contemporaries in establishing contact with French writers, he met several painters, including Max Ernst, who later claimed to have had a powerful influence upon West; West purchased several prints by Ernst, including his series *Rêve d'une Jeune Fille*.

It was characteristic of West, however, that he established the closest friendship with Hilaire Hiler, not only a painter but also a bartender and a jazz pianist. Hiler, with whom West would resume friendship in California a decade later, spoke of West as an "intimate friend of mine," and later arranged a meeting between West and Henry Miller. (That meeting, to Hiler's surprise, was unsuccessful: the two writers, both moralists of chaos, bored each other.) But West and Hiler were fast friends from the first. West, Hiler said, was "a gentle and sociable fellow with a good sense of humor." When West was killed, he commented bitterly: "Tragic about Fitzgerald, Joyce, and West. All entirely too young to go, and a loss to the world. While bastards like Hitler live. The fates seem to deal out tragedy and suffering to artists and crowns to gunmen."

French life interested him as much as its artists, however, and far more than work on his own novel did. On *Balso* he wrote only infrequently, but he roamed around Paris—in the evening, in formal dress—spending a lot of money in a short time. If he was fascinated by the sensational brothel on the rue Blondel, which catered to Americans who simply wanted to watch nude models walking about, he also was intrigued by the gaiety and rationalism of the French, particularly of the students at the nearby Académies Colorossa and Grande Chaumière, and at the Sorbonne. He remarked that their "refusal to fall into conventional tracks fascinated him." If he liked to sit conspicuously on café terraces, he also took delight in rolling French words off his tongue; he collected Paris argot and playfully talked about making a glossary of prostitute slang. In imitation of the bohemian crowd, he grew a reddish-brown beard. He had planned to write, of course, but the food was good, he was free of his family, life was interesting, there was the Louvre to visit, the Cirque d'Hiver, with its clowns, or the Luxembourg Gardens to stroll in, the music halls in Montmartre to enjoy; he did not take it all very seriously, and he didn't produce much, although he would later tell A. J. Liebling that he had completed *Balso* in Paris.

Paris was far more productive of fantasy than of literature; the fantasies he spun out of it were evidences of the joy he had had in it. Partly as a result of his taking it so lightly, he could regard Paris as providing the materials for imaginative adventure. Even years later, he would make clear how far he saw into the gaudy romance of Paris by remarking, when he went into a steamy cafeteria in New York with Sidney Jarcho, "If this were Paris, it'd be fun, wouldn't it?" But for West, as for many other American expatriates, Paris was essentially a never-never land, like those in the movies, where one could suspend his sense of reality more easily than in America. Robert McAlmon explained that he lived in France because of the "fanciful freedom" which he found there. West, too, freed his fantasy in Paris.

He made Paris a myth. From ordinary clichés about the poverty of Parisian bohemian life, West spun several autobiographical tales. In some accounts he went to Paris directly from college, or as early as 1925; he allowed the information that he had been in Paris during 1926–8 to appear on the dust jacket of *Miss Lonelyhearts*, although he was to spend less than three months there; and he told his secretary that he had spent six years there. Always, as he told it, he was poverty-stricken. In one of the elaborate anecdotes with which he amused Wells Root, he told of being so broke one winter that he could not afford any decent clothes; he could keep warm and appear in public only by wearing a Brooks Brothers plaid overcoat (which he did in fact own) over his shabby, worn-out clothes. He chuckled that he was regarded as an eccentric American bohemian from necessity rather than inclination. Another story—by this time, he had mysteriously acquired a suit of clothes —concerned a way he devised of making money. He and a friend, he told Wells Root, "would go to the Gare du Nord and meet a boat-train bringing in a wide-eyed collection of American tourists. Scanning the arrivals narrowly, they would pick out a youngish female, or two females traveling together. Preferably pretty ones and necessarily ones with the outward evidences of large letters of credit. . . . [He] would rush up to them and pretend that he thought they were Mary Jones and Eleanor Smith of Peoria, whom their parents, old friends of his mother's, had written him to meet. By the time it was clear that he had made an excusable mistake, introductions had been accomplished. Since Mary Jones and Eleanor Smith had obviously not arrived on the boat-train and since our heroes were clearly men to be trusted since they had been selected to shepherd Miss Jones and Miss Smith, it was an easy step to guide them to the Ritz or wherever they were staying. Since the boys knew French and the girls didn't, and since the girls knew no one in Paris, it was almost too easy to get the assignment to show them the town.

"Of course, there was the little matter of money. Our heroes were writers or artists, temporarily incommoded by the tardy arrival of their monthly checks from home. It might cost a little to show the girls Paris really thoroughly. Particularly if the girls wanted to see the night life. In nine cases out of ten, that was exactly what the girls did want to see, and they were more than happy to pay for it under such expert auspices. What the girls didn't know was that in various cafés and bars the boys had arranged with the proprietors for a percentage. So the boys ate, drank, and made merry—and got a nice cut on the side.

"The climax was a real bohemian party. Would the young ladies like to attend a really inner-circle shenanigan of the painters, writers, and musicians of the Latin Quarter? The kind of a party at which ordinary tourists were never tolerated. Obviously, the girls jumped at this rare opportunity. Again the unfortunate matter of money. Food and drink and music were essential to a really successful gathering. By this time they knew pretty well how much the traffic would stand, and soaked the young ladies the maximum. They hired a garret and some starving musicians, arranged with a restaurant-bar to supply food and liquor—and invited all their hungry friends, and their friends' hungry girls. The resulting brawl was, of course, sensational and lasted all night. Our heroes cleared a hundred dollars or more if the young ladies were really well-heeled. . . ."

West told this story with great gusto, declaring with conviction that "there was not the least chicanery involved" and that no harm was done to anyone. This was all the more true in that the tale was sheer invention. He told another friend, similarly, that he had traveled a good deal through France but, owing to his poverty, almost entirely on foot. In another tale, he returned to the theme of his lack of respectable clothes and declared that he had once made a sensation by appearing at a party dressed—it turned out, when he removed his plaid coat—in nothing but a hat and tie.

Apparently the Paris literary scene held less romantic possibilities for him than the rich legends of bohemian life and the romance of poverty. He spoke only vaguely about having known several great writers there. The best daydream he could manage was that he had carried with him a letter of introduction to Gertrude

Stein and that when he called at her apartment Matisse was there with her. The true life of art, perhaps, was too serious a matter for him to deal with in inventive trifles.

A tale of exotic adventure which he was still telling as late as 1939 best represents his sense of the romantic possibilities of Paris. West, Boris Ingster says, told the story "with utter conviction and utter belief," as if it were veritable fact. "As so often in his life," Ingster recalls, "West was completely on his uppers and like so many people in Paris he went to the American Express and stood waiting outside it in the hope that he would see a familiar face. After he had waited about an hour, in pain with hunger, suddenly a very distinguished middle-aged lady appears and says, 'You are Nathanael West, aren't you?' It develops that from some snapshots of himself and his roommate at Brown she has recognized him. She is the roommate's mother and the boy has disappeared. His is a wealthy family, and she has hired a Pinkerton man to try to find the lost boy. The story of his disappearance is a weird one, including drugs, etc., and she pleads with Pep to assist the detective. This person himself turns out to be a con man who decides to live off the fat of the land at the mother's expense. Nevertheless, they pick up some kind of trail which leads them to North Africa—Casablanca —and eventually to a native café. After Pep has a strange romantic adventure there, the story ends as they find that the boy is dead. West, unable to tell this to the mother, flees."

West's most finished piece of short fiction, successively titled "The Fake," "L'Affaire Beano," and "The Impostor," is set in Paris and deals with the condition of the expatriate artist there. Even artists, for the most part, West suggests, play fantasy roles; not the production of art, but the creation of a satisfactory guise has come to define art. This is the naturalistic version of the theme of *The Dream Life of Balso Snell*. The story (in its last version) begins:

"In order to be an artist you have to live like one." We know now that this is nonsense, but in Paris, in those days, we didn't know it. "Artists are all crazy." This is another statement from the same credo. Of course, these ideas and others like them were foisted on us by the non-artist, but we didn't realize it then. We came to the business of being an artist with the definitions of the non-artist and took libels for

the truth. In order to be recognized as artists, we were everything our
enemies said we were.

"All artists are crazy." Well, one of the easiest things to be is "crazy,"
that is if you are satisfied with the uninformed layman's definition of
craziness. To be really crazy is quite a job. You have to have a good
deal of mental and physical control and do a great deal of scientific
reading. We didn't have the control or want to do the reading; nor were
these things necessary. Tourists and the folks back home, not doctors,
were on our jury.

As time went on, being "crazy" became more difficult. The jury
gradually changed. Fellow artists began to sit on it. This wasn't quite
as bad as doctors would have been, but it was pretty bad. Long hair
and a rapt look wouldn't get you to first base any more. Even dirt,
sandals, and "nightmindedness" wasn't enough. You had to be original.

By the time I got to Montparnasse, the second stage was well advanced. All the more obvious roles had been dropped and the less
obvious ones were being played by experts. There were still a few gents
with long hair, but no one took them seriously and they were never invited to the important parties.

The rest of "The Impostor" tells how a sculptor, Beano Walsh,
with no artistic training or talent, devotes himself to inventing artistic roles which convince people that he is a true artist. When an
agent for the Oscar Hahn (i.e., Otto Kahn) Foundation comes to
check his progress, for a continuation of his support, he invents his
greatest role. He claims that he "had discovered . . . that all the
anatomy books were wrong because they used a man only five feet
ten inches tall for their charts. . . . Since the anatomy of all modern sculpture is based on these books, all modern sculpture is
wrong." In order to write a "new anatomy" of the human form,
Beano (a cousin-germane to Balso Snell) buys a corpse from the
French morgue. While it sits unwrapped and nude in a taxi outside
the Dôme, he gets drunk, then embroiled with the police, and is
arrested and incarcerated overnight with his cadaver. In the morning he is found mad, the corpse mutilated. Later, at an asylum, the
doctor explains to the narrator of the story that Beano has all the
while been "an insane man who knows he's insane. . . . Instead
of hiding his disease, which would be the obvious thing to do, he
hid only part of it, the more serious part, and used the part he

exposed to hide the rest." West would later base the character of Miss Lonelyhearts on psychoanalytical case studies and Beano's case also has classic psychotic outlines, which fitted in with the Paris scene, the surrealist interest in the insane, the modern interest in the artist-figure, and West's personal scorn for the phony artist.

That scorn was partially based on a fear that he might not be a true artist himself. Certainly he was a kind of Rotarian in Paris, doing the conventional things. West's persona, the narrator of "The Impostor," is, as much as Beano, implicated in the story's title. He too plays a fake role—precisely opposite Beano's. He too wants to be "invited to the important parties. What was I to do? [*Cancelled:* I wanted badly to belong.] But how was I to make the grade?"

After hiding in my hotel for about a week, not daring to show myself at the Dôme for fear of making a bad impression, I hit on a great idea. I had come to Paris from a runner's job in Wall Street and still had the clothes I had worn there. Instead of buying a strange outfit and trying to cultivate some new idiosyncrasies, I decided to go in the other direction. "Craziness" through the exaggeration of normality was to be my method. In this land of soft shirts, worn open to the navel, and corduroy trousers, I would wear hard collars and carefully pressed suits of formal, stylish cut and carry clean gloves and a tightly rolled umbrella. I would have precise, elaborate manners and exhibit pronounced horror at the slightest, *public* breach of convention.

I was a big success right from the start. When I entered the Dôme, beer was spilled at many of the tables. More important, I was asked to all the parties.

Compounding the behavior of T. S. Eliot, Jacques Rigaut, and Anatole France* with his personal incapacity for real involvements, West turned his incapacity into fantasy and, in this case, his fantasy into fiction, in which he tended both to elevate and to mock his first-person, fictive surrogate. "The Impostor" remained unpublished, but parts of it West later told as true stories about himself.

* Eliot appeared at the Dôme and other bars in 1924, William Carlos Williams declares, "dressed in top hat, cutaway, and striped trousers. It was intended as a gesture of contempt and received just that." Rigaut dressed in stylish British clothes and wore rich cravats; and Anatole France, his biographer remarks, looked like "a well-tailored boulevardier."

Paris was for West what Troy was for medieval writers—not so much history as material for variations of legend. Such indulgence in fantasy, of course, was not peculiar to him; it was a characteristic of the imagination of West's time, particularly in the kind of experimental writing which he then most admired. Margaret Anderson, editor of the *Little Review* (which moved from Chicago to New York to Paris and in which *Ulysses* was first published), remarks in her autobiography: "My greatest enemy is reality." Like her and others, West allowed the super-real to subdue the real, as the more real. Paris gave him new insight into the resources of his imagination. He would now need, and would shortly find, a reality more adequate to engage the powers of that imagination in the form of art. His adjustment to life would be through satire and fantasy, and in the years to come he would have abundant opportunity for both.

The actual conditions under which he returned to America were less romantic. Although he had been writing home continually about how much work he was accomplishing and what painters and authors he was meeting, business conditions at home were worsening and his parents were beginning to be anxious for him to return and take up a business career. West, who told this story to a friend with a "kind of pensive pride in his own irresponsibility," said that his father, whom he portrayed as a sound businessman, had lost patience with him, and that the letters from home were becoming angry ones. Finally, he agreed to return "if they would send him the passage money. The money arrived. [West] spent the money —most of it in Paris bistros—and ended up just as broke as ever, and just as far from home." At last, after more entreaties, he returned, early in January 1927, after spending less than three months in Paris. Hereafter, his life would be changed; for though until this time he had been able to define his identity by all that he opposed, now little by little he would be drawn to the fringes of the public world—as a businessman, as a writer of screenplays and novels, in politics, commerce, and marriage. His return from Paris marked the last stages of his total commitment to simple rebellion and the beginning of a new education in his obligations to public society.

During that year, everyone was singing the lastest hit tune by

Irving Berlin: "Blue skies, smiling at me,/Nothing but blue skies do I see." But the clouds of the economic crash were gathering. West's father and uncles were losing all their unprofitable, unrented properties to banks and receiverships. The family practice by which individual members gave financial help to each other until it could be returned in the next cyclical upswing to fortune now began to implicate each member in the general disaster, and they slid into an abyss of debt together, at last losing everything in an attempt to save something. The houses they had built, with their sad, grand names, were empty. The national house was tumbling down.

The year 1927 was no year for rebellion. West, who had resisted with all his might the idea of taking over a successful contracting business, now was obliged to return from Paris at once and to accept the position of night manager in a second-rate hotel. He could not have known a year earlier that this would be his fate. And now how could he foresee that it, in turn, would be part of the making of his art?

6 / "The College of Misery"

No Congress of the United States ever assembled, on surveying the state of the Union, has met with a more pleasing
prospect than that which appears at the present time. . . .
The country can regard the present with satisfaction and
anticipate the future with optimism. . . .

—Calvin Coolidge, *Final Message to Congress,*
Dec. 4, 1928

When the business cycle ends,
In flaming extra dividends,
Will he smile his work to see?
Did he who made the Ford make thee?

—Ogden Nash, *The Face Is Familiar* (1940)

Tod Hackett, the hero of *The Day of the Locust,* West wrote,
"was really a very complicated young man with a whole set of personalities, one inside the other like a nest of Chinese boxes." In
Tod, as well as in many other characters in his fiction, West analyzed aspects of himself. He possessed the same kind of personal
intricacy. It may be, as more than one friend believes, that West's
complexity resulted from the "many layers of protection around
him," by which he preserved his inner self from society. Perhaps,
too, his intricacy was in part the issue of an inability fully to
resolve his emotional life—what Lillian Hellman names the "dark
side to his nature." In short, he may have been, as Josephine
Herbst believed, "a labyrinth who concealed things, even from
himself." In any event, all his friends agree (as another puts it)
that "he was a tremendously complicated man, with many, many
facets which very few people ever saw." In 1927, when West returned to New York, this complicated young man was just preparing
to enter upon the career of writer, with layer beneath layer of iden-

tity. These must be stripped away to suggest the various facets of the kind of man he was during the period between his return to America and the publication of his first novel. In this chapter I am not so much concerned with following the chronology of West's life as with presenting a general portrait of his complexities. For *Balso Snell,* which he finished during this time, and *Miss Lonelyhearts,* which he began, may be illumined by a study of the roots which they have in West's personality.

The leading element and perhaps the chief source of West's intricacy lay in the contrast between his intellectual and emotional life, between his passive ability to understand experience and his lack of capacity for deeply active involvement in it. Philip Wylie, who met West in 1925, describes him as "thin, restless, discontent, sardonic, homely and very warm and affectionate under that." Clearly his intellectual convictions were in many ways opposed to his emotional predilections. His manner was opposed to his dreams; but, as Wylie says, he was "full of dreams," and could "shout laughter at irony." Many of his acquaintances describe him as "a very naïve man, very sweet and innocent"; as "sentimental," as "a strange mixture of savviness . . . and innocence"; as "a real natural" who pretended unsuccessfully to be an "exquisite"; as "warm, sympathetic, and sentimental," having a "simple heart" and a spontaneous boyish blush; as "childlike and wonderfully appealing"; as "soft and vulnerable"; and call his supposed cynicism "a cover-up for a real desire to make contact." Such people were, of course, shocked by the difference they felt between the person and the author, and concluded that his books are basically unlike him.

On the other hand, West had, according to others, an "intellectual brutalism" which emerged surprisingly at times—in his humor, which was often cruel; in his absolute intolerance of pretense and his refusal even to talk to people he regarded as dull or superficial; in his mockery of the emotions of others and his anxiety to suppress all expressions of sentiment. "I did not like the three-button repression of Pep," John Sanford remarks. "It stopped me. You'd want to . . . let an emotion out, [but] you'd know that if you did, you'd offend him. . . . It would be almost a physical offense." Once, when Sanford began to confess that West's influence was responsible for his decision to give up law and become a novelist, West, with a pained expression, got off the bus they were riding on rather than hear him continue. West was, those who saw this side of him concluded, one who would shout irony at laughter.

This predisposition toward a tough intellectualism at the expense of tender emotions constituted the source of West's satiric point of view. One of the characters in his first book describes himself in exactly these terms: "I am . . . on the side of intellect against the emotions, on the side of the brain against the heart." Kenneth Burke's contention that "the satirist attacks in others the weaknesses . . . within himself" suggests how West may have been seeking to resolve personality conflicts by ridiculing in art the emotions to which he was susceptible in life. As a friend of the 1927–33 period has said, "he rejected people who were expressing [emotions] . . . because he was afraid of being 'overwhelmed' by his feelings." Thus, as he again puts it in *Balso Snell*, "the ritual of feeling demands burlesque." Furthermore, West delighted in "particularized knowledge" of any kind, and so tended to emphasize knowledge, which gave him pleasure, over emotions, which brought only suffering. Anatole France, whose satiric influence on *Balso Snell* is obvious,* shows much the same conflict. France's emotions, his biographer, Chevalier, says, "were tender . . . [and] wanted beauty; his mind wanted knowledge. . . . They wanted to believe; his mind did not. His emotions were credulous; his mind was skeptical." And though West is superior to France in the range of his satirical power, at his simplest he can be similarly described. In general, of course, the writers of the twenties tended as a whole to hold sentiment in contempt and to express sophistication through wit and knowledge.

How far West might actually participate emotionally in incidents of human suffering, and with what potential suffering for himself, is fully suggested in his fiction, particularly in *Miss Lonelyhearts*; but there is plentiful documentation that such involvement was characteristic of his responses. He was, James T. Farrell and Josephine Herbst agree, "instinctively sensitive about people": what appeared to be reserve was really concern. His tender sympathies very easily led him to identify with suffering people. Wells Root has said that "West could go into a bar and pretty soon the

* West owned *Merry Tales of Jacques, Jocasta, Penguin Island, Thaïs,* and *Revolt of the Angels.*

bartender was his friend. He got along with taxi drivers, rich people, everybody . . . to a degree that very few people I've known in my life could." In particular, another Hollywood friend, John Bright, declares, West could talk with "bruised people"—"bums and criminals and Negroes. . . . He had true empathy. He didn't have a 'sociological' attitude toward them, or a political one either —he empathized with them because they were bruised people." And on these occasions, Bright says, West's "bitterness eased off. . . . He was extremely sensitive to hurting the feelings of people who had had more than their quota of hurt." He was even capable of inventing fables of empathy. For instance, in 1937 he told his secretary, who had recently lost a sister, "I know just how you felt, and my mother knows how your mother felt, because my older brother, who was seventeen, ran away in the First World War to join the Merchant Marine, and he was washed overboard in the North Sea." As this tale suggests, West tended to fantasize in compensation for unsatisfactory reality. He could never, apparently, fully indulge his emotions with people he regarded as intellectual; with them, he was wary of being mocked as a sentimentalist. And he could express his emotions only in part in his novels. But hunters, farmers, shopkeepers—non-intellectuals in general— found him extremely sympathetic. West's butcher in rural Frenchtown, New Jersey, for example, saw him as just "the kind of person you know like an old shoe—very able to sit down in the middle of a group and make everyone feel they knew him." And it is clear that West partly resumed interest in hunting around 1933 in Erwinna and later in Hollywood, as a way of establishing contact with the rural folk.

Yet, for all his sympathy, an equally fundamental principle of West's character was, as Robert M. Coates has said, "his immense, sorrowful . . . all-pervasive pessimism. He was about the most thoroughly pessimistic person I have ever known. . . . But," Coates adds, pointing to an important aspect of West's complexity, "though this colored all his thinking both creatively and critically, it had no effect on his personality, for he was one of the best companions I have known, cheerful, thoughtful, and very flexible in all his personal attitudes." He was, as another friend remarked, "rebellious about everything—but in the mildest way."

In some part, West's bitterness may have derived from his own image of what his attitude should be, for he was full of illusions, as Malcolm Cowley says, the chief of which was that he was sophisticated. But he was also, surely, acutely aware of the universality of human suffering and of the discrepancy, in America, between the real and the ideal. His bitterness and pessimism were as deep-rooted and as justifiable, he believed, as his hopes and sympathies. Like the existentialists, he was willing to let absurdity and irony be standards in an absurd world; but, like William James, he was willing for hope to prevail until the triumph of absurdity. According to Robert Coates, West "regarded the world almost as an evil place, and though he would want people to fight against its evils," he wouldn't do so himself. He was deeply pessimistic, but grateful "to those who gave him reason for hope." Yet he never yearned to have a religion, or at least never was fooled into faith by his yearnings. His hopes were adjusted to his doubts. These were balanced counterweights in West's responses and are at the basis of his irony; for in confronting the choice between faith and doubt he would, in his art, choose both. Pity and horror would be his themes; and his art, at its best, that of ironic tragedy.

Aware of suffering, he yet delighted in free fantasy, and he took a childish pleasure in telling convincing lies. The details of his stories, a friend says, "were brilliantly . . . and beautifully expressed; he could re-create a picture and present a point-of-view beautifully and effortlessly." In at least one instance, one of his myths served as the basis of another writer's fiction. In his tale, "A Meeting of Minds," George Milburn retold a story that West had related about a series of humorous incidents which had supposedly taken place on his father's (Max Westermark, West said his name was) chicken farm. So familiarly and accurately did West talk about the diseases of chickens and the hazards of chicken farming that Milburn, who had himself grown up on a chicken farm, swallowed the story whole.

West's personality, then, was pervaded by inclinations in opposition, reaching to every level of his being and actions. He was not interested in business and indeed rebelled against it; but obliged in time to be both a hotel manager and a professional screenwriter, he would succeed along businesslike lines. He loved fine things, but would make relatively little effort to possess them. Attracted to the bohemian life, he yet surrendered to it very seldom. For all his wit and geniality, he was, as he occasionally revealed, deeply serious. Committed to writing as his career, he yet would seldom discuss writing and only rarely showed his manuscripts to anyone; and in a period when theories of literature were more interesting than literature, he was singularly free from theorizing. The most precious success, he claimed, was a *succès d'estime* with a small audience; yet he was to be very sensitive about the failure of his novels to have large popular sales. He certainly became an artist from deep needs in his ego, yet his work is not permeated by ego: he never wrote autobiography (though once he proposed to do so); he could be lyrical in his praise of many other writers, though seldom critical of any. Still, in his accurate delineations of the relations between lost individuals and helpless societies, he may be said to combine a sense of the Protestant absorption with self with the Jewish theme of the abandoned community.

Physically, he "moved slowly and often seemed overcome by inertia." But, as his maneuverings to get into college show, "he was capable of fast, flexible adjustments; he was quick and bright." Socially he could be shy and hesitant—Josephine Herbst calls this a "shy grace"—pausing long for words; but he might become suddenly loquacious, gesturing with his hands in the air while he talked, his face animated; and occasionally he dominated conversations with merciless irony.

Perhaps West remained a mystery to himself; certainly he was one to his friends. Although he had a great many acquaintances, they all felt that he remained "essentially lonesome." Such was the variously divided character of the person who was now setting out to write about a world which was, apparently, nicely accommodating his talents by falling to pieces.

II

For West the thirties began in 1927. This period, one of its historians has said, "was uniquely [an era] . . . in which time outran consciousness, in which the sequential stages of depression and reform appeared too rapidly to allow for accurate fathoming. Hence, the misery of the country was equalled only by its bewilderment." It was a period of great disruption in economic life, of course, but it was also one of powerful intellectual and cultural, literate, if not literary, excitement. In the twenties, a decade of artistic experimentation had finally flowered in a stimulating literature and other achievements of culture. The thirties, whether there had been a Depression or not, were to constitute a new beginning, an intellectual readjustment, with all the mental rejuvenation this implies. Although, clearly, this readjustment was not caused by the Depression, it was certainly accelerated by it and was given a particular bent by that central economic fact of the time. Consciousness and culture were absorbing and reflecting not only a radical change in sensibility but a momentous one in economics. Combined, these brought American life and government abruptly to a crisis as decisive as those in the periods of the Revolution and the Civil War. It may be that because the new possibilities of mind outdistanced literary possibility—that because theory outran practice—there was a less brilliant flowering of literature in the thirties. Perhaps only writers like Dos Passos, Hemingway, Faulkner, Fitzgerald, and West, whose consciousness extended from the twenties across into the thirties, could survive the oblivion which has overtaken many of the writers of the thirties and into which they fell, even then, daily.

The mind and sensibility of such a writer as West, raised on the literary tastes of the twenties but attentive, as he began to publish, to the critical demands and audience of the thirties, was bound to be either enriched or immolated by the ferment of literary ideas of both periods. Undoubtedly, the seven years following December 1923, when the first number of *The American Mercury* was published, belonged to Mencken and Nathan. The prewar assumptions concerning the "innate virtue of the people and the desirability of more democracy," the inevitability of progress, the general purity of political activity, and the belief in the ultimate prevalence of moral idealism fell meteorically from the American empyrean. H. L. Mencken, whom Edmund Wilson called at the time "the civilized consciousness of modern America," mercilessly pilloried the "boobus Americanus" in issue after issue; in particular he attacked the naïve belief of reformers in placebos and programs. "The fact that I have no remedy for all the sorrows of the world," he announced, "is no reason for my accepting yours. It simply supports the strong probability that yours is a fake." The only true issue which he recognized "was that of intelligence against stupidity, the fine and developed spirit confronting the dull life of materialist America." Now, as Norman Thomas aptly said of the twenties: "The old reformer [became] the Tired Radical and his sons and daughters drink at the fountain of *The American Mercury*."

West and his friends at Brown naturally preferred intelligence, the sophisticated life. There, the students regarded the copy of *The Mercury* they carried as their green badge of courage and protection—a weapon against the athletes, the faculty, and their parents. "There were those of us," I. J. Kapstein has remarked of their feelings, "who belonged to Mencken, and those of us who belonged to the outer world." Mencken had decisively disposed of politics for West and his college contemporaries, and they—West most of all—gave themselves over entirely to matters of literary form and style. Separating life from literature, they agreed with George Jean Nathan's remarks in "The Code of a Critic": "I am constitutionally given to enthusiasm about nothing. The great problems of the world—social, political, economic, and theological —do not concern me in the slightest. . . . If all the Armenians were to be killed tomorrow and if half the Russians were to starve to death the day after, it would not matter to me in the least. . . . My sole interest is in writing." Not only in 1927 but to the end of his life, West shared, in a less extreme form, both Nathan's commitment to the primacy of style in literature and also something of his skepticism about "world problems"—a phrase which he and his friends uttered with an intellectual sneer. West admired, a Hollywood friend of the late thirties says, "the cynicism of Mencken, rather than the fervor of Heywood Broun."

Mencken stands, of course, simply as a convenient symbol of the skepticism of the twenties. The success of the skeptical comedy of *The New Yorker*, founded in 1925, would serve equally well. Its spirit and in some part its nucleus deriving from the brilliant coterie habitually gathering at the Algonquin for a round-table luncheon and calling itself "The Thanatopsis Literary and Inside Straight Club"—George S. Kaufman, Dorothy Parker, Robert Benchley, and Alexander Woollcott—*The New Yorker* proved that sharp, sophisticated humor was suitable to and could flourish in the America of the twenties. As evidence of this, it soon outdistanced its rivals, *Judge* and *Life*, whose best writers and cartoonists, like Peter Arno and S. J. Perelman, found their true place on the *New Yorker* staff.

Through Perelman, his brother-in-law after 1929, West knew many of the people on *The New Yorker,* and he was influenced by them, particularly by Perelman, in shaping his own version of savage humor. In turn, his work was admired not only by Perelman, who has made moving tributes to his talents many times, but also by Dorothy Parker, Kaufman, Woollcott, and James Thurber. West and most of the *New Yorker* writers were attracted equally by satire and sentiment. They chronicled the scandal and he the tragedies of American life, but all understood its grotesque and pitiable human character.

How close the spirit of disillusion stood to the heart of American life in this period is suggested by the history of politically radical magazines in the twenties, in contrast to the stunning success of *The New Yorker.* In the same year in which that magazine was founded, the International Union of Revolutionary Writers was organized as a branch of the Soviet, in an attempt to encourage revolutionary writing abroad. With *Masses* closed by the government and *The Liberator* languishing after a raid by the Department of Justice in 1922, *New Masses* was founded in 1926 to spread radical idealism. One of its founding editors, Michael Gold, had aspired "to make a bright, artistic, brilliant magazine that would captivate the imagination of the younger generation and rally them around something real—not the sterile mockeries and gibings at the books that Mencken had taught them." But even with such tried polemicists as Gold exhorting or admonishing a hypothetical audience, and although even Mencken praised its liveliness and Ezra Pound declared it was the best recent reason for repatriation he had seen, still *New Masses* languished. By the early twenties, "sophisticated" Americans had lost interest in both Russia and Communism. While *The New Yorker* leaped forward, *New Masses* seemed, for the moment, destined for oblivion.

But as the thirties approached, a change began to be noticeable. *New Masses,* cleverly mingling art and politics, and with Edmund Wilson and John Dos Passos on its board, was showing surprising strength. Whether the young realized it or not, the three most important influences upon them—World War I, the Russian Revolution, and the modern movement in art and literature —were all carrying them away from Mencken-like skepticism toward social concern and commitment. Mencken had prophetically chosen as the first object for satire in *The Mercury* the expatriate aesthetes. Ernest Boyd's lead article in the first number, titled "Aesthete: Model 1924," satirized such younger writers as Malcolm Cowley, Matthew Josephson, Gilbert Seldes, and John Dos Passos in a "composite portrait" which drew together the dadaist idiosyncrasies of each. At first this group answered Boyd on artistic grounds in a magazine issued only once, *Aesthete 1925*. But not long after, the same writers began to sponsor programs implicating literature with the advocacy of social justice. Their Dada aestheticism, it turned out, had been, as Daniel Aaron writes, "an act of protest rather than one of renunciation and indifference." Now their protests were mixed with renewed faiths and hopes for society. With Mencken, they had mocked reform, but now they awaited and encouraged it; though they had despaired of American civilization, particularly of the life of its masses, they now idealized the worker, to whom reform, they insisted, would give his true status. Repatriated, they insisted that America was the proper arena for their activities of protest and reformation, and they began to celebrate the popular music, cartoons, and movies—mass entertainment and culture—which they had earlier seen as evidence of the lack of culture in America. It was true, as James Agee claimed in a *New Masses* article of 1937, that both surrealists and radicals were revolutionaries, and "that there [were] no valid reasons why they should be kept apart."

John Howard Lawson, who was shocked into radical politics by the Sacco-Vanzetti execution in 1927, and who eventually would be the leading spokesman for radical writers in Hollywood, has described this switch from the Left Bank to the radical left as "the logical development of a more political point of view." "What I was trying to do in the twenties, unsuccessfully," he declares, "was . . . to discover myself. I'd been running away from myself —the bohemian phase was largely running away: the finding of all sorts of metaphysical outlets for my dilemma that I hated the middle class and yet was part of it. . . . The only possibility remaining was to turn to some long-term, realistic way of coping with the absurdity of the civilization of which I was a part." To be sure, there were many contemporary writers who experienced no such change. For some, like Josephine Herbst and Edward Dahlberg, the commitment to social justice had always been at the heart of their creativity; others, like Thornton Wilder and Robert Frost, continued to write in the spirit of the twenties or earlier periods.

But in general the period was defined by its changing minds. Now, self-professed dadaists like Malcolm Cowley and Matthew Josephson, critics like Edmund Wilson, comic writers like Dorothy Parker and Robert Benchley, novelists like Hemingway and Dos Passos, and poets like Archibald MacLeish, all followed, more or less, the same logic, experiencing, as Josephson said of himself, "a great change of heart toward the aesthetic nihilists . . . [and] a vehement dislike for their anti-social and irrational tendencies." For the first time in America, poets and politicians were in league: Roosevelt called the twenties "a decade of debauch" and Alben Barkley termed it a "carnival" marked by "the putrid pestilence of financial debauchery." Writers, similarly, were disgusted with the apparent breakdown of capitalist civilization and the values of commercial society, by the injustice and inequities which they felt between what they were calling, with Dos Passos, the "two nations" of haves and have-nots in America; some became pro-Soviet through their earlier anti-war commitments; and all criticized the gospel of individualism which they had advocated in the twenties, with its consequent separation of literature from social issues. Now many made moves to adjust their art to politics. Archibald Mac-Leish perhaps best summed up the impulses affecting writers in the thirties when he declared: "Politics is a subject for poetry because with us the public world has become the private world. The single individual, whether he wishes so or not, has become part of the world that contains also Austria and Czechoslovakia and China and Spain."

"Nihilism, dadaism, smartsetism—they are all gone"—the *New York Post* chortled when George Jean Nathan decided to discontinue his *American Spectator* in 1937, four years after he and Mencken had given up the editorship of *The Mercury*. Many of the older writers, but virtually all of the younger ones, children during the war ("youth is beginning to believe in something again," Stuart Chase announced), cheered the end of the Mencken era or, more simply, ignored its passing.

The debate between the characteristic spirits of the twenties and the thirties coincided with the divisions within West himself. Perhaps, indeed, in no other writer was this dualism so sharply defined. In most writers, the alternate impulses merged in gradual change; but for West, similarly divided, the tendencies remained separate. Coming late in the twenties—in college idealizing the life of the artist while others were leading it in Paris, and then arriving in Paris only after most of those earlier figures had departed— West was profoundly affected by the aesthetic gospel. It accorded well with the high valuation he placed on sophistication and intellectual activity, his desire to become part of an intellectual elite, and his need to minimize sentiment while stressing form in art; and most of all, it accorded with the pessimism deeply rooted in his being. On the other hand, his personal inclination toward emotions of sympathy, his feeling for tragedy, and his view of himself as an outsider—his ability to allow human suffering to become, imaginatively, his own—these all tended to draw him away from the concern with art and into life. It is certainly true that while he was naïve about politics in the mid to late twenties, he "discussed current events with great shrewdness" by the thirties. Yeats has remarked that, for the purposes of his art, the artist often adopts a mask antithetical to his person and identical to his desire. But for West, divided equally between two desires and two persons, both responses were masks, and either, in his hands, could become art. The English poet W. W. Gibson wrote in the thirties that "the proper spiritual habitation for a poet is a halfway house between the ivory tower and a soap box at the corner of the public thoroughfare." West occupied neither, nor was he between them; he shared, rather, in the more profound aspects of these extremes and made a paradoxical art out of continued concern both with the highest ideals of art-as-form and also with a willing immersion into the archetypes of human response emerging on the frontiers of consciousness in his time. Murray Kempton has argued that "the thirties were a kind of folding of banners, a surrender to formation." This was certainly not uniformly true, and it was far from true of West. Many imaginations were brilliantly lighted by the chaos of the period. Mencken demanded conformity no less than Marx. The thirties, when no society was stable enough to anchor the mind, was for many a decade of immense intellectual freedom. West preserved the revolutionary aspects of both decades—their different revolutions in style and subject—in an art that would, for this reason, have increased meaning and popularity in later decades, when others could see around and into both the twenties and the thirties, as West had done at the time.

That West was forced home from Paris for economic reasons suggests the combination of pressures exerted on his life by both art and society. Certainly for him, as for almost everyone else, the business crash was a central fact of the late twenties—although aesthetics remained a fact as central to his life. Depression came earlier and more bitterly to West than to most others. His family wealth was dissolving even while the campaign of 1928 was in progress, with Hoover stumping on Harding–Coolidge prosperity and declaring: "Given a chance to go forward with the policies of the last eight years, we shall soon, with the help of God, be in sight of the day when poverty will be banished from this nation." So bitterly ironic were such pronouncements for West that even a decade later he would speak of Hoover with vehement dislike. It is important to understand that the personal disaster of West's hopes preceded the national crash—giving him a feeling of individual bitterness—and also that the national experience of disaster followed soon after his own, imparting, to some extent, a sense of the community of disaster. In a book on Van Gogh which he owned, West marked a phrase, the "college of misery." If West had discovered the role of the individual artist in the twenties at Brown, in the thirties he was enrolled in the college of misery, where the collective disaster merged with his personal disaster.

Perhaps, as André Breton said in his second *Manifeste du Surréalisme* of December 1929, "the simple surrealist act would consist of going out into the street, revolver in hand, and firing at random into the crowd as long as one could." But many surrealists were joining parties through which to organize reform; Breton himself was a Trotskyite and Aragon a Stalinist: the latter had pronounced Breton's surrealist cry, *Changez la vie!* to have been superseded by the Marxist proclamation, *Change the World!* West saw little hope for change of either kind in America. He was certainly "very sour on the United States," a friend says, and also "fatalistic . . . toward the ills that befall us"; and he could put both the public desire to dream and its disillusionment into his fiction. At this point he needed to join no parties. He had been imaginatively released by the confusions of his time. Moreover, in many ways, the tragic nature and disillusion of the Depression suited his personal sense of tragedy; for he was, as a friend said, "very catastrophe-oriented. . . . Disaster fascinated him . . . not in a puerile sense, but from the standpoint of the human tragedy."

Certainly, he was suffering deeply himself. That the diminishment of his father's fortune shocked West is partly suggested by the schemes and plans he shaped for making a quick fortune himself through his inventive genius. If he earlier had formulated fantasies of rebellion—like the real-estate loan scheme he had described to Rafferty—he seems to have taken his speculative fantasies seriously in the period 1927–30; these were pure acts of personal desperation. He had a good business sense—he had managed his money well at college—and he knew that anxiety over how to make money was more annoying than not having money might be; still, he fretted anxiously. One of his more adventuresome plans was to manufacture and market a commodity called "Cactus Candy." He tried to get his friends to taste it and promote it, but at least one of them remembers it as "a revolting bar of stuff that looked like kitchen soap." After about two years of faith in the prospects of cactus candy, on April Fool's Day in 1930 he told a friend: "I sold out my interest in the cactus-candy business for $65 and [a] two-volume edition of Chapman's plays—very nice, printed in England. Figuring the value of the books at $10, I am out about $50. However, I know a lot about the candy business." He continued, not despairing: "Today we delivered our first batch (two gallons) of chili con carne. I think I explained the chili business to you. I'll probably make a million dollars. If that flops, I intend to start a bureau for placing stenographers in camps. Based on a very novel scheme." All these schemes failed. West told a friend that if the possibility of credit were open he would live in luxury and worry *then* how to find the money for it. But now, apparently, there was money nowhere.

West's writing during the period between his return from Paris and the publication of *Balso Snell* reflected some of these ambitions as well as the currents of that time, and was extraordinarily prophetic of his work to come. In the most immediate and obvious way, he had a need for money, and hoping to be able to give up his assistant manager's job at the Kenmore Hall Hotel, he attempted to think of writing as a moneymaking profession and so cast about for literary projects which might sell. People had spoken of his personal manner as slow or shambling ever since his days at Camp Paradox, and his ironic nickname had stuck. But that his manner was a protective mask would become obvious not only because of the enormous quantity of material he turned out in the next decade, but also in the restless mental fever of his plans and projects. Even when he planned to return to Paris in 1930, he would ask an entirely different question than before: "Could I earn anything in Paris, do you think?" Now he saw that he would somehow have to live by his writing if he was to be a writer at all. And his mind was fertile with literary ideas: he had always had a way of taking up story notions and turning them about in conversation, as if watching for the facets of their sparkle in the responses of his listeners.

One of the possible ventures for which he had even done some research in Paris was a book of popularized short biographies of painters. Perhaps later he would do one of writers as well. He was attempting, of course, to make capital as a writer from his earlier ambition to be an artist. "There was a lot of talk about art," an acquaintance of the early thirties said, "and West was always right in the middle of it. . . . He knew a lot of names . . . and he absorbed every bit of information that he could pick up." He described his project to John Sanford, and seemed to love to repeat the names of painters like Marie Laurencin, and of writers like Lautréamont and to delight in relating anecdotes about them. There is no way of knowing what painters West would have treated in this book; but his tastes in painting, as in music, centered around those pieces which evoked some literary interest. Nothing actually came of this project until nearly a decade later, when West would need to invent a protagonist with a painterly point of view for a novel about Hollywood. Tod Hackett, an art student at Yale, his mind filled with the history and implications of his craft, would be sent to Hollywood and provide the center of historical and artistic intelligence for that novel. In his proposed book on the lives of painters, West imagined the earliest form of *The Day of the Locust* by imagining the crisis each artist faced in his life.

He could not yet anticipate *The Day of the Locust*; but he was endlessly rewriting *Balso Snell*, and between 1927 and 1929 he completed it. He was also making an attempt to write short stories, but by 1930 he decided that he had no talent for short fiction, since none of his serious stories had sold. Still, night after night he sat behind the hotel desk thinking his stories through.

At least from the time that West managed to enter Tufts on forged credentials, and particularly after his essay "Euripides—a Playwright," he had been interested in the hoax. The *Spectra* hoax by Arthur Davidson Ficke and Witter Bynner, and the critical hoax which the editors of *transition* had recently played with Poe's "El Dorado," suggested that through the hoax he might seriously express some of the true principles of Dada aesthetics. Indeed, in immediate response to the *transition* hoax, West attempted one of his own. He took some lines from Flaubert's *Temptation of St. Anthony* and arranged them into free verse, then sent his composition off to *transition*, whose editors may have recognized (as I. J. Kapstein did) the fairly well-known passage. In any event, they declined to print it.

West next tried a similar hoax in prose. He had read enough tales of the outdoors in *Field and Stream* and Western magazines to understand their formulas and to realize that episodes were interchangeable. He might, he decided, write tales of the outdoors by taking various elements from many stories and recombining and amalgamating them according to formula. He would have the public pleasure of money from the sale and the private pleasure of the hoax. Later, in Hollywood, he spent some time trying to explain to a woman how he had written such tales. He told her that he "had gone to a secondhand bookstore and bought about a hundred copies of outdoor magazines"; he then cut them up and "blended and spliced several stories together."

West's interest in such a tour de force could not be sustained, of course, but in 1929 he did manage to have one such tale accepted for publication in the *Overland Monthly*, a magazine which Bret Harte had begun nearly sixty years before. Called "A Barefaced Lie"—the title is part of West's ironical private clue to the hoax—this tale is a Western in the Harte–Twain manner, consisting of a series of tall tales and plenty of good Western talk. It opens: "With my dunnage at my feet, I stood on the porch of the Circle City Hotel waiting for the stage. I had been advised by my friend, Red Patterson, the gum booter, to ride only with Boulder Bill—and to listen politely to all he had to say." The story concerns a tall tale about a bear which tops another tall tale by Boulder Bill and

which he dubs "a low-down, bare, bare . . . bare-faced bear
lie. . . ."

At the same time he was busy with several other projects. During this period he contemplated writing, out of material related to
Balso Snell, a short novel concerning the life of St. Pamphile, a
third-century Greek saint. He made a start on this book, then
abandoned it until the winter of 1934–5, when he attempted, unsuccessfully, to revise and complete it. The fact was that *Balso
Snell* satisfied his interest in both the material and the probable
point of view of the tale of St. Pamphile.

A book on painters, revision after revision of *Balso Snell* and the
effort to apply a similar point of view to the life of an early saint,
attempts to write short fiction either as hoaxes or as true expressions
of his vision of human suffering—West's work on all these, while
he worked at the hotel, shows him absolutely, perhaps desperately,
determined to preserve his imagination and his commitment to art
even in the most difficult of situations. As the conventional society
which he had despised fell apart about him, he seemed to draw
strength from its collapse, perhaps because he no longer had to
consume his energy in rebelling against it. He had, it seems, a sense
of release, and his energy flowed into his art. By the waters of chaos
he began to integrate his talent with his ambitions.

Of all his literary activities at this time, doubtless the most important was initiated quite by accident one night in March 1929,
when S. J. Perelman—now dating West's sister Laura—dropped by
the Kenmore Hall Hotel, where West worked, and suggested that
they go to dinner at Siegel's, their favorite Greenwich Village
restaurant. An acquaintance of Perelman's who wrote a column
for the *Brooklyn Eagle* under the name "Susan Chester" had described to him the kinds of letters she was receiving and had suggested that he might be able to put such material to comic use.
She regarded the column itself as something of a joke, a special
daily visitation of the vast cuckoo-cloudlands of American illusion.
That night she promised to show Perelman a group of letters.
Perelman inquired, would West go along? He would. But after
they had heard the letters, it was clear that they would not serve at
all for Perelman's point of view, which is brilliantly designed to
puncture pretension in all its forms. Perelman puts realism to
the service of fantasy; West would see in the fantasy life pointed to

in these letters a key to the real character of the time. The letters were, to be sure, romantic and shot through with fantasy thinking; but there was no pretension in them, only unbearable pathos. One, signed "Broad Shoulders," began:

> dear Susan:
> I have always enjoyed reading your column, and have benefited by your expert advice. Now I must ask you for advice for myself. I have been married for twenty years. I have a girl 19 and a boy of 17. From the very beginning I realized that I had made a mistake in marrying my husband. But the children came soon after, and I was obliged for their dear sakes to stand through thick and thin, bitter and sweet. And also for decency sake.

Another woman wrote that as she was "stooping to put the broom under the bed to get the lint and dust . . . —lo—behold I saw a face which resembled the mask of a devil—only the whites of his eyes and his hands clenched ready to choke anyone." The woman who signed herself "Broad Shoulders" added: "Susan, don't think I am broad shouldered. But that is just the way I feel about life and me."

If any one moment in his life could be regarded as absolutely crucial in West's discovery that he was an artist, it occurred during this night of March 1929. He was overwhelmed by the letters, all his elaborate personal defenses were swept away in a flood of intellectual exaltation and emotional receptivity. Perelman could not use the letters; but *he* would, West said. He believed he could do something—not comic, certainly not comic, though perhaps using comedy to heighten the tragedy in them. He was certain that he could do something with them.

III

In all these ventures, perhaps, West was learning more than anything else what it would mean for him to be a writer. He was defining himself in solitude while he sat in the night manager's office in the hotel. But collectively, too, he was defining himself in his associations with two very different groups—the one, a loose group of writers and friends living or meeting in Greenwich Village; the other, a group of young Jewish intellectuals with backgrounds and interests similar to his own. In both cases, these groups sponsored ideals importantly dissimilar from his own knowledge and inclinations; thus, consciously or not, he tested himself against them.

S. J. Perelman had moved to New York immediately after leaving Brown in 1925 and began writing regularly, first for *Judge*, and later for *College Humor*. After West returned from Paris early in 1927, they renewed their friendship. Perelman was the first professional writer whom West knew well, and he looked to him for definitions of what life as a writer—the life he yearned for—was like. "He often visited me in the Village," Perelman recalls, "curious about, though hardly envious of, the precarious life that I was leading." Almost from the first, Perelman was, Lester Cole says, an "awe-inspiring figure" for West; and from this time on, West wrote with Perelman in mind as his first audience.

Although both men could be savagely witty toward other people, they kidded each other in a gentle way. West told his friends that Perelman was a great writer whose work would live, and Perelman never failed in his support of West.

West soon brought Perelman to meet his parents, who were then living on 79 Street. At this very time, West's relationship with his younger sister was also blooming. Like her brother, Laura had an instinctive savvy, an ability to do things in the right way. Like him too, she was bright and creative. She took his side in the family against the pressure being put upon him to devote himself to business—indeed, West later declared that it was Laura who had most encouraged him to be a writer and had kept up his faith in himself by her affection for him.

It was no surprise that Laura and Sid, who shared a love for West, should also be attracted to each other. She occasionally came down from Pembroke during the school year to see him. West himself was delighted. Finally, with Perelman's first book, *Dawn Ginsbergh's Revenge*, about to appear, Laura and he were married on July 4, 1929, and moved into an apartment near Washington Square. West visited them regularly on Saturday nights and to some extent shared their social life. The Perelmans gave West, for the first time, a second and real home directly in line with his interests. There is no doubt that the kind of personal support they gave him contributed significantly to his ability to take up his writing seriously at this same time.

Besides Perelman, there were several other college classmates living downtown, including Quentin Reynolds, working as a journalist, and I. J. Kapstein, an editor at Knopf during 1926–7. Now college bull sessions were transferred to Village speakeasies, Jack Delaney's or Julius's. During the years from 1927 to 1930, as yet showing very little interest in politics, West and his friends continued their long talks about Joyce and *transition* or other little magazines, speculated over what the next movement in literary experiment would approve or contravene, and freely scorned the majority of their college contemporaries, who had gone into either advertising or Wall Street. Kapstein has a "vivid recollection" of a summer evening's discussion about Joyce in Washington Square Park which lasted for hours. To a more recent Brown graduate who joined this group, West appeared to be "a very intense person with a sardonic wit," who "was not particularly articulate but [who could discuss] . . . some subjects with great passion." Literature was West's true passion and even to Martin Kamin, the well-informed owner of a bookstore specializing in experimental modern writing, he gave the impression that he knew something about everyone writing at that time, even the most obscure authors.

West even thought of committing a genuine Dada act to advance the cause of avant-garde writing. In March 1931, Theodore Dreiser slapped Sinclair Lewis's face after Lewis had accused him of plagiarizing several thousand words from his wife's book, *The New Russia*, which had appeared one month before *Dreiser Looks at Russia*. While the controversy between Dreiser, Lewis, and Dorothy Thompson was taking place, West told Kamin: "I think I can get a good deal of publicity for the movement by going up to court and slapping Dreiser's face." He had, Kamin said, "extraordinary dedication to the modern movement." He was learning how an artist behaves, obviously his central preoccupation during this period.

Emphasizing his sophistication, as befitted one who had been to Paris, West now imitated surrealist practice by joking in French. He spoke knowingly about performing a Black Mass at Brown, and of the unveiling of a statue there by the president, at which the statue was revealed to have been covered by excrement. He might give a party but forget to provide any food or drink, provoking a hungry friend to remark at the time: "Just like him, but in his circle that goes for just forgetfulness. Oh, Nat, why he's so intense and so vital, he just natchrally loses all sense of time and space."

West did not meet only former college chums in Greenwich Village. During this time, a historian of the Village has written, the area "drew to it a wide variety of people with one quality in common, their repudiation of the social standards of the communities in which they had been reared." Their attempt to discover other values to replace those they had rejected would give the Village a multiform, many-layered character. Social or political revolutionaries, artistic bohemians, anarchists, escapists, mystics, and sensualists all mixed and mingled with the earlier Italian inhabitants of the area and with those who had no other reason for being there except that they found this amalgam "different" and "interesting." Here, among other Party members, West met Michael Gold, who was writing about the East Side in *Jews without Money* (1930) and turning out a steady stream of polemical journalism. Gold counseled him on ways to transcend his middle-class background, gave him some subjects, and offered to help him develop "articles he should write" for *New Masses* or *Daily Worker;* in collaboration with Perelman they considered starting a magazine tentatively called *Mickey Finn.* There, too, were bohemian poets like Maxwell Bodenheim, just beginning his long decline into abject poverty; novelists like Edward Dahlberg, Nathan Asch, and Dashiell Hammett; and satirists like Philip Wylie. To the Aurora Restaurant on West Fourth Street, or to Siegel's, where West and Perelman gathered with Wylie, also came Finley Peter Dunne, Jr., and several other writers from *The New Yorker,* as well as journalists like A. J. Liebling. Not far away were the offices of *The New Republic,* where West would visit Edmund Wilson, who was literary editor; here he met John Dos Passos and Horace Gregory, among others. West listened to their arguments about art, politics, history, psychology, and sex, remaining an observer. At a party where E. E. Cummings was present, his wife recalls, West "didn't utter a word, but stood in a corner of the room, very shy but listening to every word Cummings uttered, and studied him all the time we were there." West, by observing the styles of other writers, was learning to find his own. The Greenwich Village society which he thus touched gave him rich opportunities to measure his own aspirations and endowments.

More unified and very special in character, the other group important to West centered around the home of George Brounoff on Central Park West, where at least a half dozen young Jewish intellectuals would appear on Sunday afternoons to drink tea Russian style and to discuss, intensely, literature and the arts. The apartment was filled with reminders of the distinguished musical career of Platon Brounoff, George's father and "the only representative [as he described himself] of the Russian modern school of composers in America." He had brought a Russian choir to this country and had written an opera about the American Indian, based on Helen Hunt Jackson's *Ramona*. His son had absorbed many of his interests and, on an intimate scale, held a kind of European salon, at which a variety of young men appeared. Brounoff and some of the others had studied at City College with Morris R. Cohen, and had been influenced by Spengler; he imposed upon his gatherings his own interests in philosophy, music, literature, and art. This was a seriously intellectual, masculine group, interested in the most recent developments in the intellectual world. It was hardly a social group at all, and there were no overtones of homosexuality to it. It met for serious discussion or artistic entertainments. Occasionally, even papers on philosophic subjects were delivered, and regular sessions for the analysis of Joyce's "Work in Progress" were held. Here West involved himself in abstract questions of history and philosophical developments. Although by training and temperament West was little prepared to take a leading part in philosophic analysis, he did discuss literary theory. Moreover, he read a draft of *Balso Snell* to the group and pressed upon it his own interest in surrealism, along with another member, Jessie Greenstein, who brought in his collection of French, German, and Belgian Dada periodicals. Some parts of these influenced the final shaping of *Balso*. Ultimately, most of the group tended to regard Dada as escapist and to condemn *Balso* for lack of seriousness. But West also turned the discussion to his more general literary interests: Coleridge's *Biographia Literaria*, the poetry of Rilke, the fiction of Proust and Thomas Mann, Gide's *The Counterfeiters*, and the criticism of Ezra Pound and T. E. Hulme. These suited better the general intellectual spirit of the gatherings.

The main tone of the group, however, derived from an idealism based on the conviction that love is the central need of man and that in the arts the human spirit was best expressed. Its members tended to emphasize and tried to analyze the emotional responses which art evoked in them, and they willingly surrendered to sentiment. The group was influenced chiefly by pre-Marxist Russian literature and thought. Dostoevsky inevitably provided the major ideals for the group and the texts illustrating them. They read all his works in translation and were especially influenced by *The Brothers Karamazov*, but also by *A Raw Youth*, *The Idiot*, *The Possessed*, and *Crime and Punishment*. Through Dostoevsky, Brounoff "propounded the view that it was possible for deeply sympathetic human relations to exist . . . on a basis which would exclude any selfishness or personal ambition." As for Dostoevsky's heroes—and to a lesser extent, Tolstoy's—such relationships would constitute what Brounoff called "paths of salvation." The kind of Christ figure or secular saint which they found in Prince Myshkin appealed strongly to them as the highest development, along certain lines, of their ideals. Obviously, these particular books, this interpretation of Dostoevsky's Christianity, and the whole tone of the group influenced *Miss Lonelyhearts*, West's work-in-progress.

Radiating from Dostoevsky, the group extended its interest to other Russian writers. Although West declared that he could improve Dostoevsky with a pair of shears, and insisted that "the French type of short, tight novel" was the ideal in fiction, still, interested in Dostoevsky and several other Russian authors, and with a new respect for Russian culture, he resumed his reading of the major Russian writers and took a new interest in recent Russian authors. In the Brounoff group, Ehrenburg's novels, Ilf and Petrov's *The Little Golden Calf*, Ivan Goncharov's *Oblomov*, Artzybashev's *Sanine*, Andreyev, and Gorky were all discussed. Profoundly impressed, West could repeat passages of their dialogue and describe scenes from these writers even years later.

This group hardly confined itself to the Russians. They went not only to the productions of Chekhov plays but to those of O'Neill and Ibsen. They subscribed not only to the Marxist magazines *International Literature* and *Inprecorps* but also to *Hound and Horn*. They went to meetings of the John Reed Club, to Russian movies at the Cameo and Acme Theatres, to the Workers' Bookshop, and to hear Stravinsky conducting *The Rites of Spring;* but also to Georgia O'Keeffe exhibitions at Stieglitz's American Place, to the Museum of Modern Art in the Heckscher Building, where it was first established in 1929, to the Gotham Book Mart for the latest experimental literature, to hear Beethoven's string quartets and Toscanini conducting the New York Philharmonic, to the avant-garde concerts of the International Composers Guild, to Lewisohn Stadium* in the summer and Carnegie Hall in the winter. West, who generally ridiculed the romantic music then constituting so large a part of the repertory, nonetheless went regularly to the Philharmonic on Thursday nights. He liked best either pieces with literary themes—like *Harold in Italy* or *Fingal's Cave*—or opera. But he "understood music very well," a frequent female companion says, and musician acquaintances like Vernon Duke and Harry Kurnitz would listen respectfully enough to his comments during intermissions.

West moved nimbly between his Village friends and this uptown group, in many ways so opposite each other. His response to both was ambivalent. On the one hand, there is evidence that, from the serious point of view of the Brounoff group, he privately ridiculed his Village friends. In a letter of 1930, for instance, he related: "I think I told you about e. e. cummings being at the Perelmans. I think he is crazy. He sat on the floor at Seegal's and shouted all the dirty words he knew. Not funny but very loud. The other great man at Laura's saloon was Edmund Wilson. He is certainly crazy. No dirty words, but peculiar sounds, sudden gestures and violent faces. He's a great writer you can't take that away from him. I think you cannot. I guess all writers are crazy."

On the other hand, from the point of view of his Village friends, he could mock the idealistic sentimentality of the Brounoff group. In the Village he organized a short-lived group which he called "The Prince Myshkinites." Calling himself Prince Myshkin, a name sometimes applied to Brounoff by his friends, he caricatured the proceedings uptown, declaring sardonically that for himself he would spread not just the spirit but the flesh of love as widely and

* Once, at Lewisohn Stadium, West stepped far enough out of his accustomed sophisticated role for it to be memorable. Noticing a girl reading a book before the concert, and wanting to meet her, he said: "That book you're reading— I wrote it." The girl looked him over for a moment, and then said, "I'm glad to know you, Mr. Melville."

freely as possible; and in the spirit of Candide, he would treat ideal figures ironically. Here, he ridiculed emotion and insisted that this was not the best possible world, that people were victims, and that ideal figures were invented to avoid that realization. He could be his own Shrike. Alternately, this is to say, he would affirm each group by rejecting the other, while learning from both, thereby, to explore himself, his own mixture of idealism and pessimism, faith and doubt.

West's habit of investigating himself, not meditatively or through introspection but in terms of his responsiveness to groups or situations, is nowhere more evident than in a correspondence that he conducted during the first half of 1930, when the period about which I have been writing came to a climax. During the winter of 1929–30, West was introduced by the Perelmans to the Paris-fashions writer for *The New Yorker*, Beatrice Mathieu, who had come to New York for a visit as part of Harold Ross's regular policy for foreign correspondents. The Perelmans had met her in Paris on their wedding journey in the summer of 1929 and soon began to envision a match between her and West. Although the innocent bystanders had both been comically prepared by the Perelmans' enthusiasm to dislike each other heartily, they were immediately attracted to each other in New York. By the time Miss Mathieu returned to Paris late in February, West was declaring joyfully: "Please do not speak to anyone about marriage until I come and talk to you in the spring." She had agreed to hunt up a Paris apartment for him while awaiting his arrival, probably in June. Now, as one letter to her followed another between February and July, it was clear that this was a critical moment in his life. West's emotional responsiveness to a love affair came sharply into conflict with his hopes for writing, his fear of poverty, and his hesitancy about his future—in short, with his shifting idea of his role as an artist.

His affections, from the first, were connected and compounded with his writing. He was trying both to place *Balso* and to write enough of *Miss Lonelyhearts* to get an advance on which to finish his book in Paris. "I have started in working very hard at the opus," he announces in his first letter, written while she was still at sea, "and should make good progress . . . but anyway in June." He was promising to join her in June, but his foreseeably slow work on *Miss Lonelyhearts*—he would not finish it for nearly three years

—and his commitment to it were potentially in conflict with his promise, for he knew already that he might break it.

In another letter, he reports that he is still hard at work: "Nothing happens, every day is just like every other day, nothing happens. I go to the concert once a week and work at my opus on all other nights except Saturday nights." Somewhat later in March, he adds, almost hopelessly: "I am working hard. And . . . well, and," and shows that he is now thinking of Paris—perhaps in fantasy terms—as providing him a means of getting something accomplished on his novel. "Please look around for a place for me to starve in cheaply," he asks in jest, but also ominously, since West could never but in jest believe in an art that lived in poverty. At the end of March, he expresses his forlorn hope both for the novel and for his chances of making money: "I am working pretty hard at the opus. . . . Maybe I'll be able to sell it." To some extent, of course, such remarks are ways by which he was trying both to defend and to define himself. They could range all the way from serious introspection to such mock-heroic Prufrockian observations as: "Maybe I'll eat an omelette for lunch, tomorrow I may go for a walk, Saturday night to the movies, Sunday night perhaps I'll inscribe some pleasing sentiments in a lady's album. I read a book the other night." But in all, having reached a crisis of self, West was trying to resolve the conflicting demands of his own identity as an artist with those of society and marriage.

Most of all, he was trying to convince himself that he *could* be a writer. *Balso Snell* had been rejected by one publisher in the middle of March, and he had lost faith in the book. Still, he reiterated, he was "working hard. In the next few weeks I shall be ready for Simon and Schuster and the others." He comically instructed B. —as she signed her *New Yorker* letters—to go to church regularly and pray for his book. By the middle of April he had finished the first four chapters of *Miss Lonelyhearts*, but his enthusiasm was somewhat dampened by Perelman's reaction to them. "Too psychological, not concrete enough," Perelman had complained. Finally, on April 26, he brought 15,000 words of *Miss Lonelyhearts* to Simon and Schuster, where Clifton Fadiman agreed to read them. To B. he was still insisting, but now without enthusiasm, that he expected to "leave New York some time in June." He had only to wait for his "employers"—he never admitted that this meant his family—to pay him "about two hundred dollars' worth of vacation money."

By the middle of May he heard from Fadiman. "They weren't too discouraging . . . I guess," he wrote—but he was not offered a contract, much less the advance for which he had apparently hoped. Was this kind of anxiety included in the life of the artist? "I hope the places you have in mind for me are good and cheap," he wrote at the end of the month. "Oh dear! I am already sick of the cheap business. It's going to be devilish hard to be a cheapie." "But," he reassured himself weakly, with the self-mocking cliché, "an artist must suffer."

June was nearly here, but he had made no arrangements for sailing. Still, on May 26 he reapplied for a passport to reside in France for less than one year. Again, curiously, he gave his purpose as "student," but now listed his occupation as "writer." One other alteration in his application is significant. Whereas in 1926 he had given his father's birthplace as "Danenberg, Germany," he now—with the new intellectual respect for Russia he had absorbed in the Brounoff circle—gave it as "Denennenbourg, Russia." Both times, of course, he was far from accurately naming his father's birthplace—and both mistakes reveal how little he knew about his background and how much of it he had been obliged to create imaginatively. Now promising that he would sail no later than the fifteenth, he announced proudly to B.: "I'm beginning to think in, well, French again."

Still he did not sail—"the people" at the hotel hadn't found a substitute for him, he needed the vacation money and "so must await their pleasure," he could not get a ticket. He wired that he would leave no later than the eighteenth, then that he was trying to buy a ticket on the *Bremen* or the *Leviathan*, sailing on the twenty-eighth, or "if worse comes to worse, I'll go steerage on the *Mauretania*," though he was not sure he could get a ticket. He did book passage, only to cancel it at the last minute. Then all his hesitations and fears—the conflict, in essence, between his several views of the life and commitment of the artist—spilled out in a roar of self-accusation and self-defense: "Times are indeed hard. And on us, they are very hard. Ever since I cancelled my ticket, I have been in the dumps—but I guess I'm yellow. I was afraid to go out and do . . . to try and earn a living writing, hacking, I'd rather work in

a hotel, and I'm not at all sure that I could hack out enough. . . .
I feel like, I guess I am, a phoney. . . . I am afraid that I would
have spent my few hundred dollars without getting anything
done."

At the heart of West's fascination with the biographies of writers and artists and with the artistic and intellectual groups he was
seeing were his speculations about what being an artist would
mean for him, and what kind of artist he should mean to be. This
is, of course, the central issue throughout his letters to Beatrice
Mathieu. He had finished *Balso Snell*, but had lost interest in it; he
was writing *Miss Lonelyhearts*, but was discouraged by Fadiman's
indifference. He was in love, and yet he hesitated to marry or even
to go to Paris. He loathed his work at the hotel, yet was loath to
give up the meager security it provided. What should he do? What
were his prospects?—indeed, what were his talents? What would
be his fate? The letters he was writing all during the winter and
spring of 1930 were letters to himself, and these were the questions
he was really asking.

7 / "Abandon Everything!"

> Abandon everything. Abandon Dada. Get rid of your wife.
> Give up your mistress. Give up your hopes and your fears.
> . . . Give up the substance for the shadow. Give up your
> easy way of life, and that which passes for a job with a
> future. Take to the roads. . . .
>
> —André Breton, *Lâchez tout!* (1924)

Between 1927 and the fall of 1930, when West was variously confronting his own artistic identity through association with Village and other intellectual groups, through his reading, and, perhaps most of all, by assessing and deciding on his future, he continued as assistant manager of the Kenmore Hall Hotel at 145 East 23 Street. West's Aunt Susan had married a well-known physician, whose brother, Morris Jarcho, was a plumbing sub-contractor, and it was through him that West was given this job when it appeared otherwise impossible for him to get one. In the collapse of the building trades, when a general contractor (like West's father) could no longer hold his assets, his sub-contractors for plumbing, bricklaying, and the other individual crafts frequently attached the completed building and together formed a corporation to administer it. This was true of both the Kenmore and the Sutton, a hotel where West was eventually to become manager. Ironically, the same economic circumstances which ruined his father also led to the jobs which were to have other effects on West's life.

The Kenmore Hall was uniquely suited among hotels built in the late twenties to be successful during the Depression. Badly designed, with small rooms, no restaurant, and neither conference rooms nor a mezzanine, it was saved by its faults; in some ways, it had been planned as a kind of glorified rooming house, its small rooms renting at low rates, its lobby and drugstore, where all the guests necessarily congregated, becoming popular as unostentatious meeting places for young men and women.

Although most of the family recognized that hotel work was far from West's main interest, they were content to help him along. Moreover, he had the instincts of a good businessman: he was disciplined and well organized, with a love for moneyed life. His duties as night manager were not arduous—nor (for his tastes) was his salary of $35 a week a large one, even with extra benefits like his room, and meals at the drugstore. West did not hesitate to tell his friends that he "loathed" hotel work, although he sometimes concealed the fact that his family were partly running the hotel. But in obvious ways, the job was to be interesting: it gave him a certain position, and he could invite Sid Perelman, Max Bodenheim, Mike Gold, or Quent Reynolds up for lunch and a swim. It became known that Brown boys in town could stay free in rooms where the linen hadn't yet been changed. Perhaps, as night manager, he could humorously think of himself as another Stanley Sackett, night manager for the Madison Hotel, who wore only evening clothes and became a favorite of sophisticates and a model for a series of cartoons by Peter Arno. Certainly West too looked, as Arthur Kober remarks, "like someone out of Wall Street," "very formal indeed."

But most of all, the job at the Kenmore provided for West precisely what he had not had in New York before: a certain removal from his family and yet a fixed place—in short, the conditions for meditation. Infrequently in his room, more often sitting in the glassed-in hotel office—insulated from the people in the lobby, but still in visual contact with them—he was able to work on *The Dream Life of Balso Snell*. In the hotel, he developed his natural attitude of preoccupation into genuine meditation and night after night between 1927 and the last part of 1929 wrote and rewrote his book, first in pencil on yellow ruled paper, and eventually on typed sheets, correcting and retyping repeatedly. As late as 1930 he was calling it *The Journal of Balso Snell*. In some ways it was a journal of his own daily response to certain problems of attitude and definition, in art and life, then engaging him intensely. Only in minor details could *Balso Snell* be called directly autobiographical; but it is a book which does set down, boldly and directly, the character of West's imaginative life during the late twenties.

He made several attempts to have it published. At this time, of course, any avant-garde writer had real difficulty finding a publisher. Older, established firms—Houghton Mifflin or Harper, for instance—still retained certain commitments to the genteel past of New England respectability. Only a few commercial houses— notably B. W. Huebsch, Liveright, and Knopf—genuinely encouraged experimental writing, and even these leaned toward the writer who, if experimental, still had a certain position by virtue of earlier publications or frequent appearances in little magazines. A small press with a select audience was, therefore, West's only hope for publication. In one of the policy statements for Contact Editions, Robert McAlmon had summed up the credo of the small publisher: "Contact Editions are not concerned with what the 'public' wants. . . . There are commercial publishers who know the public and its tastes. If books seem to us to have something of individuality, intelligence, talent, and live sense of literature, and quality which has the odour and timbre of authenticity, we publish them. We admit that eccentricities exist." West therefore attempted to place his book with McAlmon's press. West, McAlmon wrote, "gave me a Ms. which was too Anatole France for me," and he refused it. Later, West appears to have hoped that David Moss, then manager of the Gotham Book Mart, the leading New York bookstore distributing avant-garde literature, would issue his book under the Gotham imprint, as Brentano's had done with many books earlier. In 1930, another small press, Brewer, Warren & Putnam, refused the completed manuscript, considering some sections obscene and blasphemous. That same year in a fascinating series of moves, David Moss and Martin Kamin founded a bookstore in the Barbizon-Plaza Hotel and proposed to McAlmon that "they would take on the publishing of books under the name of Contact Editions." They had collected a number of Contact Editions—books which McAlmon had difficulty getting into the United States and which he could find no way of distributing when he succeeded —and it seemed as if they might give him both an editorial and a distribution center. They suggested, in addition, that *Contact*, the magazine which McAlmon and William Carlos Williams had edited, be revived. Williams, practicing medicine in New Jersey and frequently visiting New York, was willing to become editor. McAlmon, though tempted, eventually allowing himself to be listed as associate editor of the magazine, and even taking part in one of its editorial conferences, nonetheless refused to continue editing either Contact Editions or *Contact*, and let both imprints pass into the hands of Moss and Kamin.

In the meantime, West had followed Moss to his new bookstore and was purchasing fiction and art books there. There, too, he met slightly older writers like Williams, Nancy Cunard, and McAlmon, showing, Kamin recalls, both personal intensity, even a certain brashness, and a winning commitment to their common interest in artistic experiment. Early in the fall of 1930, West mentioned to Kamin that he had finished a manuscript, and Kamin, thinking of continuing the Contact series, offered to consider it. He asked William Carlos Williams to give an editorial opinion and soon he reported to Kamin that he was impressed. Perhaps this was predictable, since West, as Josephine Herbst has observed, "had something of . . . Williams' approach to language . . . that it be living and fresh." Williams, the first critic to give West the acceptance for which he yearned, never after wavered in his enthusiasm for West's work.

In consequence of Williams's report, *The Dream Life of Balso Snell* was accepted as the first Contact Edition to be published by Moss and Kamin. As it happened, it would also be the last. West's book would stand in 1931 as the conclusion of a list that epitomized—in Gertrude Stein, Hemingway, and Robert M. Coates's *Eater of Darkness*—the best experiment of the twenties. This was historically fitting, since West would carry out in the thirties the intentions and literary hopes of the twenties.

West reached an agreement with Moss and Kamin, not to subsidize the publication, but to guarantee the sale of 150 of the 500 copies printed. (As late as 1937 he still had a few copies remaining.) Dashiell Hammett read and criticized his final manuscript, and John Sanford helped him to correct proofs in an apartment on Bank Street which West rented for this purpose. At last, in the spring of 1931, handsomely bound in de luxe paper covers, 500 numbered copies ("300 for sale in America and 200 . . . for Great Britain and the Continent") of this octavo edition of *The Dream Life of Balso Snell* were offered to the public at $3 a copy.

When West had first submitted his manuscript to Kamin, he had as his epigraph a quotation from Kurt Schwitters that sums up his attitude toward the book: "Everything that the artist expectorates is art." However ugly the material, however mundane the substance—as in Duchamp's signing of a urinal—however offensive to ordinary or cultivated tastes, whatever the true artist produces constitutes art. This is the only way in the modern world, West was saying, that the integrity of art could be guaranteed. His art is his style, his way of behaving and taking and shaping reality, his way of telling truth. Like Schwitters's *Merzkunst* collage, West's book would be an act of defiance, not a gesture of despair. If he made a fictional collage out of scraps and fragments—the garbage of modern civilization—it was to deny that civilization ultimate power, since the artist, in his own power, could still make use of even the worst aspects of his culture. Like the "garbage monument" of a colleague of Schwitters's, Johannes Baader, West's book would be implicitly dedicated to the "Greatness and Downfall" of his nation.

In his revisions he substituted for the Schwitters quotation a comic epigraph. His serious intentions, however, are expressed in an advertisement he wrote for the use of Moss and Kamin. Interesting because it states some attitudes only implied in the book, it is also a kind of manifesto. "English humor," it announces, "has always prided itself on being good-natured and in the best of taste. This fact makes it difficult to compare N. W. West with other comic writers, as he is vicious, mean, ugly, obscene and insane." However, the advertisement continues, West can be compared to French writers. "In his use of the violently disassociated, the dehumanized marvellous, the deliberately criminal and imbecilic, he is much like Guillaume Apollinaire, Jarry, Ribemont-Dessaignes, Raymond Roussel, and certain of the surréalistes." Balso Snell's journey, which may also, the ad explains, be compared to Lewis Carroll's famous work, consists of a series of "tales, [all of which] are elephantine close-ups of various literary positions and their technical method; close-ups that make Kurt Schwitters' definition, 'Tout ce que l'artiste crache, c'est l'art!' seem like an understatement."

This advertisement makes plain that in 1931 West viewed himself as an artist whose comic vision has its closest parallels in the French tradition and nicely suggests the sense of literary internationalism which he shared at this period with his peers. *Balso Snell* resembles the short, tight kind of novel which he professed to admire—imaginative, highly witty, and inventive. Many of its themes and methods have close affiliations to Continental preoccupations. Breton, Picasso, Klee, Joyce, and others, of course, had experimented with the dream life of man, the night life of the soul. Scorning ordinary social values and emphasizing man's interior life, the main tendency of experimental literature between 1924 and 1930 had been to turn values inside out—to declare the primacy of dreams over acts, of violence over order, of the sexual gospel of the Marquis de Sade over that of the churches; of arbitrary over calculated action; and of the criminal, insane man or clown over the bourgeois citizen. Reflecting these preoccupations, *La Révolution Surréaliste*, for instance, printed extracts from a collection of "beautiful crimes," as well as the depositions of crackpots and criminals, all collected in a mock-scientific way by a "Bureau Central de Recherches Surréalistes." Many of these same impulses West satirized in his Paris tale, "The Impostor."

"To be a writer, as such, was nothing, was passé," Matthew Josephson has summed up this impulse; "to be engaged in a variety of moral experiments was everything." In *The Dream Life of Balso Snell*, West conducts a moral experiment in the nature and principles of values by plunging into the underworld of the mind, where ordinary values are transformed, strangely twisted—in effect, transvalued—and alternative moralities are given painful birth. West, in America, had the same sense as his European contemporaries of this profound alteration of consciousness. He was hardly alone. The year 1931, when *Balso Snell* appeared, was the first year in American history when the number of people emigrating from the United States was larger than the number immigrating. In the same year, even so distinguished a spokesman of the establishment as Nicholas Murray Butler, president of Columbia University, described this time as one "like the fall of the Roman Empire, like the Renaissance, like the beginning of the political and social revolutions in England and in France in the seventeenth and eighteenth centuries." Now the American Dream seemed to be driving toward nightmare. West sends his "base" man, the material man, the man of smells, on a journey into this renaissance and revolution of the mind. He too emigrates, into a landscape of anguish and horror, by entering the bowels of the Trojan horse and there investigating the mental geography of the Western tradition.

The fiction of journey has built into it certain conventions or expectations, the chief of which, as in *Pilgrim's Progress* and *The Divine Comedy*, is that the journey may symbolize a moving upward, to illumination or purification; second, that it suggests a moving outward, a rebirth. In particular, the Trojan horse, whose body Balso enters, hints at epic triumphs, involvement with dangerous but successful adventuring. But in *Balso Snell*, movement is only vagrant wandering, as dream moves endlessly within dream, all equally grotesque. Instead of rebirth, the book ends merely in an unproductive orgasm, induced by the dream; what is revealed is not archetypal purity but the nightmarish corruption of the id, which West, like Freud, describes as a fetid swamp, "the swamps of my mind." The Trojan horse suggests not epic—West summarized his plans in 1924 as a "parody" of the Troy story—but deception, the deceitfulness of dreams, and thus of the life that these dreams symbolize. His favorite inscription for the book, calling attention to the universality but also to the individual applications of his satire, was: "From one horse's ass to another." All men are deceitful, base Trojan horses. If, in this context, "life," as the epigraph has it, "is a journey," then it is a journey through illusion, and the book which describes it constitutes, like France's *Penguin Island*, the anatomy of illusion, in which West uses as satiric material the ideals which his friends were sponsoring, and toward which he himself was to some extent inclined.

In this first novel West at once faced the problems which he was to take up in all his fiction: how to satirize illusions when they seem necessary in the modern world, when the future of an illusion seems only to be the proliferation of greater illusions; how to assign guilt in the post-Freudian age when even blame has been rendered difficult; and how to make these conditions tragic when both the need and the guilt for illusion lie in the very nature of man and his world. West understood only tentatively here, but with brilliant clarity in his later books, that he would need to invent new literary forms and attitudes whereby to express, for the modern sensibility, moral indignation without righteousness, and a tragic sense without a vision of redemption.

Balso Snell, the American Ulysses and successor to Cabell's Jurgen, is essentially a Babbitt of the imagination, "an ambassador from that ingenious people, the inventors and perfectors of the automatic water-closet," who gives aphoristic advice like: "Play games. Don't read so many books. Take cold showers. Eat more meat," and " . . . run about more. Read less and play baseball." Like any good American tourist, however strange the foreign customs in the bowels of the Trojan horse may be, he is not unduly impressed. He retains a calm demeanor in the face of chaos and, though declaring that "in his childhood things had been managed differently," he has ready both defenses of American life ("You call that dump grand and glorious, do you? Have you ever seen the Grand Central Station, or the Yale Bowl, or the Hollywood Tunnel, or the New Madison Square Garden?") and easy explanations for chaos ("the War, the invention of printing, nineteenth-century science, communism, the wearing of soft hats, the use of contraceptives, the large number of delicatessen stores . . ."). He is a direct descendant of Mark Twain's Innocents, and of other indigenous comic characters discussed by Constance Rourke in her *American Humor*, published the same year as *Balso*.

He comes not to Europe, of course, but to the dream world, in naïve search for principles of identity. One after another Balso encounters, and finds absurd, the major historic forms by which identity has been defined in Western civilization. A series of antagonists define themselves in terms of its major religions; in succession, here where the dream reveals the grotesque essence, Balso sees the absurdity of all—Greek, Jewish, Christian, and such modern religions as those of "Mother Eddy and Doctor Coué." All religions, he concludes, are but the human cry of the flesh against its own extinction: "I won't die! I am getting better and better. . . . The will is master o'er the flesh."

The religion of art, an alternate to these, he recognizes as similarly inadequate, a way of gaining fame, pleasure, admiration, or sexual success. John Raskolnikov Gilson, one of the fictive authors in the novel, writes a *Crime Journal* in which he describes a library as merely a vast charnel house of stinking corpses on which generation after generation feeds like parasites, and then themselves add to the steaming pile. Relying upon Otto Rank and Freud, West, in the consciousness of Balso, reduces art to its biological basis ("I need women and because I can't buy or force them, I have to make poems for them"). "Art," he concludes, "is a sublime excrement." The central theme of *Balso Snell* is that in contemporary life art has become merely a way by which each man seeks to define his individual ego; his sense of the crisis in his identity has become both his religion and his art. One by one, West will satirize, in "elephantine close-ups," various literary positions. James Joyce had concluded his *Portrait of the Artist as a Young Man* by sending out his hero, an early Ulysses, to encounter his self in experience, and he had had him cry in conclusion: "Old father, old artificer, stand me now and ever in good stead." West's hero, mocking Joyce's epic quest, begins his odyssey with the ejaculation: "O Beer! O Meyerbeer! O Bach! O Offenbach! Stand me now as ever in good stead." On his journey he rejects—since he acts out their absurdity—the kinds of archetypal figures whereby West's artistic contemporaries were conducting the search for self: the criminal figure who discovers his self through his crimes (Dostoevsky's Raskolnikov, the Marquis de Sade); the insane hero, whose insanity is a way of reaching to the truths of self; the clown, the truth of whose self is in his absurdity (Rilke's *Duino Elegies,* Picasso); and the hero whose vision of self is of a streaming sequence of selves—what Ezra Pound called "a broken bundle of mirrors"—and whose identity is defined by the roles he can choose to play, the masks he can assume (Yeats, Conrad Aiken's *Blue Voyage*). Scrutinizing each, he finds all equally absurd. One of the titles by which Balso Snell names the character of his journey, "Anywhere Out of this World," is also the title of a poem by Baudelaire. Just as in that poem, all the attempts at self-definition are rejected; Balso too wants desperately to fly out of this world. He will do so—ending his dreams in an orgasm, as if his dreams and the identity he can find through them are worth no more than that. In this sense, West accurately told an interviewer that *Balso* was written "as a protest against writing books."

But he also told his cousin that *Balso Snell* was "a very professional book, a play on styles." In its stylistic exuberance lies the positive center of the book. West may have abandoned everything in the book by satirizing everything and even giving up the ordinary goal of fiction—representation of society, scene, and character—but his style remains brilliant and accomplished, the successful end of a literary journey. Regarded thus, the book is a boldly rhetorical work in which the author, along with his hero, explores the rhetoric or style of his contemporaries. Balso's journey is of the innocent abroad, but West's is the wise artist's journey in search of a style. The styles which he encounters—a kind of coming to grips with language "with the bare hands," as Williams would say of *Paterson*—are in search of authors. The wooden horse, Balso recognizes, "was inhabited solely by writers in search of an audience."

Balso Snell is, then, a language experiment in which West tests out various styles. In its claim for style as the medium of artistic truth—its separation of satire from moral intent—*The Dream Life of Balso Snell* reflects the literary faiths of the twenties in individual expression, in wit, and in defiance of convention. West at this stage was more eloquent in his revisions of his contemporaries than in his own visions but he was brilliant in his criticisms. Easily recognizable are his parodies of Rimbaud and Baudelaire (West plays on their theory of "correspondence"); J. K. Huysmans's *Là Bas* and *En Route*; Joyce and Proust (from whom the epigraph comes); any number of "objectivist" writers, including Williams and Pound; the Dada mode of surrendering language to chains of associations in the subconscious mind, and the attempt to write prose from a poetic point of view, from Robert Desnos to Robert M. Coates; the fantastic comedy of S. J. Perelman's *Parlor, Bedlam and Bath* (originally called *Through the Fallopian Tubes on a Bicycle*); the style of the "tough" school of detective-fiction writers such as Dashiell Hammett; of realistic proletarian fiction like that of Gorky and his American followers in "socialist realism," who all, as was said of Gorky, "look at life from a basement . . . from which he sees only feet of men passing by rubbish pails that stand near his windows"; of *True Story*; of James Branch Cabell (from whom the original plot idea derived); of Rabelais and Voltaire; of dirty jokes (some of which West had told his friends earlier); and of Aldous Huxley and D. H. Lawrence. All are brilliantly etched, as West wrote on a sketch he drew of Beatrice Mathieu in 1930, "by the savage pencil of the master."

He is the master, and his book a masterful play on styles, by virtue of his ability to understand and thus to parody them all. Refusing to make an epic, a "Great American Novel," he made a lyric novel out of his violent American response to European materials. "Lyric novels," he wrote in 1933, "can be written according to

Poe's definition of a lyric poem. The short novel is a distinct form especially fitted for use in this country." West, Kamin said, could have a "brashness arising out of his idealism" about art, and "he wanted to do something terribly distinguished." His book reflects, obviously, intellectual arrogance; but, in his exploration of the styles of his contemporaries, he proves himself a distinguished stylist. For all of West's apparent disillusionment in the book, he, no less, romantically celebrates style. Gilbert Seldes complained in 1926 that American writing was lacking in satire and rebelliousness. West would uniquely fill this need. His satire and savagery, in *Balso Snell*, constituted positive claims for his ability to understand the absurdity of modern poses—role playing in artistic, mythical, or religious terms—and his stylistic dexterity was a declaration that he could see through his contemporaries' art.

In later novels West would make more refined use of his stylistic brilliance. *Balso Snell* shows his virtuosity; in *Miss Lonelyhearts* and *The Day of the Locust*, style is made to illuminate character. But this first novel is crucial to an understanding of West's development because in it he foreshadows in a rough way the attitudes and preoccupations of his later books. The phantom characters who people Balso's dreams—the sainted holy fool, the materialist, the cynic, the scapegoat, the cripple, the grotesque, the sterile modern woman, and the pervert—reappear transmuted. The Quester, Balso himself, will later become Miss Lonelyhearts, Lemuel Pitkin, and Tod Hackett. All are caught in their own or others' illusions. The paradoxical themes of the duality of body and soul, good and evil, of unfulfilling reality leading to unsatisfactory wishes, of violence and the futility of action, all first occur in *Balso*. The myths of success, redemption, innocence, and idealism West will examine again and again. In this first book West's hero enters the Trojan horse of illusion. In his last novel Tod Hackett finds among the "dream-dump" of old Hollywood sets "the wooden horse of Troy." Like Tod, West was to follow the path of Balso all along, through a world littered with the sad rubble of hopes and dreams.

II

The writings of Freud had a profound effect on Americans in the late twenties and early thirties. Not only did he make clear how complex the human entity is and the importance of dreams, and thus provide a justification for literary dream-adventures like Balso Snell's; he also provided for Americans a way of discussing (and, to a limited extent, understanding) the profound displacement of sexual life that seemed to have occurred at the same time as the equally profound dislocations in economics and democracy, and appeared to be intertwined with them. One of the most striking of social and literary phenomena during the twenties and thirties was the open obsession with sexuality—of which James Branch Cabell's exotic and Henry Miller's elemental novels, Eugene O'Neill's Freudian dramas, the omnipresent confession magazines, and movies were symptoms on various levels of sensibility and consciousness. Perhaps by spreading a popularized Freudian gospel to the effect that personal maladjustments are due to the suppression of sexual desire, some were also causes of the increasing preoccupation with sex—although social moralists were more readily pointing to other factors, like the automobile (a kind of portable sitting room), the increased drinking among women and young people that accompanied Prohibition, and modern dances like the fox trot and the grapevine.

Sex, in any event, left its collective and individual traces everywhere. Restrained by social conventions on the one hand, but incited to sexual fantasy on the other, Americans were caught in a dilemma which they found no way to resolve. By ending his novel with an orgasm, West both mocks the genteel tradition of a happy ending and points to the particular kind of happiness which his contemporaries were seeking. Balso Snell is his first voyeuristic hero. All his impulses to act are turned inward. He is a "lonely spy," compelled to take his satisfactions from his sights; his climaxes come only as consequences of his observations.

Although West had had no really steady girl during college—at least partly because regular social events took place in fraternity houses—he had dated frequently. S. J. Perelman recalls that "his taste in women, with whom he tended to be shy, was catholic enough, but he preferred those tall, rangy girls who had attended certain finishing schools and universities—the type that our generation called 'snakes.' " While strenuously suppressing any expression of romantic ideals, he was personally inclined to idealize certain women. He spoke particularly of his sisters, especially Laura, and of his mother, as feminine ideals. To the end of his life, Laura Perelman remained his standard for all women. Theirs was a truly close, sympathetic, and companionable relationship, emotionally, temperamentally, and intellectually. With most other women, West was reserved.

Generally speaking, he retained a personal reticence about sex. "Without being a Puritan," James T. Farrell has said, "there were things that he didn't like about the [openly casual] sexual behavior of some of the people he knew." Attractive to women, he was very discreet in intimate sexual relations. A woman with whom he had a brief, intense love affair declared that he "behaved very nobly" in his relations with all women.

West was chivalric, but certainly not innocent about sex. Indeed, he had apparently matured early in both sexual attitudes and knowledge. He "had already appraised" sex by the time he arrived at Brown, Brae Rafferty says. He arrived on campus with gonorrhea and suffered very intensely through the curative treatments in Providence. Nonetheless, he contracted the same disease at a college party in New York City during 1923. Sometime during these treatments, apparently, his prostate gland was slightly damaged and would cause him recurring pain for the rest of his life. In some part, then, he was led, early, to associate sexuality with pain and disease. Everywhere in his books, of course, the identification of sexuality with pain and disease is apparent. Miss McGeeney and Janey Davenport (*Balso Snell*), Mary Shrike, Fay Doyle, and Miss Farkis (*Miss Lonelyhearts*), Betty Prail and Cobina Wiggs (*A Cool Million*), Faye Greener and the scabby black hen (*The Day of the Locust*) are all related, all sterile but threatening female figures. Ironically, the nearest anyone comes to being a really complete and attractive woman in any of West's novels is the female impersonator in *The Day of the Locust*. The orgiastic conclusions to three of his novels, too, are not merely violent but also nightmarishly sexual.

Moreover, that West was by no means free of guilt feelings over sex is suggested by frequent retellings of one basic story in which he was guilty of a sexual betrayal. In *Paterson*, William Carlos Williams reports his version of a tale which West had told him:

which reminds me of
an old friend, now gone

—while he was still
in the hotel business, a tall and rather beautiful young woman came
to his desk one day to ask if there were any interesting books to be had
on the premises. He, being interested in literature, as she knew, replied
that his own apartment was full of them and that, though he couldn't
leave at the moment—Here's my key, go up and help yourself.
She thanked him and
went off. He forgot all about her.
After lunch he too
went to his rooms not remembering until he was at the door that he
had no key. But the door was unlatched and as he entered, a girl was
lying naked on the bed. It startled him a little. So much so that all he
could do was to remove his own clothes and lie beside her. Quite comfortable, he soon fell into a heavy sleep. She also must have slept.
They wakened later,
simultaneously, much refreshed.

Paterson, IV, 3

Altered, and attributed to Homer Simpson, this story appeared
first in *The Day of the Locust,* where it is closer to the truth: a
young hotel resident who couldn't pay her rent offered herself to
West. Afterward he often damned himself—perhaps a sign of both
his sensitivity and his naïveté—for having taken advantage of her.
Guilt feelings and associations with pain and disease—these mixed
powerfully in West with a personal restraint and romantic yearning—and gave a highly ambiguous and unresolved character to his
sexual identity.

Beatrice Mathieu, whom he had met in the fall of 1929, was apparently the first woman West had wished to marry, though clearly
he was personally divided between a desire to marry and fears
over the consequences of marriage, including doubts about his ability to continue as a writer. Of course, the ideals of the free life in
the late twenties and thirties generally minimized marriage. In the
intellectual circle about Brounoff's house, the feeling predomi-
nated that sexuality of any kind was frivolously opposed to con-
templation of serious issues, the true life of the mind. Moreover,
West's mother was opposed to his marrying Miss Mathieu, a gen-

tile. And though he joked with Miss Mathieu about this, it was undoubtedly one more cause of his failure to join her in Paris.

But by the time *The Dream Life of Balso Snell* appeared, West was truly in love and hoping to be married. The novel is dedicated to "A. S.," Alice Shepard, whom West had met in New York in the fall of 1930. They were introduced by his sister Laura when he ran into the two women shopping together on 57 Street. Like Beatrice Mathieu, Alice too was a friend of West's sister—Laura and Alice had met at Pembroke. A tall, attractive woman—"a *real* beauty," Edmund Wilson says—Alice had been in Paris when the Depression broke and had recently returned to New York, where she was working as the chief fashion model for Elizabeth Hawes. At this time managing the Sutton Hotel, West inevitably found time to drop around to teas and showings at Elizabeth Hawes's nearby showroom, where he was intrigued by (though also ironical about) the display of elegance and wealth. Anatomist of the psyche, West also had a keen eye for exteriors and was fascinated by fashions: he was attracted by style, an elegant finish of any kind.

West and Miss Shepard were soon dating regularly. Often in company with the Perelmans, they went to Thursday night concerts, to the theater, and to nightclubs, like the Ambassadeurs, where Clayton, Jackson, and Durante regularly held forth. Alice, who was genuinely sweet and friendly, and whose appearance and Congregational New England ancestry were both distinguished, clearly suited West's romantic ideal.

The dedication of *Balso* was also part of his image of the romantic author. He presented Alice with the first numbered copy, jokingly inscribed, on an evening when he took her to a D'Oyly Carte production of *The Mikado*. He was casual and witty and pretended not to take his book seriously.

By the following year, however, he was taking Alice very seriously and was carrying a blank application for a wedding license in his wallet as a kind of hostage to a future. There was no official engagement, only an understanding that they would marry as soon as his or the general economic situation improved. Were not all experts predicting a speedy end to the Depression? Were there not, as they all repeatedly said, "distinctly encouraging features"?

His hopes of marriage proved as vain as the predictions of economic recovery. In the winter of 1932–3, the informal engagement was broken and the relationship ended. West was deeply affected by this split, and at least once he nearly broke down in conversation about it with one of his friends. It was clear that he had been truly in love and that the separation had a great emotional impact upon him. Yet he never spoke about its cause to his friends. Those in the Brounoff group assumed from his reticence that the cause was West's religion and race, about which several were themselves sensitive. There was no basis to this belief. To more than one person West hinted at what was perhaps near the ultimate truth—that, as earlier with Miss Mathieu, he had no real hope of ever having enough money to marry; he foresaw only "a hopeless, blank future" in which he would have only his art, if that much.

He came closer to the cause when he told a California acquaintance that at a party he had compulsively taken another girl out on a balcony and kissed her, knowing that this would be seen by Alice and that it would occasion a complete break. In this evasive tale he at least suggested that continuing fears about marriage led him to find some way of dissolving its prospects. The truth is that after a party he drove Alice and another young woman uptown, dropped Alice off at Grand Central Station, where she entrained for New Rochelle, and then allowed himself to be seduced by the other woman, spending the night with her. It was a casual affair, not even compelled by passion. (In bewildered exasperation at his own stupidity, all he could say later was that she had simply been the first woman who had *asked* him to sleep with her.) By the time Alice arrived home, she had become vaguely uneasy and called West. He was not in his room. She called through the night. Then, in the morning, he finally answered. The inevitable conversation followed and West confessed that he had slept with the other woman. Alice agreed to come into the city at once to talk it over. After an emotional meeting at Longchamps, she broke off with him, deeply hurt, convinced that she was not strong enough to forgive his betrayal.

It was, for West, the great disgrace of his life. How far he may have unconsciously provoked the breakup due to a fear that he could not devote himself both to marriage and to fiction, to what extent he feared for himself his father's fate as a mere family man —this, of course, remains unclear. Perhaps, even with Miss Shepard, West had not allowed himself to become seriously involved and had at last (however unconsciously) forced a separation rather than face real involvement. It is certainly true that for several years he would be uncertain in his relations with women and wary of any genuine attachments. He became more restrained and shy with women than he had ever been before and treated lightly and jokingly several women in Hollywood who were attracted to him.

In the mid-thirties West summarized his fears by telling a friend, Sy Bartlett, that he was afraid of the pain which marriage would involve. Few marriages, he said, were happy; "and even if you found that two people had been very compatible and had had the unique luck of having had a happy marriage, in the end one had to die—and *that* would be so terrible for the survivor that perhaps his unhappiness and loneliness would negate all their happiness," he concluded hopelessly. In consequence of his fears and perhaps his self-doubt after his failure with Alice, he developed a scoffing attitude with all women but intellectuals, such as Lillian Hellman, Dorothy Parker, and Josephine Herbst, whose relationship with him centered on a shared commitment to literature. Yet, even the intellect gave him no final protection from his emotions, and his attitude, Miss Herbst has said, "was always ambiguous."

To cover over the painful guilt of his betrayal of Alice, West gave friends various versions of the reasons behind their separation. These, all extremely revealing fantasies, range from his hints that they parted because of his hopeless poverty, to the tale—reported by Josephine Herbst in her novella, *A Hunter of Doves*—that he saw at once that Alice was potentially unfaithful to him; many of his retellings include the sub-plot that he had tried to commit suicide by driving a borrowed car into an elevated pillar and that he in fact almost died from his injuries.

According to Miss Herbst's novella, West appeared at her house in Erwinna on the morning following the party and told "his story, in hints, in fits and starts, trying to find a line to walk amidst the contradictions." Since he saw Alice Shepard on the morning after the party, unsuccessfully attempting to resolve things over coffee, he did not arrive in Erwinna until the next morning. He had had a whole day to spin out the first fantasy over his personal failure.

The truth is that he made several attempts to patch the relationship, but all failed. This, too, would be part of the making of his fiction. He would translate his pain and guilt into compassion and sympathy in his art. Yet he continued to carry the New York State application for a wedding license. He still had it with him, a kind of talisman, early in 1939. But by the time he would really need it, he would be living in another state and his whole life would be changed.

8 / "A Trail through the American Jungle"

"*Contact* will attempt to cut a trail through the American jungle without the use of a European compass."

—Motto of *Contact* (1932)

Miss Lonelyhearts went slowly, although the title and conception came almost at once after the night West read the letters on which the book is based. The book weighed heavily upon West. Deeply affected by the letters, he was driven to art not for self-esteem, but from compassion. That night he had discovered what being an artist could mean for him, and so now faced the difficulties, where before he had written for the satisfactions, of art. Through the fall and winter of 1930–1, feeling (as he put it) like a "louse on myself," he continued to work on the novel. He had given up, for the sake of his book, all hope of going to Paris; yet he feared that he would never be able to complete it. The acceptance of *Balso Snell* by Contact Editions during that winter revived his hopes, and he began to devise a plan to take a long vacation away from the hotel in an effort to bring his novel to a conclusion.

Shortly after his boyhood friend Julian Shapiro returned from Paris in May 1931—he was also working on a novel—West proposed that they find a cabin somewhere in the Adirondacks and spend the summer writing. During the early thirties, with Allen Tate and Caroline Gordon farming in Tennessee and later living in upstate New York with Hart Crane, with Sinclair Lewis going to Minnesota to write, Josephine Herbst and John Herrmann settled in Erwinna, William Carlos Williams in New Jersey, and Robert Coates, Malcolm Cowley, and the Josephsons living or soon to live near Sherman, Connecticut, the New York City which they were fleeing seemed to be the sole place in the country where no one was writing serious fiction. Of course this was not true; nor was there a revulsion among writers against the city or a romantic yearning to "return to the soil." "We weren't in love with the soil, per se," Josephine Herbst remarks. "We loved the outdoors but we liked the city also. But to stay in the city meant harnessing yourself to a regular job so you could pay rent." The country alone seemed to provide some time for leisure and respite from the daily evidences of economic chaos only too apparent in the metropolis. Most writers who went to the country, then, did so both to escape economics and because of economics.

But West's plan for spending a summer in the Adirondacks suggests that in some part he was unconsciously yearning for reimmersion in the less difficult world of his childhood. Indeed, the place on which he and Shapiro settled was only a short distance from Camp Paradox, where West had first learned the power and the personal satisfactions of art. Now, in 1931, he returned to this region to complete, he hoped, the work of fiction which would bring that discovery to its first really acceptable culmination.

Before the middle of July he and Shapiro gathered the paraphernalia of frontiering, as they saw it—a .22 rifle and thousands of rounds of ammunition; targets, rods and reels; and cookbooks by two pioneer Indian trappers named Nessmuk and Kepog. Finally, they went shopping for an automobile in a used-car lot on 125 Street and Broadway, and for $195 picked up a serviceable Ford that already had license plates and a registration and had obviously been stolen. Toward the end of July they pointed this automobile, fully packed, north along the Hudson River, though still without destination, toward the Adirondack Mountains in upper New York State.

Eventually, with the aid of a state game warden whom Shapiro had previously met, they located, and for $25 a month rented, a cabin near Warrensburg, New York, on Viele Pond. Surrounded by 1,200 acres of forest and approachable only by dirt roads, this fully equipped, seven-room house near the fifty-acre pond seemed to be just what they were looking for.

From the beginning, it was clear that the trip as much satisfied West's need to escape temporarily the pressures of the hotel and his family as it promised to give him time for uninterrupted work on *Miss Lonelyhearts*. For at Viele Pond the interruptions which West and Shapiro made in their writing were so frequent that at last these threatened to consume altogether the time initially proposed for work. At first they stuck to a schedule by which they arose at 8 a.m., made breakfast and cleaned up, then fished or shot targets until about 10:00; from then until about 1:00, they wrote. Afterwards, they ate lunch, and then returned to work from 3:00 to 7:00. But the periods of work steadily shrank as outdoor activities expanded. All his life West tended to awaken slowly in the morning, as if drugged by sleep—a characteristic he would attribute to Homer Simpson in *The Day of the Locust*. He seldom began to work before ten in the morning and finished by noon. Perhaps what he wanted most was absolute freedom from a schedule.

Soon he and Scotty, as West called Shapiro, were spending their afternoons swimming from a raft they constructed from oil drums; exploring the territory with the aid of a U.S. geological survey map (once losing their way); fishing for trout, bass, and bullheads in Viele Pond or on the Schroon River from a flat-bottom rowboat they bought; and, after West took pains to make friends with the local game wardens, shooting (quite illegally) partridge, deer, and squirrels. They prepared their fish or game à la Nessmuk and Kepog and ate it along with canned beans and brown bread. After dinner, with much amusement, they read aloud the advertisements out of the issues of *The Smart Set* and other magazines dating back to 1909, which they found in the cabin.

Romanticizing his reading and his earlier summer vacations at camp and on the farm at Colchester, West talked knowledgeably of wood lore and the fine points of fly fishing (though, characteristically, he showed less skill in execution). He spoke about having eaten all kinds of wild game. But his enthusiasm was always betraying his inexperience. Once, when he brought down a sharp-shinned hawk with a borrowed shotgun, he was so delighted that he insisted on driving at once to the nearest taxidermist to have the bird stuffed and mounted. By the time they arrived, traveling more than twenty-five miles over bad roads, it was so late they had to rouse the man out of bed. But West had a trophy. He talked about hunting far better than he knew how to hunt. All this he would summarize in a self-mocking story about a bear hunt in the Adirondacks which he told to Edmund Wilson. "The whole note of the bear story," Wilson recalls, "was one of pity for the bear and disgust for himself." Wilson felt that this story was "absolutely typical" of West's imagination. The factual basis of the story was even more ridiculous. One night, thinking he heard a bear prowling about the house, West (clad in his Brooks red-flannel nightshirt) dashed out with a shotgun and pulverized a stray cat. Still, West could turn these self-parodies into the sad horror of the quail-trapping scene in *The Day of the Locust*. Little of his casual experience was lost for the serious uses of his fiction.

Even at Viele Pond, of course, there were serious occupations. In July, before leaving New York, West had picked up bound copies of *Balso Snell*, ready for fall publication. Under West's winking eye, Shapiro volunteered to try to publicize the novel by writing a review letter about it addressed to Samuel Putnam's Paris-centered *New Review*. During the previous winter Shapiro had met Putnam, along with some of the contributors to his magazine—A. Lincoln Gillespie, West's old friend Hiler, and James T. Farrell. Like the publications of all the little presses—McAlmon's, Harry Crosby's, or Nancy Cunard's—*The Dream Life of Balso Snell* would clearly be neither distributed nor reviewed widely. Perhaps Putnam would print the letter, they hoped. He did. Shapiro's notice—one of the two periodical reviews of *Balso Snell*—appeared in the winter number of *The New Review*. The book, he wrote, was among other things a deliberate insult to the genteel critics who controlled public opinion: "One of the reasons why the hiredmen, or the tiredmen have failed to understand [the novel] is because West used parts of the book to fling handfuls of dung in their faces." Still, he insisted, West's book was "a good sort of literary fooling, a nonsense both above and below what the critics sweat for." "This book," he concluded, dadaistically, "doesn't try to explain."

For his part, West worked on *Miss Lonelyhearts* in the front room of the house, writing and rewriting on his typewriter from his handwritten copy. In attempting to carry the colloquial truthfulness of the original letters into the narrative itself, he was devoting his attention at this time almost entirely to the language. He needed to achieve, somehow, a style that would be richly vernacular and also carry psychological and moral reverberations. He wanted it to be an eminently *human* style but also to have, by implication, an analytic core. Although, while he was working, West kept the door closed between his room and Shapiro's, still Scotty could hear him reading his sentences aloud, over and over again, trying each out in speech, until he perfected it. This kind of trial by voice, it became obvious, was necessary for West. And although Shapiro asked West to stop his reading aloud, when it began to interfere with his own work on the book he would name *The Water Wheel*, soon the voice from the next room began again. "He had to read it to know what it sounded like," Shapiro says. "He had to speak it." The effort which West demanded of himself was enormous, and the care which he needed to create the appropriate style was so well matched by his patience that nearly a year and a half would pass before he would finish this short novel.

II

In New York, frequenting Kamin's bookshop after the acceptance of his first novel, West had already met William Carlos Williams, who was to be his earliest admirer and advocate, and whose effect upon *Miss Lonelyhearts* would be far-reaching. Although West did not know that Williams had approved the publication of *Balso Snell* as a Contact Editions book, they soon became close friends, West immediately responding to Williams's interests in popular culture and his emphasis on precision in language, as well as to his personal appeal and social enthusiasms. Moreover, West was re-reading *In the American Grain* for hints about how to employ non-literary documents, while keeping the language fresh, in his novel. Shortly after West arrived in Warrensburg, he wrote Williams in gratitude for a letter praising *Balso* that Williams sent to Kamin. With his thanks West enclosed an absurd "Code Selznick" suggesting guidelines for motion-picture production which Perelman had sent to him. Williams was then preparing to drive to Montreal and responded in a friendly manner. West invited him to stop by on his way north. "Hardly necessary to say," West wrote, "your visit would give me a great deal of pleasure." Unfortunately, when Williams arrived in Warrensburg, intending to stop, a heavy rain made the dirt roads to the pond impassable, and he continued on.

But, for a moment, their paths did join. At the end of September, after West and Williams had separately returned to New York and Rutherford, Moss and Kamin proposed to Williams that he revive *Contact*, now to be subtitled "An American Quarterly."

They would see to printing and distribution, while Williams would take up the editorship. Beginning in December 1920, and continuing through 1921, Williams and McAlmon had issued four numbers, McAlmon publishing a fifth on his own in Paris during 1923. Williams himself liberally and generously regarded all little magazines as part of a single endeavor to free writing from the academies, as one "continuous magazine, the only one . . . with an absolute freedom of editorial policy." Williams and McAlmon had announced in their first issue: "We seek only contact with the local conditions that confront us." But by 1931 McAlmon no longer believed in the value of the experimental literary magazine: "I decided that they did not help the working artist to arrive; and they are . . . apt to create antagonism on the part of publishers and in the minds of certain people." For this reason he declined Williams's offer to edit the magazine jointly in this new incarnation. It was an important decision. For, to fill McAlmon's place, Williams chose West as his associate editor. West never ceased to be grateful to Williams, whom he would speak of even years later as a model writer for his unyielding commitment to literary experiment and his freedom from orthodoxy.

It is true, certainly, that by virtue of the publication of a book by Contact Editions, West could claim a very distinguished and special place in the literary fellowship. But the associate editorship of *Contact* was an even more tangible evidence that he was gaining a special place among his fellow writers. His enthusiasm was obvious at once. Both he and Williams not only understood their magazine as a continuation of the earlier *Contact;* they also regarded it as the legitimate successor to *transition,* which had discontinued publication in June 1930. Viewed historically, indeed, their *Contact* was to be the culmination of two decades of little-magazine publishing. In 1931, the temper and tone of the literary scene had so far changed that the venture of founding a little magazine in the thirties already had something retrospective about it. West proposed, in this spirit, that an essential feature of the new *Contact* would be the compiling and printing of a bibliography of little-magazine publishing in America. By October 10, 1931, he was boldly telling Williams that "the boundaries of our task" were the limits of the nation, but that "with the aid of my staff—two girls and an earnest young man—I expect to finish all the files in the P.L. [New York Public Library] during the next two weeks."

Before that time elapsed, his work would be briefly interrupted by another call upon his enthusiasm. In a letter to the New York *World-Telegram*, one Frank Shea criticized *Contempo*, a little magazine, for not paying contributors. West had met this magazine's editor, M. K. Abernethy, at Moss and Kamin's in 1931 and had given him a room at the Sutton. Published at Chapel Hill, North Carolina, *Contempo* was a lively journal with a distinguished list of contributors, including Kay Boyle, Ezra Pound (both contributing editors), Sherwood Anderson, Hart Crane, Dos Passos, Dreiser, Faulkner, Sinclair Lewis, Wallace Stevens, and William Carlos Williams. In it one of the two reviews of *Balso Snell* had appeared. With Julian Shapiro, West defended *Contempo* against Shea's complaint. Clearly, though the first issue of *Contact* would not appear for more than three months, West already saw himself as a spokesman for the tradition of the avant-garde magazine. His (as the editor called it) "spirited reply" appeared on October 20, 1931, in a *World-Telegram* column called "Book Marks for Today":

We have had some experience with the little magazine, and think that such a statement as the one recently made by Mr. Frank Shea in connection with *Contempo* ought not to pass unchallenged.

When he wrote about "panhandling magazines," he was taking a crack at one of the few decent things in American letters. Apparently, he is unacquainted with their sponsors and ignorant of the purpose they serve.

As to the sponsors, it would be hard to find greater idealists in the literary world. Invariably they have spent money [on] and given time to what they knew from the start was to be a losing venture. As to purpose, the little magazine in the past has found audiences for such writers as Sherwood Anderson, Ben Hecht, Ernest Hemingway (*Little Review*), Robert Coates, Malcolm Cowley, Allen Tate, Hart Crane (*transition*), Ruth Suckow, Edna Ferber, Glenway Wescott (*The Midland*)—to mention but a few.

Surely the unpaid writer for that type of magazine has little to complain of, since [only] he, and "litrachoor"—but never the sponsors—get anything out of it.

West saw himself as the inheritor and defender of the great tradition which he here described. It was a time, clearly, of great intellectual and personal exaltation for him. Suddenly the whole world of contemporary literature seemed to lie open to him, and he was tremulously perched on its brink. But with the Depression the avant-garde world of art was already closing. In his introduction to the bibliography of the little magazine, Williams would write that "it represents the originality of our generation thoroughly free of an economic burden." In 1932, the worst year yet of the economic crisis, the springs of support for advance-guard writing rapidly dried up. When the various forms of patronage available in prosperous times disappeared, the outlets for publication went with them. *Contact* was the last of the experimental magazines of the rich twenties. As West stood overlooking the valley of that world, it was turning to sand.

From the first, West and Williams were hampered by difficulty in getting contributions of quality, by misunderstandings with the publishers, and by compromises that threatened to obscure their particular aims. Their plan, basically, was to emphasize the native power of the American tradition, which, Williams felt, had been minimized by Pound and Eliot. In particular, both writers stressed the colloquial, the brutal, and—their version of surrealism—what West called "American super-realism," which was, he said, certainly "not the Frenchified symbolist stuff." "*Contact*," the editors announced on the title page of the first number, "will attempt to cut a trail through the American jungle without the use of a European compass." Their work would be, as West lectured Williams in the spring of 1932, "not only in but against the American grain and yet in idiomatic pain."

In the fall of 1931, West sent Williams "a long list of the kind of stuff I mean," for the first issue. Among those indigenous writers whose work they should attempt to print, West named John Herrmann, Archibald MacLeish, John Dos Passos ("the big city stuff"), Erskine Caldwell, Edward Dahlberg ("right up our alley— the Middle West stuff is the best"), Malcolm Cowley, Hart Crane, Hemingway, Faulkner, Farrell, Edmund Wilson, and Robert Coates, as well as a number of lesser writers. Some of these would appear in the three issues of the new *Contact*; but for the most part the editors would fail either to attract these writers or to get suitable material from them.

Both West and Williams were dissatisfied with the first issue, which appeared in February 1932. In particular, the design and printing lacked style, they thought. Still, some of the contributions were interesting. E. E. Cummings sent in a poem mocking their request ("let's start a magazine/to hell with literature . . .") and they printed it delightedly; S. J. Perelman contributed a witty sketch entitled "Scenario"; and Williams himself printed prose sketches later transmogrified into parts of *Paterson*. Williams, moreover, attempted to defend the magazine's non-political posture: "A magazine without opinions or criteria other than words moulded by the impacts of experience (not for the depths of experience they speak of but the fulfillment of experience which they are) such a magazine would be timely to a period such as this," he argued, using a distinction between literature *about* events and literature *as* an event which West would maintain in his own writing, from first to last, all through the literary wars of the thirties.

The shape of the second issue appeared more promising, since contributions came in rapidly after the first one. Even so, West wrote to Williams, few of them were " 'in the American grain.' It wasn't anything except lyric, lyric crap." West, by now, was doing the initial sorting of the material and also making the final selections. Privately regarding the second number as "an American Primitive issue," he and Williams planned to print, as earlier American perspectives, a sermon by Jonathan Edwards, a sketch of Benjamin Franklin by one of his contemporaries, and, as if it were a poem, an excerpt from an old Sears, Roebuck catalogue. West's notion of how to express the "American grain" was to "do it obviously—cruelly, irresponsible torture, simply, obviously, casually told"—a theory to which he was giving fictional shape in *Miss Lonelyhearts* and which he discussed in the third issue under the title "Some Notes on Violence."

This commentary helps to explain the interest in violence which is so striking a feature of all four of West's novels. Sent from all parts of America, "from every type of environment," almost every manuscript mailed to *Contact*, West writes, "has violence for its core." The reasons for this are clear, he declares. "In America violence is idiomatic. Read our newspapers. . . . In America violence is daily. . . . [Thus,] what is melodramatic in European writing is not necessarily so in American writing. For a European writer to make violence real, he has to do a great deal of careful psychology and sociology. He often needs three hundred pages to motivate one little murder. But not so the American writer. His audience has been prepared and is neither surprised nor shocked if he omits artistic excuses for familiar events." Violence, West saw, was at the heart of American myth, assumptions, and preoccupations, and received its expression in writing as different as Williams's and Caldwell's. Both, along with himself, West believed, avoided following the French naturalists, whom Dreiser and Lewis imitated; they followed, instead, a native American tradition to be illuminated by *Contact*'s second, "primitivist" number.

Dissatisfied with the cover of the first issue and, moreover, wanting to make his concept of American primitivism visual, West pleaded with Williams to get Charles Sheeler to do the cover for the second issue. Williams hesitated so long that finally, drawing upon his own experience in layout, West himself made the cover design used for the second and third numbers. After rejecting two "fake moderne" drawings which Kamin had commissioned, he modeled his simple and bold design on "Eliot's old *Criterion*, but not quite so conservative." Although the Edwards sermon and the other documentary pieces were eventually omitted, the second issue, of May 1932, was clearly a better one than the first, with prose by West, Nathan Asch, Caldwell, Shapiro, and Reznikoff, and poetry by Marsden Hartley, Williams, and Nancy Cunard. Now *Contact* seemed to be established as the leading active little magazine. But with the controversies which arose over the third number, the enterprise that appeared so promising was doomed to dissolution.

It was inevitable that if the magazine survived economics, it would founder on politics. For the second issue they had accepted a poem called "The Furdresser" by Ilya Ehrenburg, but West omitted it at the last moment. Now time and personalities began to insist on including literature with political relevance. Martin Kamin proposed early in the summer that a number be devoted to Communist writing, a suggestion which West and Williams first accepted but which was all the while inimical to their plans and, as it turned out, to their continuance. "Contact III," Kamin wrote to West, ". . . must be a huge issue and it must have contributions from Gorky and Rolland down to Mike Gold . . . I have lists of authors who contribute regularly to the USSR magazine of the Social Revolution and we'll have to write to them." True to the kind of commitments that would characterize much of the literary activity of the thirties, Kamin was asking questions and making proposals that made politics coincidental with art. He asked West "whether you are interested in essays and critical dissertations . . . (to satisfy the theoretician), or do you want merely good prose and good poetry . . . ? Do you want scientific application and interpretation of Karl Marx, or merely material on the proletarian awakening, unscientific, devoid of conscious formulae . . . ?" His "merely" says it all for the current tendency to elevate political rightness above good writing, an ideal which would destroy *Contact*.

Williams reacted almost immediately by writing to Kamin and "asking him to postpone his Communist number." He and West agreed, as he said to West, that *Contact* must be "a forum of good writing. All we'll get by a Communist issue is a reputation for radicalism and not for good writing—which is our real aim." But 1932 was a pivotal year in American writing. The obvious change was signaled most plainly, perhaps, by the fact that almost simultaneously four writers were using the Gastonia strike as material for fiction; or equally by the fact that many others, among them Edmund Wilson and John Dos Passos, not only supported the Communist ticket for 1932, but also issued an artists and writers' manifesto of support titled "Culture and Crisis," signed by a wide spectrum of writers, from Robert Coates to Kenneth Burke. Clearly America, as Wilson put it, had the "jitters," and the writers were responding to its crisis in ways unthinkable only a few years earlier. Now, instead of imagism, writers spoke of Musteism; instead of surrealism, of Lovestoneism; instead of vorticism, of Trotskyism, Christian Socialism, anarchism. West could joke in one of his letters to Williams: "Business is lousy and my company is close to bankruptcy. . . . I guess I'll have to go to Hollywood or start a brook farm experiment and wait for THE REVOLUTION. For Lan's sake, why don't they hurry up?" But he had, another friend has said, "a dimensional sense of the complexities of Communism" and was "completely sacrilegious about the Party's sacred principles."

In early August, Williams and West were still uncertain whether there would be a third issue, though they decisively rejected the idea of a Communist number and agreed (as Williams put it) that "everything must be put aside for the sake of interest to the reader. Ruthlessly, we've got to turn down anything that doesn't fit that purpose even though we make virtual blackguards of ourselves." By this time, West was so far the controlling spirit of the magazine that Williams complained jokingly: "Hell, I often wonder who is editor of this mag. Some day I'm going to indulge myself." Still, it was not easy to edit a literary magazine in 1932. West was picking his way among lost friendships, troubles with Moss and Kamin, and difficulties with contributors. "I'd just as soon call this third number the last," he told Williams. The third issue, however good it was, still left West dissatisfied. For this final number of October 1932, the editors had gotten Hilaire Hiler to write about art and gathered prose by Perelman, Caldwell, Farrell, and John Herrmann, in addition to their own, and poetry by Yvor Winters. With a current issue as good and as promising as this one, it seemed that the magazine might survive its controversies and as late as the end of November it still appeared that a fourth number might come out. But at last, in December, West quarreled irrevocably with Kamin, and *Contact* was ended.

III

Miss Lonelyhearts, however, emerged from the ruins. After returning from his summer in the Adirondacks, West had worked steadily on the book, and five months later, by the end of January 1932, he could announce to Williams: "I have been working hard on a novel that I intend asking you to look at soon."

Williams read it almost at once, and part of West's book, "Miss Lonelyhearts and the Lamb," was included in the first issue of *Contact*. Revised, this would ultimately become the third chapter of his novel; but at this middle stage in its composition, the lamb story was serving as the book's dramatic opening. The protagonist of this *Contact* episode, Thomas Matlock, a man ironically writing the advice column of the New York *Evening Hawk* under a female name, starts out for a drink in a nearby speakeasy; but knowing that there his editor, Shrike, will mock his attempts to give genu-

inely helpful advice, he sits down in a wasted park to ponder his
fixation on what he thinks of as "the Christ business." "He did not
want to listen to Shrike who had discovered that he still worried
about Christ and for his benefit had invented a new church, The
First Church of Christ Dentist, and a new trinity, the Father, Son
and wire-haired Fox Terrier. Shrike and his stage, the speakeasy,
made him feel that he was wandering, lost without hope of escape,
among the scenery and costumes stored in the cellar of an ancient
theatre." Returning home, he falls asleep and after dreaming that
"he was a little boy . . . praying with his head on his mother's
knees," and then that he is standing on a stage in an auditorium
crowded with his correspondents, he dreams that he is back in college and that, drunk, he performs the mock ritual of sacrificing a
lamb.

West was testing his novel in print after working on it for more
than two years. Now, with the chance to print sections of it in
Contact—and perhaps elsewhere—he worked steadily on the book.
By June he had rejected most of the elements of the "Lamb" chapter in almost completely rewriting the novel; and he had what he
now believed was the "first final draft." Still obviously perplexed by
the central problem of how to present the psyche of his hero accurately, he had redone the novel in the first person and from this
version selected two revised chapters, "Miss Lonelyhearts and the
Dead Pan" and "Miss Lonelyhearts and the Clean Old Man," to
appear in the second number of *Contact*.

Most of the first of the "Dead Pan" episode consists of the letter
from Broad Shoulders which would later become the core of the
chapter "Miss Lonelyhearts Returns." In this early version, the
hero decides to go to the speakeasy for a drink in order to escape
from his suffering. His correspondents, he explains—as West uses
the first person to make Lonelyhearts's motives intelligible—drove
him to Christ. "But," he self-analytically explains to the reader,
"don't misunderstand me. My Christ has nothing to do with love.
Even before I became Miss Lonelyhearts, my world was moribund.
I lived on a deserted stairway, among steel engravings of ornate
machinery. I wrote my first love letter on a typewriter. . . . The
joke of suffering and the joke of comforting killed this world . . .
I turned to Christ as the most familiar and natural of excitants. I
wanted him to destroy this hypnosis. He alone could make the rock

of sensation bleed and the stick of thought flower." In this chapter it seems clear that analysis might be sharper in the first person, and that the personal voice, the "I," would effectively contrast with the collective misery of the letters. But the deficiencies of this point of view became apparent in the "Clean Old Man" section, where the hero necessarily has to describe his own emotions ("I felt as I had years before when I had accidentally stepped on a frog"), and so takes on the same tone of misery as that in the letters. West would need to find a way of both keeping the immediacy of appeal and suffering in the letters and giving Miss Lonelyhearts distance from them, a kind of numbed inability to commit himself to emotional responsiveness.

In the summer of 1932, West sent a trial section of a further revision of his novel to Abernethy, calling the book of which it formed a part "a moral satire." This section, titled "Miss Lonelyhearts in the Dismal Swamp," was to be the eighth chapter of the novel; again the version published in *Contempo* differs significantly from the final one. In this episode West strikingly attempted to give his hero complexity by making him a character divided against himself. Miss Lonelyhearts contains, as aspects of one personality, both Thomas Matlock and Shrike: his own meditations are the stage on which their dialogues are played out. The satirical style of the one personality lashes out against the romantic content of the other's fantasies. As his meditation on the varieties of escape begins, Miss Lonelyhearts sits in a room—the stage of his consciousness—"walled at both ends," torn by the opposing principles of self, holding "a Bible in one hand and a philosophy book in the other. In his lap are travel, art, seed and gun catalogues." Recalling vividly Baudelaire's "Anywhere Out of This World," he muses on the varieties of escapist experience in the satirical speech which Shrike will later deliver to Miss Lonelyhearts. "Politics, drugs, suicide, golf . . . no, the street is walled at both ends [he tells himself]. Ah, Miss Lonelyhearts, your soul is sick." For his last hope, he reaches entirely out of this world and writes "J. C. a letter," the same one dictated by Shrike in the novel. For all the tension gained by such internalizations of dialogue, this narrative apparently lost, for West, the hard objectivity which he had striven, in other sections, to achieve. He was not yet entirely satisfied.

Still, the selections in both *Contact* and *Contempo* were striking ones, and soon Williams was passing along "good words about your work" to West from Gorham Munson and another correspondent, comments declaring that West's contributions had been the best in the second issue of *Contact*. Later, after Ezra Pound had written approvingly to Williams about West, Williams informed West that he had written "a short notice about you for the paper Pound is working for, said you were the best America has to offer today." This notice constitutes the first serious appreciation of West written by an important critic. Appropriately, too, it appeared abroad through the agency of Ezra Pound, who had dedicated two decades of effort to the discovery and encouragement of those Americans, like Eliot and Frost, who had been ignored on native grounds. For Pound's literary page in *Il Mare*, Williams's essay was translated into Italian by Edmundo Dodsworth and survives only in this version. Translated back into English, it follows:

A NEW AMERICAN WRITER

No. I don't mean *another* American writer, I mean a *new* one: Nathanael West. When another of the little reviews that appeared in the United States during the last quarter of the century died, I thought it was a shame. But now I think differently. Now I understand that all those little reviews ought by necessity to have a short life, the shorter the better. When they live too long they begin to dry up. But they have had at least one excuse for their existence—they have given birth to at least one excellent writer who would not otherwise have had the means to develop. *Contact* has produced N. West. Now it can die.

The special strength of West, apart from his ability to maneuver words, is that he has taken seriously a theme of great importance so trite that all of us thought there would be no life in it: I mean the terrible moral impoverishment of our youth in the cities.

But to do that he has discovered that the way to treat this theme is to use the dialect natural to such a condition. Since the newspapers are the principal corruptors of all that has value in language, it is through the use of this very journalistic perspective and everyday speech that language must be regenerated. West has taken as his material the idiom of the reporters, the tough men of the newspapers, and has counterpointed it with the pathetic letters and the emotions of the poor and the ignorant city dwellers who write to the newspapers to obtain counsel for their afflictions and poverty.

After all, what is the urban population made up of? Of seduced and corrupted, nothing more. They have been gathered together so that they may be better exploited, and this is West's material. But no, his "material" is writing itself—he has invented a new manner, he has invented a means that allows him the full expression of his sentiments in a language that a journalist would recognize. It conveys the real, incredibly dead life of the people and the incredibly dead atmosphere of the book itself and—my God!—we understand what scoundrels we've become in this century. "Don't be deceived" could be West's motto. Don't think yourself literate merely because you write long books and use correct English. Here are the problems, do something with them that will not be a lie. Don't deceive yourself: you don't see because you don't look. These things are there just the same. And if you think you can write poems while you live in a sewer, and at the same time think you're lying in a bed of roses—well, go ahead and be happy!

The cities are rotten and desperate—so is most polite, "literary" literature. So? Nothing much. Only a little review that publishes good material. I don't think that many will find it. It [West's writing] would offend the paying subscribers if it appeared in the large monthly magazines. Which makes one wonder if they will ever let it enter their consciousness.

This review suggests, as does the whole editorial history of *Contact,* how great and unrecognized was the influence of West upon Williams. It is not too much to say that, though Williams's career began much earlier, the two writers had been working along similar lines, and Williams's understanding of West's imagination helped him to sharpen his own sensibility and define the direction he would pursue in literature after this time. To West's crucial influence are directly traceable the important developments which led Williams to *Paterson.*

By the time Williams's notice came out, the third issue of *Contact,* containing "Miss Lonelyhearts on a Field Trip," had appeared. In this chapter, West finally found his solution to the narrative problem by eliminating both the personal character Thomas Matlock and the personal "I"; telling the tale from a third-person, omniscient point of view, he now threw the suffering in the letters into high relief, and contrasted to them Miss Lonelyhearts's inability to resolve his suffering and so become an "I" and find a voice.

With this solution, West turned his formal problems into aspects and expressions of the tragedy of his hero. Williams, who "admired West tremendously," generously summed up both the value of the three issues of Contact and the power of West's emerging book when he declared grandly: "I'd tie myself to a fourth Contact just for the sake of bringing out Lonelyhearts again but for no other reason. More and more it becomes apparent that your stuff is the real reason for the mag. No kidding, that's true." But West would not need a fourth issue. Having arrived at his final version in this chapter, he would now be able to bring the whole novel into line and at last write its conclusion.

All he needed was time and freedom from the hotel. He had never worked so hard before, and he yearned for leisure in which to complete his book. Although he had planned to spend another summer with Shapiro at Viele Pond, business kept him in the city. Busy with both the magazine and the hotel's pre-fall advertising campaign of pamphlets, mailings, and newspaper ads, he had taken only a four-day weekend in June for fishing in the Adirondacks, where he had been bitten all over by blackflies, caught only three trout, and returned home "with both eyes closed and my neck so swollen that I couldn't button my collar." He had vacation time coming, to begin on October 12—"and while away hope to finish Miss Lonelyhearts," he wrote Williams. But the rustic Adirondack cabin would very likely prove uncomfortable in mid-October.

Williams, in the meantime, had performed another friendly service for West in sending the young, enthusiastic novelists John Herrmann and Josephine Herbst to meet him. Herrmann, whose novel What Happens had been published as one of McAlmon's Contact Editions, and Miss Herbst, who had already published Nothing Is Sacred (1928), had bought a seventeenth-century farmhouse in Erwinna, Bucks County, Pennsylvania, intending to live there cheaply and write. For Contact 3, West had selected thirty pages from Herrmann's manuscript novel, "Foreign Born," and in late September, shortly before the issue appeared, Herrmann and Miss Herbst drove from Williams's house to the Sutton. Delighted, West came out to the car, looking (Josephine Herbst thought) "very attractive . . . with marvelously alive eyes and a face filled with wit and intelligence, but with no reservations." In his rooms, shyly accepting their praise for his *Lonelyhearts* pieces and falling under their spell at once, he told them that he was confident that in a couple of months of sustained work he could finish his book, but that he was afraid he would never be able to complete it in the hotel, where interruptions were frequent.

"She had fairly snatched at the chance," Josephine Herbst writes in *A Hunter of Doves*, ". . . to rescue [him] from the doldrums, and, when they were inside the hotel and she had admired the view from his penthouse apartment where he deprecated the big room and even the view as little more than a cage, where to see beyond rooftops merely enhanced his sense of being in jail, she listened with growing impatience to his admission that he had been working on a novel for three years with a trepidation that it would never be finished." Excitedly, they talked to him about the literary and economic felicities of life in Erwinna, and after the three had dinner in the hotel he arranged at once to come back with them the following day. "It was a delicious autumn and for three days we barely slept," Josephine Herbst remembered. "We walked through fields of tall grass, plucked the antlered horns of red sumac, talked of Pushkin for whom autumn had been the creative season. We drank Pennsylvania bootleg rye and homemade red wine; read aloud Carl Sternheim's *A Pair of Underdrawers*, recited poems by Hans Arp, 'The trap drummer,' and Schwitters's *Revolution in Revon*. John Herrmann had an autographed copy of George Grosz's *Ecce Homo*; he had known the artist in Germany. We opened the big volume flat on the table, poring over the grotesque comics of the violent Berlin world. We spoke of his *Christ in a Gasmask*. . . . Taunted with, 'If autumn could be the great creative season for Pushkin, why not for you?' [West] had decided to ask for a leave-of-absence from the Hotel Sutton, had picked up our challenge to finish the book, *now or never*." With good, new-found friends to feed him, friends with whom he could talk over the final version of his book, West found Erwinna a greater Adirondacks.

On October 12 his vacation began and he returned to Erwinna for six weeks, working in a room at the Warford House in Frenchtown, N.J., just across the river, spanned by a covered bridge. "I am exceedingly grateful to you," he wrote Williams in mid-November, "for putting me in touch with the Herrmanns. . . . They got me this place to stay, and they feed me, while I am working. I will positively be finished with *Miss Lonelyhearts* before I leave for the city next week."

9 / "The Apocalypse of the Second Hand"

> Near the close of this hearing, Senator La Follette remarked: "Your counsel is really one of despair, then." Mr. Wiggin answered: "Human nature is human nature. Lives go on. . . ." The Senator thought a moment and then commented: "The capacity for human suffering is unlimited?" The great man of affairs answered: "I think so."
> —Charles Beard, *America in Midpassage* (1939)

West's inability to finish *Miss Lonelyhearts*, and perhaps even his indecision over what narrative techniques to use, was obviously connected to his life at the hotel. It was not merely a matter of the distractions of business. Of course, there were interruptions, but they really counted for little. West had an enormous power of concentration and could, as he proved in Hollywood, successfully juggle several endeavors at one time. The truth was, as he intimated to Josephine Herbst, "that the hotel with all its occupants surrounded him with the felt mat of a persistent presence." The character and condition of the mass life around him weighed upon his imagination. By temperament and training, West was a close observer of mass life—and he was all the more imaginatively engaged by the suffering he found at the hotel, since he was unable to participate actively in it. He suffered vicariously with each sufferer; imaginatively he lived over all their inner lives.

On the surface, of course, the job was a lark. In the fall of 1930, Morris Jarcho, one of the Kenmore Hall owners, also became a stockholder in a corporation that acquired the Sutton Club Hotel at 330 East 56 Street, and West, having failed to join Beatrice Mathieu in Paris, was made its manager at a salary of about $50 a week. "Pep said," a friend reported in a letter, "he is glad to say that his family in writing has informed him of his appointment to the position of matron in the Welfare Island home for retired wealthy prostitutes," and his friends were soon referring to him as "P. N. West, the great writer and bordello-keeper."

The Sutton had been built to be leased to a women's club; but when the contractor failed, the sub-contractors formed a corporation and turned it into a regular hotel. It had arrangements for suites and eventually inaugurated a policy of separate floors for the sexes and for married couples. It had no suitable lobby. For these reasons, it could not succeed so well as the less expensive Kenmore. This gave West ample opportunity to allow friends to occupy the empty rooms, and so conferred upon the Sutton a special glamour and a place in the literary history of the thirties. The Perelmans lived in the hotel and John Sanford moved in for five months or so. Norman Krasna, Quentin Reynolds, A. Lincoln Gillespie (who had a diabetic attack and went into a coma there), Edmund Wilson, and Robert Coates all occasionally lived off the Sutton bounty. Lillian Hellman and Dashiell Hammett came, Hammett skipping from the Hotel Pierre wearing, in layer upon layer, all the clothes he owned. (Hammett borrowed, as well, and made famous, the name of Laura's dog, Asta, for the Charles's dog in *The Thin Man*.) Other guests soon arrived. When James T. Farrell and his wife were evicted from their hotel, West gave them two rooms for two weeks. Erskine Caldwell "heard on the grapevine that he had read some of my short stories and thought I would be a respectable roomer . . . to help light some of the windows so the hotel would look more live than dead." Many of these writers West saw at night, in his rooms or over coffee and a sandwich in the nearby Child's. In time, both Hammett and Caldwell would read "parts of *Miss Lonelyhearts* while it was in progress," as well as in proofs.

For West, the Sutton was a Paris of the imagination; for, like Paris, it evoked a vivid personal response in him and was a fertile source of fantasy. Even as late as *The Day of the Locust* (1939), the atmosphere and meaning of this hotel would retain a hold on his mind, and early in his planning he would switch the scene of this book from a boat to a rooming house, and at last to an apartment hotel. The Sutton clientele fascinated him. Indeed, since they were his subjects, they were more important for him than the writers who might be his companions and critics. He drew upon them for emotional energy. A half dozen had committed suicide by throwing themselves off a terrace—one crashing spectacularly through the glass dining-room ceiling just as the guests were sitting decorously down to dinner. Why couldn't he have at least waited until dinner was over, West moaned sardonically. But more seriously, he was asking, why at all? The hotel was filled with grotesques, to hear his account of it: "It was not a place for the successful." An elderly couple regularly paid a high price to take over the swimming pool. What pleasures were they seeking? A good-looking young woman, formerly a movie extra, gave her services to both men and women, famous Hollywood people. What drove her to it? Young men went grimly each day to struggling advertising agencies. How could they bear to sell when they themselves had been utterly sold? Even in the Kenmore, he had watched "shabby, lonely men and women reading pulp magazines in the lobby, and inventing elaborate daydreams as a result of their vicarious thrills derived from the reading." What was the pleasure in this and how far could it satisfy them? He had selected night duty to have leisure for work, but he was drawn from his work—and from the work of wit like *Balso Snell*—by such questions and awakened to the tragedies of lonely, frightened, desperate people. Still, there was the hotel to manage, bills to collect, food to order, waiters to hire and fire—and West did all this well. It was, as Michael Gold says, "a weird combination"—West's business obligations merged with his awareness of the human tragedy. "He had," Gold says, "to *pretend* to be a hotel manager." More and more, however, the hotel seemed to him to be symbolic of the whole culture.

For out on the streets misery and tragedy, the economic effects of the Depression, were everywhere. In December 1930, as West took over his Sutton job, New York City officials declared that begging on the streets had become a menace: a man might expect to be asked for money four or five times in a ten-block walk around West's hotel. From three or four million in the spring, unemployment had increased by this time to five or six million. Among patients admitted to certain health centers in New York, malnutrition had increased by sixty percent. Others were leaving the city altogether, while some lingered in it, hopelessly, in search of food and work, a solvent friend, or a generous relative. The march upon Washington of the Bonus Expeditionary Force was only the most striking evidence of a migratory population that was estimated nationally at one million. Shades of men and women blowing aimlessly in and out of the hotel, masses wandering the continent —these meant the same; from the individual case, West worked imaginatively to a vast vision of the general purposelessness. Individuals, the city, the nation—all were implicated in drift and misery. In New York, 32,000 families—with an average family income of $8.20 a month in 1932—waited patiently for local aid to trickle down to them. In December of that year, a couple was discovered living in a cave in Central Park, where they had remained for months. No wonder that many sensitive people felt, as Rexford Tugwell wrote in his diary in December 1932, that "no one can live and work in New York this winter without a profound sense of uneasiness."

In Europe similar misery was leading or had led to revolution. But in America, as foreign observers like Philippe Soupault were quick to notice, only confusion resulted. People were asking, "Do you think we are going to have a revolution?"—but asking this, Elmer Davis remarked, "apathetically, as if nothing they might do could either help it or hinder it." The refrain of Archibald MacLeish's "Land of the Free" would be: "We wonder . . . We don't know . . . We're asking. . . ." Americans were appallingly lost in a world they had lost all expectation of understanding.

They were suffering not only from economic but from spiritual poverty—from what W. H. Auden has named "West's Disease" after its discoverer—a spiritual illness to which West devoted a decade of reflection and fiction. In the thirties, there were many writers and economic analysts dramatizing sheer material misery; but West, more accurately than anyone else, measured the malady of spirit. His novels are the fever graphs of its hectic increase. Auden has described it accurately. "This is a disease of consciousness which renders it incapable of converting wishes into desires. A lie is false; what it asserts is not the case. A wish is fantastic; it knows what is the case but refuses to accept it. All wishes, whatever their content, have the same and unvarying meaning—'I refuse to be what I am.' " This rejection of self, situation, or position erodes desire and consumes belief, for whatever the individual wishes, Auden concludes, "he cannot help knowing that he could have wished something else."

Wishes were everywhere: the speculative desires for wealth typical of the late twenties—fed by bond salesmen, Old Counselors on the radio, and newspaper hucksters—exploded into uncontrolled wishing on all levels of life in the thirties; for now a gulf wider than ever before, an unbridgeable gulf perhaps, lay between the ideals of society and the possibilities of fulfilling them. If Theodore Dreiser could say in 1919 that the speed and complexity of modern civilization "wearies and stultifies the moral nature . . . induces a sort of intellectual fatigue," what would he say of the complexities of the thirties? How little surprised he would be at the varieties of escapist experience. Even literature, which West had regarded as civilization's most intense vehicle of truth, now seemed designed only to provide its chief means of escape. During the Depression, circulation at the free public libraries increased forty percent. Historical novels (Willa Cather's *Shadows on the Rock*, Hervey Allen's *Anthony Adverse*) led all others in popularity, by offering escapes into the costumes and guises of the past. On the newsstands, with circulations ranging up to four million copies a month, pocket-digest magazines or newspapers like Bernarr MacFadden's *Evening Graphic* were made up of a mélange of articles on sex, success, strange hobbies, and self-health remedies mixed with crime stories. The *Graphic* contained not only an "Advice to the Lovelorn" but a "Lonely Hearts" column, in which (the editor declared) "lonesome girls were enabled to meet equally lonesome boys, meetings were held, dances were conducted, and 'Lonely Hearts' strove mightily that all might have Love."

Heated interests in dance marathons, various stunts, and miniature golf flared up, while visiting between families, a survey showed, dropped off sharply. Gambling increased noticeably—the largest salary in the United States in 1934 going to Moe Annenberg, owner of *Racing Form*—as people tried to win back, by good luck, what, as it seemed, they had lost by bad. At the movies, fantasy was compounded on Banko, Keeno, or Screeno nights, when the assistant manager would come out on stage and spin a carnival wheel while the audience, like the rest of society, waited anxiously for a winning number.

It is not surprising but indicative that in 1933 the jigsaw puzzle craze began. By the end of that year, more than two million puzzles had been sold. All over the country, people were trying to put the pieces together, to get the picture organized. But in culture there were puzzles too difficult for even a master to solve. Some of the pieces were missing, thrown away or never manufactured; and such puzzles, even if completed, would have shown only pictures of chaos.

Sublime order seemed to reign, however, in both fraternal societies and the movies. By the early thirties, almost half the adult population belonged to at least one of the 800 active secret orders. Every week, Americans were dressing themselves as Brahmins, Knights, Pharaohs, Redmen, Vikings, Furies, Hermits, Owls, Odd Fellows, Galahads, Maltese, and Tibetans—an exotic army of men and women fighting, with all their power, boredom, inertia, and nonentity. In their Hives, Grottoes, Forts, Nests, and Mystic Dens was no confusion: the rules were clear, the process of initiation and the rituals were securely ordered and eternally fixed in a kind of living historical novel, put together once a week.

Moviegoers averaged more than once-a-week attendance. Even in the twenties, of course, movies had appealed to the desire for wish-fulfillment satisfactions. In *Middletown* (1929), the Lynds quoted a revealing *Saturday Evening Post* advertisement: "Go to a motion picture . . . and let yourself go. Before you know it, you are living the story—laughing, loving, hating, struggling, winning! All the adventure, all the romance, all the excitement you lack in your daily life are in Pictures. They take you completely out of yourself into a wonderful new world. . . . Out of the cage of everyday existence! If only for an afternoon or an evening—escape." Attendance was bound to increase in the thirties. As the Lynds pointed out in *Middletown in Transition* (1937), the movies then became the major source for emulative ideas. In them, escape became the very image of reality, "authentic portrayals of life" that ultimately consisted of "a medley of vague and variable impressions—a disconnected assemblage of ideas, feelings, vagaries, and impulses." Screened in a darkened theater, where gorgeous architecture and furnishings helped narcotize the sense of reality, movies not only romanticized life; they transformed its conditions and gave them simplicity and order. It was no wonder that when all else was so complex, twenty million people, one out of every six Americans, found time to go to the movies every day of the week.

These, then, were the symptoms of West's Disease, whose contagion was everywhere. Like D. H. Lawrence, West had a brilliant, intuitive grasp of anti-rational behavior and a less dogmatic knowledge than Lawrence's of its importance in human affairs. Isaac Rosenfeld wrote that West's two centers of sensibility were "the poetic and the popular": his own identity and "the secret inner life of the masses." His ability to combine the two in fiction produced, Rosenfeld says, "the nearest thing to a new art form ever to be derived from the materials of a mass culture."

West's "wound" lay, as I have suggested, in his incapacity to relate directly to one person. Except for his deep affection for Laura and S. J. Perelman, he regarded himself as "a lonely spy" —above emotional displays, "outside" social life. But this wound, if it was such, combined in West with his "bow": an extraordinary capacity for imaginative involvement. His experiences with ordinary people at a time when general suffering was acute gave him a special material for his imagination to explore. He turned his inability to relate fully to individuals into an enormous capacity to understand and identify with mass life in general. What may have begun as a personal incapacity, then, he turned brilliantly into a triumph of art. "As the mass man grows in ratio to man," Philip Wylie writes, "Pep seems to me to have drawn the floor-plan of that descent, early, and in ways, first." West's perception of the fact and implications of the birth of mass man and his ability to give his understanding form in fiction constituted his interest for his contemporaries and explains his special fascination for us.

II

In a remarkable group of unpublished stories which West wrote between 1930 and 1933, he turned forcefully from the theme and methods of the private sensibility to investigate the collective "secret inner life of the masses," from which anarchic voices, frustrated in dreams and wishes, rise in pain and confusion. Reversing his focus in *Balso*, West now concentrated his vision on the vagrant lives of the inarticulate and attempted to originate an art form whereby to express a new state of mass consciousness. His stories show the defects of concentration upon a particular point of view. But he sensed that the older forms of fiction would no longer serve. Experiment was worth the cost of failure and would be the expense of success. Henry Seidel Canby expressed (without himself knowing how to solve) the new problems of form for novelists in the thirties. "It is folly to suppose," he said, "that a society which reads a daily paper, sees a newsreel weekly, and hears the radio every other hour, is going to be novelized successfully by the old-time story teller who assumed that a 'character' was an independent personality instead of a consciousness, floating on a stream of impressions."

West's tales are not stories in the ordinary sense; for he set out in them to define form and character anew. They deal singlemindedly with the lost lives of the masses, as *Balso* had dealt with the estranged individual self. Still, they possess the excitement, and bear the conviction, of West's discovery of this alternate theme. He knew, as few others in his time did, not only that the individual was lost but that the masses who had defined themselves through their society were lost too, now that society itself was drifting and undefined. And he treated both themes.

To explore mass life empirically was more difficult, of course, than to analyze one's self. Yet West's vision rests upon real observation, however subsequently altered by imagination. His position as a hotel manager during the Depression, when the whole of society seemed as transient as hotel life, gave him a strategic advantage. Again, he was stalking his quarry. He told Josephine Herbst that "a hotel like this was jam-packed with broken hearts, broken pocketbooks, too, and as the hotel was a genteel one, with a gilding upon it, one could imagine the pride of the victims who, finding themselves slowly drained of their substance, tried to keep up a front, sallied past the door, hummed, pretended light-hearted gaiety, delay of checks from rich uncles, alimony, or the imaginary sale of imaginary real estate that would put them on easy street." The hotel, West realized, could symbolize the fantasy life of the masses; he would spy on this.

He was not content, however, with merely imagining the wishes of its guests. He interested himself in entertainments in which the masses were interested, and now reassessed movies, cartoons, popular literature, and jazz as expressions of collective yearning. He attended closely to individuals; the writer George Milburn, for instance, says that West "probably got to know me better than I know myself." He had particular compassion for loneliness and suffering; and while he still maintained a cynical, scornful pose with intellectuals, he freely indulged his emotions in observing collective life. With great tenderness and sympathetic feeling for detail, he described to a friend, for instance, an incident he saw in the street. "Pep saw a man 'pick himself up after a fall on the sidewalk and his whole face was dirty like a hand from a very dusty book. But where the nose and mouth ordinarily are, there was a wide smear of blood. He moved slowly, very carefully, and seemed just mildly surprised, and touched slowly—twice—his hand to his face and looked at it, hesitatingly, gently.' " On occasion, West even feigned ungrammatical speech, and his shambling characteristics seemed, to at least one observer, to have been purposefully adopted and emphasized in imitation of desolate, inert mass man.

Finally, the mail of the hotel necessarily passed through West's hands, and he did not hesitate to steam open letters addressed to people whom he regarded as particularly interesting, even enlisting the aid of Lillian Hellman. In this way, he followed the private lives of the hotel guests and so could accurately assess the tragic difference, which he pointed out to Josephine Herbst, between their true inner situations and their outward pretenses. In his solitary consciousness he kept the secret diary of the wishes and dreams of the whole hotel. He had probably first thought of doing this after reading the Susan Chester letters. Now, in the hotel, his friends say, he would often point out people who, he told them, would make "wonderful characters for fiction," and he would seem to make up stories about them. But it is clear that often these stories were true and his proposed fiction was simply the tragedy of fact. Only West understood how far his fiction was factual.

The central tale of West's vision of mass life is called "The Adventurer." Of this sketch West was never able to make a completed story; it has the structural waywardness of wish fantasy, without logical end, once begun. The "Adventurer," Joe Rucker, is simply an order clerk in a wholesale grocery house. His adventures consist of daydreams and memories of earlier daydreams. West was the first writer to discover, or at least the first to dramatize in vivid fictions, the psychological fact that once a fantasy is perfected, it may be lived over and over in further fantasies precisely as if it had been a real experience. Such a life feeds on collective fantasy and adjusts the self to it, so that the personal sense of self becomes at last coincident with the general daydream. Character, as West defines it in "The Adventurer," is constituted by: "Buttons, string, bits of leather, a great deal of soiled paper, a few shouts, a way of clasping the hands, of going up steps, of smoothing a lapel, some prejudices, a reoccuring dream, a distaste for bananas, a few key words repeated endlessly. With time . . . memories pile up, hindering action, covering everything, making everything secondhand, rubbed, frayed, soiled. The gestures and the prejudices, the dislikes, all become one and that one not itself but once removed, a dull echo. The trail becomes hard to follow, not grown over, but circular, winding back into itself, without direction, without goal."

Joe's story concerns his memories of various fragments of this secondhand self. His father, a janitor, "spent a great deal of time picking over the rubbish sent down in the dumbwaiters. . . . What he searched for were mementos of pleasure. Fans, perfume bottles, an embroidered slipper, a gilt dance card, theatre programs, elaborate menus, things of that sort." These, which he collected in barrels, gave him some strange satisfaction. Like his father, but in more subtle ways, Joe has spent his life collecting pleasurable fantasies, storing them up in his mind like debris, where he can sift through them over and over again. When he was seventeen, he recalls, beginning to redream and relive past fancies, he was a messenger boy. He valued his uniform since he could pretend it was "a disguise I wore to fool my enemies." Much of the time between his hurried deliveries he spent in the public library, there assuming his true imaginative guises as Argonaut or African explorer. "From ancient Greece to nineteenth-century Africa was just a quick thumbing through the card index, a scrawled request blank and a few minutes' wait for my number to be flashed on the electric call board." Joe is merely acting out, wholly in his mind, adventures he acted out physically as a child in the secluded recesses, the "secret nests," in Central Park.

Now, however, he sees "the corruption, the monstrosity," of both the library and the park: of all life. The library is filled with grotesques who search books for pornography or facts about strange diseases, innumerable spiritual cripples with "rubbed, soiled faces," pursuing "ten thousand deliriums." The library, as he now sees, is his "father's barrels multiplied by ten million!" It is "The Apocalypse of the Second Hand!"—the symbol of soiled, fragmented, mass dreaming.

Even the park "seems filled with cripples of many kinds. . . . [They] congregate on the benches that line the walks. Some with pencils for sale and others with gum. Do they live by selling to each other?" Now, in horror, he watches a continuous stream of furtive adults moving like animals into hiding places in the dense thickets where he had played as a boy.

Yet his own need to enter that collective dream which they are all pursuing is so great that he must both torment himself with his vision of horror and surrender to the horror. By day he habitually returns to the library; and by night he finds a secluded place to "lurk in the brush, hiding and dreaming." As he looks out on Central Park Lake, he tells himself dream and myth tales of magical transformation, the apocalypse of renewal—for instance, the story of the Waste Land: "How quick I was to name it all. Lake Elsinore, the Chapel Perilous, the Singing Wood. A swan boat was anchored by the boat dock at the pergola, its faded white paint a rosy silver in the magic light. Within, I knew, a king lay sorely wounded in the groin, and it was his loss of manhood through this grievous wound that had made a desert of the once rich meadow land.

"I didn't tell myself this story. . . . A story is—and then something happened. And then something else happened. This was simultaneous, like a great picture. My head and heart were full of one, great timeless image. . . ."

But for Joe there would be no *Datta, Dayadhvam, Damyata*— only the repeated reimmersion in his dreams, in the library and the park, "without direction, without goal." This "Adventurer" is West's objectification of his wound; his story—a revelation of the seething and numbed desires of mass life—is the ecstatic trembling of West's bow, his art.

"Mr. Potts of Pottstown," another of West's unpublished short stories, treats the comic aspects of wishing at such length that they become absurd and tragic. In these tales, clearly, West was experimenting with various perspectives upon a single theme. Potts, a man divided between his love of comfort and his imaginative passion for adventure, lives in a house filled, museum-like, with weapons and books recounting "heroic deeds." He has organized a local Hunt Club which feeds solely on fantasy, since there is no game in the nearby woods. In an attempt to duplicate in fiction the contradictions in the streaming consciousness of Potts, West attempted to write simultaneous, parallel interior monologues. The truth is, he writes, "that two entirely different men occupied his stout body. At one and the same time he was Quixote-Potts and Sancho-Potts . . .":

Quixote-Potts	*Sancho-Potts*
(*Highly excited*)	(*Quite calmly*)
Cover yourself with glory, Potts.	Potts, cover yourself with flannel.
(*Still more excited*)	(*Still more calmly*)
O for the terrible double-barrelled rifle! O for bowie-knives, lassos and Moccasins!	O for knitted waistcoats! O for the welcome padded Caps with ear flaps!
(*Above all self-control*)	(*Ringing for Nancy*)
A battle-axe! fetch me a battle-axe!	Now, then, do bring me a bowl of chicken broth and shut that window.

The equilibrium between these selves—both aspects of the mass mind and collective yearnings—is disturbed when the local lawyer forms an Alpine Club (even though there are no mountains nearby) in competition with Potts's Hunt Club and, aided by their wives, gets all the men to desert Potts. Potts immediately responds with fantasy action. After ordering "a complete climbing outfit in the latest mode down to ice glasses and spiked shoes" from Abercrombie and Fitch, and reading a library of mountain-climbing books, Potts attempts to regain his local leadership in the new club, but he is hooted out. As a result, he tries the dangerous experiment of contacting reality by swearing to climb a real mountain.

What he discovers—a secret hidden from Joe Rucker of "The Adventurer"—is that there is no reality, only pretense. The collective dream is all that exists; meaningful individual action is impossible. As he is preparing to climb the Jungfrau, he hears a yodel which, he realizes, is a tune familiar to him from his home in Tennessee:

"It's me, Jimmy Larkin," the Swiss peasant went on. With these words, he removed the large, luxuriant mustache he was wearing.

"Sure enough," exclaimed Potts. "But what the devil are you doing here, Jimmy?"

"I'm local color; I'm atmosphere. I work for the company."

"Herding goats?"

"Oh, these goats are props, too; local color . . ."

". . . What is this company you're telling me about? Are you an actor?"

. . . Jimmy explained to the amazed Potts.

"Switzerland," he said, "is nothing but a fake, an amusement park owned by a very wealthy company. The whole show is put on for the tourist trade—lakes, forests, glaciers, yodlers, peasants, goats, milkmaids, mountains and the rest of it. It's all scenery. . . . It's like the opera." . . .

"The mountains, too, eh?" asked Potts. . . . "But how about the avalanches and crevasses?"

"All fake," said Jimmy airily. "If you tumble into a crevasse, you fall on soft snow, and there is a porter at the bottom of every one of them to brush your clothes and ask for your baggage."

"My," said Potts.

Even the possibility of tragic consequences stemming from Potts's engagement with real life is eliminated. There is no real life to which Potts can awaken—only a collective dream life in which dream feeds on dream, monstrously.

In another comic exploration of the dream world, "Tibetan Night," West deals with the collective mythmaking, during the Depression, of the wealthy classes. At a time when President Hoover was declaring that few emergency measures were needed to restore healthy economic conditions, when businessmen announced regularly that the Depression would soon be over or was already ended, it was clear that the economic wishing of the wealthy classes was as much a part of fantasy life as anything else. West never made the mistake, characteristic of the proletarian novelists, of regarding misery as confined to the working classes; he knew that poverty is spiritual—and that its effects are total. "Tibetan Night" is West's comic version of James Hilton's *Lost Horizon*. He plays imaginatively with the comedy of wealth-fulfillment thinking in the last Shangri-La of the capitalist classes. In all parts of the world but Kaskaz, Tibet, the proletarian revolution has been successful. Only here a group of Americans, refugees from the Red Terror, keep an isolated outpost of gentility. One former director of investment corporations (now "quite naked under his Prince Albert") declares: "I hope, Mr. Morand . . . that you will excuse our inability to entertain you properly. Soon, however, we will return to our Connecticut estates. . . ." They all live in a world of myth—in Tibet—in which their memories are their only future, as their wishes had been their only past.

How easily such wishing can lose its comic veneer and become what West was to call "the truly monstrous" is shown in a tale entitled "The Sun, the Lady, and the Gas Station." "This story is all of a piece," West begins, "yet that may be a hard thing to make you see." The pieces which make up the tale, all recalled by the narrator, are indeed widely disparate, related only by his similar emotional response to them, A visit to the "Streets of Paris" exhibit at the 1933 Century of Progress Fair in Chicago; a memory of building, in a vacant lot, a boat to play in as a youth; a ride along Hollywood's "Miracle Mile"; a Beverly Hills dinner party; and, finally, a story told there—these all, he sees, point to the deadly heart of delusion in modern life. In each case, the sun exposes the ghastly, rotten unreality and pretense of things. Even the real is only a mask of the corroded core of existence. At the fair, the "exhibit looked very badly in the bright sun, very cheap and phony, but then even the real Paris would have probably looked the same way." As for the boat, it is made from dreams and debris, and "looked really horrible. I learned then never to look at junk or machinery when the sun is shining. Don't even look at people." The Miracle Mile, in the exposing sun, "looked just like the main street of Asbury Park, New Jersey," except for its vivid banners. At the dinner, as the sun shines into a "glass-enclosed room," in its glare "those of us who were fat looked greasy and soiled, those of us who were thin looked rubbed and faded."

Finally, a guest tells a tale about "an old actress" who wants to sleep with a handsome gas-station attendant. To revive her faded beauty, she has her face built up: "Incisions were made under the skin and paraffin was poured under the parts to be built up. In this way the doctor made her a new nose and a new chin." She arranges a private meeting with the young man: "Well, the sun was very hot that day. While they were talking and drinking, the paraffin in the old lady's nose and chin began to melt. The gas-station man watched in amazement as her chin sagged and became long and pointed. When her nose slipped, it was too much for him . . . then he burst out laughing and he laughed and laughed."

III

That kind of uncontrollable, hysterical laugh in the face of terror, the misshapen visage of things, runs fitfully and uneasily beneath all these stories, whether their surface is comic or tragic. It is a laugh rising out of a horror, though not a revulsion; from an intellectual hatred mixed with deeply wounded emotions; from a kind of personal hysteria, but also from a clear vision of the hysteria in the contemporary mind. It runs through the letters addressed to Miss Lonelyhearts and the jokes (even the punning name) of Shrike, and it would recur in *The Day of the Locust* as Tod's imitation of a police-car siren. It is undoubtedly one of the evidences of West's Disease, but also one of the ways of treating it.

Fantasy life—led in the library or in Central Park, in equally phony Switzerlands or Tibets, or in Hollywood—the dream lives of all kinds and classes of people: this West took as his theme in these stories, as in "The Impostor" and "Western Union Boy," also written during 1930 to 1933. In a very clear sense, there are no characters in these stories, any more than *Pilgrim's Progress* has an individuated hero. The "characters" are types. Either they are named Joe, Potts of Pottsville, or Harry—names pointing to their typicality as mass men—or they are, frequently, not named at all: merely "a lady," "my agent," or—in West's best use of this device for suggesting archetypal anonymity—simply "Miss Lonelyhearts." And there are no "stories"; the narratives are parable-like occasions for revealing the meaninglessness of both characters and story, and the way that delusion has eaten away all semblance of the existence of either. In the thirties, when fantasy infested American life, West dealt in fiction with mass life on the deepest possible and most relevant level by concentrating on this phenomenon.

Other writers were setting out in search of the mass folk, the proletariat, or the American peasant (as the people in general were being named); and Americans were sorted, sifted, arranged, classified, and characterized in various ways. Sociologists, social psychologists, novelists, and investigators of many kinds sent back their reports. The "folk" were even encouraged to speak for themselves, and did so in such books as *These Are Our Lives, We Too Are the People, Youth Tell Their Story,* and *The People Talk.* People were talking as never before, and people talked endlessly about their talk. "Indeed the public world with us has become the private world, and the private world has become the public," one writer declared. When the public economic crisis seemed so overwhelming, as a historian of the New Deal has written, "private experience seemed self-indulgent compared to the demands of public life." Not only the Communists but also the government talked about masses. Not only statisticians but novelists gave the appearance of devoted but laborious scholarship in their books about people.

Disorders in the public world were so immediate and apparent, and remedies for them so obviously necessary, that the crisis of self and personality which now became a collective crisis threatened to be ignored altogether. West was one of the few writers who turned his attention from portraits of either the artist's personal crisis or the economic crisis to the exploration of the collective disasters of consciousness in the thirties. His short stories serve, for us, as reminders of how frequently and with what consistency and urgency of purpose he endeavored to do this. For West, they were useful trials of attitude and definition, "work in progress" which he did not need to complete. Not themselves entirely successful as fiction, they were the necessary bridges between *The Dream Life of Balso Snell* and *Miss Lonelyhearts.*

10 / *The Miss Lonelyhearts of Lonely Hearts*

> Now I possess . . . something else, called soul. I am told
> that the soul never dies, is always searching and searching.
> . . . Instead of succumbing to my homesickness, I have
> told myself that my home is everywhere, and instead of
> giving myself up to passive melancholy, I have chosen
> active despair. . . .
>
> —Vincent Van Gogh, quoted in Julius
> Meier-Graefe's *Vincent Van Gogh* (1928).
> Passage double-ruled by West in his copy

"Did I tell you that Miss L. is finished, and being typed?" West
wrote to William Carlos Williams in a letter of mid-December
1932, in which he also announced that he had broken decisively
with Moss and Kamin over *Contact* and that there would be no
fourth issue.

Although he had told a Brown classmate in late summer that he
despaired of ever being able to finish his novel, and that his father
and Morris Jarcho disapproved of his writing at all, still, working at
the Warford House between mid-October and late November, he
was free from the psychic pressure of the hotel and in a burst of
energy and artistic clarity completed the book.

Miss Lonelyhearts, he told Josephine Herbst, was really about
the people of the hotel and his personal relation to them, his feelings of sympathy and guilt. As manager he had to be merciless in
collecting rents from the deadbeats, yet he loathed his duty. His
was a conscience and consciousness haunted by its own sensibility.
Confronted by the plight of the individual caught in the commercial debacle, should he be passive in his acceptance of this fatality?

Or, if not, how and to what extent could he individually mitigate its effects?

In any event, in Bucks County such questions had had less immediate power over him and he was freed from the artistic paralysis which kept him ever revising—since it prevented him from finishing—his book. Now, in December 1932, the novel was ready for publication.

As the first move in a campaign to promote his book, West had signed a contract with an agent, Maxim Lieber, who also represented (at various times) Albert Halper, John Fante, Richard Wright, Robert M. Coates, Erskine Caldwell, John Cheever, Thomas Wolfe, Carson McCullers, Josephine Herbst, and Tess Slesinger—writers, chiefly, with liberal sympathies. Lieber himself had earlier published books at Brentano's, by Huysmans among others. He had a reputation for working extraordinarily hard for his clients and for selling stories even after their authors had lost all hope of a sale.

Now West was concerned about a publisher. During the summer of 1932, Angel Flores, then an instructor at Cornell and editor of the Dragon Press, wrote to West praising the sections of the novel appearing in *Contact* and *Contempo* and asking for the complete novel for one in a series of short books which he was issuing. He proposed to publish books by West, Williams, and Shapiro—and did eventually publish Shapiro's *The Water Wheel* —during 1933. West, however, was well aware that his book might have a chance for commercial success. He had been counting on Horace Liveright, Inc., for several reasons. Perelman had published two books there and through him West had become friends with Louis Kronenberger, who in 1932 was chief editorial adviser for the firm. Lillian Hellman had worked there several years earlier; and Isidore Schneider, the poet, was in charge of advertising.

Liveright had been a distinguished house—at that time the American publisher whose history was most closely and fruitfully intertwined with experimental writing—publisher of O'Neill, Dreiser, Pound, Cummings's *The Enormous Room* and Eliot's *The Waste Land,* Sherwood Anderson, Ben Hecht, Hart Crane, Hemingway's *In Our Time,* and Faulkner. But in recent years Liveright had attracted few new authors of stature. Horace Liveright himself had neatly juggled many marriages, theatrical enterprises, and stock speculation into personal insolvency. The internal, financial machinery of his firm was grinding slowly away. Arthur Pell, who had been treasurer, was rapidly becoming financial manager, until, exchanging cash for Liveright's stock, he finally owned the business and Liveright went off to Hollywood. Pell began to reduce costs. Still, revenues continued to decline. In 1931, the employees were asked to take cuts in salary, and Pell was inviting them to purchase stock in the company in order to shore up its lagging resources. West did not know much about this except for the gossip. But he did know that, on the very day he finished his novel, in late November 1932, Kronenberger was fired for reasons of economy. He had heard good reports about the judgment of Charles Pearce, an editor at Harcourt, Brace, and now was wondering if he might take a chance on the novel.

But Liveright was interested after all and in late January 1933 offered to publish the book in a first edition of 2,200 copies priced at $2. Production moved quickly. Even while the contracts were being drawn up—they were signed early in February—the book was being set in type. By the first week of March, West was rewriting in galleys, still eliminating lines and inserting words, always condensing, with an almost faultless skill in revision, and showing endless patience even in the last-minute hurry. Finally, on April 8, 1933, slightly over four years after West had first seen the Susan Chester letters, *Miss Lonelyhearts* was published.

As his letters to Beatrice Mathieu show, West was concerned over the reception of the book; even while his experience of mass life in the hotel provided the emotional source of the book's power, he yearned to escape from the hotel through a good sale. Although it was true that writers in the twenties and thirties often regarded popular success with suspicion—"success," Lionel Trilling says, "was not . . . thought to be naturally compatible with purity of intention"—West made an absolute distinction between his own purity and the public reception. Once the book was completed, he regarded it as subject, like any life, to the accidents of popularity or failure: neither would affect the book or his pride in it. But he decidedly preferred success to failure.

To some extent, he counted on success as part of his vision of a literary career. His dreams of the future danced freely. Since it was a short book, with good reviews *Miss Lonelyhearts* might sell well.

Moreover, a popular reception for his novel might give a sales boost to his stories. Perhaps there was a chance for a sale to the movies. With a well-received novel, he might be a successful candidate for a Guggenheim Fellowship or some other form of foundation support. A year away from hotel work, a year in the country— Josephine Herbst and John Herrmann had the perfect solution to the artist's economic dilemma, he thought—and he might produce another novel. He already had the idea for one.

With these considerations in mind, West had attempted to choose a publisher thoughtfully. Moreover, he helped to prepare for a good critical reception by arranging to have several carefully chosen friends write blurbs for the book's jacket. Edmund Wilson commented on the cosmopolitan character of the novel's humor: "It is not in the least like the work of even the best American humorous writers because Mr. West has a philosophic-poetic point of view which our humor usually lacks. . . . Though he has evidently been influenced by the irony of Dada, he strains less and goes deeper than Dada. Mr. West is, in short, an original comic poet; and he has made . . . a miniature comic epic." Dashiell Hammett spoke of its originality: "In his work there are no echoes of other men's books." Erskine Caldwell, on the other hand, pointed to its core of seriousness: "I can easily imagine that the bulk of its audience will applaud it for being a clever and amusing novel, and I believe it will have a large audience; but to me it is a tragic story." Josephine Herbst characterized it aptly as "concentrated reality," and pointed to its surreal and serious truths: "This story . . . is a sort of morality play in which characters stalk a little more conclusively than in life." West gathered such a varied abundance of praise that he even rejected the comment of William Carlos Williams: "A distressing book, relieved by some of the best writing of the day. Here is a city's violent distress caught livid upon the gates of God!" The other comments would suffice for the jacket. Any reviewer confronted by this varied phalanx of approval, West supposed, would at least have to take it into account if he would be critical.

II

An accurate judge of his own work, as his skill in revision proves, West was confident that he had written a good book. It is the tale of a newspaperman who casually takes on the job of giving advice but thus finds himself confronted by needs which he had, like his fellows, been able before to avoid facing. "Perhaps I can make you understand," this young man tells his fiancée. "Let's start from the beginning. A man is hired to give advice to the readers of a newspaper. The job is a circulation stunt and the whole staff considers it a joke. He welcomes the job, for it might lead to a gossip column, and anyway he's tired of being a leg man. He too considers the job a joke, but after several months at it the joke begins to escape him. He sees that the majority of the letters are profoundly humble pleas for moral and spiritual advice, that they are inarticulate expressions of genuine suffering. He also discovers that his correspondents take him seriously. For the first time in his life, he is forced to examine the values by which he lives. The examination shows him that he is the victim of the joke and not its perpetrator."

The novel (as Miss Lonelyhearts, though too simply, describes his own transformation) begins in comedy and ends in an exploration of the archetypes of suffering. Perhaps West's own phrase, "moral satire," best describes the character of his novel. But both the satire and the morality grow out of a comic vision. Not only does Miss Lonelyhearts play lightly and ironically with the obvious fact of his situation as a supposedly female columnist and spill forth several witty, joking replies to his correspondents and friends; his editor, Shrike, is also a master comedian and ironist, whose monologues, improvisations, and games are brilliantly witty. He is Miss Lonelyhearts's Buck Mulligan. Toward any kind of affirmative impulse on the one hand, or any effort at imagining escape from the pain of disillusion on the other, Shrike shows a wit so devastating that it is close to hysteria and implies, what Miss Lonelyhearts never sees, that Shrike himself is undergoing torments similar to his own, but has learned to conceal them (even from himself) in sallies of humor. As a result of their numbing of sensibility, Shrike and his followers, the hero does understand, are merely "machines for making jokes. . . . They, no matter what the motivating force, death, love, or god, made jokes." If he is to learn anything, the hero must learn how to go beyond jokes, as Shrike cannot. For Shrike's bitterness can neither deny human suffering nor relieve his own pain.

For both men, the central problem is that of value. How and what can one affirm? "Life *is* worth while," Miss Lonelyhearts writes in his first intended reply—saying in his italics all that we need to know about the unsteadiness of his beliefs. Asking for guidance, his correspondents really demand gospels, want him to be an evangel of value. Why is there evil in the world, Desperate asks. What are the principles of religion, Sick-of-it-all wants to know. What, above all, nearly all the letters ask, is the nature and use of love? What good is love? How far love may be perverted in this dead world—a world of doorknobs—all the letters show.

But the verbal wit with which Shrike has treated questions of meaning has robbed Miss Lonelyhearts of the power satisfactorily to state principles of value and to test these through the responses of others to them. Instead, all his quests are internalized, they are mock quests like that in *Balso Snell*, and to that extent are finally useless to his correspondents and even to himself. He realizes that "when he did speak, it would have to be in the form of a message," but his attempts to reconcile Fay and Peter Doyle sound clichéd and are either versions of carnal mysticism or highly rhetorical and symbolic talk, imitations of Shrike's talk. West's intentions, in the very structure and style of the novel, are anti-mimetic: West conceived of *Miss Lonelyhearts* as "a 'novel in the form of a comic strip.' The characters to be squares in which many things happen through one action. The speeches contained in the conventional balloons." Imitating a cartoon, he keeps altering normal sequence and proportions and isolates his characters in time, space, action, and language. West believed, as the French symbolists and surrealists did, that perfect words could rejuvenate man's spirit and imagination. But, like them, West knew that vague, overused language is destructive and unholy. None of the characters converse; they can only write letters or give orations. Somehow, Miss Lonelyhearts's meaning strives to transcend the limits of verbalization; he has to get around Shrike's words in order to express his affirmation. Yet Shrike, even in his similar-sounding name, is a mock Christ, the Jesus Shrike (but also shriek) which is all he really can have instead of God.

The novel is concerned, then, with the possibilities and the usefulness of religious consciousness in contemporary life. Just before the publication of *Balso Snell* in 1931, West told A. J. Liebling in an interview that he had already "ceased being the author" of this novel. He declared (doubtless, rather ironically) that "he personally has reverted to the mystical" in wanting now to write a "wholesome, clean, holy, slightly mystic and inane" book. He was convinced, he concluded, that "the next two thousand years belong to Dostoevsky's Christianity."

But two years later he produced a very different book from the one he proposed. For West was a sharp observer of the perversions of consciousness, and whatever his convictions or hopes, he was obliged to face the truth that not Christ but the Grand Inquisitor was resurrected in his time. He has Miss Lonelyhearts speak of his job as part of "the Christ business"; and certainly his column is part of a journalistic enterprise arranged on business principles. Accepting nineteenth-century success ethics, many Americans had made a business of Christ. The most striking popular expression of the alliance between religion and business had come in Bruce Barton's *The Man Nobody Knows,* a book portraying Christ as the first modern business and advertising man, "the founder of modern business." In this book, the leading seller of 1925 and 1926, Barton, himself an advertising man, declared that Christ's parables are brilliant examples of advertising, that he had known and used "every one of the principles of modern salesmanship," and that his great triumph was that he had "picked up twelve men from the bottom ranks of business and forged them into an organization. . . . Nowhere is there such a startling example of executive success as the way in which that organization was brought together."

West knew Barton's book, of course. But he would not have needed his example. In the thirties, the "Christ business" was everywhere. Had not Henry Ford announced his belief that "there is something sacred about big business. Anything which is economically right is morally right"? And would not Ruth McKenney quote another commercial leader as shrewdly telling a Toledo businessmen's meeting: "A man with Christ in his heart can outsmart all others"? Other books, all in very different ways, pointed to shifts in attitudes toward religion. A tract like Henry C. Link's *Return to Religion,* which answered the question, "How can religion make life more tolerable?" and made a tidy package of religion and psychiatry, was a best seller, as were Harry Emerson

Fosdick's *The Power to See It Through* and Emmett Fox's *Power Through Constructive Thinking*. In his earliest attempt at a column, Miss Lonelyhearts repeats their clichés: life is worthwhile, "for it is full of dreams . . . and faith," without asking what dreams and faith are for. Religion had become either a guide to business success or a consolation for missing it. "All will be fragrant and quiet in heaven,/Like the best real estate in Westchester," Kenneth Burke wrote, in summing up both attitudes.

Of course, there was opposition to this kind of happy acceptance but debasement of Christianity. H. L. Mencken's *Treatise on the Gods* (1930) attacked religions as the excrescence of human cowardice, and there is no doubt that in part Mencken's ironic sallies went into the shaping of Shrike's. But in the thirties the need for faiths and the sudden upsurge of religious evangelicism, growing out of a loss of material security, went into the making of the figure of Miss Lonelyhearts, who attempts to get around Shrike's cynical rationalism. With the dadaists or with Randolph Bourne, Shrike can declare that the ironic life is better than the religious life; but, like the increasingly powerful and numerous followers of Mary Baker Eddy, Frank Buchman, Evangeline Adams, or Aimee Semple McPherson—like members of the New World Water Cult, Vedanta, Baha'i, Rosicrucianism, Theosophy, and Yoga—Miss Lonelyhearts wishes to find what William James called an "altogether other dimension of existence." So, inevitably, irony and idealism go together in the novel, interwoven as inextricably as they had been earlier when Shrike and Miss Lonelyhearts were a single person. While Miss Lonelyhearts searches for viable religious ideals, religious cults on every level are satirized not only by Shrike but even by Miss Lonelyhearts himself: meditating on Father Zossima's sermon, dreaming of the abortive ritual lamb slaughter, psychoanalyzing himself ("I've got a Christ complex . . .").

Most of the faiths of the period, with women as their leaders, pointed conclusively to diminished male authority in spiritual matters, underscored by West when he made "Miss Lonelyhearts" the sole name of his male columnist—a name even he uses in reference to himself, so far has it become his true identity. "On seeing him for the first time, Shrike had smiled and said, 'The Susan Chesters, the Beatrice Fairfaxes, and the Miss Lonelyhearts are the priests of twentieth-century America.'" On the universal, Tiresias-like character of Miss Lonelyhearts, West based the structure of the book: he is balanced between two married couples, the Shrikes and the Doyles, inversions of each other; he must encounter now the male of one couple, now the female of the other, in episode after episode. If he himself must be a priest, he must also be a female columnist.

Miss Lonelyhearts can find only remnants of religious institutions—only the newspaper office, a "comfort station" in a park, and a speakeasy. But tabloid newspaper columnists like O. O. McIntyre, Dorothy Dix, and Dale Carnegie gave merely gossip, sentimental advice, and instruction. West's vivid mock presentation of the comfort station in terms of a church—with the toilets as altars and the booths as confessionals—suggests how low the Church can be reduced in modern life. The speakeasy is used repeatedly to suggest the final degradation of the Church. Here Miss Lonelyhearts goes for refreshment, here he has virtually the only "drinks" in the sterile land that he inhabits. It was a brilliant choice, for it was clear that the speakeasy had a mystic, initiatory glamour in the twenties and early thirties. At the entrance, bells were to be rung in a special way, and a face would suddenly appear as a panel slid away, behind an iron grill. (Miss Lonelyhearts "pressed a concealed button and a little round window opened in its center. A blood-shot eye appeared glowing like a ruby in an antique iron ring.") Introduction by someone who had been there before was usually required. Then the new patron's name was registered and he was issued a card, sometimes given occult distinction by a signature or a cabalistic sign on its back. "Once inside, a man was among kindred souls. The speakeasy was nothing like the bar we know today. It was more like a club. You could talk to the elbow bender alongside you quite easily because he had the same entree, the same special status that you had. He was 'one of the boys' in a closely knit group of insiders. . . ." This is, in West's broad joke, the place where the modern everyman is obliged to seek his spiritual refreshment.

Reminders of the religious impulse in modern form flit through the novel. The hero, son of a Baptist minister and inheritor of the temperament of the New England Puritan, has an "Old Testament look." In writing sermon-like letters to querying congregations, he is in the New Testament tradition of the epistler. Like Saul/Paul, he is on a road that will lead either to his transfiguration or to his destruction. But he also appears as a modern version of Christ. Crossing a park, he "walked into the shadow of a lamp-post that lay on the path like a spear. It pierced him like a spear." Clearly he is, as he later tells himself, "capable of dreaming the Christ dream." And near the end of the novel, he sees himself as completely identified with God: "His heart was the one heart, the heart of God. And his brain was likewise God's." However, as a priest of Christ (the lamb) he has performed a ritual sacrifice badly, even mocking the Holy Family by singing an obscene version of "Mary had a little lamb." His room, containing only "a bed, a table, and two chairs," is monastic as well as characteristically urban. "Eating only crackers, drinking water, and smoking cigarettes," he begins an anchoritic retreat in his room. He smiles at Shrike "as the saints are supposed to smile at those about to martyr them." His final disaster comes when he succumbs to the third temptation offered to Christ, desiring to win the hearts of the masses by virtue of a miracle for their sakes. West could have drawn this incident, of course, from the Bible, but it is even more likely that it derives directly from the Grand Inquisitor chapter of *The Brothers Karamazov*, a novel which Miss Lonelyhearts reads. There are, certainly, several Dostoevskian overtones running through the book. Above all, Shrike is a modern, less grand Inquisitor of Miss Lonelyhearts's Saviour.

In short, West compressed into the person of Miss Lonelyhearts suggestions of several roles and figures of religious tradition. In fifteen chapters, the first of which is a prologue, he made a parallel, as Robert M. Coates has suggested, "to the symbolism of the four-teen Stations of the Cross, for the progression does become a kind of modern Calvary." But, as it ironically turns out, West writes, "his prayer was one Shrike taught him and his voice was that of a conductor calling stations."

Miss Lonelyhearts's inane and ultimately insane vision consists in a belief that he can still be the Christ for the yearnings once contained by the Church and expressed in religious terms, which now have been dispersed among movies, books, and such other forms of escape as those in "The Adventurer" and "Mr. Potts of Pottstown." All "these things," he understands, "were part of the business of dreams. He had learned not to laugh at the advertisements offering to teach writing, cartooning, engineering, to add inches to the biceps or to develop the bust." "He saw a man who appeared to be on the verge of death stagger into a movie theater that was showing a picture called *Blonde Beauty*. He saw a ragged woman with an enormous goiter pick a love story magazine out of a garbage can and seem very excited by her find." The yearnings in modern life to return Tolstoy-like to the soil or to escape, like Gauguin, to the South Seas; to pursue other forms of pleasure, like Huysmans's Des Esseintes, including sexual gratification; to be an artist or live a life devoted to Beauty; or to believe in a God—all these yearnings, satirized by Shrike, Miss Lonelyhearts now sees, are important not so much for their particular content as for the strivings of the human spirit which lie behind them. To these he will be the Messiah, he believes; he dreams that the crowd is fashioning his name out of the debris of their dreams—from the kinds of mementos of pleasure which Joe Rucker's father collected in barrels—"faded photographs, soiled fans, timetables, playing cards, broken toys, imitation jewelry—junk that memory had made precious." He will be the Saviour to the pawnshop of the spirit.

Using his sense of the violence and collective dreaming at the heart of mass life, about which he wrote in his stories, West here is able to give the suffering of his hero real tragic stature; he convinces us that Miss Lonelyhearts has stumbled upon a vivid awareness of the permutations and transformations of the religious consciousness in the twentieth century. Aware of Eliot—and producing a cameo image of *The Waste Land* in the sterile little park— West gives a more elaborate sense than Eliot could in 1922 of the possibilities for the redemption, by love, of sterile modern civilization. (Interestingly, he read Eliot's *For Lancelot Andrewes* of 1928 while he was working on *Miss Lonelyhearts*.) Eliot would balance *The Waste Land* with another poem, *Ash Wednesday* (1930); West kept the balance in this one book.

But, of course, the possibilities raised in *Miss Lonelyhearts* only increase the intensity of West's moral satire on their hopelessness. The hero unmasks fictions only to find that people cannot live without them, and write to Miss Lonelyhearts in order to keep faith in illusions or to be given greater ones. Insane (but compelling) illusions constitute the only sanity. The hero himself is at last appealing because he has committed himself to the greatest of illusions—personal redemption of the mass. Yet, though his emotional needs drive him to the Christ dream, his intellect drives him from it. He is impaled—by the butcher-bird, Shrike—on the thorns of this dilemma. In the series of episodes, he moves, helplessly, from each compulsion to its opposite. Indeed, West deliberately structured his book not only on the model of the popular cartoon strip, as he professed, but, more seriously, upon the serial form then widely employed in experimental poetry by Eliot, Conrad Aiken, Ezra Pound, Wallace Stevens, and Hart Crane. West's one long poem, "Burn the Cities," is in the series form. From Pound, he took the conception of modern identity as a broken bundle of mirrors and in his fiction fitted it to the multifaceted series form. His own imagination was essentially sequential, and all his novels are built loosely on the same serial structure.

West made an art form of popular myth by putting to serious fictive use the lessons of the hitherto unabsorbed materials of his stories; he found literary ways of presenting the secret life of the crowds who "moved through the streets with dreamlike violence"; and, thereby, he pushed close to the archetypal experiences (as Jung put it) of "modern man in search of a soul." He would no longer need to cry with Joyce, "Old father, old artificer, stand me now and ever in good stead"—or even to satirize this invocation as he had done in *Balso*. For he was writing directly out of the "uncreated conscience" of Americans; and while he would need extraordinary art to turn this into fiction—as his trial versions in *Contact* and *Contempo* show—his vision of the archetypal power of religious yearning was all the father to fiction he would require.

W. B. Yeats has asserted that "every writer . . . who has belonged to the great tradition has had his dream of an impossibly noble life, and the greater he is the more does it seem to plunge him into some beautiful or bitter reverie." West brooded over the degradation of the collective dream; his book combines his dreams of a noble life and his bitterness over its betrayal. He had moved beyond the Dada satire and rebelliousness of *Balso Snell* to moral indignation. The wit and satire of Sinclair Lewis and George S. Kaufman, the anger of James T. Farrell and Dos Passos, the pity and sympathy of Dreiser and O'Neill, the stoicism of Hemingway —compared to these, West's work shows a power of beauty and bitterness which places him in Yeats's "great tradition." His true peers were writers like Sherwood Anderson, Fitzgerald, Eliot, Faulkner, and Williams.

The archetypes were not necessarily drawn from the original Susan Chester letters, although upon the publication of the book some critics complained that West, in the tradition of *The People Talk*, should have simply reprinted these "real" letters, and let the surrounding fiction go. Yet the original letters are much revised: he made them seem more "real" through the power of his fiction. From the original letters West derived two things: first, a suggestion for fiction written in a form matching the vision he had achieved in his stories; second, the realization that the journalistic convention of using a representative signature for the letters—concealing but, by its choice, revealing—could symbolize the anonymous, archetypal needs out of which they were written. West was deeply affected when he first read the letters; later, reading them aloud to the Brounoff circle, he betrayed considerable—to his friends, surprising—emotion in his voice and manner. He had obviously been, as one of his audience on that occasion says, "terribly . . . hurt by them." But he did not surrender to them; from them he made a novel that included this emotion but also the hard calculations of fictive technique. The actual letters addressed to Susan Chester were signed with names like "Daily reader," "Misery," "Down-hearted wife" and "Broad Shoulders"—all names suggesting how people had themselves, within the convention, named their own typicality. Some of these names West used in the book, of course. More important was his realization that they represented the anonymous, hopeless and yearning cry of pain raised up to an equally anonymous listener—the genuine, modern, collective prayers offered to a distant God. In an acknowledged source for *Miss Lonelyhearts*, *The Varieties of Religious Experience*, William James wrote: "Here is the real core of the religious problem: Help! Help! No prophet can claim to bring a final message unless he says things that will have a sound of reality in the ears of victims such as these." West expanded on this principle: his letters cry, piteously, "Help! Help!"—while Shrike cries "Jug! Jug!", bitterly mocking them. Out of the tension between Shrike's mock prayers and the apparently real letters arise the chief ironies of the novel.

Pressed between these two, Miss Lonelyhearts must "say things" that will "have a sound of reality" to the victims—both his correspondents and Shrike himself.

The skill with which West heightened the effect of reality in the original letters is demonstrated by his alterations in them, his deliberate cutting of all stylistic pretenses in order clearly and boldly to stress the pain of the writer, and his heightening of the shy, genteel attempts to conceal the pain evident just beneath a reasoned surface. Compare the following passages. The original letter reads: "I am a girl, sixteen. I am sometimes very unhappy due to the fact that I have a weak knee and am obliged to walk with a cane. Of course, I am not greatly disabled, but walk with a slight limp. I have hopes of becoming gradually improved, but none of becoming completely cured. . . . I have several acquaintances among boys but no special boyfriend. I know that I am young to think of this, but all of my girlfriends have boys who like them a little better than the others. . . . Do you think my lack of a special boyfriend is because of my physical disability?" West used this as the basis of the first letter Miss Lonelyhearts reads: "I am sixteen years old now and I don't know what to do and would appreciate it if you could tell me what to do. When I was a little girl it was not so bad because I got used to the kids on the block making fun of me, but now I would like to have boyfriends like the other girls and go out on Saturday nites, but no boy will take me because I was born without a nose—although I am a good dancer and have a nice shape and my father buys me pretty clothes." The repetitions, the calculated intensification of pain, and the pitiable, conscious reiterations of clichéd phrase and pattern all hint at a kind of torment far deeper and more significant than that suggested by the language of the original letter. West expands a question and comment in the original—"Will any man want me, as I am? I . . . can scarcely believe that life would be so cruel to me"—into questions concerning the nature of, and justification for, pain and evil in the universe. What was a sad letter, West, using every device of the novelist, transforms into a tragic one. He invented for the letters as well as for the rest of the novel a literary manner through which he could express collective torment.

West, in this sense, attempted himself to be the true Messiah of the lonely hearts by giving voice to the pain of alienation. West's personal melancholy, his almost irresolvable solitude, was deeply affiliated and responsive to the loneliness of the crowd.

Personally, he looked upon himself as a kind of Messiah, Beatrice Mathieu says. He regarded the publication of *Miss Lonelyhearts* as useful to people. By stripping the original letters of their surface, he explored the style of mass dreaming, and in his own prose he practiced a similar rich and full bareness of style. He was creating essential, typical reality. Not surprisingly, therefore, late in April, less than a month after the book's publication, West answered a phone call and heard a voice say: "This is Mrs.————, and I'm suing you for using a letter in your book which I wrote to a woman who runs an advice-to-the-lovelorn column in a Trenton, N.J., paper." She hung up, leaving West bewildered. Then he called his publisher and discovered that another woman had threatened to institute an action based on the same letter, which, she said, she had written to a New York newspaper. There were no suits, of course, but these incidents show how close West had struck to the general pain.

Another response to West's book points up the extent to which he had hit upon a subject essential to the imagination of the thirties. Loneliness and personal alienation, he showed, were as pervasive in that era as economic disaster. Moreover, in the person of the lonely-hearts columnist he had found the perfect symbol whereby to express this. Shortly after the appearance of *Miss Lonelyhearts*, Irving Berlin and Moss Hart put together a revue, *As Thousands Cheer*, which opened at the Music Box Theatre on September 30, 1933. West and his book were known to them through the Perelmans, Beatrice Mathieu, and other acquaintances they all had in common. For the sixth scene of the first act, Hart wrote a "Lonely Heart Column" sketch, and Berlin wrote lyrics and music for a ballad entitled "Lonely Heart," which became one of the hits of the show.

As Thousands Cheer was deliberately meant to mirror and comment on the time, 1933. It was staged in front of newspaper headlines flashed on a screen. Berlin and Hart's "Lonely Heart Column" was accompanied by other sketches, such as "Franklin D. Roosevelt Inaugurated Tomorrow," "Joan Crawford to Divorce

Douglas Fairbanks, Jr.," "Unknown Negro Lynched by Frenzied Mob," and "Gandhi Goes on New Hunger Strike" (in which Gandhi meets Aimee Semple MacPherson). No less than these contemporary figures, West's Miss Lonelyhearts was part of the daily news, integral to the imagination of the time. Hart and Berlin wrote the news report on the suffering of the lonely crowd; West penetrated to its archetype.

West could write a novel out of his own experience of suffering: going beyond satire, scorn, or rhetoric, he typified not merely the women who believed his letters to have been theirs, but, more generally, the representative experience of the thirties. Unlike West, of course, Miss Lonelyhearts fails. For while he can make some progress toward expressing his new sense of mass pain by clasping hands with Peter Doyle, and while he too runs at last "to succor them with love," he is never able to give expression to his insight in language during an age when language seemed altogether to have lost its power for truth-telling. Miss Lonelyhearts had looked, like Ahab, into the blank face of nature for an object of hatred or desire. "But the gray sky looked as if it had been rubbed with a soiled eraser. It held no angels, flaming crosses, olive-bearing doves, wheels within wheels. Only a newspaper struggled in the air like a kite with a broken spine." The gun with which Peter Doyle kills him is fittingly wrapped in a newspaper; for the newspaper column which pushes Miss Lonelyhearts toward his vision ultimately withholds it, since he cannot get around its false language and can speak only its appalling banalities.

Many critics have pointed to the passage in which Miss Lonelyhearts describes to Betty the seriousness of his task as an apt summary of the novel. But the very simplicity with which he can describe his mission is a sign of the too simple way in which he regards it. Far from a summary of his dilemma, this passage points directly to his confusion—it is another indication of the simplifying lie of language. Even at his clearest, he cannot give his spiritual condition adequate expression. Indeed, his "religious experience" precisely turns religious tradition inside out. Christ he symbolizes as a "bright fly," and the "black world of things as a fish," which "suddenly rose to the bright bait on the wall. It rose with a splash of music and he saw its shining silver belly." But the fish traditionally symbolizes Christ, and the fly, man (the profane flies clustering around the bloody lamb). Miss Lonelyhearts's perception of himself, of tradition, and of reality is totally disorganized. He has never understood what it would mean to be a Messiah. Like Betty, he wants order rather than transcendence: he is a Betty without knowing it. Thus, he conceives of himself at last as a rock. But he is no Peter, only a conglomerate of confusions, yearnings, and self-delusion. The rock is West's brilliantly graphic symbol for the numbing of sensibility, the modern, psychological version of despair. Unlike Eliot's, West's "peace which passeth understanding" is madness.

The experiences of Miss Lonelyhearts thus remain a kind of "psychological case," part of the modern myth, as West saw it. As an aspect of the novel's structure, he psychologically dramatized the helpless confusion of Miss Lonelyhearts, who unconsciously associates the body (which is ill, diseased, and troubled), or objects related to the body, with ideals, religion, and spiritual states; from the beginning, he holds both fleshless and violently sensuous images of Christ, for instance. Moreover, he thus identifies cruelty, a physical sensation, with pity, a spiritual attitude, and oscillates between pity and cruelty. Apparently, West had been struck by Freud's analysis in the first chapter of *Civilization and Its Discontents* (1930), and designed Miss Lonelyhearts as a character fixated at the oral level of development, unable fully to distinguish between flesh and spirit. Oral imagery—of food, the mouth, the breast, and so on—predominates in the book. The masochistic fantasies of Miss Lonelyhearts, resulting from this confusion, thus seem to be defenses against deep-seated sadistic impulses. These are the lines along which a full-scale analysis of Miss Lonelyhearts would proceed. West himself did not go so far in the psychological analysis of his own book—though he was certainly aware of the outlines of Miss Lonelyhearts's "case." West, indeed, explicitly denied that the novelist should construct a web of psychological motivation for his characters; psychology merely provided one more storehouse of character and fable. "Psychology has nothing to do with reality, nor should it be used as motivation," he insisted. Freud's analysis simply gave him a clinical background which could be made metaphorical.

West explained the relation between the novelist and the psychologist by reflecting on his intentions in *Miss Lonelyhearts:* "The novelist is no longer a psychologist. Psychology can become something much more important. The great body of case histories can be used the way the ancient writers used their myths. Freud is your Bulfinch; you cannot learn from him. With this idea in mind, Miss Lonelyhearts became the portrait of a priest of our time who has a religious experience. His case is classical and is built on all the cases in James' *Varieties of Religious Experience* and Starbuck's *Psychology and Religion.*" Unable to give expression to his vision, Miss Lonelyhearts is himself an instance of the tragedy which he has recognized. Although he speaks of himself as a rock, it was hardly one upon which a new Church might be founded. West recognized his indebtedness to the psychoanalysts for instances of this experience. "The psychology is theirs, not mine," he says. But in his fiction he could give their psychology power and relevance— his novel could itself be a kind of religious experience. And so, decisively, he adds: "The imagery is mine. . . . I was serious, therefore I could not be obscene. I was honest, therefore I could not be sordid. A novelist can afford to be anything but dull."

III

The reviewers agreed that West had not been dull: even those few who criticized the book responded to its vividness. But, in the important reviews, there was little negative criticism. "It is a brilliantly witty and ironic picture of Dostoyevsky's 'Poor People' transferred to the chaos of New York in the present century," John Preston wrote. "It is," another reviewer concluded, ". . . one of the most profound, intense novels an American has produced about America." Basil Davenport added: "It is brilliantly executed, so that one is constantly forced to admire the technique of its torture of one's nerves. . . ." "Chapter after brilliantly written chapter," the reviewer for the *Herald Tribune* declared, "moving like a rocket in mid-flight, neither falls nor fails." Robert M. Coates, in *The New Yorker,* spoke of West's style as "a prose that is like glass for transparency and that is lit by the most fantastic and colorful imagination." (Soon after this, West met Coates in the apartment of Leane Zugsmith, then working at Liveright's, and formed a lasting friendship with him.) The critic for *The Saturday Review*, speaking of West's humor, called the book "a comedy with tragic implications." And the anonymous reviewer for *The New York Times*, after unabated praise, announced his conviction that " 'Miss Lonelyhearts' stands to be one of the hits of the year, to win both popular and critical approval."

Congratulations from friends began to come in. The poet Bob Brown told him it was "a breathless book." "I'm glad to see your book getting such good notice right off the bat. It's damn fine," Caldwell wrote; and Frank O. Hough, himself on the way to becoming a popular historical novelist, wrote admiringly: "If I could turn out a piece of sustained writing comparable to what you've done, I'd be willing to take it on the chin almost indefinitely." West would indeed soon have to learn the difficult art of taking it on the chin, but for now praise alone was coming from all quarters, and success seemed certain.

For a moment it seemed that all of West's hopes for the book were going to be realized. However, contrary proceedings were underway at Liveright. Arthur Pell, who had been firing one employee after another, including staff members who had purchased shares in the company to the limit of their capacity, suddenly instituted bankruptcy proceedings as a legal technicality to clear away his debts, while he arranged to buy back, at a low rate, rights to the most profitable assets of the firm, like Dreiser's novels and the "Black and Gold Library," and later to reestablish it as "Liveright Publishing Company." Unlike Miss Lonelyhearts, Arthur Pell did not ask: What would Christ do? His was not a financial manipulation as astounding as many investigated by the Pecora Committee, but its effect upon West's book was crushing.

On April 29, M. K. Abernethy, the editor of *Contempo*, wrote to West: "and listen Pep, IF LIVERIGHT OWES YOU ANY MONEY GET IT WHILE THE GETTING IS POSSIBLE." But the blow had already fallen. Just as the favorable reviews began to come in, the printer of *Miss Lonelyhearts*, one of Liveright's creditors, seized 2,000 copies of the first edition of 2,200 and refused to release them until he had been paid. Thus, while demand for the book increased under the pressure of the favorable reviews, no copies were available to bookstores.* Eliot's famous description of April, though by then already a cliché, was indeed appropriate for West.

Moreover, the publication of West's novel and the contrived failure of Liveright, Inc., coincided with the period of the greatest financial cataclysm in the history of America. Only a month before publication, at 4:20 on the morning of March 4, Governor Franklin Roosevelt had declared a limited, two-day moratorium on banking in New York. As he rode to his Presidential inauguration that day, "the huge mechanism of American finance had almost ceased to function. In forty-seven of the forty-eight states, banks were either closed completely or, with few exceptions, were doing business under severe restraints. . . ." Soon after taking office, he declared a national "bank holiday." Roosevelt began his inaugural address with the words: "This is a day of national consecration," and bringing his address to a close he invoked divine aid: "In this dedication of a nation we humbly ask the blessings of God."

West's hero had also sought personal and collective "consecration," "dedication," and "the blessings of God"—and in this sense, *Miss Lonelyhearts* as directly reflected the yearning of the early thirties as did Roosevelt's speech. But only a few copies of the book had reached the stores—and even these found few buyers. The tight-money situation had not yet abated. After four years of preparation, *Miss Lonelyhearts* appeared just as the Depression reached its lowest point. Fifteen million persons were unemployed and six million were on state or municipal relief rolls. Schools were closed by the thousands, construction ceased altogether, and apple peddlers, the symbol of the Depression, lined the streets of the lost Eden.

West found all this, he later told Leonard Fields, "brutal and heartbreaking." He had believed, momentarily, that he would "be able to live in peace . . . on a farm and write his next novel with the profits from this. Instead, he was still broke." In the spring of 1933, Fields, a reader for Universal Pictures, had read West's novel

* In early May, prompted by the tragedy of the publication of West's novel, the Authors League of America rewrote its model contract to include a clause by which "all rights of the contract revert to the author in case of bankruptcy, receivership, assignment for the benefit of creditors or liquidation for any cause of the publishers." But this was too late for *Miss Lonelyhearts*.

in New York and recommended it to the studio. Convinced that the novel could be turned into a movie, he even wrote a trial outline which made it the story of how the letters affected a newspaperman's personal life. Fields won approval for the purchase, but he approached Liveright when its affairs were chaotic. At the same time, four other story departments—those of Twentieth Century, Fox, M.G.M., and Paramount—were recommending purchase of options on the book, and James Geller of the William Morris Agency was working hard to sell it. But the state of the publication and subsidiary rights was hopelessly confused.

West, with a potentially popular book in print but not in the stores, with movie rights for sale but unsellable, toiled on at the hotel.

He worked desperately, of course, to free the copies held by the printer. Legally, the copyright and the copies were both controlled by the trustee in bankruptcy, as assets of the estate-in-bankruptcy. West's cousin, Sidney Jarcho, a lawyer, went to work early in May to separate the book from the estate so that the film rights could be sold and the book taken over by one of the several publishers who were, following the favorable reviews, anxious to have it. With the help of Eugene O'Neill's lawyer and Arthur Garfield Hays, Jarcho finally persuaded the trustees to release the publication and subsidiary rights and assign the copyright to West for the "consideration of one dollar lawful money." With no little sense of bitter irony concerning the legal writhings of the capitalist system in 1933, West gave Sidney Jarcho, as a token of thanks, a two-volume edition of Trotsky's *History of the Russian Revolution*.

Almost immediately, on May 26, West signed a new contract with Harcourt, Brace, Inc., providing for a "royalty of 12½ percent on the regular edition and an additional 2½ percent on all copies of the regular edition after 2,000 copies." By June 5, 1933, Harcourt had purchased Liveright's electrotype plates to produce the novel under their own imprint. By this time, two months had elapsed since publication. It was too long. The sales of *Miss Lonelyhearts* trickled along until the Outlet Publishing Company—under the imprint of Greenberg: Publisher—put the copies on hand in its "popular copyright series" and sold them out at 75 cents. Of course, West received a reduced royalty for these copies, as is customary when a book is remaindered.

Persons, events, and history in general had all conspired against the sales and success of *Miss Lonelyhearts*. With good reason, West could have written letters to the Miss Lonelyhearts of authors, signing himself, "Betrayed." But his novel had said enough of betrayal, and he would need to say no more. Whatever else around him dissolved, his novel remained.

11 / *Return to the Soil*

"You are fed up with the city and its teeming millions. The ways and means of men, as getting and lending and spending, you lay waste your inner world, are too much with you. The bus takes too long, while the subway is always crowded. So what do you do? So you buy a farm and walk behind your horse's moist behind, no collar or tie, plowing your broad swift acres. . . . You plant, not dragon's teeth, but beans and greens. . . ."

—Shrike, in *Miss Lonelyhearts* (1933)

The two characters in *Miss Lonelyhearts* who had given him the greatest difficulty, West told a friend, were Miss Lonelyhearts himself and Betty, his fiancée. Betty serves as a dramatic counterbalance to Shrike; where he satirizes, she proposes a simple life as an escape for Miss Lonelyhearts. Betty tells him long stories about life on a farm, conceiving of his moral illness as simply an urban malaise and believing "that if his body got well, everything would be well." She has, as Miss Lonelyhearts realizes from the first, the "power to limit experience" and thus to give it apparent order. Still, he believes too that "his confusion was significant, while her order was not": the moral perplexities through which he goes, he believes, might lead to transcendence of both the perplexities and ordinary schemes of order. Nonetheless, he agrees to vacation with her in the country and test the curative power of nature.

The farm in Connecticut where Betty has grown up represents, of course, the simpler childhood world and the kind of childlike order which Miss Lonelyhearts had himself imagined as the universal dancing of grave children, an image of the garden of Eden, not only ordered but innocent. Betty proposes that they camp together in this house—to reenter the childhood of Eden.

At first, indeed, nature seems to be pure and ordered, "bright with gladness," as Darwin put it. The "pale new leaves, shaped and colored like candle flames, were beautiful and . . . the air smelt clean and alive." But, like Darwin, West unmasks the innocent appearance of nature to reveal its terror. He had experienced this terror himself. When he was twelve or thirteen, in Colchester, Connecticut, he and his cousins had followed out their bizarre interests in deciding to make a ritual sacrifice of a goat—a plan they gave up only because no one would cut the animal's throat. This incident stayed with him as a reminder of pastoral terror and, altering the goat to a lamb, he adapted it to *Miss Lonelyhearts*. Almost immediately he begins to stress in his images the extent to which his Adam and Eve have been expelled from the Garden. They do not have the key to the house and must enter by force. Inside, the furniture is musty with wood rot. Although they observe a pastoral scene of tranquillity by the pond, there they see, too, the Darwinian struggle for existence, nature "red in tooth and claw." A heron hunts frogs, and their presence frightens away two deer and a fawn. Later, although they do not make love after Betty confesses that she is a virgin, in self-mockery they do eat an apple.

The next morning, Miss Lonelyhearts goes to the lasciviously named "Aw-Kum-On" garage, where the attendant blames the disappearance of deer on "the yids." Now Miss Lonelyhearts sees clearly that the nature which had seemed eternally ordered and permanently pure is only in a cycle of perpetual decay. "Although spring was well advanced, in the deep shade there was nothing but death—rotted leaves, grey and white fungi, and over everything a funereal hush." Even the new leaves droop in the hot sun "like an army of little metal shields," and a thrush makes an obscene sound, "like that of a flute choked with saliva." At the last, when Betty and he do make love, the ground beneath them smells of "sweat, soap and crushed grass." The country has failed as an escape. There is no Eden to go home to, and Miss Lonelyhearts returns to the city; to Christ, the new crucified Adam; and to the letters and his correspondents. Shrike was right: the soil was no answer, and he feels "like a faker and a fool" in attempting to escape to it.

West had anticipated the ultimate failure of the pastoral for his hero in the elaborate pun of the second chapter's title, "Miss Lonelyhearts and the Dead Pan." His hero's world is a comic-grotesque, vaudeville one; Shrike's wit, which defeats Miss Lonelyhearts's capacity for assertion, is classically deadpan. The god of fecund nature, Pan, is dead: the world (the Greek *Pan* means "all things") is sterile. Relying on the myth* that Pan died simultaneously with the rending of the veil at the crucifixion of Christ, West associates Miss Lonelyhearts's futile attempt to redeem the dead spiritual world with the similar failure of the natural world to rejuvenate him. For West, this myth had personal associations. He and his cousins had been interested in Schiller's works. Early, West knew Schiller's poem "Götter Griechenlands." Later West's course at Brown in Victorian poetry reminded him of this poem, since Elizabeth Barrett Browning had been inspired by Schiller to write a lyric whose very title West punned upon: "The Dead Pan." Mrs. Browning detailed the myth in stanza XXVII:

> 'Twas the hour when One in Sion
> Hung for love's sake on a cross;
> When His brow was chill with dying,
> And His soul was faint with loss;
> When His priestly blood dropped downward,
> And His kingly eyes looked throneward—
> Then, Pan was dead.

In her conclusion, she advised poets to "Look up Godward; speak the truth in / Worthy song from earnest soul!" For her, Pan's death was richly compensated for by the saving powers then initiated by Christ. But West, dramatically, took the myth literally: both Pan and Christ were dead possibilities for Shrike's world. Neither can Miss Lonelyhearts be a Christ nor can nature restore. In this light, Miss Lonelyhearts's final meeting with Betty, when he sardonically pretends to accept nature (they have strawberry sodas and plan to have children and "farms in Connecticut") as well as myth (they decide to have "a love bed, an ornate double bed with cupids, nymphs and Pans"), reveals in all its horror the empty tragedy to which he has given himself.

Nature is not simply sterile—the disorder so evident in the rest of the world is a principle of nature. "Man has a tropism for

---

* This well-known tradition is mentioned, for instance, in a treatise by Plutarch, *De Oraculorum Defectu*, according to which, at the hour of the Saviour's agony, a cry of "Great Pan is dead!" swept across the waves in the hearing of certain mariners—and the oracles ceased.

order," West writes, but "the physical world has a tropism for disorder, entropy." It is not simply that Miss Lonelyhearts cannot
find relief in the country: that ease itself is delusive; Betty is an Eve
whose persuasions would lead him into another form of pretense.
Whatever principles of value he works out must come in terms of
his relation to man—who desires order—in imitation of Christ, not
of nature. West took this theme directly from William James's
Varieties of Religious Experience. "There are," James writes,
"people for whom evil means only a maladjustment with *things*, a
wrong correspondence of one's life with the environment. Such
evil as this is curable, on principle at least, upon the natural plane,
for merely by modifying either the self or the things, or both at
once, the two terms may be made to fit, and all go merry as a
marriage bell again." Miss Lonelyhearts's rejection of Betty and the
"natural plane" which she represents hints at his continuing efforts
to know truth; for, as James concludes, "healthy-mindedness" like
Betty's fails as a philosophical doctrine, "because the evil facts
which it refuses positively to account for are a genuine portion of
reality, and they may after all be the best key to life's significance." For Miss Lonelyhearts, things cannot go merry as a marriage bell; he must reject Betty and nature, and go back to suffering
and the city. Betty has the smiling face of nature; but in the girl
born without a nose the mask is stripped off: that horror is nature
itself.

II

West's social personality, however, was never so unyielding as the
personality which drove his fiction. In life, he was ever willing to
suspend the disbelief of his novels; life was West's fiction, an illusion—his tough reality was in his books. He had spent the summer of 1931 writing in the Adirondacks and during the following
year had driven to Connecticut to look at a house for sale—the trip
after which Miss Lonelyhearts's trip to the country with Betty was
modeled. Moreover, he had finished *Miss Lonelyhearts* in the
country, where his childhood feelings of summer release allowed
him for a moment to believe in the power, for literary creativity, of
nature; contrasting it to his hotel work made it seem all the more
attractive.

Among the Bucks County houses for sale in the neighborhood of

Josephine Herbst was one that Mike Gold had purchased only a few years earlier with his profits from *Jews without Money* (1930). Gold sent out a mimeographed description of his farm, a copy of which came into West's hands. "The farm consists of 83 acres of tillable farm land, twelve being in excellent timber," Gold began a rosy description of the property. "The soil is rich Southern hillside land. There are fruit, nut, and persimmon trees, berry bushes, and a large garden. A creek flows through the meadow in front of the house, and several natural springs furnish a constant supply of fresh, clear, pure water. . . . There is a large dwelling house, five out-buildings, three studios and a large stone barn. . . . It is two miles from Frenchtown, New Jersey, where there are chain stores and shopping at cheaper than city prices. Erwinna is an old canal town on the Lehigh Canal, one mile from the farm. The Delaware River is one mile and a quarter away. There is fine swimming, canoeing, and fishing on these waters. . . . This is fine, hilly country, inhabited by old Pennsylvania Dutch farmers and a colony of well-known New York writers and artists. The farm is a mile away from the State Game Preserve and the hills are full of deer, pheasants, quail and other game." For all this, the property was priced at a modest $6,000. No wonder that, shortly after West returned to New York with his book completed, he was discussing with Josephine Herbst the feasibility of buying the farm.

Unlike Miss Lonelyhearts, West could believe partly in the curative powers of nature—at least he could convince himself that he did. On December 19, 1932, as co-owner with the Perelmans, he purchased the farm from Gold with a down payment of $500, and set out to improve it with paint, hardware, tools, and furniture liberated from the Sutton.

At the same time that *Miss Lonelyhearts* was appearing, West was having the farm refurbished, a septic tank installed, and other improvements made. But he would not often live there. When Liveright's bankruptcy ruined any chance for a popular success, West found himself still at the hotel, with the little money he had saved invested in a Pennsylvania property seventy-five miles away, and no prospects of settling on it. As the troubles in Eden began to mount, West would be signing his address "8-Ball, Ottsville, Pennsylvania."

It appeared that West would again have to be content with literary prestige. All through the spring he awaited the issue of *Contempo* devoted to a critical symposium on *Miss Lonelyhearts*. Appearing late in July, this issue included essays by Angel Flores, S. J. Perelman, Josephine Herbst, Bob Brown, and William Carlos Williams. Brown, recommending the book to young writers as a kind of manual of the art of fiction, praises it heartily as "a lesson in expert typewriter-poking, and cheap . . . at only two bucks the complete course." Williams defends it against charges of obscenity and sordidness. He begins by pointing out that the true sordidness of the subject lies in the way the newspaper management capitalizes on human misfortune for the sake of sales, "while it can do nothing but laugh at those who give it their trust." He speaks of the need to create an audience for serious writing. And he concludes by pointing to what West had most in common with Williams himself—West's fresh use of common, clichéd language: "It's plain American. . . . Anyone using American must have taste in order to be able to select from among the teeming vulgarisms of our speech the personal and telling vocabulary which he needs to put over his effects. West possesses this taste."

Expanding her earlier blurb, Josephine Herbst accurately named *Miss Lonelyhearts* an allegory in the form of a moral detective story, in which realism has become nightmarish and people grotesque, "representatives of a great Distress." West was writing, as she saw it, the inside narrative of international distress. She sees this distress in the particular context of the modern insanity evidenced in the daily papers, while Angel Flores detects in it a background of world-wide malaise, with historic roots in the eighteenth century. He brilliantly places West in the company of his European predecessors. West, he says, is most obviously indebted to Dostoevsky—but also to "that pervasive uncanniness which hovers over the canvasses of Giorgio di Chirico and Salvador Dali. In literature it existed coarsely in the terrorists of the XVIIIth century . . . particularly, in Lewis' *The Monk*. Later, it entered the chapel of the Symbolists via Poe–Coleridge, and now reigns, stylized, in surréalisme." West, Flores concludes a little patly, has combined the anguish of Dostoevsky with the fantasy of Cocteau to make a new and distinctive artistic vision.

"Nathanael West: A Portrait," by S. J. Perelman, is a truly provocative piece. There are really two Wests, Perelman intimates. Earlier and perhaps more accurately than anyone else, he hinted that West's personality was divided between self-deluding fantasy and scorn for illusions. The first of West's two personae is a "ruddy-cheeked, stocky sort of chap, dressed in loose tweeds . . . six feet in height"—a man of contradictions, but above all, a romantic dreamer, "a dead shot, a past master of the foils." This man, Perelman says, is not in any part the author of *Miss Lonelyhearts*. He is the exterior, romantic self—Nathaniel von Wallenstein Weinstein —the man of illusions, the ordinary hero. But the West who wrote the novel, Perelman continues, only apparently joking, "is only eighteen inches high. He is very sensitive [and] somewhat savage." He is a kind of eternal figure of revolt—having been seen at Austerlitz and Jena—savage, close to madness, a man out of the world of dreams, the creative dwarf, the inner man. This, Perelman says, is the true Nathanael West.

In *Balso Snell*, West wrote a similar speech in which he tried to explain his own duality. "When you think of me," a character says, "think of two men—myself and the chauffeur within me. . . . From within, he governs the sensations I receive through my fingers, eyes, tongue, and ears. . . . Imagine having this man inside of you, fumbling and fingering your heart and tongue with wool-covered hands, treading your tender organs with stumbling soiled feet." Perelman's analysis of the savage, impish sensibility inhabiting the body and trying (not with complete success) to influence the temperament of the romantic dreamer is a more accurate description of the split in West's being, where each aspect of his personality could only briefly hold sway.

Certainly, both the romantic and the satiric self were to be fully indulged in the summer of 1933. For while the *Miss Lonelyhearts* issue of *Contempo* was being prepared, other developments were underway whose effects on West's life would be profound. Although the critical notices of *Miss Lonelyhearts* had not been able to sustain public interest long enough to give the book a popular sale, they had nonetheless attracted interest in Hollywood. In some ways, 1933 was the last great year, economically, for writers in Hollywood; the industry was just then completing its adjustment to the introduction of sound, when dialogue writers suddenly became essential and a literary migration from East to West started on a grand scale. As a novelist with a recent *succès d'estime*, West glowed briefly in the visions of Hollywood producers.

III

In the spring of 1933, Samuel Goldwyn began to plot a triumph for his newest film discovery, the Russian actress Anna Sten, who he believed was destined to become another Garbo or Dietrich. To publicize her arrival in the United States, Goldwyn considered "plastering a facsimile of her head on 10,000 or more billboards around the country . . . the most lavish introductory gesture ever accorded a screen personality." Moreover, he hired West to write, in the East, an original screenplay for what was planned as her initial triumph. Early in June, Perelman was writing from Hollywood to ask: "Have you submitted your outline yet? Don't worry about clichés and familiar situations, you go to enough movies to see what kind of fare they dole out." In the permutations of film planning, however, West's original was eventually dropped, and Anna Sten returned to Europe after appearing in a heavy-handed adaption of *Nana* and in other undistinguished films.

But the studios remained interested in *Miss Lonelyhearts*. On the day after Harcourt, Brace completed arrangements for the transfer of the novel, Darryl F. Zanuck paid $4,000 for the right to produce the movie at his newly founded studio, Twentieth Century Pictures. After the cruel failure of *Miss Lonelyhearts* to reach a wide public, this sale gave a real boost to West's morale, as well as a significant lift to his slim capital. Now, he felt, he would show his mother and his family that he could make writing his profession. It even seemed, as Perelman told him, that "the book [would] be aided in sales by the picture, even if the latter has nothing to do with the book."

West was counting on movie-derived money to give him the leisure to write another novel. For almost immediately after the publication of his second book, he had begun to think about satirizing the myth of success lying, psychologically, behind Miss Lonelyhearts's tragic perfectionism. West had tentatively titled his prospective novel—mournfully and mockingly—*America, America,*

and in preparation for it he was reading schoolbooks like Mc-
Guffey's Readers. But while he was still working in the hotel, he
made little progress on the book.

The sale of *Miss Lonelyhearts* allowed West to think seriously
of quitting his job. When this sale was followed by a contract from
Columbia Pictures to write an original screenplay, he calculated, as
he told Robert Coates, that since hack work is necessary when one's
books don't sell, the higher the pay for it the better. And he accepted the Hollywood offer at once.

In this, there was nothing unusual. Several of West's friends,
even the painfully shy Erskine Caldwell among them, had already
gone to Hollywood as junior writers. S. J. Perelman, of course, had
an established reputation as a writer of brilliant dialogue and had
already written *Monkey Business* and *Horse Feathers* for the
Marx Brothers. He openly regarded films as "an occupation which,
like herding swine, makes the vocabulary pungent but contrib-
utes little to one's prose style," yet saw in film work an opportunity
to make enough money to continue serious writing on his own. On
the other hand, some of West's friends regarded work in movies as
a sellout. Both Josephine Herbst and James T. Farrell had refused
contracts. Coates himself chose to do book and art reviews for *The
New Yorker*. But equipped with a list of movie terms that he asked
Perelman to type out for him, West chose to go to Hollywood and
work in the Junior Writing Department at Columbia Pictures.

On July 26, 1933, a Hollywood gossip columnist wrote: "No
matter where they plan to go they end up in Hollywood. Some
years ago three young people planned to settle on a Pennsylvania
farm and start a literary settlement. . . . [The] humor writer S. J.
Perelman and his wife have been in Hollywood for some time,
Perelman having written *Horse Feathers* and *Monkey Business* for
the Marx Brothers. . . . And now the third member of the group
which once dreamed of a Pennsylvania farm has come out to join
them. He is Nathaniel West, author of *Miss Lonelyhearts*."

West had arrived in Hollywood at the very beginning of July, on
leave for the summer from the Sutton. He moved into the Perelmans' large, Mexican adobe-style house at 5734 Cazoux Drive, and
started to work at Columbia on July 7. His first assignment was on
a studio-owned property titled *Beauty Parlor*.

West amusingly summed up his earliest reactions to Hollywood in a letter to Josephine Herbst: "This place is just like Asbury Park, New Jersey. The same stucco houses, women in pajamas, delicatessen stores, etc. There is nothing to do, except tennis, golf or the movies. . . . In other words, phooey on Cal. Another thing, this stuff about easy work is all wrong. My hours are from ten in the morning to six at night with a full day on Saturday. They gave me a job to do five minutes after I sat down in my office—a scenario about a beauty parlor—and I'm expected to turn out pages and pages a day. There's no fooling here. All the writers sit in cells in a row and the minute a typewriter stops someone pokes his head in the door to see if you are thinking. Otherwise, it's like the hotel business." Still, West worked on his first script with an enthusiasm not merited by the original story idea itself, but derived from his interest in collective fantasies, a long-standing interest in their expression in films (and elsewhere in American culture), as well as a personal talent for easy adaptability. Within a week he had submitted an eleven-page "treatment" of the original story idea—that is, his version of how the picture should be conceived, with brief indications of dialogue, scene, and characterization, but relying chiefly on suggestions concerning plot development. Departing widely from standard Hollywood formulas, this treatment shows that West regarded his assignment as an interesting, curious game. He knew Hollywood terms, but didn't bother about Hollywood rules. Allowing his invention to roam freely, he produced a treatment that violated enough film conventions to make it certain that the film would not be produced.*

Astonishingly, however, West's treatment was accepted by the studio and he went on to a first-draft screenplay, which he submitted at the end of another week. Perhaps the studio always regarded the original material as unusable and saw his treatment and script merely as a way of allowing West to try his hand at film storytelling and accustom himself to movie procedure. His completed screenplay, in any event, was the last interest the studio took in the property except for a brief period a year later when a director considered interpolating some of West's more conventional material into another movie titled *Blind Date*.

None of this was uncommon in the production of motion pic-

---

* For a chronology of West's film-writing and summaries of the plots of his films, see Appendix, p. 401.

tures. It was not at all unusual in Hollywood for work on a script to be stopped after a first draft, or even for a final script to go unproduced. At all times, many more scripts were written than would be used—a policy first pursued by Irving Thalberg, who had nearly sixty writers working at M.G.M. so that finished scripts would always be ready to go into production.

On the day after West submitted his first draft of *Beauty Parlor,* he began to work on the original screenplay he had come out to do. This he titled first *The American Family Anderson,* and later *Return to the Soil.* All the satisfactions and powers which West denied to rural life in *Miss Lonelyhearts* he would be able to attribute to it here in the free fantasy-world of a Hollywood movie. If his work at the hotel and his life in New York had given him insight into the collective wishes inspected coolly in his novels, picture writing allowed him to indulge his own deep personal attachment to fantasy. The divided nature of his imagination, then, meant that he could work happily and successfully in Hollywood and that this would not only not detract from his novels but would lead him more fully into a personal exploration of fantasy by which his novels would thrive. Thus, while *Return to the Soil* was to be West's last script until he resumed film work at Republic Studios in 1936, in the interim he kept active his membership in the Screen Writers Guild, knowing that the Hollywood experience could be useful to him and that he might return to it. He wrote his novels out of the imagination of personal and collective disaster, but his film scripts out of his imagination of fulfillment. His novels were a pain and torment to him, a concentration of energy, written carefully and in language so precise and condensed that his books, as Malcolm Cowley has said, read like telegrams sent to distant lands. But his scripts would be a delight, dictated rather than written, spun off freely and rapidly in a release of energies and in language virtually indistinguishable from that turned out by his fellow writers. It is undoubtedly true that in one way West's career crystallizes the dilemma and fate of scores of fine writers who have gone to Hollywood; it is equally true that his case was special and that his talent for scriptwriting was so different from his novelistic skills that the one never interfered with the other. West always recognized the differences between the two forms. He knew that fiction is essentially language, but that the characters and incidents in films are visual events, detached from language—the script, a series of rec-ommendations to the director and the actors concerning their feel-ings, motivations, speeches, and actions. It was not unusual, he dis-covered, for a scriptwriter to read only the synopsis prepared by the Story Department when a novel was being adapted for the screen —not because he was uninterested in books or "culture," but be-cause the movie could truly draw only on the aspects of the book capable of synopsis. For this reason, some of the most successful screenwriters for the early talkies were the same "men who used to write those snappy, to-the-point subtitle captions in the silent days of the films." Ideally, words were to be avoided—both Eisenstein and Chaplin had insisted on this principle. Instinctively knowing this, West wrote masterful novels with the one hand, and with the other, movies of visually realized fantasy.

Return to the Soil, essentially one long paean to the curative powers of nature, is not without hints of the possibilities of disaster —there is a suicide, and the son of the hero robs a theater. But these are the complications of Hollywood convention; even the son redeems himself by surrendering to the police and saving his fa-ther's farm. In general, West's script contrasts rural values with ur-ban life and wholly affirms the former. "Father" Anderson is a kind of farmer-Bryan, who declares: "Everything comes from the soil. Without the farms, the cities could not be built. . . . Men lived from the soil in the beginning and will continue to live from it until the end. When Mother Earth stops giving forth, the world will end." Many years later, after the film's hero, "Father" Ander-son's son, has failed in the city, he returns to the soil with his own children and reemphasizes his father's speech with a kind of natu-ral mysticism. "Nature," he announces, "will always provide for those who love her. Soon she will give us potatoes, corn, sweet but-ter, eggs . . . everything that man needs in this world. Not slimy stuff from cans, but rich, beautiful vegetables and fruits that are loaded with life." The script single- and simple-mindedly drama-tizes human disintegration in the city, rejuvenation in contact with the soil.

On August 25, West submitted his third draft of this script. The studio was not about to press it into production, and since no pro-ducer had another project for him, his week-to-week contract was terminated the following day.

However, he remained briefly in Hollywood, sketching out his next novel and watching to see whether *Miss Lonelyhearts* would have better success in reaching production than his scripts had had. For all their faults, even these seemed more suited to film production than *Miss Lonelyhearts*. Yet it was to be produced, though always hedged by doom. Coincidentally, on the very day that West's Columbia contract terminated, the editor of a movie-industry sheet, *Harrison's Reports*, editorialized on the coming production of this movie: "During the three years of my publishing . . . I have read more than five hundred books, plays, or magazine stories. Among these there have been some very dirty ones: William Faulkner's 'Sanctuary' .. . . is one of them. . . . But I have never read anything to compare in vileness and vulgarity with Nathanael West's 'Miss Lonelyhearts,' announced by Twentieth Century Pictures. I am surprised that its publication should have been permitted, particularly because of its implications of degeneracy. It cannot be defended on the grounds of art; it has none: it is just low and vulgar, put out undoubtedly to appeal to moronic natures." Harrison proceeded to warn exhibitors that the screening of this picture would anger newspaper editors and bring both movies and exhibitors bad publicity. This was a sensitive time in the relations between movies and the public, and Harrison apparently believed that he had a mission to save the movies from the stigma of West's novel. He sent letters to all the leading dailies and newspaper associations asking them to protest the production of the film. Most important, he urged exhibitors to request that NRA director Hugh S. Johnson declare the standard production practices of blind selling and block booking unfair, since such pictures as this one could thus be forced by the studios upon unwilling or unwary exhibitors.

West, who saw a copy of *Harrison's Reports* at once, was aghast and sent it to Charles Pearce at Harcourt, Brace, asking about the possibility of legal action. Pearce replied sadly, "You couldn't sue . . . on the grounds that his review was hurting the sales of the book because there have been too few sales during the past two months." But he released a "Literary Note," listing the critics who had praised the book along with some of their comments; it was reprinted widely in newspapers, and so gave the book a brief flurry of publicity and a few more sales.

Still, *Harrison's Reports* had had its effect. West had never anticipated that his novel could successfully be reproduced on the screen—a hack writer had been assigned to the script—but now even his least hopes for the film frittered away. To appease newspapermen, the director engaged a reporter as technical adviser and promised both accuracy of detail and a production that would reflect the journalistic profession's high image of itself. The film was turned at once into a comedy-melodrama in which the hero, finally named Toby Prentiss, a tough, fast-talking reporter resembling Shrike of the novel, is assigned as punishment to the "sob-sister" desk, and decides to treat his job seriously. He takes one letter, explores it, and uncovers a melodramatic mystery plot, which he solves. Included among the novelty scenes is an attention-getting earthquake in the city room. One gossip columnist even referred, during production, to " 'Miss Lonelyhearts,' that rip-roaring yarn of a newspaper's love-lorn column." Perhaps, West meditated, the studio had bought his novel only for the publicity value of its title. But finally, in early October, even the title was changed, to *Advice to the Lovelorn.* All semblance of West's book had been so removed that Zanuck's film was far closer to the Warner Brothers recent film *Hi Nelly,* also about a love-lorn column, than to West's novel. His book had been scaled down to the standards of the *Evening Graphic.* On December 13, 1933, *Advice to the Lovelorn* opened in New York's Rivoli Theatre on the same bill as "that delightful Disney prismatic cartoon, 'Santa's Workshop.' " While *Variety* criticized it as "an unauthentic newspaper story," *The New York Times* reviewer had the final ironic word. "It is obviously a story which would have been infinitely more satisfactory," he said, "had the lighter vein been sustained."

IV

The day before the movie based on his book was released, West took the train back to New York.

During this first trip, he had learned many useful things about Hollywood, its industry, and its product. Immersed in Hollywood, he began by thinking it ridiculous and ended by seeing that it was grotesque. Most of his friends, including Dorothy Parker and Dashiell Hammett, scorned the Hollywood scene publicly. They pointed to such incidents as the famous credit line for Mary Pickford's and Douglas Fairbanks's *Taming of the Shrew:* ". . . by William Shakespeare, with additional dialogue by Sam Taylor." It was comically and absurdly true, they pointed out, that bad movies had reduced the public to such a paralysis of discrimination that in 1933 the two most popular movies were Mae West's *She Done Him Wrong* ("I'm tired, I just laid a cornerstone") and *Little Women.* And they regarded movies—even their own—more as a subject for jokes than as a career.

Indeed, the studios were, it appeared, controlled entirely by commercial considerations. Did not Rouben Mamoulian announce his belief that "the picture industry is no different from the underwear business," itself a curious and revealing comparison? Hollywood was a vast business enterprise, controlled financially by the owners of theater chains which distributed pictures nationally and run by men like Fox, Zukor, Selig, Loew, Goldwyn, Lasky, and Mayer, who had risen from the "marginal and shabby zones of enterprise, from vaudeville, nickelodeon parlors, theatrical agencies, flea circuses, petty trade." By the early thirties, the studios had gone through "a fantastic maze of inside manipulations that made some . . . screen stories tame in comparison." Here, as Dos Passos would soon affirm, was the Big Money. If the screen offered images of an "escape, opiate, ready-to-wear dreams," behind the screen the shadow of commerce fell heavily on romance and from the first qualified the potentiality of movies for art.

By 1927, moviemaking had become one of the ten leading American industries, with invested capital of a billion and a half dollars, a work force of 235,000, a yearly expenditure of $155 million on new pictures, and profits of one billion dollars from ticket sales as well as $250 million from film exports. (All told, there were 2,800 million paid admissions in 1933.) The profits of movie production depended on the economics of theater ownership. The balance sheets of the major producing companies in the thirties show that from half to three-fourths of their total assets were "land, buildings, and equipment"; the dreamland created by movies rested on heavy investments in real estate and theaters. This had important effects on the movies themselves. Financiers early showed an interest in the cinema and applied to it the same corporate methods that had resulted in profits (to financiers) in other industries. Moreover, since most of the theaters were acquired with the aid of bonds and other forms of long-term debt, the principal corporate officers of four out of the five major studios* were bond holders or their representatives; due to the regularity with which their heavy fixed charges had to be met, the film producers opposed all innovation or experiment. Certainly, nothing distasteful to corporate trustees was to flicker on the silver screen. Nor were there to be stories affronting the citizens of Nazi Germany or Fascist Italy, Communist Russia or totalitarian Japan—countries forming a large part of the very important foreign market, which brought in forty percent of the earnings of a picture. (In consequence, for instance, M.G.M., which purchased Sinclair Lewis's *It Can't Happen Here*, would announce in 1936 that it would not make the picture.) None of the many special interest groups in any country should be offended, the market thereby limited, and the legality of the profitable practice of "block booking" questioned.

Thus, paradoxically, as a consequence of these interests, the movies of the thirties portrayed a world in which economics, politics, race, and religion were absent, a world strangely polarized between historical-Western adventure and bedroom farce, attempting to convince its patrons that this was the normal lot of mankind. In one of the thirteen volumes of the Payne Fund Studies of the movies, conducted in 1933, Edgar Dale tabulated the "individual goals" of movies heroes. These, he showed, had importance in this order: "Winning Another's Love," "Marriage for Love," "Professional and Vocational Success," "Revenge," "Crime for Gain," "Illicit Love," "Thrills, Excitement," and "Conquering of Rival"—a primitive, Darwinian world in which, as Dale concluded, "only 9 percent of the total goals are social in nature . . . [and even some of these] are probably inimical to the best interests of society." Liberal writers often saw in this a capitalist plot for thought control; but it was simply the nature of business enterprise inexorably at work. For as the Lynds showed in *Middletown*, what the average

---

* The five "major" studios were all theater-owning enterprises and produced an average of fifty pictures each per year during the mid-thirties; these were M.G.M. (Loew's), Paramount, R.K.O., Twentieth Century–Fox, and Warner Brothers. Columbia, United Artists, and Universal, owning less property, were essentially production-distribution companies, most of whose films were booked into the theaters owned by the "majors." The majors were also known by the cost per picture—at M.G.M. in 1938, an average of $683,000—while the minors like Republic or Monogram spent $100,000 or less per picture.

moviegoer demanded was "the opportunity to escape by reverie from an existence which she finds insufficiently interesting." Alfred Kazin suggests that in the mid-thirties film images provided man's chief escape from social nightmares: ". . . in the smoky balconies of Forty-second Street, where they specialized in triple-features and where I often spent half the night, people sat glued together in a strange suspension but depending on each other's presence." Realism was of little interest, either to the audience or to the conservative producers. Even the sound process, at first rejected by all the major studios, had at last been used by Warner's in 1927 as a desperate means of averting bankruptcy. Romance or escape, simply, was the commodity that executive boards believed had the greatest saleability. Movies were the last artistic stronghold of the genteel tradition.

Hollywood, then, was a glamorous company town in which the economic interests at the heart of production strikingly affected both political and social life. Perelman called it "a dreary industrial town controlled by hoodlums of enormous wealth." Social status was measured almost wholly in terms of salary or profit. Money was social power. Alvah Bessie has related this "classic gag": "Following a violent argument between producer and writer over a story situation . . . the producer . . . leads [the writer] to the window of his office. . . . 'Which is your car?' says the producer, pointing to a Cadillac. 'That's mine. The situation stays in.' " In this socio-economic hierarchy, the ego could rest securely only at the very top of a well-publicized salary scale. West's salary, from the beginning, was closer to the bottom. If one writer could say: "In this town, I'm snubbed socially because I only get a thousand a week. That hurts," West in turn would probably have been ignored by that writer. Even among liberals, economic distinctions prevailed. Joseph Freeman, then editor of *New Masses*, has said that when he went to Hollywood in 1937 to collect funds—he was advised to speak as an anti-Nazi rather than as a Communist— he was taken to a party by J. Edward Bromberg, who left him at the door. "I haven't been invited," Bromberg explained. "I only make a thousand dollars a week. There won't be anyone there who makes less than fifteen hundred dollars. They'd resent it if I came in."

West, though he had been invited to the Hollywood "party"

for the summer of 1933, had not really come in. He was, after all, more interested in Hollywood as material than as a career. He knew that fiction had been written about Hollywood—Carroll and Garrett Graham's *Queer People* (1930) and Elmer Rice's *A Voyage to Purilia* (1928) were classic excursions into this scene. Yet he recognized that its richest materials were largely untapped. These lay, he saw at once, in the underworld of Hollywood life. The Hollywood gold rush of the 1920's, like that of 1849, had brought with it a mob of pleasure and fortune seekers, active exploiters of Hollywood or the Long Beach oil boom, weary exploiters of the sun, aged citizens of the Midwest, and the sick from all parts of America—as well as those who would prey upon them: confidence men and women of every variety, embezzlers, yoga and faith healers, gamblers, prostitutes. All these swarmed promiscuously together in the City of the Angels.

The grotesque character of this underworld appealed to West's pessimistic view of human life, and when he arrived back in the East he impressed (and often shocked) his friends with tales of the oddities of the golden scene; for him, Hollywood had been a museum of curiosities. He spoke, with obvious interest, of the peripheral characters of Hollywood, of hunchbacks, dwarfs, and variously deformed people, told several stories about Lesbian actresses and curious sexual practices. He even started a short story which he called "Three Eskimos." A studio brings an Eskimo family to Hollywood to star in a romantic adventure film which subsequently flops. "It was about Eskimos," the narrator, from the studio publicity department, explains, "and who cares about Eskimos?" Now the family is stranded in Hollywood. "And they were a headache. I don't know who picked me, but I was supposed to ride herd on these four pus-pockets. Well, I dumped them in a cheap hotel. . . . Then the trouble began. Joe, the papa, went to house and got everything. He started to rot on me. He gave all he had to Mamma and she began to stink." Here the sketch ends: like the Eskimos, it had nowhere to go, except that ultimately this fragment of imitation gossip would go into the background of the Gingo family in *The Day of the Locust*. Certainly, as Philip Wylie, who was seeing him in Hollywood around this time, later recognized, West had already begun to collect "the Locust cast-and-anecdote without having a frame for it. . . . Not, perhaps, thinking of a book—just observing (and recounting) the ways and types he knew." But, for now, West was interested chiefly in the scandals of Hollywood.

He summed up his attitude of fascinated but revulsed wonderment toward Hollywood when he told his cousin "that a trip to Hollywood was like a ride in a glass-bottomed boat in the waters near Bermuda, where you could see garish, improbable fauna swimming about."

V

His first attempt to use Hollywood materials in fiction came in a tale titled "Business Deal," published in the October 1933 issue of *Americana* magazine. Behind the publication of this story is the story of the magazine itself, and of West's associations with its editor, Alexander King. King, at that time probably the best-known book illustrator in America, was a man of ironical temperament, with talents well suited to a period that obviously called for satirical treatment. Perhaps laughter was the only weapon remaining whereby people could deal with the Depression; for the economic crisis, as Peter Drucker said, revealed "man as a senseless cog in a senselessly whirling machine which is beyond human understanding and has ceased to serve any purpose but its own." Satire and comedy began to predominate in American literature. Art, too, was turning at just this time toward laughter—and on all levels, from the cartoon to the sprawling murals installed in 1932 in the Whitney Museum of American Art. When people could not cure confusion, they attempted to laugh it away.

King, sensing this mood of satire, decided to begin a magazine, patterned after the German magazine *Simplicissimus*, satirizing the American scene. In 1931, just after the publication of *Balso Snell*, a book which King admired, he and West met, and West subsequently spent many evenings at King's 21 Street apartment. King was attracted to West at once, and for many months, while West was planning the first issue of *Contact*, they discussed the prospects for a journal of pictorial satire. In West, who had first learned to regard himself as an artist in his drawing of satirical cartoons, the idea found a ready response. The first issue of King's *Americana* appeared in February 1932, almost simultaneously with the first number of *Contact*. King's magazine, as experimental as

Contact, was its satirical counterpart. Both sought to unmask American pretenses. Working on the one, West was watching and discussing the developments on the other. While he was writing *Miss Lonelyhearts* for *Contact,* he was surely also looking to *Americana* for standards of satirical, Shrike-like attitudes. *"Americana* sees all. Hears all. Tells all," the first issue announced. Work by George Grosz, José Clemente Orozco, John Sloan, E. E. Cummings, Gilbert Seldes, William Steig, and James Thurber appeared in the early issues. In the fourth one, of November 1932—the date of *Contact's* last issue—*Americana* found its style: Grosz and Seldes became associate editors, and they and King announced their policy. Criticizing Republicans, Democrats, Socialists, and Communists with equal vehemence, they declared: "We are Americans who believe that our civilization exudes a miasmic stench and that we had better prepare to give it a decent but rapid burial. We are the laughing morticians of the present."

Before West went to Hollywood, he selected two pieces from John Gilson's "Pamphlet" in *The Dream Life of Balso Snell* for reprinting in the August and September issues of *Americana,* and agreed to gather together materials for an "All Hollywood Number" from those writers who "are at present exiled in the Athens of the West." Ever mythmaking, he wrote to the Brown alumni monthly for December 1932 that he had gone to Hollywood expressly "to collect materials for . . . that indignant monthly." It was true, in any event, that in August 1933 West joined Seldes and Grosz as an associate editor and was especially influential in putting the Hollywood issue together.

West's Hollywood tale, "Business Deal," a satirical sketch influenced by Perelman's "Miss Klingspeil, Take Dictation," appeared in the Hollywood number of *Americana.* This sketch begins as Eugene Klingspeil, head of Gargantua Pictures, falls into a "gentle reverie," in which he dreams of "Gargantua Pictures swallowing its competitors like a boa constrictor, engulfing whole amusement chains." He is a vulgar parvenu. The screenwriter, Charlie Baer, who comes into the office to discuss his contract, is no better: both are described in animal images—gorilla, bear, cobra, stag, and bull —since both are engaged in a fierce battle to realize their dreams of wealth. The sketch is amusing, but West would go far deeper into the Hollywood dream world than this. Klingspeil and Baer are the surface of the violent life he was to treat in *The Day of the Locust*, with Charlie Baer transformed into Claude Estee.

In the following issue of *Americana*, King played his final joke upon his audience. "Attention," he wrote. "The next number . . . brings momentous information on a change in editorial policy." But King had run out of money. And there would be no next issue —a momentous change, indeed!

It is unfortunate that the magazine did not continue, for it was the last true outlet West would have for his "particular kind of joking"—anarchistic like that of Gilbert Seldes, witty and pictorial like King's, vivid like Cummings's, and characterized by a sense of the grotesque similar to Grosz's. All these men admired West's writing, and with all, moreover, he shared a distrust of panaceas and reform movements. Although many of the artists who worked for *Americana* had shown in the "Social Viewpoint in Art" exhibit of the John Reed Club, their radicalism was bohemian and anarchistic, their viewpoints were influenced by visions of dissolution and decay. They wanted only to unmask. Perhaps this explains why photography became so important a part of the magazine. When speech seemed to have become merely rhetoric, pictures alone told the truth. The work of Stieglitz and his followers was in the background, of course, but Laurence Stallings's *The First World War* (1933) pointed the way to techniques of visually demonstrating horror, while the popularity of picture and comic books indicated how large an audience they might reach. West's original conception of the comic-strip form of *Miss Lonelyhearts* allies him to these interests. He and the other editors of *Americana* combined an awareness of the collapse of society with a desire to force an awareness of it upon the democratic masses. Weimar and New York were in the same moral depths. Especially at this time, when other intellectuals were allying themselves with movements for social reform, West and the other editors *cherished* no illusions (though they might *have* illusions) about attempts to transform man or his world. "Western Union boys" was West's phrase for reformers, and "boyscout" his adjective for their activities. West, a friend who was deeply involved in labor problems says, shared the excitement of his friends, but continued to laugh cynically at their efforts. West felt that "the real enemy was the pervasive boobocracy which overhung everything."

To King's, and more particularly to Grosz's, sense of the grotesque, West responded with a shock of recognition. Grosz, whose satire was no longer welcome in Germany, came to the United States in mid-1933 and found a place at once in the mental orbit of *Americana*. He possessed a sense of the violence and ugliness of his disintegrating society similar to West's. To be sure, the vision of the grotesque shared by West and Grosz had very different sources. In Berlin, Grosz had been able to see on a vast scale the evidences of suffering from war and inflation, and he reproduced its visual expressions. West, working from the evidence of the chaotic fantasy life of Americans, dramatized mental anguish. Still, Dos Passos's description of Grosz's style is a remarkably accurate characterization of the effect of West's: "Looking at Grosz's drawings you are more liable to feel a grin of pain than to burst out laughing. Instead of letting you be the superior bystander laughing in an Olympian way at something absurd, Grosz makes you identify yourself with the sordid and pitiful object."

Generally speaking, *Americana* fed the aspects of West's imagination from which *Balso Snell* grew. "Business Deal" is closer to his first novel than to his unpublished short stories, which are reflections of the imaginative impulses at the center of *Miss Lonelyhearts*, a book nourished by *Contact*. Between the very different temperaments of Alexander King and William Carlos Williams, West's own temperament and creativity moved, exploring the poles of his personal imagination.

West's imagination, even at the time, was growing, as experience brought fresh materials for it to explore. In 1933, politics was an everyday experience. At about the time *Miss Lonelyhearts* was published, West had tried to write a sketch which he called "Miss Lonelyhearts and the Communists," but he had been unable to find an appropriate form for his satire of Communist evangelism, and had left the sketch uncompleted. But in March 1933, when the German Reichstag passed the Enabling Act, which conferred absolute power upon Adolf Hitler, Fascism seemed a good deal more of an evangel than Communism, whose candidate, William Z. Foster, had polled a mere 102,991 votes in the 1932 Presidential elections, and West began to think of satirizing the Fascist spirit in America. He decided to take a young Miss Lonelyhearts figure, full of unbounded faith and confidence, and put him among the capitalists and Fascists. He had, he believed, found a form and fable appropriate for this tale, *America, America*. America was falling into ruin? Very well, against this he would shore the fragments of art. And, for this, he would return to the soil and matrix, the groundwork of American myth, to Horatio Alger, whom he called the "Bulfinch of American fable and the Marx of the American Revolution," the comic Messiah of the American Dream of Success.

12 / The Black Hole of Calcoolidge

> Oatsville is in Vermont. The Vermont of nutmegs, blue-
> berries and maple sugar. The Vermont of potbelly stoves,
> and cracker barrels. Cal Coolidge's Vermont.
>
> Joe Williams is one of Oatsville's nicest boys, blue-eyed,
> fair-haired, with a back as straight and strong as one of his
> mother's hickory chairs.
>
> A hero out of Horatio Alger.
>
> Only fools laugh at Horatio Alger, and his poor boys who
> make good. The wiser man who thinks twice about that
> sterling author will realize that Alger is to America what
> Homer was to the Greeks.
>
> —*A Cool Million: A Screen Story.* Treatment by
> Nathanael West and Boris Ingster (1940)

In the fall of 1933, anxious to begin his third novel, West was back
in Erwinna. Having resigned by letter from the managership of the
Sutton early in August, while he was still working for Columbia
Pictures, he now settled in the same area where he had finished
Miss Lonelyhearts.

West looked upon the farm chiefly as a place where he might be
free to write, by living what he believed to be the artist's style of
life. Among other things this would include friendly converse with
the "colony of . . . writers and artists," which Michael Gold had
noted. As it turned out, Miss Herbst and John Herrmann were the
only genuine writers around. The poet Isidore Schneider gave up
his house at about the time West moved in. Charles Sheeler had
paused there in the twenties to paint and photograph Bucks
County scenes and then departed. Gold never returned. John

Coffey, though a fascinating character and an anarchist fur thief, was a subject for writers rather than a writer; Conrad Aiken, Maxwell Bodenheim, Josephine Herbst, and William Carlos Williams all wrote about him. New Hope, where George S. Kaufman and Moss Hart lived, was some distance away. Only somewhat later would Dorothy Parker, the novelist and playwright Melvin Levy, the dramatist Joseph Schrank, and the novelist Daniel Fuchs live in the Erwinna area. For the moment, what literary society West would have beyond that of the Perelmans, Miss Herbst, and John Herrmann would come by invitation: Dashiell Hammett, Lillian Hellman, Robert Coates, and Edmund Wilson all visited from New York.

In 1933, conversation about art inevitably turned to politics; but in Erwinna, the conversational atmosphere and tone were far less ideological than in New York, where, as Daniel Aaron has remarked, "To champion liberal economic and social legislation was not merely undangerous, it became highly respectable." While in Erwinna "at that time," Josephine Herbst has said, "everyone thought himself a Communist," this was so only in the loosest, most non-regimented way, because only the Communists seemed interested in the plight of the people, whereas the propertied classes sought only to save their property. If West had been thinking of satirizing the Communist evangel in New York, in Erwinna he regarded the world-and-national situation non-ideologically, as a kind of morass from which to escape. In ways roughly parallel to those of Malcolm Cowley and John Herrmann, West would follow out in the thirties the logic of the dadaistic disgust with the middle class characterizing the twenties. Earlier, this generation had written out of desperation, "like soldiers . . . betrayed by their commanders," and many now turned to Marxist, agrarian, or other forms of planned opposition to capitalist society, as well as from European to American themes, myths, and institutions.

West was a part of all this. In the lingering spirit of the twenties, he regarded politics with traces of suspicion, yet for the rest of his life he was to be involved in politics. When one of his Erwinna acquaintances asked him about his politics, West told him: "I'm like the guy who stands on the outside and observes. I like to observe. It really makes little difference to me. I want to interpret, I want to understand. I'm not going to be able to change the course of anything, I just want to know." In a time when "there were no neutrals," as Murray Kempton has described the ideal of the thirties, West was committed to his freedom to be neutral, though never indifferent. Hesitant about engaging personally in political activity, as, for instance, Gold or Herrmann could, West turned politics into a concern of the imagination, the visiting mind. The inarticulate and seething hopes for revolution, fear in the propertied classes, the proliferation of nostalgic or utopian schemes—all that marked the politics of the early thirties—implied, he saw, widespread political wish-fulfillment thinking not essentially different from the delusions in the letters to Miss Lonelyhearts. On different levels, both were the natural consequence of the chaos in the American mind. Pressed by extreme situations in spirit or society, feeling both victim and victimized, Americans were struggling simply to keep from being inundated by history. Although by temperament West stood aside from political activity, his mind still roved over the fundamental ground of the early thirties and he chose to satirize the American folklore of success which had constituted, traditionally, part of the foundation of American political and economic ideals. The new novel, as he planned it, would fall partly into the native traditions into which other writers had pushed early explorations. But specifically he would again diagnose the symptoms of West's Disease in the political and economic body of the country.

More interested in people than in ideas, West was interested in Communism because his friends were, because he was interested in them. And because the Bucks County economy was agricultural, he developed an imaginative interest in farm problems and farmers. The Depression had really begun in agriculture in the early twenties, brought on by overexpansion from foreign demand and governmental price supports during and immediately following the war. President Hoover warned in 1932 that if a Democratic tariff were put into effect, weeds would "overrun the fields of millions of farmers," but during his own administration many farms became wastelands and farming districts wards of poverty. Between 1929 and 1932 alone, the gross annual income of farmers fell fifty-seven percent. Nonetheless, by the early thirties, although still hobbled by departures to the cities and by remnants of Populist economics, farmers were beginning to organize protest movements. Josephine

Herbst had covered the Iowa Farmers' Holiday Strike led by Milo
Reno, and in the September 1933 issue of *Scribner's Magazine*
called her article about it "Feet in the Grass Roots." But the farming situation was exploding everywhere. In New York State, Edmund Wilson remarked with amazement on the way that even
Adirondack farmers began to talk of "brutal state troopers" and
"cossacks" in their denunciations of state authority.

Near West, in Ottsville and in Erwinna, the farmers struggled to
keep their heads above water. Certainly, their cooperative drive
to achieve the barest way of life for themselves was remarkable. By
the early thirties they organized under the leadership of Russian
Jews like Leo Ars and Joe Tenin, or of Quakers, some of whom had
gone to Russia in the late twenties as agricultural advisers. They
first organized into the United Farmers' Protective Association and
later were chartered by the Farmers' Educational and Co-Operative Union of America and became associated with organizations
like the Delaware Valley Co-Operative. Ars, who farmed his own
as well as West's land, was elected a delegate to the Farmers'
Union and served on its educational committee. Occasionally he
and other farmers would meet at John Herrmann's house to consult with him and other radicals like Bud Reynolds and Herbert
Benjamin about their problems. They formed study groups to discuss tactics during a drive to get decent prices for milk. Three hundred of these farmers forced the foreclosure sale of John Hanzel's
Bucks County farm for $1.18, then leased it back to him. At the
Herrmanns', West too would appear, drinking and talking with the
farmers, but mostly listening. He heard them speak vaguely of revolution, since even the farmers' most urgent needs had not been
satisfied. They presented a grotesque spectacle of spiritual and physical mutilation caused by farm life and farm accidents—like angry
Ahabs meeting in mid-ocean. They "were so damn poor," Gold
later said, "they weren't scared of anything—you couldn't hurt
them any more."

West was excited by the militancy of the farmers and deeply
moved by their poverty. But he was also interested in the local response to them, the conservative reactions of the Ku Klux Klan and
Silver Shirts. The farmers were forbidden by "the better class of
taxpayers" from using the Erwinna school house for gatherings.
There "was a sense of hysteria in the air," Josephine Herbst says.

Circulating among the people of the neighborhood and sensitive to persons and situations, West absorbed their spirit into the structure and tone of his work-in-progress. He brooded on these meetings and conversations, as well as on the dissolution, everywhere apparent, of the tradition of the yeoman farmer, the noble creature of the soil. "Let me tell you something, my son," he had made Father Anderson say early in *Return to the Soil*, ". . . everything comes from the soil . . . men lived from the soil in the beginning and will continue to live from it until the end." His script, written in the summer of 1933, had seemed to prove Father Anderson right. But the autumn revealed to West how far men had been dismantled by the soil and by American enterprise, and how far he had been romantically yearning in Hollywood, for a noble, pastoral, but impossible, life in the country. As he had done with the authors of the Susan Chester letters, West began to associate himself imaginatively with the farmers-as-victims. For him the farmers were neither sons of the soil nor distressed proletariat. He was drawn to them, as to Desperate or Sick-of-it-all, by the enormity of their suffering: for him, they were simply desperate people. He made some attempts at imitating country talk in his conversation, and he daydreamed of leading successful, epic farmers' movements and thus restoring prosperity to his neighbors. Of course, he took no active part in any of this, but his fantasies were so strong that even years later, in Hollywood, he confided to Darrell McGowan, a screenwriter at Republic, that "he had led some farmers' labor radical movement back East, earlier." He added, shyly, that he had had "some degree of success."

II

Clearly, too, West was imitating the local farmers in taking up hunting at this time: in Bucks County, hunting was exploration, not escape, for him. Outdoor tales recalled from magazines read in his youth; incidents of adventure, doubtless much altered, drawn from his Adirondack summer; memories of camp; and sheer invention—these all give him material for hunting conversations with his neighbors. Not with calculation, but because he was deeply moved by them, he identified imaginatively with the farmers. West, Josephine Herbst writes, "was shy and he was very introspective, and it is significant that he got on so well with the extrovert characters with whom he hunted and all of them loved him. . . . For Pep, hunting was a way to be easy and natural with people very different from himself. He wanted to get into that world, so much less complicated than his own, and he was lonely." "In a bar or talking just to an average bunch of hunters," a later hunting friend said, "nobody would ever suspect that [West] was an intellectual at all." He admired, with few reservations, Hemingway's work; but his own passion for hunting was derived not from Hemingway's appealing dramatization of the hunt as a ritual or sacrament, but from the easy opportunity it gave him for establishing human communication. West never hunted alone; he was often careless about his clothes and equipment; though by instinct he was an excellent shot, he never really practiced to improve his aim, as many hunters do; and he never wanted to shoot big game. In 1933–4 he owned only a double-barreled, 20-gauge shotgun, and hunted grouse, pheasant, and quail in the fields in back of his house, shooting only often enough to keep his dogs sharply trained. West, in short, had no code for hunting; it was an activity of life rather than of art. (Only at the very end of his life would he consider writing a *Sportsman's Sketches*.) Hunting, simply, was fun for him, and he delighted in saying that he had discovered in the early writings of Lenin that Lenin himself had been passionate about duck hunting and came at last only sadly to give it up in order to devote his life to politics. Lenin gave his life (perhaps unwisely, West joked) to politics—but he would give his to hunting. While other intellectuals talked *about* farmers, he would talk *to* them.

He did talk. "He was quite a storyteller," a local carpenter says. West told him that he had gone "to the Adirondacks and to Kentucky to get material for his writing. And he had lived among the natives." Drawing, most likely, on conversations with Erskine Caldwell and upon his reading, he described the way Southern farmers lived. The people in both regions, he said, "were the original [American] people," and his buddies remember his "vivid stories about living in Kentucky, and about the hillbillies and those who lived off the land." With a jug of applejack purchased from the moonshiners, West, sitting on a log, would talk for hours about dogs, hunting, guns, and farming, while his own dogs bayed after coons miles away.

These dogs became aspects of his pastoral imaginings. His tales of his life in Kentucky were associated with (and probably ultimately inspired by) the brownish-red, white-ticked coon hounds he purchased, in company with a neighbor, from a mail-order Kentucky kennel. He described his dog of the pair, Lulu, to Robert Coates as "a first class, slow-trailing coon hound from Kentucky— a real hound with a beautiful bell-like voice." But his actions were always betraying the limitations of his knowledge. He was so excited by receiving his dog, for instance, that according to Miss Herbst, "when it arrived in a stuffy boxcar, shivering, tail between legs . . . he could not wait to acclimatize the brute but had to give it a workout that very night. What a comical sight it had been, with deep snow covering the world, and all the traditional fixings culled from a book rigged up for the occasion! There had to be a bonfire, there had to be a bottle of whiskey. . . . Deep into the woods they had ploughed." But the dog whimpered with cold and abject homesickness, pressing near the fire, "as though the raccoons had been mythical." West lost interest in the dog at once. Although it turned out to be an excellent animal, subsequently winning many field-trial prizes, it was his other dog, a pointer, Danny, which West loved and which has become part of the West legend.

When friends came to visit, Danny was the dog they took out and hunting the occupation they shared. Peter Blume, the painter, came to Erwinna in the fall of 1933 and was started on hunting by West, who seemed to Blume to have "a great deal of esoteric knowledge and the lingo of hunting." All in all, with friends or neighbors, West was, as Josephine Herbst has said, "a hunter of doves," on the track of the human spirit. And in the midst of all these activities on the farm, he was beginning to write his third novel.

III

"I finally got started on my new novel and have been doing nothing else since," West wrote to George Brounoff in October. "I like it, and I think it'll be alright. You know I never wrote steadily before, taking a month to do five pages in the past, and find it hard to keep going. However, I'm doing five hours a day steadily now and expect to be on Harcourt's Spring list." He did move rapidly and by late autumn, still conceiving of this novel as a satire on the

American Dream of Success, he was well along. Surely, never before in America had success seemed so unlikely or hope for success so vain. It was no accident that Josephson's *The Robber Barons*, Lewis Corey's *The Decline of American Capitalism*, Edward Dahlberg's *Those Who Perish*, and West's novel should all appear in the same year, when the extent to which Roosevelt's legislative program ran counter to *laissez faire* doctrine was becoming clear. Earlier American writers like Twain and Dreiser had rejected the Gospel of Success; but now this gospel was opposed very widely in America.

But West's anatomy of success had deeply personal as well as widely social roots. He could trace the effects of the gospel of success in his own life. Humbert Wolfe, among other theorists of satire, has suggested that "the satirist must have love in his heart for all that is threatened by the objects of his satire." There is no doubt that the idea of success was highly charged for West. As a violent inversion of the American dream, *A Cool Million* provided West a means whereby he could adjust his desires to reality, by viewing both in fiction. As a child, he had read Horatio Alger and Oliver Optic. More important, he had absorbed from his parents a devotion to the ideals of success.

In the twentieth century, immigrants like West's parents gave renewed vitality to the dream of success. East European Jews in particular came from villages where economic individualism was as pervasive as social and religious cooperation, and while social and religious bonds were often severed by relocation, a commitment to free enterprise persisted in the new land, the Promised Land. A popular guidebook advised the immigrant in terms drawn, like West's novel, directly from Horatio Alger: "Hold fast, this is most necessary in America. Forget your past, your customs and your ideals. Select a goal and pursue it with all your might. . . . You will experience a bad time but sooner or later you will achieve your goal. . . . A bit of advice for you: Do not take a moment's rest. Run, do, work and keep your own good in mind." Perhaps, as some contemporary Jewish commentators suggested, Puritanism was but a version of Old Testament teaching suited to America. In any event, West's family was saying in all its actions and in its hopes for the children what one of the heroes of Mike Gold's *Jews without Money* shouts: "I will work alone. I will show you . . . how a man makes his fortune in America! Look at Nathan Straus! Look at Otto Kahn! They peddled shoe laces when they first came here!" The American Dream was the immigrant's faith.

That faith, moreover, had been apparent at De Witt Clinton and at Brown. "John D. Rockefeller would give a cool million to have a stomach like yours," the epigraph and source of the title of West's third novel, was an "old saying" at Brown and satirized one of the college's most illustrious graduates, who had subsequently chosen a Baptist minister, William H. P. Faunce, to be president of Brown. Three times each week, at 8:30 a.m., West and his classmates were required to gather in the college chapel to hear Dr. Faunce preach, in mellifluous tones, the gospels and evangels of success. While West was a Brown undergraduate, Rockefeller himself had written a letter to the students, declaring: "I believe that the Golden Rule is the best principle upon which to conduct a permanently successful business, and that its application offers the only real solution to the problem of capital and labor." Such platitudes seemed confirmed by plenty. In the golden glow of the twenties, businessmen rode a wave of confidence, made of high tariffs, decreases in tax on upper-bracket incomes, easy corporate regulations, and a favorable share of international markets. Calvin Coolidge of Plymouth, Vermont—the acknowledged model for West's Shagpoke Whipple—put the assumptions of these men into secular creeds like "What we need is thrift and industry," "Let everybody keep at work," "The man who builds a factory builds a temple. The man who works there worships there." These were all nicely summed up in Coolidge's classic remark: "The business of America is business." Not long after the announcement of this dogma, West's father, then millions of others, were put out of business altogether. What, they all asked, was the business of America now? Even while he was writing *A Cool Million*, his mother, who periodically lived with him in Erwinna, was still harping upon the virtues of success and encouraging him to go back to his job at the hotel or to take up some serious occupation. She had been disappointed in his writing from the beginning. When he had given her a copy of *Balso Snell*, she had complained that now, after telling all her friends that she had a son who went to Paris to write a book, she couldn't even show it to them, "because all it says is 'stink, stink, stink.'" She thought his books were "dirty." Well, that was the gap between generations, West had remarked lightly to I. J. Kapstein. But in the fall of 1933, he was more concerned and asked Josephine Herbst to talk to her about the life of a writer and the function of literature. Although he was determined not to go back to the hotel, he told Miss Herbst, his family was putting pressure upon him to do so. Perhaps she would convince his mother that important critics respected his work? She tried, and Mrs. Weinstein listened silently. Then she said, "How's he going to make a living?" "It doesn't matter," Josephine Herbst said, ". . . he has to have a chance." Mrs. Weinstein repeated, "How's he going to make a living?" She loved him, but she didn't recognize his qualities. In her eyes, he had been far from a success except in the brief period of scriptwriting, when his salary had seemed enormous. In his own eyes, he made clear in letters and remarks to friends, he was like the hero of James's story "The Next Time," fated to produce one shameless masterpiece after another and yet go unrewarded and unrecognized.

West himself had early and absolutely rebelled against success ideals, of course; and he had later seen his father prematurely aged and sickened by overwork. One of the essential facts behind the bitterness of the new novel was his helpless despair over his father's death from bronchiectasis in June 1932. Edmund Wilson recorded West's feeling in his journal:

Nathanael West (Weinstein): Father a building contractor—died in the tool house in spite of the fact his heart was weak and the family had tried to persuade him not to go to work—gave him half-Hebrew half-English service at funeral church, up on Riverside Drive—West was horrified when he found that they had rouged the old man's cheeks and cut off his shaggy eyebrows and put a great big white tie on him. He couldn't see that there was much in the funeral service that could comfort you very much. The first spadeful of earth that he had to throw down on the coffin gave him an awful jolt.
"From shirtsleeves to shirtsleeves in one generation."
"In this business you've got to know the value of $1.49."

West himself wrote to William Carlos Williams just after his father's death: "I've been heartsick since. He was building an extension to the Fordham hospital in the Bronx—and although sick for the last two years seemed pretty fair lately—when he dropped dead on the job."

Still, however he rebelled, whatever his bitterness, West could never entirely rid himself of an itching desire for success and certainly never from love of the fruits of success. Now the popular failure of his book and the desperate situation of the Bucks County farmers raised again the issue of success so meaningful for West.

In 1933 and 1934, West headed his letters "Ottsville, Bucks County." In choosing to have the mock hero of A *Cool Million*, Lemuel Pitkin, begin his career in Ottsville, West showed that he identified himself with his dismantled hero. Lemuel takes a room at the Warford House, the Frenchtown hotel where West completed *Miss Lonelyhearts*. One of the prostitutes in Wu Fong's all-American brothel is the fictitious Lena Haubengrauber from Perkiomen Creek, Bucks County, Pennsylvania. Lemuel's failure was an analogue for West's own, his way of viewing himself from the outside and so reducing the tensions to which the idea of success subjected him.

Even as West wrote, hurrying his third novel along, the papers daily brought him confirmations that his own involvement with success and failure was the central issue of his time. America itself, like West's comic hero, seemed to be in the process of dismantlement. The revulsion against business practices that inevitably accompanied the Depression, moreover, was intensified by the Senate banking and currency investigation, whose counsel, Ferdinand Pecora, began early in 1933 to lay bare the diseased tissue of commercial corruption. While West's earliest plans for A *Cool Million* were taking shape, one after another the Lords of Creation testified revealingly to their public irresponsibility and private greed. Pecora put on a sensational national show in which he proved, as he later said, that the Stock Exchange "was in reality neither more nor less than a glorified gambling casino where the odds were weighed heavily against the eager outsiders." These disclosures concerning capitalism and its folklore were striking and provided an important background to West's book. The effects on public opinion were immediate. Floyd Olson, fiery governor of Minnesota, declared that if the traditional American system, the code of Alger and Coolidge, could not prevent depressions, then "the present system of government [should] go right down to hell." But in what direction would the government go? How would the shattered, dismantled nation be pieced together? Who would direct its mending? And what principles would be its cement? Everywhere, people felt a change coming. Had not a group of New York rabbis, in April 1930, announced their confidence that a new Moses was soon to appear? Did not some New Dealers, Berle and Wallace among others, believe in the Social Gospel hope of a kingdom of God on earth? Had not Father Coughlin excoriated Mellon, Morgan, Meyer, and Mills as the "Four Horsemen of the Apocalypse"? Perhaps an apocalypse was at hand. But what would be avenged? And what millennium would it issue in?

Floyd Olson believed he knew. In November 1933, as West was completing a draft of his novel, Olson told a convention of the Farmer-Labor Party that the true aim of radicalism was "a cooperative commonwealth." West's Communist friends in New York believed that they too knew and prepared poems, essays, and fiction meant to accelerate the coming dictatorship of the proletariat. The New Dealers believed that they knew, and through the NRA and similar organizations sought to regulate individual enterprise. Indeed, instead of speaking of individuals, they referred to "each individual sub-man," regarding the individual as useful "not for his uniqueness, but for his ability to lose himself in the mass." The credit system devised by Major Douglas, proposals for huge bond issues and public works, for "hot money" which would decline in value if not spent, for work-sharing schemes—these all piled up in congressmen's baskets and editors' desks. Shortly after taking office, Roosevelt told reporters, "There are about 350 plans here in Washington, public and private. I should say that they are still coming in at the rate of twenty-five or thirty a day." On all sides people agreed that individual effort was as outmoded as the antiques which Henry Ford was now fervently collecting from every dusty nook and cranny of the country.

West ended his novel with an apocalypse of a very different sort. He remembered what most of his contemporaries had forgotten: that myth is more important—since it goes deeper into the emotions—than belief, and that in a contest between traditional and radical ideals, the former would prevail. Alger, he believed, not only was the "Bulfinch of American fable" but also would be the guide to change, if change was to occur—"the Marx of the American Revolution." Perhaps it was symptomatic that Ford, like one of the characters in *A Cool Million*, was hunting antiques. In a time which critically threatened their traditions, Americans were more likely to revert to antique ideals than to overthrow them.

The revolution, then, West believed, would be by and for the middle classes—what his radical friends called, sneeringly, a Fascist revolution. Shagpoke Whipple, a kind of nightmarish excrescence of the bourgeois clichés of the American Dream, was West's symbol for what that dream implied. The phantom world of Ottsville and Rat River over which Shagpoke presides includes meaningless proverbs, outworn symbols, vain oratory, usury, and perfidy—and he is determined to keep these at the heart of American life. Its enemies, in Shagpoke's view of history, are the international Jewish bankers on the one hand and the Communists on the other; both oppose "the American spirit . . . of fair play and competition," and in this satiric novel both cooperate to destroy the middle-class way of life. The Depression is only "an un-American conspiracy."

However comic they seem, such appeals could have deadly serious consequences. Had not Adolf Hitler, at first regarded as a clown, succeeded in becoming the dictator of Germany by playing upon similar emotions there? Alger's books, West saw, have much in common with *Mein Kampf*; he modeled his own novel upon both. Shagpoke, who upholds for "American citizens their inalienable birthright; the right to sell their labor and their children's labor without restrictions as to either price or hours," decides to found the National Revolutionary Party, popularly known as the "Leather Shirts," whose uniform is a coonskin cap, a deerskin shirt, a pair of moccasins, and a squirrel rifle. His party will be made up, as he puts it, from "the revolutionary middle-class." Shagpoke takes the field against the combined forces of the Communists (whose officers are West Point graduates), the I.J.B. (International Jewish Bankers), and the Indians, agitated by both groups. He begins by fomenting wild riots in the South ("The heads of Negroes were paraded on poles. A Jewish drummer was nailed to the door of his hotel room. The housekeeper of the local Catholic priest was raped"), then triumphs elsewhere, and ultimately demands a dictatorship. Finally, Lem, his dupe, completely dismantled, an American Horst Wessel, is assassinated and becomes a martyr in the triumph of Whipple's forces. At the end of the tale, this "American Boy" has fulfilled his dream of success, since "through his martyrdom the National Revolutionary Party triumphed, and by that triumph this country was delivered from sophistication, Marxism and International Capitalism."

Although on the jacket of the first edition of *A Cool Million* West accurately declared that his novel "was written without malice," nonetheless it did raise serious political issues in ways that continue to be relevant. West was concerned with the exploitation of the individual American under unrestrained free enterprise, as well as with the ways in which propagandists and publicists had manipulated patriotism to conceal this danger. In *Miss Lonelyhearts* he had written of desperate cries for faith and belief; here, he wrote of the American faith, and of its perversions and perverters. In the fall of 1933, he told the butcher in the American Store in Frenchtown: "You're going to see a lot of trouble. We're going to get into a big war, sure as hell, you can bank on it." He "didn't believe in making predictions," he said, but he was "sure of this: the social and psychological conditions were exactly right for it." While it was undoubtedly true that West personally feared and despised the Fascist disease, and was well informed on the subject of European and native Fascism, still he could regard its increase clinically and, in fiction, with comic objectivity.

More shrewdly than most of the social prophets of his time, West saw the sudden, surprising upsurge of native Fascist movements as a genuine folk movement which had connections, however distant and indistinct, with fraternal societies, clubs, evangelical religions, patriotic symbols, and the scarcely suppressed American love of authority, tradition, and ceremony. West saw that a time when only a handful of intellectuals voted the Communist or Socialist ticket but hundreds of thousands belonged to what were being called Fascist organizations was rich in wishful thinking. The American way of dreaming took form in such organizations. Americans treated Fascism as one more half-comforting fantasy which offered hopes of ordered security, not scripts for revolution. Plans of all kinds were a major form of mental activity in the thirties, the most hurried and hasty decade of intellectual restlessness in our history. To list the semi-Fascist versions of social security is to catalogue the sometimes comic but always desperate and hopeful uto-

West's parents, Max and Anna Weinstein, with young Nathan

West and his sister Hinda

West as a schoolboy (*left*)

At Camp Paradox, Paradox Lake, New York, in 1920

An illustration from the *Paradoxian* for August 1920, drawn by
Nathan "Pep" Weinstein, "Art Editor" of the magazine

From the 1924 *Liber Brunensis*, the yearbook of West's class at Brown. In 1926 he used this photograph in his passport

"Do I love what others love?" (*"Lieb' ich wass andere lieben?"*): The bookplate of Nathaniel von Wallenstein Weinstein, which S. J. Perelman designed for West while they were at Brown

West sailing for Paris, 1926. Inscription in his handwriting to "Mon Amour Alice"

Alice Shepard (*right*), modeling for the designer Elizabeth Hawes

Passport photograph taken in 1930

atrice Mathieu aboard ship with the
West gave her, 1930

st in 1931, the year *The Dream
of Balso Snell* was published

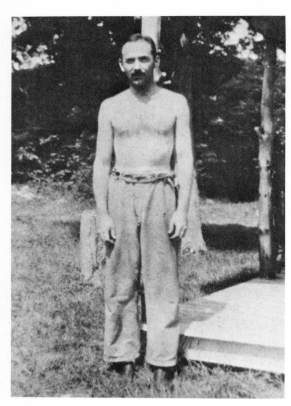

At Viele Pond, near Warrensburg, New York; August 1931

On the roof of the Sutton
Hotel, *c.* 1932

Nathanael West, *c.* 1931

West at the farm in Erwinna, Pennsylvania, *c.* 1932. (*Below*) Robert Coates, Dashiell Hammett, West, Laura and S. J. Perelman, and Danny at the farm, *c.* 1932

West, at the Erwinna farm

"Eight Ball," the Erwinna farm bought by West and the Perelmans in 1932. West's writing studio was the small white building to left and rear of the house

Laura and S. J. Perelman in Hollywood

During West's first trip to Hollywood, 1933; at Cazaoux Drive. (*Below*) West photographed against a process shot on a Hollywood set

With his sister Hinda, in Hollywood, *c.* 1933

The photo of West used on the jacket of *Miss Lonelyhearts*

Fishing in California

West on a hunting trip made with William Faulkner

West, with a guide, on a fishing trip in Oregon

Eileen West

Eileen at the station wagon in which she and West were killed.

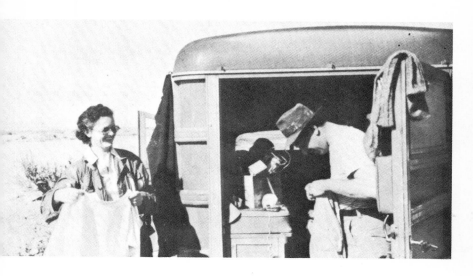

Eileen and West on a hunting trip

Where Two Died, Three Met Injuries Sunday

Two Hollywood residents met death in the station wagon shown at the left when it collided with a sedan, shown at extreme right, at the intersection of highway 80 and the Central Valley highway Sunday afternoon. Three persons in the sedan were injured. Speeding through a boulevard stop was said to have caused the accident. Nathaniel West, 36, Hollywood scenarist, and his wife, Ruth McKenney West, 30, were killed.

A Calexico (California) newspaper photograph of the wreck

Nathanael West; Mexico, 1937

pias of the day, most of which made their first appearances just before the publication of *A Cool Million.*

There was the venerable Ku Klux Klan, by this time generally discredited, but still representing—as its leader in the twenties, Hiram Wesley Evans, put it—"the great mass of Americans of the old pioneer stock," who "have broken away from the fetters of the false ideals and philanthropy which put aliens ahead of their own children and their own race." Like Shagpoke's, the Klan's slogan was "Native, white, Protestant supremacy." By the thirties the Klan had spawned organizations like the Black Legion of Michigan (active from about 1932 to 1936), the White Legion of Alabama, the Nationalists of Texas, and the Vigilantes of California, all terrorist clubs with avowed intentions to fight Communists, Catholics, Jews, and Negroes. The Knights of the White Camelia were revived under the leadership of George E. Deatherage. Fiery preachers of social doom like Gerard B. Winrod of Kansas and Gerald L. K. Smith of Louisiana ("the greatest rabble-rouser . . . since Apostolic times," Mencken said) stumped the backwoods, and later the cities, with gospels of suspicion, and with enemies inherited from the Klan. In New York, New Jersey, and the Middle West, organizations like the Friends of the New Germany and the Amerikadeutscher Volksbund (complete with uniforms, dues, and ceremonies) ultimately multiplied into a series of uniformed groups—the Gray Shirts (or "The Pioneer Home Protective Association," incorporated in 1932), the White Shirts ("Crusaders for Economic Liberty," 1931) the Khaki Shirts (1932), the Gold Shirts, the American White Guard, the Order of '76, Father Coxey's Blue Shirts, the Brown Shirts, and the Black Shirts.

The largest and most fantasy-ridden of the organizations uniformed on the Nazi model was William Dudley Pelley's Silver Shirts. Pelley had been a scenario writer for Lon Chaney, Tom Mix, and Hoot Gibson movie thrillers, as well as a popular writer of fiction for such magazines as *Redbook, The American, Collier's,* and *Good Housekeeping.* He put this experience to work in creating the myth of the founding of his Silver Legion. One night in April 1928, according to his own account in 1933, Pelley died for seven minutes, during which he learned, from "The Oracle," of the international Jewish conspiracy and of his own mission to return America to Americans in the form of a giant corporation, with Pelley as president and all "100 per cent Americans" as stockholders, each receiving $12.50 per month in dividends. Moreover, The Oracle told him, "when a certain young house-painter comes to the head of the German people, then do you take that as your time symbol for bringing the work of the Christian Militia into the open." After reading of the appointment of Hitler to the Chancellorship of Germany on January 30, 1933, he announced, "Tomorrow, we launch the Silver Shirts!" Spreading rapidly, the organization soon numbered as many as 75,000 members in forty-six of the forty-eight states. As in all such groups, the uniform (costing $10) was vivid and ceremonial—silver shirts, blue corduroy knickers, with gold stockings or puttees.

There would be more than a little of Pelley in Shagpoke Whipple. Like Shagpoke, Pelley made appeals to Indians—he saw subversive influences at work on them—and he recruited a redskin branch of his legion to stamp out Communism on the reservations. Although his appeal, like Shagpoke's, was patriotic and racial, still it had the same seething background of evangelical mysticism, endocrinology, radio therapy, evolution, astrology, and myth. Like Shagpoke, Pelley had affiliations to avowed Nazi groups, such as the Order of '76 and the Friends of New Germany. "If you are a weakling, or given to compromise, sentimentality, and docile acquiescence to intimidation," Pelley wrote, "you are not wanted in the Silver Legion. . . . But if you are . . . not afraid to risk your life and limb for your country, you are asked to take the Oath of Consecration upon you and step out as a True Christian Soldier, garbed in a shirt of Silver, with the great scarlet 'L' emblazoned on your banner and over your heart, standing for Love, Loyalty, and Liberation."

Observing movements like the Silver Shirts, a European visitor commented that Americans "move in a world of illusion of which, outside the lunatic asylums, there is no longer the faintest trace in Europe," where the dangers of Fascism were apparent. In *A Cool Million* West wrote a novel dramatizing that lunatic world—presenting it in a solemn, innocent way, until its nightmarish horror and comedy all at once break through the appearance of sanity. Beginning in the familiar American scene, the reader is abruptly plunged into the suddenly strange American dream world, hissing and writhing with absurd hates and fears, both grotesque and hilarious. West sent his "All-American Boy," successor to Balso Snell and Miss Lonelyhearts, to encounter a new set of dissolving faiths.

IV

West's problem in the composition of *A Cool Million* was to find or invent a literary form mirroring the character and structure of this wish-fulfillment thinking. Quite consciously, he set out to gather the clichés of success literature together in a comic, ironic plot. Though the result would be far from naturalistic, naturalist-like he explored the wilderness of American myth, notebook in hand, to record the strange specimens there. Before departing for Hollywood, he had consulted with his friends about "success" books. Charles Pearce had given him some information about collections of American schoolbooks, and on his way to the Coast, West stopped in Chicago to see the schoolbook exhibition at the Century of Progress Exposition. Josephine Herbst loaned him her copy of Horatio Alger's *Andy Grant's Pluck*, and on his own he found *Tom Temple's Career, Erie Train Boy*, and other Alger books. S. J. Perelman's influence upon West's method is obvious, of course. Perelman says of himself: "I . . . became a great reader as soon as I was able to appreciate the beauty of Horatio Alger and Oliver Optic." His own use of such books as vehicles for satire in his "Cloudland Revisited" series suggests the parallel lines along which his and West's imaginations might work. West also read more recent books that appeared either to satirize success stories or to be genuine recent examples of the traditional theme, like Abraham Cahan's *The Rise of David Levinsky*. He made notes on the pronouncements by the two recent Republican Presidents concerning success, as well as those by John D. Rockefeller, Sr., and the other "Robber Barons," as Matthew Josephson was then naming them.

"These fragments I have shored against my ruins," T. S. Eliot had written at the end of *The Waste Land*, suggesting that in his ability to gather and unify in his consciousness fragments of universal wisdom, he (or his hero) had seen shards of permanent value in what had appeared to be ruin. West made his novel out of fragments of the success story. *A Cool Million* is literally constructed of altered and purposefully arranged fragments of his reading in Alger and the others. In effect, he made a prose, American

Waste Land—one, like that poem, which is composed of fragments of knowledge and belief. But in West's book the source of the fragments is hardly the wisdom of the Gospels, the prophets, or the Orient—only of Horatio Alger, Calvin Coolidge, and similar savants. And in the thirties, their "wisdom" was no longer strong enough to shore against the ruins of history. Eliot's poem has coherence because Eliot believed that there was useful wisdom in all the areas of belief called forth by his sensibility. West, on the contrary, brilliantly contrived his book to fall back at last into the useless fragments of which it is made. As the morality, advice, and situations of American success stories are tested, from episode to episode, by confrontations with the facts of the thirties, the book crashes into glittering fragments—of dream, hope, and illusion. West's Waste Land is truly, finally, and unutterably sterile. *A Cool Million* is ostensibly, as S. J. Perelman, to whom it was dedicated, has said, the most comic of West's books; but with *Candide, Gulliver's Travels,* and *Penguin Island,* it belongs to the tradition of tragicomedies, since at its core lies bitterness and disillusion. Hart Crane, in *The Bridge,* and Van Wyck Brooks, in his literary histories, were finding what they believed to be a "usable past" in American myth; but West found only deceit in the past. "Only a man who had been hurt deeply," as one of West's friends says, "could write so comically."

For the narrator of *A Cool Million* West created a conventional-minded youth who shows an air of patient wonder before the monstrous. A descendant of Swift's, this Lemuel Gullible still believes in the sham of success. While the tale in general seems to be predominantly narrated from an omniscient point of view, a personified speaker ("It might interest the reader to know . . .") frequently appears, to remind us that the "mind" that could accept and relate the details of this story has entirely lost the ability to recognize the absurd and ironic gulf lying between the words of success—Alger's dream words—and the realities of the thirties imbedded in West's plot. But West's surface realism, on close inspection, is cracked and riddled by the incongruous and bizarre; for, though appearing to have committed himself to observation of a deadpan surface, West lets cosmic jokes explode through it and tear it apart. He had been reading Kafka as he was completing *Miss Lonelyhearts,* and Kafka continued to influence him. Lemuel Pitkin is an American Joseph K., so innocent he cannot know he is condemned. All the daily news of the thirties is in his book, the dreams of his time; but we fall through them from moment to moment into the cosmos of nightmare. What begins as observational at once becomes imaginative truth.

Like Balso Snell, Lemuel Pitkin walks through a dream landscape in which strange, ridiculous characters appear without reason or consequence, seeming to have common identities but ever taking on new shapes; where the apparent logic is nightmarish, the action is inexplicable except by dream standards. The speech on horses by Sylvanus Snodgrasse and the description of the "Chamber of American Horrors" suggest that if the focus of West's satire has narrowed from Western civilization (the Trojan horse) to American society ("in the center . . . was a gigantic hemorrhoid . . . lit from within by electric lights"), it has gained in intensity. Both *Balso* and *A Cool Million* share the savage quality of reversal possible in dreams. Both take place almost entirely in the dark. Lemuel, in summing up his insane experiences, remarks, "It all seems like a dream to me," and thus strikes at the central theme of the book, that the American dream is a monstrous nightmare.

The comic absurdity of the dreams of modern man, then, provides the source of humor in West's third book. He made no claim that he was saying something politically new. Although his novel preceded Sinclair Lewis's *It Can't Happen Here* by a year, it was by no means the earliest warning of the possibility of Fascism in America. West was attempting to be neither a Party man nor a prophet. He was writing humorously and freely in well-defined traditions of satire. When he discussed the book with his friends, he spoke about its comedy, its technique, of the comic usefulness and irony of dealing with an "inverted fable," but never of his book as a tract for the times.

Herman Melville wrote in *Pierre* that "in the hour of unusual affliction, minds of a certain temperament find a strange, hysterical relief in a wild, perverse humorousness, the more alluring from its entire unsuitableness to the occasion." West's particular kind of joking in *A Cool Million* combined his reading in satiric traditions with the brutal comedy of American burlesque. With Robert Coates, an aficionado of vaudeville, West had frequently gone to Harlem nightclubs, to burlesque, or to performances of Jimmy

Durante (of whom he gave a fair imitation); and of course he had attended carefully to the Marx Brothers scripts written by Perelman. He frequently spoke of burlesque comedy as classical in form. Perhaps recollecting his college essay on Euripides, he talked to Melvin Levy in a "scholarly and accurate way" of the connection between burlesque and Greek comedy; he knew the standard routines and traced them to *The Birds* and other plays. He even knew some performers, and took Levy backstage at the Los Angeles Follies Burlesque to introduce him to the comics. Combining his native, grotesque sense of the absurd with the comic techniques of vaudeville, West wrote the kind of diabolic humor that Melville described.

In addition to the basic comedy of the deadpan narrator wandering unaware in and unresponsive to a fantastic world, West exploited several other kinds of comedy in *A Cool Million*. Most obvious is the slapstick comedy of plot. Lemuel Pitkin, an innocent young man living in Ottsville, Vermont, determines to come to the city to make his fortune. He is cheated by Lawyer Slemp, who forecloses on his house; by Nathan "Shagpoke" Whipple, the aphoristic mock-Coolidge-Pelley figure, once President of the United States, but now president of the Rat River National Bank; by confidence men, and so on; deceived repeatedly on his "way to wealth." Wealth never comes, but Lem is arrested and loses his teeth; he saves a rich man from a runaway horse and loses an eye; he joins Whipple's Fascist National Revolutionary Party and is kidnapped by the Communists. Later, he is scalped by Indians. The literary analogue of this novel, Poe's "The Man That Was Used Up," makes clear that *A Cool Million* follows in the tradition of grotesque comedy, from Poe and Melville through Kafka and Gogol, rather than in the traditions of social or political satire. That Lemuel is (as the subtitle puts it) "dismantled" rather than "dismembered" suggests the inhuman, mechanical quality of man's fate. At last, killed during the first stage of their uprising, Lemuel becomes the martyr-hero of the Leather Shirts. " 'Hail the Martyrdom in the Bijou Theatre!' . . . 'All hail, the American Boy,' " Whipple's Party roars out at the end.

In the framework of this plot, West wrote several kinds of supporting comedy. The names of all the characters, of course, are ridiculous. West also plays with the comedy of taking banality seriously. Within his overall savage reversal of expectations, he treats various forms of the comedy of reversal: the firefighters who let the house burn, the Chinese laundry-and-brothel owner who speaks Italian and was educated at Yale-in-China, the Indians who scalp instead of save Lemuel. A basic device of comedy, the sudden revelation of the difference between appearance and reality, West uses again and again in situations ordinarily not comic—in particular, on each occasion when Lemuel appears to have been lucky. Each instance of luck dissolves into misfortune, a further stage in his dismantlement.

In his comedy of "the dismantling of Lemuel Pitkin" West reminds the reader that brutality has been a basic feature of American comedy. From the time that Lem is knocked off the porch steps into the cellar by Lawyer Slemp until he joins the team of Riley and Robbins near the end, Lem plays the comic victim—although, of course, West regarded him as seriously as he did the victims in the Susan Chester letters. As Lem joins the vaudeville act, the simple-minded narrator remarks: "'. . . there was much to laugh at in our hero's appearance. Instead of merely having no hair like a man prematurely bald, the grey tone of his skull showed plainly where he had been scalped by Chief Satinpenny. Then, too, his wooden leg had been carved with initials, twined hearts and other innocent insignia by mischievous boys. 'You're a wow!' exclaimed the two comics. . . . 'You're a riot!' " The comic act they develop, emphasizing each "punch" line by beating Lem violently until he is completely dismantled, suggests that life for Lem-as-Everyman is merely a violent but comic routine, a ludicrous stage affair or tent show, the bad joke of a clichéd vaudeville act.

West begins in comedy and ends by showing that beneath the comic froth lies the bitter, salt tragedy of betrayed ideals. This is particularly true of his stylistic comedy. Obviously, characters who are trying to speak sense in a nonsensical world, to act like humans when a measure for humanity is absent, provide abundant materials for comic speech. Neither the narrator nor the characters seem to be able to relate two sentences—each utterance, in this atomistic, incoherent world, is a distinct unit. The irony resides in the reader's perception of the contradictions from statement to statement. West develops this dark comedy into the even darker suggestion that the primary use of language in modern America is deception. The novel is inhabited by confidence men and their dupes; but ultimately even the confidence men are duped by their own oratory when cunning prevails over honesty, but force and violence master cunning.

Like Lem's body and the minds of the characters, *A Cool Million*, made out of bits and pieces of Alger novels, falls into fragments. The very form of West's book is a violent, mocking reversal of the American tradition of the National Novel—John DeForest called it the "Great American Novel"—whose major practitioners had been William Dean Howells and Henry James. (While working on *A Cool Million*, West was reading James as well as Alger.) Their kind of novel was based on the amalgamation, in an American (or American-European) setting, of the widest of diversities: Howells, James, and their followers had written scores of novels—constituting a definable genre—in which Southerners, Northerners, Westerners, and Europeans meet in train stations, resorts and hotels, or great cities—novels in which, as a result of this mixing, unity is won out of conflict.

Of course, by the twenties the attempt to write this kind of novel had itself become part of the body of literary cliché. In 1923, Contact Press published William Carlos Williams's *The Great American Novel*, which Williams described as "a satire on the novel form in which a little (female) Ford car falls more or less in love with a Mack truck." In his first letter to Williams, in July 1931, West mentioned this sketch, and the idea for carrying out a full-scale reversal of the form seems to have been part of the impetus for *A Cool Million*. The celebratory tradition of the National Novel, as treated by West, is seen to be one more deception. For West, the chief images of American unity become the "Chamber of American Horrors," and "The Pageant of America, or A Curse on Columbus"; Lem takes part in both. Best of all is West's description of the brothel that has been transmuted from the famous "House of All Nations" (in Chicago as well as Paris)* into a brothel of American regions: "Wu Fong . . . saw that the trend was in the direction of home industry and home talent, and when the Hearst papers began their 'Buy America' campaign he decided

---

* West refers directly to the Paris landmark, but in making his white slavers and Wu Fong speak Italian, he alludes also to Big Jim Colosimo's famous Chicago operation, overseen by John Torrio.

to . . . turn his establishment into a hundred per centum American place." West's novel not only reveals the deceptions of the American dream; it is in every way a precise reversal of the very literary form in which that dream had been best expressed.

V

Having read widely in success literature and having followed the daily news of the stirrings of native Fascism since the spring of the year, and deciding upon the technique of piecing together, in various ironical ways, fragments from Horatio Alger, speeches by Coolidge, and pamphlets by Pelley—all altered to heighten their effect —West moved rapidly through the writing of *A Cool Million*. By early November he had finished the first, handwritten draft. In Erwinna he spoke marvelously in telling friends about his book and was clearly feeling a return of confidence. He announced to his agent Maxim Lieber that this book would be "better than 'Miss Lonelyhearts.' "

Through November he toiled with increasing confidence, and with Lieber's encouragement, on a second, typewritten draft. Harcourt was anxious to have his book on its spring list, Lieber kept telling him, and needed the manuscript by December 1; "otherwise spring publication will be out of the picture." West, as it turned out, was not able to complete the second draft by then, but he did send Lieber a typescript comprising about half the book, with an outline of the balance. Cap Pearce had agreed to make a decision on the novel quickly and Lieber hurried the materials on to him. With the money West had saved in Hollywood rapidly running out, and with his mother, now back in the city, intent that he take a regular job, he was anxious to get an advance on the royalties for his book. While he waited to hear from Pearce, he continued to work on it.

Toward the end of December there was not only snow in Erwinna, appropriate to the Christmas season, but a spell of bitter, freezing weather. During this time West, not yet finished with the second draft and by now lonely on the farm, learned that Pearce, disappointed in his novel, "felt *Miss Lonelyhearts* was one of those brilliant cries without echo, a tour de force from an author whose future looked too uncertain, etc."; that, in short, his book had been rejected. Years later, West would claim that *A Cool Million* was written as a kind of parlor amusement for his friends, and that he sent it to Harcourt, Brace only in order to fulfill the option in his contract. But such tales were only masks he assumed to cover over the bitterness he felt. At the time, West was crushed by the rejection.

Again, he would turn his pain and—for all his semblance of toughness—his considerable reservoir of self-pity, into myth and fantasy. This disappointment and his anxiety about money and his future made West later speak of his bitter desolation during this time in Erwinna. He talked of this period as if all of it had been nightmarish, and of himself as if he had been trapped and immobilized. His anguish, in any event, was vividly present to him, like a recurring, terrible dream—the dream of creative impotence and failure. He told Wells Root that the farm had been "a kind of last-ditch refuge" for him. "There wasn't anybody else around—it would be winter—and he would have nobody but his dogs and nothing to eat out of but cans and he'd be trying to write something and didn't have any future or any place to go, because his books would not sell, yet *this* was all he could do." He told another friend that in Bucks County he had lived "off the land" for a whole winter, without a dime, "poaching deer and birds and rabbits," and cutting thousands of cords of wood to keep one room, the kitchen, warm. He pictured himself as going down to the pond for water, having to break the ice, and living "like a wild, primitive Indian."

These fantasies reflect West's sense of desolation and abandonment, his fears of poverty, and his almost absolute loneliness. All these he summed up in the final detail of the story he told Root— "one of the most tragic comments on loneliness I've ever heard," Root says. "He would be so lonely in the winter down there," West told him with a kind of sad, puzzled, and wistful irony, "that he'd dance with his dogs. He didn't feel sorry for himself—he spoke of this only as an example of the dreadful, lonely, pent-up life he led, when a human being got to the spot that he was eating out of cans and dancing with his dogs."

Most of these stories, of course, were not literally true. Josephine Herbst and John Herrmann were in Mexico, but West was intimate with his neighbors, the Richard Pratts, all that winter. He had no pond, only a small brook. West's re-creation of this time in fantasy reveals, rather, the hopeless anguish he was experiencing and would embody in these stories.

The snow fell fast on the Erwinna farmhouse while West worked hopelessly to finish his novel.

13 / "Vote Red, The People Are Goofy"

> ". . . Myself, I'm frankly after two things: truth, regardless of propaganda; and art. . . ."
>
> "Art," cried Jeffrey, "art as propaganda! Of course! Art as a weapon. . . ."
>
> "No, art as art," said Bruno grimly. . . .
>
> "But we've got to change our ideology," cried Furman, "to fit the times!" "Aesthetics were all right in your day," cried Cornelia impolitely: "but this is wartime! we need ammunition, not poetry."
>
> ". . . Why must a depression put an end to art?"
>
> "Art can't make a revolution," cried the Black Sheep.
>
> —Tess Slesinger, *The Unpossessed* (1934)

Around the West Washington Street Covici-McGee bookshop in Chicago, a distinguished group of writers, including Maxwell Bodenheim, Ben Hecht, and Sherwood Anderson, gathered during the mid-twenties. In time, Pascal Covici began to publish books himself; and finally, in 1928, he moved to New York to join with Donald Friede, a vice president of Horace Liveright, Inc., to found a new firm. In December 1932, this publishing house had put in a bid for *Miss Lonelyhearts*, just after it had been submitted to Liveright's. Now, slightly over a year later, Covici-Friede asked to consider West's recently rejected 200-page manuscript.

A Cool Million was accepted early in March, the contracts were executed by March 15, and the book was hurriedly scheduled for publication at the earliest possible date, in June. Once again West revised the manuscript while preparing it for the printer, making minor but careful changes on nearly every page, eliminating whole pages here and there, moving what was originally Chapter VII back in the novel where it finally became Chapter XXI, giving his book its final shape.

By early May, he had read and corrected galleys, and on May 20 he received page proofs. The publishers were moving at top speed and issued the book on June 19, 1934, in an edition of 3,000 copies priced at $2 each. Another in the series of failures connected with this novel came when West was not able to be present at his own publication party since he had to stay in Erwinna to repair the damage caused the previous night when an oak tree crashed down onto his front porch in a storm.

Once the novel had been accepted for publication, James J. Geller of the William Morris Agency, who had sold *Miss Lonelyhearts* to Twentieth Century, suggested to West that he be allowed to work on a picture sale. Somewhat more dubiously, he was prepared to try to get another Hollywood job for West on the strength of the film sale of his novel. West "was frank enough to admit that he didn't think it possessed any motion-picture possibilities." But the book's title sounded romantic enough to have already raised some interest in Hollywood, and several producers had asked Geller about it. In any event, Geller told West, "with a copy of *A Cool Million* under my arm it might be the means of getting you another job out here."

The novel, in fact, had already been turned over to the Joyce-Selznick Agency by Maxim Lieber and was submitted to Columbia Pictures in galleys on May 19, 1934, and purchased shortly thereafter. The book was in no danger of being filmed, however, except as a slapstick burlesque or, possibly, as was once suggested by the Columbia Story Department, as the basis for a musical comedy. The first studio report on the plot of the book summarized West's theme as "Honesty will buy you pain and disgrace," a thesis wholly unacceptable to the Hays Office. (Years later, even West himself would fail to make a producible script from his novel. It was never to be filmed.) Thus, even though West kept up his membership in the Screen Writers Guild all through 1934, no Hollywood offer was prompted by the purchase of another unproducible novel.

The movie sale, to be sure, made a much needed addition to West's dwindling capital. Still, he was really counting on the reviews to consolidate the position he felt he was winning in critical regard. The novel had been brought out with such rapidity that West could not arrange to have blurbs written about it in time for printing on the jacket. But his reputation was given a timely boost by a survey conducted by Malcolm Cowley in *The New Republic* in April 1934. Cowley had asked several writers to send him short lists of books that had been unjustly overlooked by the general public. *Miss Lonelyhearts,* in the result, was singled out by Cowley himself and by F. Scott Fitzgerald.

Still, the critics were not entirely prepared for a book so different, on the surface, from *Miss Lonelyhearts* as *A Cool Million.* On the jacket and in their catalogue the publishers sought to influence the critical reception by speaking first of *Miss Lonelyhearts* as "a brilliantly conceived and executed satire on one special phase of American civilization." In *A Cool Million,* they suggested, "[West] widens his scope, and few aspects of the picture presented by America today escape his biting and outrageously funny pen."

But the reviews were disappointing. Most of the local newspapers picked up the United Press review by Allen Smith, which flatly concluded: "The book is funny in spots, but there are not enough spots." Leftist reviewers felt that the material was too serious to be treated lightly; one declared, in familiar rhetoric, "I should prefer [to humor] a searing sense of justice which would unite free men everywhere against cruelty, oppression and tyranny." More conservative critics, on the other hand, felt that the humor was too broad and West too critical. The reviews in *The New York Times Book Review* and the *Herald Tribune* were favorable, but both declared *A Cool Million* to be a performance inferior to *Miss Lonelyhearts.* The single warm and perceptive review was written by John Chamberlain. Reading the novel, he aptly said, one must "either laugh . . . or go mad because of the insane reality that lies behind it. . . . There is no Falstaffian humor, no genial, all-dissolving laughter, in Mr. West, as those who have read his *Miss Lonelyhearts* know. His . . . satire is wry, piercing, painful. . . . [His] humor is a way of getting revenge for the indignities which one suffers. . . ." Although he was aware of the sharp differences between this and West's previous novel, "West's imagination," he declared, "is as fecund as ever."

Generally speaking, however, the reviews hardly stimulated sales, which trickled on through 1934 until the book was forgotten altogether and at last, in 1935, remaindered for 25 cents. Ironically, this kept the memory of the book alive in a certain Midwestern liberal circle. "When I was in Detroit last summer," the novelist Jack Conroy wrote to West, "I found A Cool Million . . . in a Kresge store amid some two-bit remainders. I bought every copy I could lay my hands on, and have been doing so since. I hand the books out with the stipulation that they must be passed on . . . and every book has been passed around till it fell to pieces. I hope you'll turn out another book soon," Conroy concluded.

West, for all his efforts, was no closer than he had been in 1930 to supporting himself through his writing. His first three novels, he calculated, had earned total royalties of $780. Although never doubting that his talent lay in fiction writing, he now cast about for other ways of making money by writing—an effort that would return him to screenwriting, though not before he experienced further disappointments and almost absolute poverty.

II

West's first attempt in this period to reap harvests of gold from his awareness of the basic drives of the American mind promised in some ways to be his most successful. He had, so he believed, a sure-fire commercial idea for a theatrical revue based on American folk materials. The devaluation of the dollar and the spread of Fascism in Spain, Germany, and Italy had helped to make Europe a less desirable resort for American intellectuals. More important, the economic crisis in America helped to turn their interests homeward. In 1932, Thomas Hart Benton declared: "No American art can come to those who do not live an American life, who do not have an American psychology, and who cannot find in America justification for their lives." Unintentionally, he thus signaled the increase in interest in American folk materials during the Depression, as American artists absorbedly probed their past in order to understand their present. Benton himself had studied in Paris and experimented with abstract styles; but by the thirties he was painting, representationally, the rural South and Western American scenes, sharecroppers, the Mississippi River, Negroes. In 1934, the year when West's novel satirizing American myth was published, several other Americans completed works based on native American folk materials. Howard Hanson's opera *Merry Mount* was produced by the Metropolitan, and a nostalgic regional literature began to revive with Carl Carmer's *Stars Fell on Alabama,* the best of a large number of similar journalistic ventures into the local lives of Americans. George Gershwin's masterpiece, *Porgy and Bess,* was less than a year away.

As an outgrowth of his study of American myth in preparation for *A Cool Million,* and as the natural issue of his own involvement in American literature and folklore, West had hit upon a "notion . . . for a novel sort of review or theatrical entertainment based on traditional American material." An "American Chauve Souris," he called his notion, pointing to the way European materials had similarly been used, with some popular success, in a recent Broadway revue. Early in April he mentioned this idea to the New York producer-director John Houseman, whom he met through the Perelmans, and who became excited about it. On April 11, with Houseman's encouragement and his promise of aid, he sent into the Leland Hayward office an outline of the kind of revue he envisioned, "utilizing American folk songs, dances and legends." "I feel," West wrote the agency, "that the material should be authentic as possible . . . in no case should it be permitted to deteriorate to the 'folksy' or 'arty' in a Cape Cod Tea Shop sense."

The design he proposed combined choreographed musical numbers with a one-act play in each half of the show, given continuity through the presence on stage of and occasional monologues by "a master of ceremonies." As the sequences most elaborately to be developed, he suggested "Nantucket during the great days of the whaling industry," centering the scene in the sailors' chapel and the drama in Father Mapple's "sermon about the nature of delight . . . one of the most dramatic speeches in the English language," and including a ballet of a whale hunt. Second, "Natchez-Under-the-River at the time of the land pirates . . . full of horse-thieves, gamblers with lace cuffs . . . river men . . . Creoles and planters. . . . The songs would be the whore house ballads of the period, boastful and extremely sad." Next, the celebration of the Resurrection in the "ancient Moravian church at Bethlehem, Pennsylvania," a "folk event, older than the American Revolution." After this, the scene of "the Erie Canal at the time of its construction . . . in a canteen on one of the company barges pay-day after-

noon. . . . about as good ballet material as anything that exists."
Another would be a "gathering of mountaineers," ending in a coon
hunt and the "Hound-Call Song." Last, he suggested the use of
jazz in a sketch about "a Harlem rent party, using real scat music."
"I could keep this sort of thing up forever," West wrote, and he
went on to suggest "a barber shop of the nineties," "a group of
Louisiana, French English patois songs," "a Salvation Army
group," and an Oregon Trail scene. For the one-act interludes he
suggested works by Paul Green and Eugene O'Neill. And as the
basis for the speeches of the master of ceremonies, he proposed
"the wonderful comic monologues that Nye, Artemus Ward and
Mark Twain used to recite on their tours." The only difficulty
West foresaw was "in an embarrassment of riches." His imagination was soaring, and he was thinking, too, that "this material, arranged chronologically and combined with the history of an American family as the plot, would make an excellent moving picture."

Problems concerning the structure of the revue soon became apparent, however—namely, how "to give [the show] some kind of
form and progression and contrast." After working casually with
Houseman for two months, West had achieved a loose structure
that satisfied them. For a brief period, more than one producer
seemed sufficiently interested so that some thought was given to
casting; West suggested the humorist Irvin Cobb for the role of
the master of ceremonies. By the end of June, however, nothing
had developed. All the commercial producers to whom the outline
was submitted at last turned it down, and West himself lost interest.

But it had been a plan reflecting elements just ready to emerge
in American culture, one which again demonstrated how close
West was to it. "Within a few years," Houseman writes, "every
single item [in West's proposal] had been used and abused—first
by the folk singers and later by the show-business exploitation of
these same themes and subjects. Actually, a short time later, the
Theatre Guild produced a not dissimilar entertainment." West, no
doubt, watched these developments with some irony, but not without puzzlement and disappointment.

III

During the summer of 1934, while the first unenthusiastic reviews of *A Cool Million* were appearing and the prospects of the revue were dimming, West and S. J. Perelman, in Erwinna, began to talk about collaborating on a play—Perelman having written a novel, more than one screen play, and a stage play, in collaboration. West and he were sympathetic in their tastes: Perelman had advised him in his work on *A Cool Million* and *Miss Lonelyhearts*. West, a generous critic who spoke well of his contemporaries, was especially enthusiastic about Perelman's work, praising it above his own. Theirs was a real meeting of tastes and knowledge and their collaboration gave every promise of success.

In 1934, George S. Kaufman's play *Merrily We Roll Along*, in the tone of personal confession, traced the compromises a dramatist might make for success, winning popularity, wealth, celebrity, and prestige at the sacrifice of his personal and intellectual integrity. One of his old friends warns him: "You're getting away from the guts of things into a whole mess of polite nothing." But West and Perelman believed, as Perelman puts it, "that it would be possible for an audience to absorb a play on a very high level." They believed that they could write a first-rate play together and worked through the summer to be ready for a possible production during the fall season.

They first called their play *Guardian Angel* and finally *Even Stephen*. The heroine of the play is Diana Breed Latimer, a female novelist, author of *Stone Walls Do Not*, the forthcoming *Orchids of Evil*, and other similarly sensational novels. She quotes her own works continually, having absurdly confused her fiction with real life. As the play opens, she arrives at Briscoe, a girls' college in New England, to complete her current book, an exposé of flaming youth in college. Looking for publicity material, her publisher, Marcel Schwartz, follows her there. Obviously, both West and Perelman had in mind the sensation caused at Brown by the publication of Percy Marks's *The Plastic Age*, regarded by the public as a college exposé. Diana Breed Latimer—a triple-named woman author like those mocked in *Miss Lonelyhearts*—is a female, calculating version of their Brown instructor. "Vice exists everywhere," she announces, "but in the hothouse atmosphere of a womens' college . . . it becomes intensified. It thrives, it spreads like a giant

creeper twisting and torturing the loves of its unfortunate victims.
. . . [The girls] are helpless victims of the hypocrisy that hems
them in with iron-bound rules—chains their amorous little bodies
so that they writhe with repressed desires." Distorting and inaccu-
rately piecing together scraps of information, she and Schwartz release a story of midnight orgies to the press, which leads to several
complications. West and Perelman's broad comedy expands along
several lines. *Even Stephen* satirizes publishing and publicity practices ("Diana Breed Latimer Week! Why, for Christ's sake, I'll get
your picture on a postage stamp!"), sensational novels of expo-
sure and sex, college professors and their wives, newspapermen,
romantic young poets, and mad scientists.

By September, West and Perelman had completed a first draft,
but it met with little enthusiasm from producers; Max Gordon,
among others, rejected it. Still, they worked on a final version, hoping to find backers through Kaufman, their Pennsylvania neighbor,
or through other friends in the theater, like Woollcott or Marc
Connelly. In any event, they still held real hopes for eventual production.

IV

For a brief period at the end of the summer, West and Perelman
also talked about collaborating on a novel, but Sid and Laura returned to Hollywood before anything could come of this. At the
same time, West set another project in motion. As the author of
three novels—one of them, at least, highly praised by influential
critics—and by now beginning seriously to need a source of support
if he was to avoid returning to hotel work, he determined to apply
for a Guggenheim Fellowship. His application and project are of
the greatest interest, since both reveal the desperation and sense
of failure which West was beginning to experience at this time.

In his application, sent in before the end of September 1934,
West gave his occupation as "writer" and his correct year of birth,
1903. Among "Unpublished Work" he mentioned, in hope of bol-
stering his file, "several dozen short stories," "*St. Pamphile. A
Novelette*," and "*Guardian Angel. A Three Act Comedy.*"

His project, he told Malcolm Cowley, was to be a kind of *Exile's
Return* for his own generation. Cowley's "narrative of ideas" (as
the subtitle defined it), which had appeared that very year, traces

the progress of a young man from Pennsylvania through Harvard to Europe and back to America in search of personal and artistic commitments and values. Cowley looks back upon his dadaism in the twenties tenderly but not nostalgically, as if upon his own rebellious child. Preserving an air of bemused detachment, he suggests, in his own progress, the way that Americans in general were moving toward discovery of their true identities. Similarly, West summarized the novel he hoped to write with Guggenheim support as "a novel about the moral ideas of the generation which graduated from college in 1924." It would be an essay in the form of a novel.

The fuller statement of his plan indicates the extent to which West's novels have ideas, myths, facts, and situations as their foundations. Despite his early professed interest in the aesthetes of the 1890's and in Dada experiments, all of West's writing is marked by its concentration upon intellectual concepts. His books are truly narratives of ideas. West began with simple actualities; his novels turned these into rich webs of the surreal and symbolic. The idea came first, the imagery second. The actual writing was the difficult discovery of adequate symbols. In "Some Notes on *Miss L.*," West had hinted at this. This novel, he said, could be described as his own imagery imposed on William James's psychology: "Chapt. I—maladjustment. Chapt. III—the need for taking symbols literally is described through a dream in which a symbol is actually fleshed. Chapt. IV—decadence and disorder; see lives of Bunyan and Tolstoy. Chapt. VI—self-torture and conscious sinning: see life of any saint. And so on." Now, in similar manner, in his Guggenheim proposal he suggested that he would write an autobiographical novel, with Joyce's *Portrait*, Adams's *Education*, and Pierre Drieu La Rochelle's *Le Jeune Européen* as his models.

I intend to tell the story of a young man of my generation; that which graduated from college just before the boom and became thirty years old during the Depression. I want to show the difference between it and the one that came before; the famous "lost generation."

Chapter One
Elementary school in New York City. First ideas of American history, the world, or what is worthwhile.

Chapter Two

High School during the war. Introduction to sex. Ideas about conduct. The morals of sport.

Chapter Three

College in New England. The post-flapper period. A first attempt at definitions, including that of Beauty. Arguments over whether anything is really worth while. A discussion of values. The necessity for laughing at everything, love, death, ambition, etc.

Chapter Four

Business and the objectives involved. An attempt to love, and the difficulties encountered. The impossibility of experiencing genuine emotion.

Chapter Five

Europe in 1927. The ideas of Spengler and Valéry. The necessity for violence. The composition of a suicide note as an exercise in rhetoric.

Chapter Six

The return to America. A discussion of values and objectives at a class reunion. The discovery of economics.

This is a very brief synopsis. I hope, however, that it suggests something of what I mean to do.

No attempt has been made to describe what actually happens to my protagonist because I think that an outline of adventures is meaningless. Nevertheless, the ideas I have briefly described will be hidden as carefully as possible in the body of my narrative.

By September 1934, even after repeated commercial failures, West had by no means lost his acute sense of vocation as an artist. But he had been brought to a crisis of identity in which he began to think consciously of his fiction as a way of resolving the personal difficulties which the practice of fiction had brought on. Superficially, West held decided opinions opposing autobiographical fiction. When John Sanford had written, in *The Water Wheel*, an account of a love scene with a girl who was easily recognizable, West told him with considerable force that it must be deleted or masked. "People don't write about their friends like that," he insisted. Indeed, the models he proposed for himself, books by Joyce, Adams, Cowley, and Drieu La Rochelle, are all far from confessional autobiography. Each, in a different way, is a model of how art can transmute an individual life into a symbol through which the implications of that life, but not the life itself, may be revealed.

Doubtless, there were personal reasons for West's unwillingness to write directly autobiographical accounts of his life. He may have hesitated to do so simply because he could neither discover nor invent an artistic form suitable for treating his own life as a Jew—a theme and situation only then beginning to come into American literature, when he was interested in perfected, finished writing. At that time, as Lionel Trilling has said, "Jewish writers were not yet numerous and such novelists as there were did not find it natural and easy to take their subjects from their own lives." More deeply, it may be that West was opposed to an art form which plunged into the chaotic life of self, since as a writer he cultivated an art free from personal emotion. He regarded art as identical with form and as resulting in escape from emotion, though his own emotional responses were always deeply involved in the groundwork of his art.

West, planning his application carefully, asked F. Scott Fitzgerald, Malcolm Cowley, Edmund Wilson, and George S. Kaufman to write letters to the foundation recommending him. He could not know, of course, what they would write, but he felt sure of favorable responses from all.

He was right. "I consider [West] a writer of great promise, with a viewpoint and style of his own that are quite likely to elevate him to significance," Kaufman wrote. Wilson, who had been asked to recommend three writers, pronounced *Miss Lonelyhearts* "quite extraordinary" and West "the most original of the three . . . a very finished writer." Cowley pointed out that in the recent *New Republic* survey of excellent neglected books, *Miss Lonelyhearts* "was mentioned so often that it became almost a refrain," and concluded that "West writes brilliantly, but I think his special quality is a keen sensitiveness; perhaps 'tenderness' would be a better word."

West had told Fitzgerald, in asking for a reference: "I am writing to you, a stranger, because I know very few people, almost none whose names would mean anything to the committee, and apparently the references are the most important part of the application." If West was right, Fitzgerald's letter should have assured

him of an award. Fitzgerald reminded the trustees of the Guggenheim Foundation that in his 1934 preface to a Modern Library
reissue of *The Great Gatsby* he had specifically mentioned West as
a younger writer "being harmed . . . for lack of a public"; and he
pronounced West "a potential leader in the field of prose fiction."
The Guggenheim Foundation, Fitzgerald implied, could give
West the support which recent criticism had failed to provide.

With so many projects underway in 1934, West had held a
guarded optimism about his prospects. But as he waited out the
fall in Erwinna, he saw one hope after another fritter away. Despite
the enthusiasm of Donald Friede, *A Cool Million* failed to sell.
West's idea for the folk revue found no backers; but, in being
talked around, it found a certain currency and soon began to appear bit by bit on the stage and in clubs. Maxim Lieber had been
trying very hard to sell some of West's stories since West had an
understanding with Covici-Friede concerning the publication of a
volume of his stories in 1935, hinging upon the appearance of some
in magazines. All during the summer and fall, Lieber sent West's
stories to such magazines as *Vanity Fair, The New Yorker, Harper's
Bazaar, Esquire, The Magazine*, and *Story*—but did not succeed in
placing a single one. The fall season passed by without any producers showing interest in *Even Stephen*.

After the cruel failure of *Miss Lonelyhearts* due to circumstance
in the spring of 1933, West had believed that his fortunes could
only rise. But now, at the end of 1934, a year and a half later, he
seemed to have been moving backwards all along. Was *Balso Snell*,
whose 500-copy edition had sold quickly, to be his only success? He
had written two better novels since that one; yet *Miss Lonelyhearts*
was out of print and *A Cool Million* was about to be remaindered.
He had edited two magazines; yet now he could not place a story.
He had been alive with ideas for novels, schemes for publicity, and
anticipations of success; still, all had been shades, ghosts of hope,
rather than forecasts of achievement.

V

Indeed, West might have felt in 1934 that his kind of talent for
fiction was being shouldered aside by some aspects of the political
interests of the time. Were not writers being asked in influential

New York literary circles to write the proletarian novel, as if that were the only form appropriate for any imagination? Leftist critics simplified issues and recommended directness rather than depth. To produce fiction satisfying the new standards, Edwin Seaver announced, the writer needed to possess "the revolutionary comprehension and resolve that the future belongs to the workers," and must be "equipped with the Marxian analysis of the decay of the bourgeoisie and the predicament of the petty bourgeoisie under the impact of the capitalist crisis." In *The Great Tradition*, Granville Hicks summed up the dogmatic aspects of such literary values by fulsomely praising novels like Clara Weatherwax's *Marching, Marching* as "richly poetic," while speaking of Faulkner's books as "dangerously close to triviality."

Such critical convictions were patently silly, of course, and affected only the art of less talented writers. Such criticism hardly touched the public, which was buying books like *Goodbye Mr. Chips, Of Time and the River,* and *Tender Is the Night,* during this period. Nor did it much affect friends of West's like Edmund Wilson, Cowley, James T. Farrell, or Josephine Herbst. Like West, Faulkner, Robert Penn Warren, Katherine Anne Porter, and others all followed their individual talents. Most of these writers, of course, had either established reputations or a traditional sense of society to strengthen their resolve. But West, in taking for his subject exactly the same mass materials as proletarian writers did, continually had to justify to himself his way with fiction against theirs. While West was interested in the mass mind, the new novelists were advised to treat collectives; while he was interested in American myth, they were investigating American economics and politics; while he was concerned with suffering, they were acutely conscious of exploitation; while West's imagination, informed by wide reading, was rich with the traditions of literature, the new novelists were advised by V. F. Calverton and others to make a "literature dominated by a dynamic revolutionary idea." West was a true revolutionary in refusing to deal with revolutionary materials in orthodox ways.

In *A Cool Million*, indeed, West satirized the political success fictions of the proletarian novels; for these, as much as Alger's books, were wooden contests of vice and virtue. Yet proletarian novels, as George Milburn says, were "paying off" with liberal critics in the early and mid-thirties. James T. Farrell and West more than once discussed and agreed upon the limitations of such fiction during 1934. Though the novels they both wrote vibrated with complex political, economic, and social implications, Farrell was soon attacked in *New Masses*, while West's books were virtually ignored by Marxist critics, who, as Alfred Kazin says, "hated no one so much as intellectuals . . . who still preserved revolutionary ideas in the form of honest personal judgments." After the decline of the experimental literary magazine, West had no real outlet for his work; such little magazines as replaced the defunct *transition* or *Contact* were, like *Anvil*, *Left Front*, or *Blast*, decidedly left wing. To their editors, West's complex work seemed trivial when economics seemed so relevant.

West, certainly, was not entirely unschooled by leftist friends. Michael Gold frequently attempted to convert him to proletarian convictions. "His writing," Gold says, "seemed to me symbolic rather than realistic and that was, to me, the supreme crime." Gold declared that West had psychological problems and that he wrote symbolically rather than realistically in order to cover them up. But, Gold encouraged him, he was not a cynic, "he was fundamentally on the side of people," and if he would commit himself to the proletarian cause, he would be cured of his "modern diseases."

Several of West's activities during 1934–5 suggest that he half-heartedly attempted to make this accommodation. The first evidence is a review of Gene Fowler's biography of Mack Sennett, which West published in *The New Republic* in November 1934. He began, in the tone of *A Cool Million*: "From Shirtsleeves to Shirtsleeves in one generation is just as true an American legend as from Ploughboy to President or from Poland to Polo. Moreover, we, who are without ambition, prefer it." Mack Sennett, he continues, built his success on the assumption of the stupidity of the masses. Of course, many things can be said in defense of the masses, West concludes: "Gene Fowler wisely leaves that to Gilbert Seldes; we prefer to leave it to Mike Gold, and no offense meant." Still, there remains a hint of irony regarding both views of the masses.

Early in 1935, however, West was actually prodded into leftist activity on behalf of workers. A few years earlier he probably would not have bought his shoelaces in Ohrbach's department store; now he was to be arrested for marching in a picket line outside it. The year 1935, when picketing waiters, cooks, and busboys from the Waldorf-Astoria sang "The International" as they marched, was marked by daily reports of strikes, and picket lines were familiar sights. If West would not follow Gold's advice in his writing, perhaps he could nonetheless, like many of his friends, enlist as a private in the war of the classes.

During the winter and spring of 1935, West was living in the Hotel Brevoort on Fifth Avenue, a block north of Washington Square. In the same hotel, he frequently saw Farrell, who was bringing his *Studs Lonigan* trilogy to its conclusion with *Judgment Day* (1935). Friendly and intelligent, Farrell frequently came to West's room to read him recently completed portions of his novel, and occasionally they met for breakfast in the drugstore across the street. After breakfast one cold Saturday morning early in February, Farrell said, "Come on along with me, Pep, and get arrested." Theirs was a kind of holiday mood, and when they ran into the novelist Leane Zugsmith, they brought her along, taking a cab to strike headquarters.

The Office Workers Union publicity organizer for the strike at Ohrbach's, one striking writer remembers, "felt that the strike was not being adequately covered in the New York press because of Ohrbach's substantial advertising budget. She thought that there would be a few stories if she got some authors together and had them do the picketing." Moreover, by putting writers on the picket line, the union hoped to circumvent or break a court injunction against labor picketing. There had already been over 150 arrests.

The turnout was somewhat disappointing, but by the time West's party arrived at the union office, about a dozen other writers were there, including Tess Slesinger, Herbert Kline, Edward Dahlberg, Edward Newhouse, and Isidore Schneider. They were instructed by the union lawyers that if they were stopped by the police they should demand that the whole of the injunction be read, while they continued to picket—Dahlberg volunteered to make the demand. They gathered together in front of Ohrbach's and (*New Masses* reported) "carried signs which protested the injunction and marched in double formation in front of the store. The picket line was augmented by several hundred workers who joined the writers . . ." When the police ordered them to disperse, Dahlberg demanded a reading of the injunction, which took forty-five minutes, while they continued to march. Upon the termination of the reading, they simply went across Union Square to Klein's department store, where another strike was in progress, and continued to picket.

West had insisted that Leane Zugsmith not get involved in any of this, since there was some danger of being hurt; he advised her to go home, promising to call later. This was fortunate, since at Klein's "they were assaulted by the police and ridden down by mounted cops. Newhouse was clubbed . . . and a girl picket was knocked to the ground by a horse's hoofs. The pickets, though they tried to hold their line, had little chance against the cops, who finally loaded the writers into a patrol wagon and took them to the station house, where several policemen and detectives explained that everybody who picketed was a Red and all Reds ought to be dumped into some old ferry boats and sent to the bottom twelve miles out. They couldn't imagine how a 'good Irishman' like Farrell could have been implicated in such a scrape." Dahlberg, charged with violating the injunction, and the other writers, booked for disorderly conduct and obstructing arrest, were locked in cells. Edward Newhouse recalls that West and Dahlberg were put into the same cell, where West sat disconsolately, "his face morbidly wretched," even though among the other writers "there was a certain amount of exhilaration: singing, fun and games. West took no part in any of it. . . . When a turnkey came by on some routine errand, West told him to go to hell." West could not be happy even as a proletarian-novelist-on-a-picket-line.

The union had mobilized a formidable array of legal talent as part of the publicity campaign and after a few hours, when the writers were brought into night court, Arthur Garfield Hays and others came prepared for a defense. "Quantities of forensic eloquence were lost to the world," Newhouse says, when Judge Linderman, who was impressed by West's natty appearance, put the arresting officer on the stand, asked him two questions—how they had marched (two abreast) and how wide the sidewalk in front of the store was (20 or 30 feet)—and then announced: "Case dismissed!" West got back to his room in the Brevoort at midnight

and called Leane Zugsmith, telling her nonchalantly about what
had happened.

He played a minor part in one other important left-wing activity
at about this time. Like most of his friends, he had occasionally
gone to meetings of the John Reed Club and he had followed its
metamorphosis into the League of American Writers. In 1935
West was one of the signers of the call for the first annual congress
of the league. This manifesto, proclaiming a "Congress of American revolutionary writers" to be held in New York late in April
1935, "invited all writers who . . . have clearly indicated their
sympathy with the revolutionary cause; who do not need to be convinced of the decay of capitalism, of the inevitability of revolution." In his Guggenheim proposal West spoke of "the impossibility of experiencing genuine emotion." There is no doubt that in
1935 he was still unable fully to commit himself to social action.
Even while he was being drawn more and more into society, he was
not able to respond to it freely except on the deepest emotional
and imaginative levels. Still, he wanted to help liberal causes and
he was happy to allow the congress to use his name for whatever it
was worth. Henry Hart, the chief organizer of the congress, says
that West "seemed to me to regard the Left as cynically as he
regarded the rest of life, but [he] felt [that] a sufficient proportion
of the Left meant sufficiently well for him to withhold his fire."

Papers were read at the congress by friends of West—Cowley,
Josephson, Conroy, and Farrell, among others—but West was not
present to hear them. A paper called "From Dada to the Red Front"
was sent by Louis Aragon—but West was going his own way, and
that way would not be toward Aragon's "socialist realism." West
may have wished that he could sacrifice his sense of suffering for a
belief in socialism; he may have regarded the programs of the
League of American Writers as desirable but impossible for him;
he may have thought of the 1935 congress as he had of the fraternities at Brown, wishing to belong, yet somewhat scornful of those
who did. However far left his hopes may have slanted him, he still
remained intellectually detached. He could be neither a socialist
nor a Communist, since he wanted ultimately to be nothing but a
novelist.

VI

When the Congress of American Writers opened, West was back working in Hollywood, where he hoped, in his spare time, to resume being a novelist. His "American Chauve Souris," *Even Stephen*, his stories—all these, however interesting, had been only diversions from the true center of his talent. By diligent effort he might have made a success on the stage or in magazine fiction. He had made sporadic efforts toward both, but finally persevered only in the novel. Now he turned back to the ideas that had been stirring and turning in his imagination since his stay in Hollywood in the summer of 1933.

In March 1935, when Alfred Kazin stopped by Farrell's room in the Brevoort, he met West, "a young man comfortably draped on the couch who said he was going out to Hollywood to write films, and that he had dropped in to say good-bye. . . . He was cool and humorous, lying there with ankles comfortably crossed and his arms under his head. . . . [West] kidded Farrell, he was easy, and Farrell . . . soon melted and lost something of his professionally tough stance." Still, when they were alone, Farrell was tough with West, saying over and over about Hollywood, "I wouldn't do it, Pep."

West defended himself, Farrell remembers, by saying that "he was interested in the odd characters, the clowns there," as material for fiction. Hollywood possessed a misshapen uniqueness appropriate to his special attitudes and talent. During the Depression, it was a boom town presenting remarkable parallels to the lavish earlier periods of the Gilded Age and the Robber Barons. "There is an air of false prosperity out here that makes news of breadlines and starvation unreal," Perelman wrote. Well, West had had his fill of breadlines and picket lines. His subject was spiritual, not material, poverty.

Hollywood was a mecca of prosperity, and West was drawn to the fantastic, restless people who were attracted by it—all, like Lemuel Pitkin and the correspondents of Miss Lonelyhearts, desperately seeking wealth, success, ease, pleasure, and entertainment. Perhaps Hollywood, huddled near the sea, was the last resort in America of such values and dreams, just as movies themselves, guided by the Hays Office, gave new prestige to Alger-like stories of the universal triumph of good. Perhaps Hollywood was the final

resting place of the American Dream; and perhaps there the grotesque lives and the violence which issued from the frustration of
that dream could be more sharply seen and more accurately put
into a novel.

Certainly, this was West's hope. West had a way of taking up
many ideas for books in conversation before he settled upon any of
them; and his final choice often included fragments of earlier possibilities. He had been full of exotic and erotic stories about Hollywood in 1933. He once told Farrell about displays of sexual relations in public. He spoke to Peter Blume, with obvious fascination,
about the surrealist movie sets; and he added, after writing *A Cool
Million*, that he believed that if there was to be a Fascist revolution
in America, it would begin in Hollywood. West's response to
Hollywood—his convictions, his observations, and his attitudes—
was still half formed, but he was convinced that he could make a
novel from Hollywood materials.

He already had sketched out the plot for the book he wanted to
write, and he was going back to Hollywood to explore its elements.
He "was full of enthusiasms," Josephine Herbst says, and "wanted
to get a boat and sail around the world." "There's a trip I would
like to take. That's to the Indies," he wrote to her. "But," he
added darkly, "I wouldn't be able to start until about Xmas and
then I don't know what year." This scheme related directly to the
plot that was churning in his imagination. In a California newspaper he had found an account of a yacht named *The Wanderer*
which (as West told it) had been chartered as a pleasure boat by a
group of grotesque pleasure-seekers, including a family of Eskimos,
dwarfs, prostitutes, movie cowboys, and a gigantic Lesbian. The
hero, as West envisioned this book, was to be modeled after a soldier of fortune who ran the actual boat and the story was to tell the
fantastic adventures of these sensation-seekers on one trip. The
point of view would be sardonic in the classical sense, emphasizing
the reversal of expectations. Setting out on a joyful sunny day, the
yacht would soon be engulfed by dark catastrophes, ending in multiple murders. Far from settled, this plan was always shifting prom-
isingly in West's accounts of it. Sometimes he outlined a notion to
make the yacht into an offshore speakeasy and gambling ship, en-
riching the possibilities for violence and an exotic mixture of
strange characters. At other times he spoke of having his ship

founder on a desert island in the Pacific, instead of returning to California, and disgorging all his misfits onto it, then watching the grotesque results. (In one form or another, the idea of the voyage of fools engaged West's imagination over a long period of time; and in 1940, planning another never-to-be-written novel, he would return to it again, under new influences and with a changed heart.)

Then, too, his sardonic point of view toward this material sometimes melted into the kind of deadpan humor he had used in *A Cool Million*. "Slapstick weighed upon him heavily. The goofy guy (versus the fast-talking gagster who punctuates his jokes by hitting the innocent over the head) was a symbolic figure for him," says Robert Coates. In yet another version of this novel, then, West replaced the yacht impressario with an old slapstick vaudeville comedian, a bedraggled harlequin, and set the scene in an old vaudevillians' rooming house. The whole action in this book, as he described it, would consist of "a sort of endless double-take," with people clowning at funerals, sad at weddings, always acting.

There were other ideas or fragments of ideas tumbling about in his imagination. He spoke to an Erwinna neighbor "a number of times about a character to be in his next book who was conscious of her hands, her hands seemed to her enormous and at times as though they had nothing to do with the rest of her, she was ashamed of them and frightened by them." This character would be metamorphosed into Homer Simpson. West also told Peter Blume of a sketch he was planning which involved a man sitting on a box of dynamite peeling an apple. And he wrote Perelman about the comic usefulness of the connecting bath. He mentioned to Michael Gold a notion for a novel dealing comically with building construction. These notions had connections with the double-take and the comedy of appearance and reality.

All these plans, of course, in one way or another affected *The Day of the Locust*, in which West was ultimately to transmute his Hollywood materials into fiction. Each, it turned out, was not so much a projection for a book as a way by which West opened up his imagination. In the spring of 1935, as he left New York, his mind was roving over the possibilities for his novel. The past year and a half had been splintered with disappointment. Latest of all, in the recent announcements of Guggenheim Fellowships for 1935, his name had not appeared.

A wanderer again and, it seemed, a failure, he would write of wanderers and the disinherited. Despite the commercial failure of his novels, he knew that they had been his only successes, and he now returned to his own truest self, in the craft of fiction.

14 / "Caliphonia, Here I Come"

> Female, 24, white, college senior. —During my high-school period I particularly liked pictures in which the setting was a millionaire's estate or some such elaborate place. After seeing a picture of this type, I would imagine myself living such a life of ease as the society girl I had seen. My daydreams would be concerned with lavish wardrobes, beautiful homes, servants, imported automobiles, yachts, and countless handsome suitors.
>
> —Herbert Blumer, *Movies and Conduct* (1933)

> Why, tell me why, I dare you, we should spend half a million dollars on it, what fresh ideas have we got to sell?—it isn't funny enough to make them piss in their seats—it isn't sad enough to make them snuffle, and there's no message for them to carry away. Go back and put a message in it.
>
> —Burt Kelly to Nathanael West, concerning West's script for the film *I Stole a Million*, April 1939

For millions of motion-picture fans, Hollywood was a luminous center of blazing romance, of dazzling possibility, of beautiful people. If thousands of correspondents asked the Miss Lonelyhearts of America for help, thousands more found their dreams realized in the golden legends of Hollywood, chronicled in such magazines as *Photoplay, Movie Mirror, Screen Guide, Silver Screen, Screenland, Motion Picture,* and *Movie Story,* each of which, in the thirties, boasted a monthly circulation between 250,000 and 500,000.

But Hollywood's romance and legend, as West had learned in 1933, were confined to the magazines; behind films were business realities and commercial calculations, and in 1935 the profitable business of making movies did not seem to require the efforts of

Nathanael West. He had written, as we can now see, some of the true legends of his time. But if his novels could not sell in the thousands—Hollywood producers may well have asked—how could he write for the millions? He had been cool and comfortable talking to Kazin, Farrell, and others in New York about writing films, but in Hollywood he was unable to find a job of any kind.

During the summer and fall of 1935, increasingly desperate, impoverished, and bewildered, he was living at the Pa-Va-Sed apartment hotel on N. Ivar Street, just above Hollywood Boulevard. For all his personal suffering there, this scene was to be crucial to his work, since it provided the model for Tod's hotel in *The Day of the Locust.* Even more important, the emotions he experienced there went into the inception and black heart of that novel.

At the Pa-Va-Sed lived bit players, stunt men, and more than one midget. Vaudeville was dead but several seedy comics lingered on, some employed occasionally on radio but most waiting for film jobs that never came. West himself was often sick and alone. For a time he was cared for by one of the midgets, who brought him chicken broth, and by a blond female bit player who was also a part-time prostitute. A stunt man tried to convince him that he could get a job as an extra if he was really desperate for money. This period was probably the darkest in West's life. He had gone to Hollywood certain that he would get a job on the strength of his recent novel sale to Columbia, but Geller seemed unable to get him an assignment and he was being supported entirely by Perelman. "Maybe I'll get a job before you really run out of dough," he hopelessly wrote to Perelman. "Geller is trying hard and Warner's has again promised a job. . . . I told Jim to take anything he offers and that I'll work for as low as fifty a week, anything, even a reader's job." Then, too, West was feeling angry and ashamed about a recent love affair—the echoes of recrimination had not yet died down.

That summer he contracted gonorrhea, which was not completely cured when he developed a congested prostate gland in the fall; the two conditions combined to cause him excruciating pain. "Even if I got a job now," he wrote Perelman, "I couldn't accept it. I can't walk and am in continuous pain. . . . I can't work during the day; I can't sit in a chair for more than ten minutes at a time, and at night I can't sleep. The doc gives me morphine, but it gives me headaches and I lie awake all night in a half doze waiting for it to get light." Still, from moment to moment he could summon up wit, even at his own expense, as in this letter to Perelman: "I have had a very bad week. My prostate gland became swollen to the size of an orange—On l'examinet avec interet et curiosité comme un bel orange—as one much greater than I has put it—causing me acute discomfort, even when I lay stretched out on my back. . . . The doctor says it is nothing, or almost nothing, a thing that can happen to anybody, God forbid, even those who have not contracted the disease I have. It is caused by a simple (?) congestion of the gland brought on from a lack of intercourse (may he rot in hell) made acute by the irritation caused by the membrane of the penis giving a false erection (as a woman's heart I suppose—science, or rather scientists, are so sentimental—this is to show how sick I am) without natural relief."

But, for the most part, he was deeply melancholic. He took the name "Melvin Apple" for himself and in a kind of absurd and witty hysteria sent dark telegrams to Perelman, like: "Shadows deep enemies lurk everywhere stop unable to walk must soon surrender no terms possible with fate stop." In a letter he attempted to express (but also make comedy of) his despair by parodying Dostoevsky: " 'Brother, brother, how shall I know God?' sobbed Alyosha, who by this time was exceedingly drunk—nothing less than the greatest of Russians can find words for it, I'm afraid." The congested prostate affected his energy and he was losing weight, eventually twenty-five pounds. His clothes did not fit him any more, and they were ragged. "My striped flannel," he wrote, "is completely worn out, the seat gave way; the cloth disappeared in that important spot, silently and without residue or fuss." He asked his sister to send him "a couple of the cheapest Brooks button-down collar sport shirts. . . . I have only two left and no white ones, the collars fell apart." He summed up what he felt to be his self-pity, his tattered appearance, and his emaciation by quipping: "I talk like Gandhi already and when you see me again I'll probably look like him."

One irony seemed to compound another in his despair. "Here's the twisteroo," he wrote to Perelman. "It's a hummer; hold your hat. (I hope it's the last twisteroo and not the twisteroo before the last twisteroo.)" A man came to his door asking "if there was any shoes to be fixed. . . . My shoes needed heels so I gave them to him." Several days later, West came upon a story in the paper about a gang of shoe thieves. They were even stealing his shoes now, he moaned.

More serious by far, of course, was his failure to find a job. The author of three distinguished novels, he saw nonentities and opportunists busily at work. Even this was not so painful as his recognition that in the hierarchies of Hollywood he had no status at all. Dashiell Hammett, he was confident, would get him a job on a Hunt Stromberg picture, *The Foundry*, for which he was assistant producer; but, West said, "he made me eat plenty [of] dirt." Hammett "had some kind of party and I sneaked out early and spit all the way home to get the taste of arse out of my mouth. I couldn't drink and had a miserable time of course, drinking wouldn't have helped and he did his best to rub it in. One of the girls there tried to make up to me and for some reason or other he said, 'leave him alone he hasn't got a pot to piss in.' Another time when I tried to talk to him about Stromberg and a job, he made believe he didn't understand what I was saying and called out in a loud voice so that everyone could hear, 'I haven't any money to lend you now, but call me next week and I'll lend you some.' "

West grew more and more desperate about money. "Sid, I don't know if I ever thanked you adequately or can thank you," he told Perelman. He would pay him back, he said—but how? "Something has got to happen, if only I don't get run over. I'm very careful when crossing the street these days, but they'll probably run up on the sidewalk to get me." Such despair inevitably affected his confidence even in his Hollywood novel, which was progressing slowly in an early draft. "I spend my time thinking of how much money I owe you," he wrote to Perelman, "and how it seems to be impossible for me to ever get on my feet again. My new book will be a failure. I can't possibly get a job. I have deteriorated mentally. I have nothing to say, and no talent for writing, then I get up and take two more tablets of morphine, against the doctor's orders. I fall asleep for half an hour—then wake up and find myself laughing quietly."* He wrote Josephine Herbst that he was "fed up with

---

* Cf. West's early story "Western Union Boy" in which he uses a semi-autobiographical tale as a symbol of the state of automatic, mechanical failure: "All Western Union boys do not deliver messages. Some are lawyers, writers,

books." The one he was writing, he said, was "going to be the last even if it sells two thousand copies, even twenty-five hundred."

His room in the Pa-Va-Sed, decorated in "Spanish and quite horrid," had a bed that pulled out of the wall. In the kitchenette he made himself breakfast and lunch, and he went out for dinner. The heat was terrific; there were fires every night in the canyons. The city itself seemed ready to burn up; flames were licking around its edges. Once a house across the street caught fire and West ran out of his apartment to watch it burn. "It was like a furnace," he said. But all day and night, generally, he lay on his bed, unable to sleep and unable to work. It was a dry time.

In return for sewing on his buttons and doing his dishes, West, with grim amusement, loaned the girls in the hotel his car to use on their business engagements, and he revived the idea he had had much earlier in Paris of compiling a dictionary of prostitute speech. He even told Wells Root that "he had gathered a glossary which he proposed some day to publish—very privately—for the benefit of H. L. Mencken." (This glossary would be compressed into a few pages of Faye Greener's and Mary Dove's talk.) Before long, as a producer friend says, West "knew a lot of tarts and madams around town in a nice way—I think he liked to listen to them. . . . They used to talk to him . . . they trusted him. I knew the same people—not in a 'nice' way—but [West] was an intimate of theirs. I'm certain that they must have told him all kinds of things that they would tell to no one else."

West knew extras, grips, madams, and all kinds of back-lot people. One of these acquaintances, Albert Hackett remembers, "asked Pep to take care of a suitcase for him. Pep kept it for months and months. Something happened . . . that made Pep

---

and so forth. But all of them are busy doing something under their regular occupations, and it is this something that makes them 'Western Union boys.' What they are doing is failing. The mechanical part of it is very important.

" 'Western Union boys' are very eager. They try hard to please. They permit themselves dreams—I have proof. They have adventures. But what they are really doing is failing. You know it and they know you know it. They even laugh at themselves! Not often, I admit, but the thing is that they do laugh. It is a peculiar sort of laughter. It can be dismissed with something about a breaking heart and a jester's motley, but it shouldn't be."

This is the kind of horrible, helpless laughter accompanied by visions of failure that West was laughing all through 1935.

suspicious. He went quickly to the closet, took out the suitcase, and opened it. It was filled with dope." West managed—perhaps through other friends—to dispose of it. He led the visiting Matthew Josephson through a string of bars along Hollywood Boulevard. He seemed to know all the shabby people there and related to Josephson the stories of their lives. These tales may have been, like so many others, products more of fancy than fact; now, more than ever, West's vision of the tragedy of mass life was tied to his own despair. In one bar, "a resort of extras, there was a large man with cauliflower ears who [West said] had been in an episode of heroism in Chicago . . . [and had] come to Hollywood and made one film." "There he is," he told Josephson in conclusion, "he's waiting here—like everybody else—like me." West, Josephson says, "made this case sound like a parable of [his] own coming there with high hopes of money and fame, having written *Miss Lonelyhearts*, a brilliant book, and then only remaining there doing his dreary hack pieces and being utterly unknown and disregarded, except by a few of us."

II

Located only a few blocks from the Pa-Va-Sed was Stanley Rose's famous Hollywood Boulevard bookstore. Actually owned by Charles Katz and Carey McWilliams, Rose's shop had opened early in 1935. It was an exotic, Hollywood version of Moss and Kamin's; West responded to it with similar enthusiasm and appeared in it with singular devotion. Located opposite the offices of the Screen Writers Guild (then on Cherokee Street), and next to Musso and Frank's restaurant, where West often ate, it was the only place in Hollywood where writers could gather entirely apart from movie and studio life. With Rose himself, a character who held great fascination for him, West became close friends. Rose had not gone beyond the fourth grade and had not learned to read until he was wounded in World War I; he moved so much more slowly than even West did that West himself called Rose "Jeeter," after Caldwell's character. A frustrated confidence man, Rose loved to think of himself as an "operator" and became involved in a wide assortment of swindles. For one of these—pirating an edition of Chick Sales's *The Specialist*—he had been sent to jail for a year. Yet he had impeccable, intuitive taste in literature and appeared at the studios regularly with two briefcases full of books to sell; for all his pretenses of insensitivity, he loved writers, lent them money, let them sign his name at Musso and Frank's, and eventually became a literary agent, with William Saroyan as his most prominent client.

In the rear of the shop, Rose cleared a room where writers (and readers) could sit and talk literature. Here, too, he held exhibitions of contemporary art which attracted prominent collectors like the Arensbergs and the Maitlands. Calder, Klee, Moore, and Brancusi had their first showings on the West Coast there, where original work by Picasso and Matisse was also to be seen. Occasionally, someone would play recordings of modern music—of works by Shostakovich, among others. Rose would often hand around a bottle of orange wine. The back of the shop had the atmosphere of a club. At different times West sat there with such writers as John O'Hara, Horace McCoy, Jo Pagano, John Fante, Meyer Levin, Guy Endore, William Saroyan, Jim Tully, F. Scott Fitzgerald, George Milburn, Gene Fowler, William Faulkner, John Bright, Budd Schulberg, John Sanford, Erskine Caldwell, and Dashiell Hammett. In contrast to his position at the studios, West was a distinguished man in this group and to some extent he was able to draw the energy to continue work on his new novel from his pleasure in this admiration. In a sense, he wrote for the approval of this group.

Rose also led West to material for fiction. Among his acquaintances, Rose numbered not only bookstore and literary friends, but also friends from certain segments of the Hollywood underworld. Through his brother, who had been a bootlegger during Prohibition, but particularly as a consequence of his own time in prison, Rose had become a familiar in what Lillian Hellman calls the "whorish, drunk, dope-taking world" that centered around Hollywood Boulevard. Small-time gangsters occasionally mixed with writers in the shop, each group pursuing its own errands. At times, however, some of Rose's friends crossed into the other group. Apparently Rose sold or rented pornography to his literary friends, and was known to have slot machines in the back. Less frequently, he introduced his friends among writers to his acquaintances in the Hollywood underworld. Erskine Caldwell recalls that he and West "used to go to Stanley Rose's when everything else closed up." John Bright, who had been "intimate with the underworld in Chicago" and had written *Public Enemy*, says that West "met a lot of bums and derelicts and criminals through Stanley Rose. . . . The 'respectable' criminal he loathed, and he would say that a bank robber was a much more honest man than a banker." True criminals, West said, were at the least not hypocritical. Moreover, with Rose and some of his underworld friends he went to the boxing matches at the American Legion Arena and to the cockfights held illegally in the Hollywood hills and at Pismo Beach.

From Rose's circle, West moved outward. While he was working at Republic Films in North Hollywood between 1936 and 1938, he lived some distance away from the studios, near Hollywood Boulevard, or just north of it, in the Hollywood hills. When Raymond Chandler chose a violent and vivid location for Philip Marlowe's office, he put it at 615 Cahuenga Boulevard, almost exactly in the same neighborhood where West generally chose to live. After the Pa-Va-Sed apartment hotel on N. Ivar Street, West lived on Alta Loma Terrace just north of Hollywood Boulevard near Highland, at the nearby Cahuenga Terrace, on N. Stanley Street, and on Canyon Terrace. Nor did West confine his excursions to the Hollywood hills. He was also, it is clear, interested in the Mexican-American life in central Los Angeles. One friend who had served time for manslaughter, then later became a screenwriter and married a Mexican woman whom he had met in a brothel, introduced West to the downtown Mexican community in which they lived. West, who visited frequently, was interested in (but not at all amused by) the sordid aspects of that often degraded, minority life, and he inquired about the latest doings of the local punks, pimps, and tarts. Possibly through these acquaintances, he made contacts with a group of smugglers working along the Mexican border. During that period, it was illegal to take a rifle or a hand gun across the border, but West managed to do so innumerable times with no difficulty, while other Hollywood people were caught and had to pay thousands of dollars in blackmail to stay out of jail. Leonard Fields, who watched these operations in fear and trembling, says that, in Mexicali, West knew "all kinds of offbeat people, [including] smugglers . . . [and] Americans south of the border, offbeat guys. They ran cantinas, or fishing boats that looked fishy. There were a couple of brothers who ran the Mint Café—which was a gathering place [for such people] and he knew them and they trusted him, and did things for us." On one occasion, when one of West's acquaintances had had a serious automobile accident in Mexico and was thrown in jail—"then synonymous with death"— West got him released overnight through these brothers, after all legal attempts had failed.

Sy Bartlett, a screenwriter friend at Republic and later Columbia, opened up to West insights into still another aspect of the life of the masses. Bartlett, who had been a police reporter in Chicago, was good friends with the Los Angeles crime reporters and in the evenings spent a lot of time in the homicide department of the police station. West soon began to accompany him downtown after work to have dinner with the reporters and officers, and to go with them on police calls. He was, Bartlett remembers, "terribly anxious to go out on these calls." One of the routine investigations on which he frequently went along involved the inspection of the downtown Filipino dance halls. He was, Bartlett says, "a keen observer, always looking for bizarre backgrounds, and always attempting to improve his knowledge of the human race." To the subject of crime, as to so many others, West seemed to have already devoted some study. He surprised the reporters and officers by repeating crime statistics and patterns of crime. He was obviously "very interested in . . . the really seamy side of life." Bartlett recalls vividly that one night, a few days after Christmas 1937, they were in the homicide room when a call came, "and when we arrived we entered a room where there was the body of the husband, with a breadknife plunged into his heart, a cheap artifical Christmas tree, two beds, and his wife. They had argued about money. West had an incredibly accurate and understanding eye, and while we were going back he not only spoke with great feeling about the large number of domestic murders soon after Christmas, when the family has to pay the bills incurred living up to what he called the fraud of Christmas, but he said that he had seen a cheese sandwich on the mantel with a perfect bite out of it and knew that the husband had artifical teeth—and from that symbol he re-created the whole quarrel and the tragedy of this death."

He was, as Bartlett concludes, "a great people-watcher." However strongly he had resisted settling in Hollywood, however much he yearned for the East and for freedom from screenwriting to work on his book, it is clear that the life which had chosen him was proving fruitful and that he was absorbed by it. Arthur Strawn, another Hollywood acquaintance, remembers West in a characteristic posture: "I can see Pep now, as I not infrequently encountered him on Hollywood Boulevard after dinner, standing in front of Musso & Frank's eating place, frequently alone, idly chewing a toothpick and eyeing his surroundings." All through this time, West was shrewdly "eyeing his surroundings" and assessing their implications for the state of man. Might not these too fecundate his novel? It was the novel toward which he was going in going to Hollywood.

In his earlier novels, West had been an observer of dreams; watching Hollywood people, he was again exploring dream life. But now he was to be a maker of dreams, a screenwriter, and his new book would have in it the starers and dreamers, as well as the performers, the creators of dreams. His life on the fringes of Hollywood and his work on the margins of the movie studios, then, would merge in the book he was writing all along.

III

One evening, Tod Hackett and Faye Greener, characters in *The Day of the Locust*, discuss fantasies. "She told him that she often spent the whole day making up stories. . . . She would get some music on the radio, then lie down on her bed and shut her eyes. She had a large assortment of stories to choose from. After getting herself in the right mood, she would go over them in her mind, as though they were a pack of cards, discarding one after another until she found the one that suited. . . . While she admitted that her method was too mechanical for the best results and that it was better to slip into a dream naturally, she said that any dream was better than no dream and beggars couldn't be choosers."

West's screenwriting was very similar to Faye's dreaming. He too had a pack of fantasies to thumb through mechanically. Every studio had files that were a jungle of dreams—stories, synopses of novels, "original" story ideas, treatments never turned into screenplays, screenplays never produced, and even successful screenplays ready to be remade into slightly different movies. West had, in novels and short stories, investigated such mass dreaming. But he also had a personal deck of dreams. Into the rich and soiled packs of studio files and his own sense of mass fantasy, he dipped during five years of screenwriting, pulling out dreams, like strange, wriggling, tropical creatures, to set down on paper.

All during 1935, West had trouble getting a job: the hierarchical organization of Hollywood excluded him. But on January 17, 1936, two and a half years after his first employment at Columbia, he signed a contract with Republic Productions, Inc., at a salary of $200 a week, on a week-to-week basis, with no provision for salary increases. On May 18, 1936, having proved satisfactory to the producers, he signed a standard contract for six months, beginning at a salary of $250. The provisions of a Hollywood screenwriter's contract at this time are revealing. West contracted to give his "exclusive services" to Republic, to write, as required, "stories, adaptions, continuities, scenarios, and dialogue," and to assign the authorship of these and all other original, literary material to the studio; to suspend his contract in case of lockout and to give his studio injunctive powers in case of breach of contract; to agree to be loaned to other studios; and to give the producers the exclusive rights of exercising options on the continuance of his contract. Options providing for salary increases at the end of every six months were always contractually dazzling. West's Republic contract provided that after five years his salary would be $1,000 a week, but in fact no writer there made more than $400, and some worked for as little as $25 a week. In return for this paper promise, the writer gave himself and his work into studio thrall. West had been forced into the Republic job since it seemed there were no other possibilities open to him. His attempts to write novels and stories that might sell, his flirtations with stage production, his hope of getting a Guggenheim Fellowship had all been disappointed. *A Cool Million* was apparently not to be filmed. Finally, since he was a member of the Screen Writers Guild at a time when producers and studios were bitterly trying to crush it, he found the major studios uninterested in him.

The management of Republic Productions, one of the minor studios, had seen in the war between the guild and the majors an opportunity to employ highly paid guild writers at low salaries by silently instituting guild demands in their contracts and so taking on writers who would not submit, elsewhere, to non-guild contracts. Representing the producers at Republic, Leonard Fields met with officials and members of the guild late in 1935 at the Hollywood Athletic Club and proposed unofficially to accept guild demands. Under this scheme, around the same time that West arrived, Lester Cole, Wells Root, Horace McCoy, and Samuel Ornitz were working at Republic.

The president of Republic, Herbert J. Yates, also owned Consolidated Film Laboratories, which had processed and financed the films of such small independent studios as Majestic, Mascot, Monogram, and Liberty Productions. In a shrewd manipulation, Yates had foreclosed these four, amalgamated their organizations under the name Republic Productions, and housed them in a former Hal Roach studio on Radford Avenue in North Hollywood. While he remained in New York at Consolidated Film, sending a succession of producers to head Republic, it was clear that the studio was devoted to money- rather than to movie-making. No A-budget pictures were produced—most films were made for less than $100,000, their artistic standard residing in simple formula questions, as summarized by one Republic producer: "Where's the good guy? Where's the good woman? Where are the white hats? and Where are the black hats?" It was, in short, a factory for the quick and cheap production of dreams to be consumed in all-night theaters, warm sanctuaries on winter nights, where two dreams might be purchased for a quarter. It was no wonder that most writers called it "Repulsive" Studios and spoke of it as a prison.

For West, it was both the worst and the best place to work. The product there was so antithetic to art that he was in no danger of ever learning to aspire to write good movies; he learned early to regard movie work as a commercial craft. Certainly, Republic was a school for learning the handicrafts of fantasy. Working on a tight budget, producers kept contract writers busy, switching them from one script to another in the frantic churning out of movies. In two years, West worked on more than a dozen movies and, in brief collaboration with other writers, in story conferences, and in friendly talks, he was associated with many more. As the contract writers at Republic came back to their offices from a general story conference, sometimes discovering that they were rewriting each other's scripts, they joked about what they had "drawn" in the dream lottery. But the business of dreams touched deep responses in West, since through them he could indulge, as he could not in fiction, his emotional identification with mass men.

His first day at Republic, dressed in a reddish Norfolk jacket, he was assigned to share an office with Lester Cole at the rear of the studio, with windows overlooking some trees. West immediately recognized that the birds there were shrikes—butcher-birds, killers of other birds—and was "terribly angered." He had, to Cole's astonishment, "a particularly intense hatred for this bird," and "the next day he brought an air rifle to the studio and spent half the day killing them."

Like Faye Greener, West literally daydreamed his scripts. The Republic offices were of the barest, and West's cubicle had no linoleum on its floor; but when he discovered that Sy Bartlett had a rug, he frequented his office in the afternoons, stretching out on the floor with his hands behind his head and letting his imagination drift. Later, when Bartlett moved a lumpy orange-striped couch into his office, West claimed it at once. Producers believed that scripts were aided by "talking them out," and in Bartlett's office, West and others conversed in the language of dreams.

The very titles of West's pictures hint both at their quality and at their character: *Ticket to Paradise*, West's first produced film, was succeeded by *Follow Your Heart*, *The President's Mystery*, *Gangs of New York*, *Jim Hanvey—Detective*, *Rhythm in the Clouds*, *Ladies in Distress*, *Bachelor Girl*, *Born to Be Wild* (based on an "original" story by West), *It Could Happen to You*, *Orphans of the Street*, and *Stormy Weather*.

Only in two of these pictures was West able to express on film aspects of his personal commitments. *The President's Mystery* was based on an idea conceived by President Franklin Roosevelt, which had inspired a series of *Liberty* magazine stories by Samuel Hopkins Adams, S. S. Van Dine, John Erskine, and others. Roosevelt had questioned whether it would be possible for a wealthy man, weary of a wasteful life, to convert his estate into cash, disappear, and begin life anew in some worthwhile activity. West and Cole ignored the series of stories and wrote a script with Roosevelt's speculation as their starting point. Jim Blake (Henry Wilcoxon), ashamed of his lobbying activities in Congress, disappears. "A strange series of circumstances brings him into a small New England industrial town where he is able to observe at close range the disastrous results of his lobbying activities. . . . Men loiter about in idleness, and over them rumbles the distant thunder of mob rule and violence. By fearlessly risking his own happiness and safety and doing what he believes right, he quells the forces of capitalistic greed and revives activity in the local canning factory," as well as winning the heart of its young owner (Betty Furness).

West often spoke with amusement (and occasionally with some pride) about this film. Although he was generally opposed to injecting political elements into movies, in this film he and Cole— later jailed as one of the "Hollywood Ten"—wrote a script far to the left of Roosevelt, who was then campaigning for reelection. West indulged himself in the mass dream of a political utopia, popular in America at least since Bellamy's sensationally popular *Looking Backward* and Jack London's *The Iron Heel*. He and Cole turned a story of disappearance into one, as they regarded it, about "the struggle of workers and farmers against the oppression and depression of their times." When Yates viewed his most recent film in New York early in September, he was outraged. A supporter of Alf Landon, he declared that the picture—made for $105,000, the most expensive Republic picture until that time—had cost him less than he had bet on Landon, and he was determined not to release it. Nevertheless, economics prevailed, and the picture, finally released on September 27, 1936, was highly praised by liberal reviewers, Meyer Levin calling it "the first Hollywood film in which a liberal thesis is carried out to its logical conclusion."

West and Cole began *The President's Mystery* with a striking opening series of scenes using newsreels, a device which Orson Welles would imitate in *Citizen Kane* (1939). Set in 1936, the film opens as people are entering a movie theater. On the screen inside flashes a shot of the White House, over which is superimposed the caption "HISTORY IN THE MAKING." As the announcer begins speaking, the newsreel switches to the capitol dome, to "Men in the Street," to scenes of idle factories, farms, and the city:

Announcer's Voice: Washington, D.C. Within two weeks Congress will vote on the Trades Reconstruction Corporation Bill. This important legislation is of vital national significance. It will be determined whether or not the Government will lend money to communities all over the nation thru local banks to again put in business those small industries which have gone bankrupt during the depression. For upon them entire communities, from factory workers to farmers, are dependent for their livelihood. The right to work is demanded by these people. Senator Randolph Gilmore, determined proponent of the bill.

Senator Gilmore: The idea of the T.R.C. bill is to bring small industries back to life. Running co-operatively, they will benefit all classes, the farmer, the worker, the salesman, the store-keeper, and the consumer. Despite the evident advantages of this bill certain greedy monopolists are exerting their influence to defeat it. But they're going to learn that there is something just as sacred in these United States as Property Rights, and those are HUMAN RIGHTS.

Announcer's Voice: A cross section of inquiry brings contrasting opinion. . . . Let's hear now how the man in the street feels about it.

Workman: I'm the man in the street all right, that's the trouble. And I gotta get off the street and back in that factory if I'm gonna keep these kids fed and get 'em back to school.

The scene shifts to Jim Blake, who, disgusted by his lobbying activities to defeat the bill, is practicing fly casting into an inverted silk hat—a scene which delighted West.

At a preview of this film, John Sanford mercilessly called it a "cheapie," and his friendship with West, slowly withering, was over. In fact, this movie "set the industry buzzing," a reporter declared. "It may possibly bring about serious consideration of the screen as an editorial medium."

West editorialized even more in a movie of 1937, *It Could Happen to You.* This was the Republic Studios version of *A Cool Million* mixed well with Sinclair Lewis's *It Can't Happen Here* and with large doses (via Samuel Ornitz) of immigrant sociology in New York City. The idea was apparently conceived by the film's producer, Leonard Fields, who got West working on it as an original so that the executive producer would exercise West's upcoming option. Fields, who apparently had not read *A Cool Million,* told West that a good picture might be made about the rise of Fascism in America. "Naturally we didn't have the money to go to Germany," he says. "What we did do . . . was to take a street in New York City and symbolize [with] that a breeding ground for Fascism. With that one street we told a story that could have taken place in Berlin or Munich or Hamburg, of the rise and development and horrors of Fascism." West worked on a treatment and a 134-page script for about two months, aided in the final draft by Ornitz.

The picture opens with a scene depicting the pastoral joys of the "Foreign American Institute Picnic." "The Professor" announces that he has sold his "citizenship school" to Robert Ames, and Bob declares: "Folks, this school's gonna be run on the American plan. . . . [Immigrants will] learn to be citizens by mail . . . can't you see it? . . . Those swell Magyars in the coal fields of Pennsylvania. . . . The Swenskas out in Minnesota. The Portuguese fishermen in New England . . . and the Polack tobacco farmers in Connecticut. They'll all make fine citizens." But his hopes are crushed when he accidentally kills the father of his best friend. Blackmailed by the power-crazed Professor, a Nazi sympathizer, Bob is forced to extort money from the immigrants. He will make the school a gold mine, the Professor tells him, by following the precepts of Nietzsche and Treitschke, for they taught that "if the meek will inherit the earth, you can take it away from them." Finally, desperately attempting to solve all the troubles he has caused, Bob commits suicide in what the publicity department called "a powerful and unusual climax which will hold the most hardened picturegoer spellbound." *Variety* did not agree. "So-so melodrama," its reviewer declared, "with an old-fashioned plot. No marquee names and word-of-mouth won't be so hot. Looks destined for below-decks dualer, where it should carry its share." It hardly did even that. "Only about three people in the world ever saw it," Fields says. "It was the most heartbreaking and resounding flop that ever took place."

West did other film work between 1935 and January 1938. In accordance with his contract, he gave the studio manager at Republic a list of the literary works he had written before being hired. This list is obviously padded with invented titles to provide for the possibility that he might write a script for another studio on his own time; under the heading "Short Stories and Original Screenplays" he listed the following: "The Red Barn," "Upsie Daisie" (a musical), "The American Chauve Souris" (his 1934 idea), "Mud in Your Eye," "Serene," "The Hour Glass," "The Black Drink," and "Osceola."

However many of the others may be invented, "Osceola" was a seventeen-page "original" which West did write, probably in 1935, but failed to sell to a studio. Beginning around 1930, there had been a reawakening of interest in the American Indian—signalized by the popularity of Oliver LaFarge's *Laughing Boy* (1930), the first volume in a whole library of books sympathetic to the Indian.

Certainly, "West was much impressed with the Indian and the bad deal he had received," S. J. Perelman says. And even as late as 1939 West told Boris Ingster that "he might write about the Indian because no one else seemed interested." *Osceola* is, West wrote, "a story of one of the greatest heroes in American frontier history. The story of a soldier who never lost a battle, of a statesman who never made a mistake, of a lover who was always generous and loyal, yet, in the end, lost everything. . . . This is the story of Captain Powell, called by his (Seminole) people Osceola . . . who was destroyed, like an ancient Greek hero, by inevitable destiny." Osceola is the Indian Lemuel Pitkin, another of West's dismantled innocents. The idea came from Whitman, who described the Indian as "a young brave . . . [who] literally died of a 'broken heart' " and in *Leaves of Grass* set down "a line in memory of his name and death." But the studios at this time were still working on Melville's alternate formula of the "Metaphysics of Indian hating," and West's script found no takers.

He had other ideas for originals; always fertile with stories for fiction, he now turned his imagination to stories for pictures. He spoke to a Republic producer of wanting to adapt C. S. Forester's *African Queen*—later adapted by James Agee—and Crane's *Red Badge of Courage*. And once, when a director mentioned an idea of his own to make a comedy out of some of the typographical mistakes being reprinted in *The New Yorker*, West declared that the idea was "worth a million" and vowed to write Perelman for advice. Somewhat later, he worked up a treatment for a musical screenplay, called *Broadway Bible*, on the life story of Sime Silverman of *Variety*, which Warner Brothers considered briefly but refused.

IV

Economically, the screenwriter of that period was caught in a kind of moving box. While under contract, he would see his salary gradually increased with each renewal of the studio option, but it was very difficult for him to move from one studio to another at increased salary; if his option was not taken up, his job elsewhere would begin with what would then be known as his "established" (or last) salary. Likewise, it would be almost impossible for his salary to increase rapidly while he was under contract. Nonetheless, since there was always a certain gold-rush atmosphere in Hollywood and considerable evidence of big killings, the solution for most ambitious writers was to work on a week-to-week contract basis while attempting to write and sell screen originals on their own time, and then to parlay such a sale into a screenplay job for another studio at an increased salary.

Like many other writers, West was divided about remaining tied to a studio and striking out independently. The predictability of the work and salary at Republic was comforting and allowed him to allot time for his novel. He knew that most writers had found freedom illusory, since they merely devoted more time to movie politics, story ideas, and the writing and peddling of originals— in short, to what they called *the biz*. Moreover, he was trying to square accounts with Perelman, who had supported him through his worst times. (He kept accurate records and eventually paid everything back.) On the other hand, freedom from routine was decidedly appealing and West believed that free time would allow him to devote more time to his novel, at a crucial stage early in 1938.

When West's option came up in January 1938, he asked the executive producer to drop him, although his contract was slated for renewal. Accordingly, on January 31, 1938, after two years at Republic, his contract was terminated.

If he had been uncertain about this step, it appeared to be justified at once when his agent—Feldman, Blum—placed him at Columbia Studios to work on a script called *The Squealer* for a contract producer named Harold Wilson. This assignment, however, lasted only a week, from February 2 to February 9, and West left his first-draft script unfinished. In it he worked some interesting variations on the gangster-movie formulas. As West wrote in his preface, the film would deal with the psychological conflicts of an old gangster caught between "the ways of crime in the roaring twenties when tough, merciless gangsters ran their rackets according to a code of their own," and the new, "modern, efficient, business-like methods." For Max Adamic, the unit man in one of the collection districts, the new ways are difficult to accept. He idealizes the old ways, and when one of his collection men squeals, he has him machine-gunned according to traditional methods. The head of the organization is angry. "It can't happen again," Pawling tells Max. And to make certain that it won't, Pawling appoints one of his younger men, Ford, to be Max's assistant and charges him to keep Max's unit running on modern lines. "Max is alone in the office when Ford comes to work. He has been there for hours, brooding, brooding. . . . Rage fills him, blinds him for a moment, and Ford is knocked down with a crushing blow. Max calls one of his men to come in a few minutes later and take care of Ford." At this point, just when the latent conflicts begin to unfold, the screenplay breaks off. Whether the producer decided to take up another project or simply lost faith in this one is not clear: the property was completely terminated.

West, once more, was out of a job—his unemployment coinciding exactly with the recession of early 1938, when about nine million others were unemployed with him. The Federal Reserve Board index fell to 79, only 10 points higher than it had been in 1932. Finally, after four months, on June 6, 1938, he was hired for his "established" salary of $350 a week by R.K.O. Pictures—the first of the five major studios to employ him—to make a screenplay from an original story by Richard Carroll. Putting everything else aside, within a week he outlined his plan for treating the material. He had seen his contract dropped after one week on his last job, months ago. He now made the mistake of handing in his treatment on Friday; in real need of a steady salary, he fretted all weekend over whether his outline would be accepted, knowing that he could be out of a job again on Monday. He waited in his office for most of Monday, until late in the afternoon he was persuaded to telephone the executive producer, Lee Marcus—who told him to go ahead at once to the screenplay.

On July 20, West finished a first draft for what would be one of his most successful films, *Five Came Back*. It is the story of a group of people—all running away from the law, society, or themselves—whose plane crashes in a South American jungle. Surrounded by savages, the pilot (Chester Morris) and crew repair the damaged plane to make it barely adequate to take off with only five people aboard. West, obviously, had learned the craft of movie writing at Republic. He gave some complexity to the original story by adding the character of an anarchist-murderer, and he invented an effective scene whereby suspense is strikingly achieved in the last part of the movie. Here, he reversed the usual formula by which native drumbeats stimulate fear in the audience, by directing that the drumbeats be woven into the musical score, building up to the moment of fearful silence when the drums stop. After eight weeks in all, having polished his script, West was released by R.K.O. It appeared that he had a good chance to earn a single credit for this high budget, B-quality movie. Moreover, it would have been a prestige credit since, as the *Hollywood Reporter* declared, *Five Came Back* had had "competent scripting" and its "playwrighting [is] colorful and graphically effective throughout."

But the studio called in a hack writer, Jerry Cady, to polish West's script; and after Cady's work on it proved unsatisfactory, Dalton Trumbo, then under contract, came in to do a revision before the film went into production. Trumbo eliminated most of the revisions made by Cady, restored some of West's material, and made still other alterations, changing, for example, the anarchist from villain to hero. By this time, West had returned to New York, and although his secretary demanded that he ask the guild to arbitrate the credits, he appeared indifferent and nearly missed getting any screen credit at all. Finally, he shared credits with Cady and Trumbo, just at a time when a solo credit would have helped him to get another job.

In the meantime, he had written, in collaboration with Gordon Kahn and Wells Root, an original fifty-one-page treatment first titled *Flight South* and later *Heritage of the Wild* that M.G.M. bought for $7,500. This, it appears, was the one time West made a sale through friends. Frances Goodrich and Albert Hackett, important contract writers at M.G.M., became enthusiastic about West's treatment and convinced the studio head to purchase it. As with so many other properties, that was virtually the end of interest in the story, and a movie was never made from it. Even so, it has historical interest. The treatment provided a kind of Hollywood version of the films by Pare Lorentz, *The River* and *The Plow That Broke the Plains*, both of which had grown directly out of a revived concern with conservation. Prompted by the monographs and reports of Stuart Chase, Paul B. Sears, the Mississippi Valley Committee, and the National Resources Committee, these films, issuing from the recognition that floods and dust storms were largely the result of a reckless misuse of the land, were counterparts to the Agricultural Adjustment Act and its successor, the Soil Conservation and Domestic Allotment Act.

Lorentz's films were blacklisted by Hollywood as "unfair competition" and "socialistic experiments," since they were produced by the Department of Agriculture and distributed by the federal government; but West's treatment is in the Hollywood tradition. The original title, *Flight South*, refers to the migration of waterfowl over North Carolina, where a gang illegally hunts wild fowl for sale to markets and restaurants. James Emmett Kane, special agent for the Department of Justice, is assigned to investigatory work at the Department of Agriculture's Conservation Bureau to help solve the murder of four game wardens in the Black Eddy, North Carolina, area. Disguised as the pilot for the wealthy Norman Seaforth, Kane works his way into the confidence of the local folk and infiltrates the gang of market hunters, who are slaughtering the birds by the thousands. He not only breaks up the gang but wins the heart and hand of Joan, Seaforth's beautiful daughter. "All the outdoor scenes in this story can be made on the Tulare Lake wildfowl sanctuary here in California," a note at the end of the outline reads, ". . . and the authors understand that the bureau in charge will be glad to cooperate to the fullest possible extent."

West's involvement in film fantasy had educated him not only in the economics, politics, and sociology of the film industry; he learned, primarily, what was involved in professional film writing, and newly defined for himself what being a writer meant to him. Long treated shamefully by producers, screenwriters began their counterattack against Hollywood in 1931, when Theodore Dreiser —distressed that Eisenstein had not been permitted to film *An American Tragedy*—sued Paramount for misrepresentations of his book in the Von Sternberg production. Though he lost his suit, in a public statement Dreiser called upon writers to insist on the integrity of their work when it was turned into films.

It had long been true, as a contemporary observer noted, that "Hollywood at present is very much like a milltown. The writers, shut up by day in small cells in large buildings, which, like mills, have armed guards at the doors, compelled to collaborate in twos just as a pair of weavers is given so many looms and reporting like school-children to supervisors who commend or suppress or censor, display, even outside the studios, a psychology of millhands or children." It was said "not to be uncommon to have up to twelve writers working [on a story] consecutively"—sometimes many of them simultaneously. Of these, some might even be writing on approval, with no salary guarantee.

All this was changing rapidly. Dramatists from the East—where unions controlled stage productions—and newspapermen turned movie writers recognized how great a change was needed and they took the lead in forming the Screen Writers Guild. Unrecognized by the producers, and hampered by internal dissent, the guild made little progress initially, though many prominent writers, among them Nathanael West, joined at once in 1932–3.

During the period 1936–8, no other group of movie people manifested so total a rejection of their work as the writers. (In part, this dissatisfaction accounts for the tradition of the anti-Hollywood novel, well-established even by 1936, when Madeleine Carroll complained about "those many novelists who come out to Hollywood expressly to write a book on the place and who, in the short time they are here, must get a very superficial knowledge of it.") There were obvious reasons for the writers' discontent. F. Scott Fitzgerald was right in telling Matthew Josephson in 1938 that "the individual writer's part in the 'regime' of a motion-picture production amounts to only ten percent of the finished job, after the rest of the team have done their work." And writers often felt that their scripts were being accepted, revised, or rejected by illiterates. "Nobody," as Alvah Bessie said, "seemed to know a good screenplay . . . the producer least of all." The result, inevitably, was the scorn and cynicism bristling in the comment made to Bessie by Daniel Fuchs, novelist turned screenwriter: "The first thing you have to learn out here is that you can't make anything good . . . but if you play it right, you can be . . . making big money." (In 1938, 165 Hollywood writers earned a median salary of $25,-000.)

West's view of screenwriting had varied from despair to resignation to ironical delight, but he was almost unique among Hollywood writers in his complete indifference toward the artfulness of his own films. Movies, as a younger contemporary of West's declared, "had nothing at all to do with *him*, his interior life." He recognized the aesthetic differences between fiction and scenario-writing and he had set out to be a screen craftsman with the same determination and enthusiasm he would have applied to bricklaying. His novels had failed to sell, he could not place his stories, and he had not gotten any foundation support. Only radio and movies were left, and, in the thirties, radio work paid less than pictures. Therefore, he had turned to movie work, but he never confused the formulas of photoplay with the art of his fiction; he could talk well about the European film and about film technique, but he never associated his own movie aspirations with the art-film tradition. Indeed, in order to concentrate his energy on his fiction, he explained to Robert Coates and Budd Schulberg, he preferred to work on B or even C pictures, since writing these was mechanical and did not involve creative energy at all. On such films, he said to Josephson and Ring Lardner, Jr., "there was no sense in getting up enthusiasm . . . since you were subject to the whims of people who really wanted to stick to the formula."

Certainly, West never played Hollywood politics, the only sure avenue toward higher pay and better films. (On at least one occasion, he chased down in his car a writer and director who had abused a hunting site he had gotten them permission to use, tongue-lashed them, and demanded they go back and clean up— though these were people whose good will would have helped his rise.) Indeed, though he was naturally friendly, he was deliberately cool toward influential Hollywood people. Perhaps he was fearful of Hollywood success.

West had found that writing movies was easy for him, while his fiction was pain and torment. His novels he wrote out by hand, he typed and corrected them himself, and he worked them again and again. His film outlines and treatments he dictated quickly and even gaily, often in happy collaboration, and almost always in running conversation with Jo Conway, his secretary. He regarded these as experiments in hack work, ways of making money; and he neither had illusions about the value of his screenplays nor felt that he had been exploited in doing them. He worked hard and attempted to draw a paycheck regularly, and had soon become a competent enough craftsman to toss around the script ideas on which friends like Darrell McGowan and Sy Bartlett were working. But he seldom discussed his own movie work (in *The Day of the Locust* he satirizes shop talk). When he did speak of it, as he did to Matthew

Josephson, it was with "sad, joyless mirth," describing "an absurd, almost Dada world," Josephson says.

Outwardly, West had accepted Hollywood. The essential, inward, savage contempt he felt for its films, of course, was part of the emotional matrix of the novel he began to compose in 1935 and 1936. While he resisted the condescension then regarded as typical of the *New Yorker* attitude toward movies, he clearly, on the level of consciousness that was the source of his fiction, detested the studios and their product; he felt tied to them by economics but never by affection; and if fascinated, he was also disgusted. When he and Hilaire Hiler met Robert McAlmon at a John Ferren show in Hollywood, he talked, McAlmon says, as if he "seemed to think he had prostituted himself." But he also spoke warmly to McAlmon about the future of fiction and "the sin of being too lazy or negligent to learn the craft." West needed the money he had earned in Hollywood, in some part he was glad that his mother was proud of what she regarded as his success—a high weekly salary—and he was not above being pleased by the minimal status that being a screenwriter had conferred; but he had long before assessed all this and found it empty for the deepest needs of his self.

The year 1938 had been a slim one for dreaming and for West's purse. He had labored long on the production line of the dream factory and had learned, particularly during the last year, that movies could make distracting emotional demands on the writer. But the principle of West's integrity still lay—as a younger screenwriter, Milton Sperling, says—in his "total selfishness about his work in fiction. He was one of the few men I met in Hollywood who filled me with a sense of awe—for he knew that he had something to write about. He affected fellow writers as Bogart did actors, with his reserve and rock-like integrity. He threatened them with his avoidance of both scorn and enthusiasm for movies, since he regarded them as an immense fountain pen, as an adding machine, a vehicle whereby to sustain his own real interest in creative writing. He was ahead of his time in knowing that Hollywood was impermanent and literature lasting, and in never confusing the two."

All in all, it had been fun to shake loose the fragments and wisps of dreams from the edges of his imagination, and to see his fantasies made into films. If it was like thumbing through a deck of cards, he had played through some amusing hands. No game had been won but he had taken a few stakes and ventured little, a year or two. He was still a young man, and this was all material for the novelist—it would all be useful and usable in one way or another. After all, Hollywood had served him as the background for his novel, drafted and rewritten in the evenings while he was working on movies during the day, and finally finished during his long layoff in the winter and spring of 1938. "Business Deal" had been, he now could see, but an excursion in a park at the edge of the jungle. Now he had explored many of its lush recesses. He had led a life strangely but fruitfully divided, plunging daily into commercial dreams and nightly into the seething life of the crowd that made the manufacture of dreams necessary. Day and night he had pondered over the novel that would illumine this connection. He was calling it *The Cheated*, and under that title it was accepted in May by Random House. The novel was one, certainly the most important, result of his stay in Hollywood. Surely the next in importance, he believed at the moment, was his collaboration with Joseph Schrank on a play called *Gentlemen, the War!* This play, West hoped, would free him forever from films and fantasies. On August 5, 1938, a few days after finishing up at R.K.O. and selling *Flight South*, West returned to New York by train to work with Schrank on final revisions before *Gentlemen, the War!* went into rehearsal. It was scheduled to begin production in the last part of August and to be ready for the stage by early September. He was finished with Hollywood. It had served his purposes and he could give it up, without bitterness or regret, to its sprawling, vacant, violent dreams.

15 / "Gentlemen, the War!"

> The rest stayed and talked about the theatre, Flaubert
> making fun of it rather rudely, as is his wont. "The theatre
> is not an art," he said; "it is a secret; and I have got hold
> of that secret from one of the people who possess it. This
> is the secret. First, you have a few glasses of absinthe at the
> Café du Cirque. Then you say of whatever play is being
> discussed: 'It's not bad, but it wants cutting.' Or you say:
> 'Not bad, but there's no play there.' And you must be
> careful always to sketch plans but never to write a play your-
> self. After all, once you write a play, you're lost."
>
> —*The Goncourt Journals*, January 12, 1860

The play that West and Schrank wrote in collaboration seemed to
have every chance of popular success. Originally called *Gentlemen,
the War!*, later *Blow, Bugles, Blow*, and finally *Good Hunting*, it is
in the popular tradition of anti-war plays, a subject that deeply
touched the American imagination for two decades after World
War I. If John Dos Passos's novel *Three Soldiers* (1921) had signalized a new spirit in the treatment of war, that spirit thereafter
frequently stalked the stage, almost always to applause.

Perhaps the first play mixing cynicism and criticism in its treatment of war was Maxwell Anderson and Laurence Stallings's *What
Price Glory?* (1924). In the next year, Channing Pollock's *The
Enemy* similarly advocated the thesis that the real enemy of mankind is fear and selfish diplomacy, not any other nation. These
were followed by such grim or satirical plays as *Journey's End*
(1928); the musical *Strike Up the Band* (1930), which dealt with
"The Henry J. Fletcher Memorial War to End Wars"; and George
Sklar and Albert Maltz's *Peace on Earth* (1933), which argued the
current Communist thesis that war results from an economic system based on private profit, and which showed labor unions pre-

venting war by refusing to handle munitions. In 1935, there was Sidney Howard's successful adaption of Humphrey Cobb's novel *Paths of Glory* (1935), which, more traditionally, showed war as cruel and senseless. In 1936 there were at least three important anti-war dramas. The least successful, Paul Green and Kurt Weill's *Johnny Johnson*, presented a veteran of the world war trying to allay the rising war fever. Robert Sherwood's *Idiot's Delight*, its title stating Sherwood's view of war, won the Pulitzer Prize for 1936 with the thesis that intelligent people abhor war. Finally, a one-act play, Irwin Shaw's *Bury the Dead*, fiercely attacked the confusion, horror, and betrayals of war. In 1937, Sidney Howard returned with another war drama. In *The Ghost of Yankee Doodle*, set "eighteen months after the commencement of the next world war," Howard shows the dilemma of a liberal manufacturing family whose refusal to make arms throws their employees, whom they are seeking to protect, out of work; and whose subsequent resumption of production provides jobs for everyone, but only through the manufacture of weapons.

Such plays coincided with the distaste for war that marked the period from the twenties to the late thirties in America. By 1930 there were, as one historian puts it, "some three hundred organizations existing for the solitary purpose of puffing at peace pipes in the wigwam of isolationism." Organized opposition to war during these years ranged all the way from the Socialists' 1936 platform declaration of "unconditional opposition to any war engaged in by the American government"; to the National Peace Conference, which convened anti-war societies in Washington during April 1937; and to the organization of the Veterans of Future Wars (beginning at Princeton but spreading rapidly), based on a demand for immediate payment of $1,000 to each male citizen between eighteen and thirty-six, since most of these "future veterans" would otherwise lose their service bonus by being killed in the next war. In 1937, 500,000 students took part in a pacifist strike and pledged themselves never to support any war declared by the United States government. In that same year, a Gallup poll disclosed that two-thirds of the people questioned believed that American participation in World War I had been a mistake. Had not the Nye committee hailed J. P. Morgan and the Du Ponts to the stand and concluded from their testimony that the United States had entered the war, not to save the world for democracy, but as a result of the intrigues of profiteers who reaped unconscionably rich harvests from it? Nye himself had stated bluntly: "When Americans went into the fray they little thought that they were there and fighting to save the skins of American bankers who had bet too boldly on the outcome of the war and had two billions of dollars of loans to the allies in jeopardy." Had not revisionist historians like Mauritz Hallgren and Stephen and Joan Rauschenbush agreed? And was not the public's agreement itself palpable in the fact that Walter Millis's *The Road to War* (1935), based on such revisionism, was a best-seller? This widespread sentiment helped to guarantee popularity for lively dramas about the tragedy or absurdity of war.

While the anti-war successes of 1936 were playing in the theaters of New York, even before Howard's newest play opened, West was developing what he believed to be a matchless idea for another such drama. Near the end of that year, Joseph Schrank, who had had a hit play in *Page Miss Glory*, was brought to Hollywood to write screenplays for M.G.M. Schrank, who had moved to Erwinna after West left, was sent to him by Perelman for guidance in Hollywood. West amused (and terrorized) Schrank with his collection of curious Hollywood lore, and they got along so well that one evening at dinner West told him that he had a notion for a play they might do together.

West had happened upon a book on military strategy called *The War in Outline: 1914–1918* (1936) by Liddell Hart, a well-known English military commentator whose London columns were also printed in *The New York Times*. Hart fully and ironically analyzed the tactical mistakes in this "War of the Masses," in which strategy was still bounded by outmoded organization, a separation of the high command from the war experience, misuse of men, and misunderstanding of recently developed technological innovations like the tank and the machine gun. "You wouldn't believe how stupid these generals are, how behind the times," West told Schrank. In the First World War, he said, the British general staff had been outraged by proposals to use tanks, strategy innovations, or surprise attacks, and instead depended entirely upon the mathematics of a war of attrition, the inevitable victory of the superior power. With the multiple ironies abounding in Hart's book as his starting point, West had conceived the idea for a play which would concern, he said, "the suicidal absurdities of the military mind, the most stupid of all minds." Instead of wasting their evenings talking, he proposed to Schrank, why not write this play together?

Schrank was enthusiastic and they began work almost at once, meeting four or five nights each week to turn over ideas for plot, scene, and characters. After a few weeks, they had gotten far enough along so that they hired a secretary and Schrank rapidly dictated a forty-page outline of the story they had come up with. West took this outline and alone wrote out each act of the play fully, then gave his manuscript to Schrank to polish. West was occupied with this work from the beginning of February 1937 to the end of May. In June, he returned to Erwinna for a brief vacation. (As he would always do, he took the train East but flew back. This, he jokingly explained, was because he did not care what happened to him *after* his vacation.) By the time he returned, Schrank had finished his polishing, and together they rewrote the third draft in September and October.

West, Schrank says, was a "deliberate worker" who would pick out and brood over certain ideas among those Schrank poured out. He "polished and debated every word." West would later tell some of his friends that the concept and most of the material of the play was his, for he turned over and assessed every detail in his imagination, including those that originated with Schrank. He was more than casually informed about military strategy. "He knew all about the absurd pretensions of the English," Schrank says, "but he shared some of them himself." Were not his interest in shotguns and dogs, the military mustache, and his English clothes aspects of this? Had not a girl in Hollywood complained that instead of making love to her in his parked car he had spent an entire evening explaining the intricacies of deployment and strategy at Austerlitz? In some measure, West was again satirizing in this play what, intellectually, he considered weaknesses in himself. Despite this, or perhaps because of it, the writing went smoothly to its conclusion.

Although West said ironically that, by Hollywood custom, Schrank, an M.G.M. writer, should not even be talking to him, they flipped a coin to determine whose name would come first on the manuscript and West won. Finally, on November 19, 1937, to protect their unpublished script, they were granted copyright on *Gentlemen, the War!: A Play in Three Acts*, and turned it over to an agent.

From the beginning of the collaboration to the toss of the coin, everything seemed, for once, to be going smoothly for West. There was almost immediate interest in the play and, early in February 1938, Jerome Mayer, producer of *Noah* and *Russet Mantle*, agreed to stage it, intending to have it ready for an April opening in New York. Could West come East to work on the production at once, Mayer asked. West, in fact, had recently been released by Republic; but he was absorbed in readying his new novel for submission to a publisher. This led to some early delays. Moreover, there were additional delays and a crowded schedule in New York, and Mayer, though still enthusiastic, was nonetheless inclined, as the season drew to an end, to postpone the play for a summer-stock tryout, with a Broadway opening to follow early in the fall.

While West was in the midst of work on *Five Came Back*, late in July, the production finally began to take shape in New York. "I have been thoroughly immersed in this job I am doing at the studio, but those few parts of me, eyes, ears, nose, that have been exposed are concentrated on the play," West wrote to Mayer, anxious for details. The news was glorious. Mayer encouraged him to return for final polishing as soon as possible. "Up to the neck in actors," he wrote excitedly. But his mind had changed again, and the opening was pushed back slightly. "It looks more and more like we will try it out of town instead of in a summer theatre. I think the old ladies and tourist crowd is not the proper audience for a play with these sophisticated qualities. Perhaps it might be amusing to open in Washington."

West had hesitated about returning East at once since he appeared to have a chance to catch on with his treatment of *Flight South* at M.G.M. Moreover, the many delays in the production already looked ominous. But he was happy about the play and joked easily. "It is important for me to get some definite idea about when rehearsals will start," he wrote to Mayer. "I would hate to go to New York City and just hang around waiting when I am sure I can continue to work out here and make some money. It has always been my contention that money is a very valuable commodity, and that those who scoff at it or its power will someday have their fingers burnt or their snook cocked. Money is really a wonderful thing. I can't say too much in praise of money. I adore it. Good old money. Good young money, too. Folding money and hard money alike transcend the common distinctions which make of our life one continuous round of humiliation." Prompted by Mayer's and his own confidence, however, West arrived in New York around the middle of August and went almost directly to Erwinna, where he stayed with Schrank while they worked out a new version of the ending.

West was counting on the success of the play to turn his fortunes, and it looked as if he had taken the anti-war fervor of America at its tide. His novels hadn't sold, his stories were refused, and on the movie lot he was so far removed from the actual shooting that he seemed to be working in a vacuum that allowed no echo to return. Now he would see the rehearsals, he would be rewriting on the spot, he would watch the play take shape, and he would hear the applause. His dramatic urge was, of course, no recent impulse. He had written *Even Stephen* with Perelman and had suggested to Josephine Herbst that they dramatize her novel *Nothing Is Sacred* (1928). The theater, he told her, was "a bonanza, an El Dorado, a Golden Hind." But now his ambitions seemed more intense. He intimated to his Hollywood friends that he wrote the play solely for money, but they easily saw through this claim and understood that what he really hoped for was acclaim. With Perelman he had often laughed at a passage in *The Goncourt Journals* which described the envy of Flaubert and his circle for fourth-rate nonentities who were having successes in the Paris theater. But for a moment West too yearned for success, and it seemed as if he would have it. George S. Kaufman, dean of successful American playwrights and an unusually accurate judge of theatrical chances, read the play and told West that it would be a triumph.

There were hints, however, that West was brooding over the possibility of failure. Certainly, he was preoccupied. Once, when driving with Schrank into New York to consult with Mayer about some changes, he went through eleven consecutive stop lights after leaving the Lincoln Tunnel, once swerving around a trolley, and finally hit a taxi that was just starting across an intersection. He settled on the spot for the slight damages, but Schrank, convinced that West was trying to kill both of them, walked the rest of the

way to Mayer's office. Then, too, in New York he began to call on
Ann Honeycutt, who had been married to the *New Yorker* writer
St. Clair McKelway. He didn't seem nervous about the success of
his play, she says, but he was very serious, and one evening he became so obsessed with a need to hear Mozart's *Eine Kleine Nacht-
musik* that although it was quite late they went all around town
trying to find an open record shop, and finally did. At her apartment, he lay straight out on the rug and played the record again
and again. He said that it was his favorite music—clearly, at this
moment it appealed to something deeply melancholic in him—and
added that he wanted it played at his funeral. Later, when James
T. Farrell ran into him at 40 Street and Lexington Avenue in September, West seemed to Farrell changed—"dispirited and apolo-
getic," more ironical than ever, uninterested (Farrell thought) in
fundamental political matters, and inclined only to small talk.

If West, hoping for a success, was dispirited and preoccupied by
September, he had good reason. Mayer had run into financial difficulties. West wired his agents to "see Sisk and Frank Davis at
Metro about a job for me" but delayed returning to Hollywood
when Mayer turned up the necessary money, after some further
delays, by convincing Leonard S. Field, the theatrical producer
(not West's Hollywood friend), to co-produce the play. By the
time that still more money was needed, with "the casting going
ahead full speed," it was too late for West to return, and he was
forced to sink his $1,000 remaining from the sale of *Flight South*
into the show. "Pray like hell," he wrote to Jo Conway. "It may be
a case of throwing good money after bad, but I felt I had to do it. I
had so much time and money in the damn thing already that I
could not let it fall through for another thousand bucks as it looked
it might. Moreover, I couldn't go back to Hollywood, I felt, after
all the talking I did unless the damn thing went on at least, even if
it were a flop."

Finances offered only one of the problems. Mayer, who had
never directed a play before, was determined to direct this one. He
rapidly proved to be inept and lacking in force, and in September
West watched the rehearsals break down completely. At Mayer's
insistence, he and Schrank rewrote feverishly, but pointlessly, since
they had no clear directions from him. Brooks Atkinson's opening-
night judgment, that the "direction is disastrous," pinpointed the

difficulty, and George Tobias, one of the actors, made a private backstage hit by giving an "impression of Mayer directing—like a fighter who starts out pretty well, gets one sock and then is punch drunk for the rest of the fight, hitting out wildly, aimlessly until the final bell." Late one night in Schrank's hotel, the Edison, West declared that Broadway was a place only for maniacs and that he would never again become involved with a play; then, leaving the revisions to Schrank, he went to his room at the Seville, where, Schrank says, he slept for about fifteen hours. As a culmination to the delays and the general chaos that prevailed in the production, the tight budget made an out-of-town tryout impossible and sent the players untried to their opening-night audience.

The play was set to open at the Hudson Theatre on November 21, 1938, in "the busiest week of the season, with a première every evening." The two playwrights, Wolcott Gibbs, Dawn Powell, Albert Halper, and George Milburn ate a nervous dinner at a saloon on Eighth Avenue, and everyone got pretty high.

West and Schrank were prepared for the worst while hoping for the best. But West's bright and lively idea had to fail. The direction of the play, and, more important, delay, proved fatal. For although, as recently as January 1938, seventy percent of Americans queried were opposed to war, this persuasion was dissolving with astonishing rapidity under the pressure of international events, particularly those surrounding the last stages of the Austrian crisis, followed by the German threats against Czechoslovakia. While the play was in rehearsal, on September 28—several months after it had originally been scheduled to open—world leaders met with Hitler in Munich and agreed to the dismemberment of the Czech Republic. This was an important turning point; for intellectuals saw it not only as a betrayal but as a decisive step toward war. Emotional reaction, particularly in New York intellectual Jewish circles, was intensified early in November when Hitler initiated violent pogroms against Jews, following the murder of the Third Secretary of the German embassy in Paris by a young Polish Jew. Synagogues in Germany were burned, Jews were barred from high schools and universities, even from theaters, and the German Jewish population was fined a billion marks. Recalling Ambassador Hugh Wilson from Berlin in protest, Roosevelt told a news conference: "I myself could scarcely believe that such things could occur in a twentieth-century civilization." Between August and mid-November 1938, the climate of opinion concerning war, at least among those who constituted a New York first-night audience, had virtually been reversed. Suddenly, the play seemed to be expressing an outmoded, post-World War I attitude, at the very moment when only a pre-World War II, pro-war play could have succeeded.

II

Still, the curtain opened on an impressive set, designed by Norris Houghton, of the ruined Cathedral of the Twenty Virgins in Millefleurs, France, occupied as a brigade headquarters by the British Expeditionary Forces. The audience, as the stage directions say, "finds itself sitting where it would if it had come to worship instead of applaud." There is a large battle map drawn across the pulpit, with flags showing the positions of the troops, a field-telephone switchboard, and two crates of carrier pigeons. Colonel Jarvis, "roast beef to the heel," is busy changing the map flags and a British journalist is telephoning news from the front to Paris. Here indeed is war.

But as soon as the characters begin to speak, they sound like idiots. The British journalist—like one of the officers in *The Red Badge of Courage*—concludes his report with thanks for the cigars and chocolates. A "sloppy and disreputable" American journalist sends messages of violence and terror, which he invents on the spot, to his Paris office. A French officer, who was in the tourist business before the war, speaks only of the beauty of France. An Indian officer has for months been speaking a language incomprehensible to everyone; and a Scottish officer is only barely understandable. General Hargreaves, brigade commander, refuses to talk shop before breakfast, and he cannot at all understand the desire of a Canadian major to try to take their objective—called the "Pepper Mill" because it grinds men up—by surprise attack or tactical innovation:

FITZSIMMONS: We've got to change the plan.

JARVIS (*a little hurt*): It was most carefully prepared, Fitzsimmons. (*Moves to a map and points to it.*) We attack with the first, second, and third battalions in the assault wave. The fourth, fifth, and sixth will form the support and mop up. When the objective has been taken, the support will pass through the first wave and pursue the enemy, so that the assault can dig in and consolidate the positions won. They will pass through the tip of the salient here, rolling back the flanks and . . .

FITZSIMMONS (*interrupting*): Williamson's *The Art of War*—page 63. [. . . The] Germans have the same textbook!

JARVIS: Williamson is the accepted authority on trench tactics involving limited objectives. [. . .]

FITZSIMMONS: We've been trying to take the Pepper Mill for months with that plan. We've held up the advance on the whole front. We've been hurled back again and again . . . routed . . . destroyed!

KILBRECHT: An attack is never entirely wasted. Experience under fire, you know, has moral value.

FRENIQUE: Marvelous training.

JARVIS: After all, we *are* turning a rabble of bookkeepers and farmers into an army of battle-tried soldiers.

FITZSIMMONS: What's left of them. [. . .]

JARVIS: What would you substitute?

FITZSIMMONS: Stop the barrage and attack under cover of the fog.

JARVIS: You know how strongly General Hargreaves is opposed to innovations.

KILBRECHT: Besides, the Ordnance would be hellish mad.

JARVIS: They're a highly organized unit—to ask them to cease firing prematurely would be an imposition.

KILBRECHT: We'd never hear the end of it.

JARVIS: It doesn't pay to get into the bad books of the gunners—they can make a lot of trouble. [. . .]

FITZSIMMONS: It's like a timetable! When it starts, the Germans look at their watches and go to sleep. Eight hours later, their officers yell: "Fix bayonets, here come the British!"—and a few minutes later, sure enough, here we are!

JARVIS: Really, Fitzsimmons, you exaggerate.

At a time when the worsening war in Spain and the even more threatening possibility of war against a powerful Hitler were in the minds of most of the audience, they listened stunned to the ludicrous debates of these British officers. Albert Halper "sat between [West and Schrank] . . . and heard them grinding their teeth" over the puzzled response. "The play," Halper recalls, "contained a lot of original humor—in fact, black humor, as it is called today"; but at this moment the audience would have wished not for absurd but for reliable officers, not for comedy but for confidence.

The idiocy continues. Fitzsimmons's request for a surprise attack is refused; but when a female spy, who has escaped from a boarding school in Germany and claims to be a Javanese temple dancer, appears, Fitzsimmons prepares an absurd plan of attack, partly based on principles out of Lewis Carroll, for her to "steal" and give to the enemy. General Hargreaves discovers that his wife is coming to the front—he has gone to the front to escape her, and now orders her arrested—and that the inventive American journalist has sent in a dispatch saying that the Pepper Mill has been taken. Now the division commander is also arriving to decorate him. In desperation, he attacks, conventionally, but fails again.

At intermission, West left off grinding his teeth long enough to go across the street for a drink and he did not return to the theater until the second act was underway. As the curtain rises, Jarvis, on the day following, is again moving the flags to new positions, while Grace Hargreaves occupies herself redecorating the church. Faced with disgrace, Hargreaves orders the map flags placed as if the Pepper Mill were occupied, only to find that now, from this supposed position, the commander-in-chief, Sir Arthur, plans to launch his spring offensive. The silence in the theater by this time was ominous—but for one man in the third row whose hearty guffaws were unechoed and sounded strange and horrible in the alien, silent air. West slipped out for another drink. In the confusion of the division commander's arrival, the "Lewis Carroll" plans are taken to the front and executed—and surprise (along with tactics from *Macbeth* and *The Odyssey*) wins the Pepper Mill for the British. Just as this absurd result seems to have concealed Hargreaves's stupidity, the audience learns that the zany plan also calls for the troops to continue hundreds of miles to Berlin—and they are suicidally attempting to follow it.

West later told his friends in Hollywood that he stayed in the bar after the first act and got comfortably loaded; but he was back for the third act—as the result of Mayer's suggestions, the weakest part of the play, although the original ending had been strong. Headquarters has lost contact with the entire 9,000-man brigade; all, clearly, are captured or killed. Suddenly the telegraph begins to click: "Gott strafe England"—"God destroy England"—repeated three times, the German test phrase of the apparatus. The British officers put on full-dress quickly and prepare to be captured—by, as it turns out, old German friends with whom they have often been on maneuvers. It is nearly a joyful class reunion, and Hargreaves looks forward to internment at the German commander's *schloss*, where he can visit excellent mineral baths. When Sir Arthur comes on the phone bellowing curses, Fitzsimmons calls into the receiver, "Gott strafe England," saying that for a moment he forgot which side he was on. Thousands of men have died; but for the general staffs, incompetent, conventional, and tasteless, it has been merely a game, a "good show," "good hunting."

The final curtain rang down to puzzlement. Were these the kind of warriors who would defeat Hitler? This audience, at least, refused to think so and was not amused. The critics were uniformly affected by this cool response of the audience and went off to write icy reviews, although Gibbs for one was prepared to review the play favorably if it lasted until the next issue of *The New Yorker*.

Good Hunting closed after two performances, before a *New Yorker* review could appear. Convinced that it was a better play than events made it seem, West read the reviews in despair, bitter about the power of critics, of the opening-night audience, of history. "I sure would like to go out to the farm," he said sadly more than once after the play closed. It seemed like a good idea. With the Schranks and the Milburns, he went to Erwinna for a Thanksgiving celebration. But he was restless and unhappy, still dazed over the failure of the play and disinclined to see any of his friends.

From Erwinna he wired Burt Kelly, a director he had been good friends with at Republic, who was now working at Universal: "If you have an assignment for me, I can get out." Against the inclinations of the front office, Kelly, who was beginning a remake of *Tom Brown of Culver*, wired back a promise of a job. West was anxious to go. He never again spoke of writing for the theater. He was a novelist and to that he would hold. He drove Schrank back into New York in a blizzard—now driving with great skill. And with George Milburn he started driving back to California.

Before he left Erwinna, he stopped to see Josephine Herbst and it was like old times. Erwinna stirred old hopes, memories of the triumphant completion of *Miss Lonelyhearts,* and his earlier dreams of settling quietly on the farm to write. Now he was driven East and West, restlessly. "But, will you be able to write in Hollywood?" she asked. He was solemn about that. "Yes," he said, "I'll be writing, but a writer needs to lead a writer's life. It isn't just a sitting down—it's the whole business of thinking and reverie and walking and reading, and you can't do that in Hollywood, so I don't know what my future will be. But I'm going to be working," he concluded. For a start, his fourth novel was soon to appear. He was working on the proofs and, as he brightened up, he said that *this* would be the book to reverse his fortunes.

16 / The Cheated

The other thing I remember . . . is [T. S. Eliot's] answer
when I asked him what future he foresaw for our civilization. "Internecine fighting. . . . People killing one another in the streets."

—Stephen Spender, "Remembering Eliot,"
Sewanee Review, 74 (1966)

As he drove back to California, West brightened with hopes for his
new novel. "This is the real stuff," he was later to write in a
friend's copy, and there is no doubt that it was his favorite among
his books. From the inchoate plans for a novel with which he had
returned to Hollywood in 1935, he had methodically eliminated
the superfluous and sheerly sensational by recognizing that his material held implications not only for the perversions and grotesque-
rie of the moviemakers, but for the ordinary masses drawn to Hollywood by the sirens of wealth, glamour, sun, and sexuality. Here,
he saw, was another South Seas dream, another embarkation point
for the Sargasso of escape.

He retained in his book many of the odd characters, the clowns
in whom he had been interested from the first; but he added the
frustrated world of Miss Lonelyhearts's correspondents, anonymous persons whose "name was Thompson or Johnson and [whose]
home town [was] Sioux City," and who had come to California in
passionate and desperate yearning for the paradisiacal life promul-
gated by the movies. The purveyors of dreams he balanced with
their purchasers, and showed both equally consumed by their
wishes. As his need to bring these two worlds vividly together grew,
he found the plot of the outward-bound ship unworkable, and he
eliminated the figure of the soldier of fortune who ran the boat—a
character who was split into Claude Estee, a scriptwriter, creator of

dreams, and the omnipresent "super-promiser," Dr. Know-All-Pierce-All, godlike impresario of violent wishes and illusions.

Along with the plot, other elements of West's original design were subtly altered or given focus. The strange company of grotesque characters became friends of Tod Hackett, who emerged as the chief character only in the last draft. The ship became the microcosmic hotel where Tod lives, while some of its surreal qualities found proper embodiment in the strange scene of the Hollywood "dream-dump" of leftover props and sets. West's notion of writing a novel about the construction business he brilliantly subordinated in the architectural imagery which is the foundation of description in *The Day of the Locust*. For his sense of disaster—comically manifested in his plan to write a story about a man sitting on a box of dynamite—he now found serious use, in a vision of general apocalypse. Speaking to a friend in justification of the violent materials of his book, West explained "his theory that the ordinary person . . . the people who supposedly worshipped the glamorous stars, really wanted to kill them, murder them [since] they were jealous of them. . . . He described to me [Henriette Martin says] a Hollywood opening on Hollywood Boulevard at the Chinese, and . . . the seats outside and the fact that these people who were coming to see the opening were there early in the morning waiting to see the glamorous stars. My feeling then was, you know, that they worshipped from afar. But he said, 'They want to kill them, they hate them, they'd like to tear them to pieces. If they could shred their flesh as much as their clothes, they would.' And he went into lengthy descriptions of the kind of expressions on the people's faces when the stars came in." West told her that he had haunted premières, that he had "watched the whole thing." Here was West's revived vision of what he had earlier, terrifyingly called, "the apocalypse of the second hand."

Now, West's Hollywood characters were stripped of even the decadent glamour proposed for them in his earliest plans. While most novels about Hollywood—including Fitzgerald's work-then-in-progress, *The Last Tycoon*—involve persons with power, wealth, and prestige, West ironically refused to include in his Hollywood any level of status higher than the screenwriter's. Beneath whatever minimal glamour Claude Estee can manage, West set not only the Midwestern pleasure-seekers (and Torchbearers) but also the Hollywood underworld which preyed upon them. He told a friend that this was "as real and perhaps a *more* real side of Hollywood than the phony glamour that *was* written about." He had made it his business, he said, the business of the novelist, to know this aspect of the Hollywood scene.

By choosing with calculation to live in the seamy area around Hollywood Boulevard and by seeking out underworld contacts through Stanley Rose and other friends, West reached into a rank and tangled life where dreams, violence, and deception mixed. Obviously, the novel he was planning was to have a realistic foundation, however monstrous the real was at last revealed to be. People familiar with the Hollywood scene—Budd Schulberg, planning his own Hollywood novel, among them—found the scene "extremely authentic," not finding in it "a single wrong detail." The novel, as Allan Seager put it, "was not fantasy imagined, but fantasy seen. All [West] had to do was recognize it and know when to stop." National Studios, where Tod works, seems to be a combination of the location of Columbia Studios—where West himself first worked in Hollywood—and the back lot or "dream-dump" of Paramount Studios or M.G.M., where the Perelmans were often employed. Near Columbia, opposite radio station KNK, in what was called "Gower Gulch," was the saddlery store outside which real Hollywood cowboys, models for Earle Shoop, gathered. The geography of streets and canyons in the novel can be mapped, and both are accurately described. West had lived in the same kind of apartment hotels as Tod; and such institutions as "The Cinderella Bar" or Audrey Jenning's (i.e., Lee Francis's) brothel are easily identifiable. The setting is rich with the specific—as the novel comes to suggest, with the specificity of the monstrously true.

Moreover, the novel contains several scenes and characters that West had earlier described to friends as real. No doubt, first in his conversation and ultimately in his fiction, he made the fantasy derived from actual events more memorable than the events themselves; but, obviously, much of this fantasy had roots in West's experiences. He intimated to George Milburn and others that he had made some investigations into the "industrial packaging" done by Lee Francis. And when a friend criticized some of the materials which he planned to use in the novel as too odd, he reached into his own experience for a suitable example of the strangeness of the real. "At that time [West told her] he was living in a seedy apartment . . . not just because it was cheap but because it was at the center of the world about which he was writing. . . . He told me one night—in justifying the kind of people he was writing about—of an episode. . . . He said he was coming home about three or four in the morning, walking down the dim corridor leading to his apartment, when he heard screaming and yelling and cursing in a woman's voice. Suddenly the door opposite opened and one of the prostitutes whom he happened to know, and knew was a prostitute, said something like 'You goddamn son of a bitch, get out of here,' and kicked something out of the door that looked like a dirty bundle of laundry. It started rolling down the hall and suddenly it got up and walked off." West found this scene too good to lose and appropriated it for his book; it introduces Abe Kusich, whose character is modeled on that of a well-known dwarf who peddled papers on the corner of Hollywood Boulevard and Wilcox Street for years.

Then, too, like Tod, West was fascinated with the back lots of the studios and often wandered through them. He wanted to know, Charles Katz says, "what went on in the costume, scenery, and special-effects departments. He was constantly talking about the crazy business he could see." In particular, "he would always talk about the business of striking a set. You would smash Paris and wind up in Tucson, Arizona, at the same spot. . . . He seemed never to be able to talk enough about it." Talking about the experience which he was putting into fiction, West was, his friends agree, extraordinarily vivid and "utterly convincing." His fantasy, like his interests, reached into every aspect of Hollywood life.

West's analysis of the barely suppressed frustrations and hatreds of the Torchbearers was based, of course, on the obvious signs of restlessness among those who (as West puts it) "had come to California to die." A gauge of the accuracy of West's analysis was the suicide rate in Southern California in the 1930's, twice as high as that of the Middle Atlantic Coast. He was interested, obviously, not simply in suicide but in the evident death wishes of "the cultists of all sorts, economic as well as religious . . . who can only be stirred by the promise of miracles and then only to violence . . . a great united front of screwballs and screwboxes. . . ." West's imagination was accumulative and synthetic. Drawing into *The Day of the Locust* the materials and attitudes of his earlier novels, he dealt now with cults both religious and economic; and he sent another Miss Lonelyhearts to inspect them.

Among the native economic movements that gained considerable support a short time after West satirized similar cults in *A Cool Million* was that of the Townsendites, obviously the group which gave West a hint of the economic frustration of the Torchbearers. In January 1934, an elderly physician of Long Beach, California, Francis E. Townsend, proposed that the federal government pay $200 monthly to all unemployed persons over sixty. This sum, which had to be spent within sixty days, would assure a wave of spending and return prosperity. His plan, Townsend declared, drew five million supporters within the year; and by 1936, his petitions begging the government to enact his plan had been signed by twenty-five million Americans. Three thousand Townsend Clubs had been formed, and Townsend buttons, stickers, automobile plates, and copies of the *National Townsend Weekly* were familiar sights west of the Mississippi.

The movement was particularly strong at its source, around Los Angeles and Southern California, where at least one half of the population of three million people had come from Middlewestern states. Farmers from Iowa, Illinois, and Missouri who found themselves unexpectedly rich from the rise in wheat and corn prices during the war retired to California and were followed by a steady stream of friends and neighbors. Combining the remnants of Populist economics with evangelism, and referring easily to Townsend as a "Christ reincarnate," they boycotted California merchants who would not extend credit on the basis of future Townsend checks. By the 1936 election, as West was polishing the first draft of his novel, Townsend's followers formed the most powerful group in the Union Party, an amalgamation of the supporters of Father Coughlin, William Lemke, and Gerald L. K. Smith. It is true that the discontents of the aged had been written about earlier —Josephine Lawrence's *Years Are So Long* (1934) deals with the fate of old people in the Depression*—but West saw the dreams of collective society divided equally between the romantic, adoles-

---

* The 1930 census revealed that nearly one-fourth of all Americans were forty-five or older; life expectancy was 18.3 years greater than it had been in 1911.

cent dreams of Hollywood and the restlessness of the middle-aged; and he made his novel, like Tod's painting, out of the tensions arising from their contact.

Rivaling the popularity of Townsend's cult were the religious cults so much in evidence in California. Tod "spent his nights at the different Hollywood churches, drawing the worshippers. He visited the 'Church of Christ, Physical,' where holiness was attained through the constant use of chest weights and spring grips; the 'Church Invisible' . . . the 'Tabernacle of the Third Coming,' where a woman in male clothing preached the 'Crusade Against Salt'; and the 'Temple Moderne,' under whose glass and chromium roof 'Brain-Breathing, the Secret of the Aztecs' was taught." The most successful and best-known of such institutions, combining many of these features, was Sister Aimee Semple McPherson's $1,500,000 Angelus Temple, which seated five thousand and found places for a radio station, a Lonelyhearts Club, a Miracle Room for discarded crutches and braces, an employment agency, a publishing house, a parole committee, and a Bible school. About Sister Aimee's mysterious disappearance, *Variety* quipped: "Plenty indications of smart showmanship in the whole affair," and it was true that few Hollywood people could match her for the variety and flamboyance of her cultist appeal. Hollywood itself borrowed touches from her by advertising new theaters as "The Cathedral of the Motion Picture" or "The Sanctuary of the Cinema," and she in turn made movie-like entrances in her Temple—appearing once on a motorcycle with blazing headlights and shrieking siren, in the uniform of a traffic policeman, to dramatize the text of her sermon: "Stop! you're speeding to ruin!" Her success spawned, predictably, scores of minor but even more extreme cults. It is no wonder, then, that a speech Tod hears during one of his visits to the "Tabernacle of the Third Coming" is "a crazy jumble of dietary rules, economics, and Biblical threats. He claimed to have seen the Tiger of Wrath stalking the walls of the citadel and the Jackal of Lust skulking in the shrubbery, and he connected these omens with 'thirty dollars every Thursday' and meat eating."

In *Miss Lonelyhearts*, West had been able to associate several traditional if now meaningless religious tales and persons with his hero's quest to communicate spiritual wisdom. Not even these remnants, only the grass-eaters and brain-breathers, remain in *The*

Day of the Locust. There is but one exception, and this, in the recognizable tone of *Miss Lonelyhearts*, is distorted and degraded. At Harry Greener's funeral, "an electric organ started to play a recording of one of Bach's chorales, 'Come Redeemer, Our Savior.' " It is not simply that the hymn is played electrically and distantly, but that even the music's plea for grace is, as Tod puts it, polite: "The God it invited was not the King of Kings, but a shy and gentle Christ, a maiden surrounded by maidens, and the invitation was to a lawn fete, not to the home of some weary suffering sinner." Tod knows that the "music would soon change its tone and grow exciting," but the organ is silenced "in the middle of a phrase" by the beginning of the meaningless ceremonies. Bach's chorale is the novel's only real remnant of the Christ hope. All the narrator can say, darkly, is: "Perhaps Christ heard. If He did He gave no sign." The churches and religious rites in West's Hollywood parallel the studios: they are the *Merzkunst* of the Spirit.

West was almost as fascinated by the architectural as by the human mélange of Hollywood. He spoke vividly of the bewildering mixturesque qualities of Hollywood architecture, drawn from every period and place: pagodas, castles, casinos, châteaus, chalets, huts, and haciendas were all assembled there in a strange world's fair of houses. Until he eliminated it in galley proof, he proposed to place an epigraph from Lewis Mumford at the head of his novel: "From the form of a city, the style of its architecture, and the economic functions and social grouping it shelters and encourages, one can derive most of the essential elements of a civilization." He was interested in the screwboxes only slightly less than the screwballs. He had worked for his father, of course, held an apprentice bricklayer's union card, and gained a certain skill in plumbing. He even wrote out a series of notes about construction entrepreneurship, on which Edmund Wilson based a character in his play *Beppo and Beth*. While the construction business itself evoked no response from West, he had internalized his father's concern with honest construction and he would be an architect of a fiction accurately recording images of houses, rooms, and streets. Acquainted with national and decorative styles of ornament, West was both appalled by and—as a novelist—delighted with the architectural chaos of Hollywood. In *A Cool Million* he had symbolized America, the "Chamber of American Horrors," by its misuse of materials: "Paper has been made to look like wood, wood like rubber, rubber like steel, steel like cheese. . . ." This satire now provided the tone for his treatment of Hollywood. In the new subdivisions that shot up in the twenties, builders had run riot through the styles of the past, with Spanish Renaissance as their favorite; Southern Europe in general seemed to have exploded and settled helter-skelter on the Western shore of America. West, to be sure, was hardly the first critic to notice this. Perelman had written bright comic captions for curious California scenes and Edmund Wilson had brilliantly satirized them: "And the Be-Happy-with-a-Home Realty Company is just a brokenne-downe ole picturesque cobwebby comfy shacke recalling the quaint olde toy-makers of Nuremberg who would plan you a little gingerbread cottage that the oil-trailers pass at high speed on their way up the macadam highway for about $9,000, including Paris-green blinds, a roof oh so lovingly peaked in spots, a weathervane shaped like a frolicsome seal and a view that takes in both the blue-blue sea where every little floozy wave croons, 'Sunkist Caliphonia, here I come!' and the brown papier mâché hills where every prospect appeases and the goofs hang like ripe fruit."

For all his similar astonishment at this scene, West saw that, like the cults, the architectural mélange was an expression of yearning for a life heightened by novelty, richness, and excitement. Homer's cottage, for instance, is gruesome in its sad mechanical effort to duplicate the exotic. In Tod's painting of the eruption of the Torchbearers' frenzy he includes "a great bonfire of architectural styles"; for the houses in which they lived, West recognized, were both the source of their frustration and the compensation for their poverty. His satire of the one was no more intense than his sympathy for the other.

West's various excursions into the realities of Hollywood life inevitably altered the plans for the novel he had carried back to Hollywood in 1935. He had begun with gossip and tales interesting enough as conversation but useless for fiction. These he had seen shift and grow in response to his engagement with the life about him. He saw around it, he saw his novel through it, and he found, slowly, the language by which he could express the true imaginative character of these materials.

For each aspect of Hollywood life he found appropriate expression in a colloquial style rich in diversity and implication. Not simply the dictionary of prostitute lingo, which he had long proposed to collect, but an encyclopedia of glosses on common speech is imbedded in the novel. The talk is vivid and alive, evocative and complexly symbolic of the characters. Faye's talk, clogged with glittering affectations of word and phrase from movie magazines; Harry's vision of the world as a harlequin show, a wider vaudeville merely; Abe's talk of gambling in all its forms; the shop talk of Hollywood workers; the vatic speech of cultists—talk on all levels, tragic and comic, fills the novel with a life of words as varied and quick as the chaotic, multitudinous scene. West, who was a watcher of people, was clearly a listener as well. By listening, he was able to take the rhetorics of traditional, popular, and proletarian novels and wring their necks. The originality of this prose style arises from his ability to understand individual and collective imagination through speech.

West's first endeavor to give shape to these materials came in a story called "Bird and Bottle," which appeared in Lincoln Steffens's *Pacific Weekly* in 1936. It would eventually become Chapter 14 of *The Day of the Locust* and is interesting both for what it reveals of West's progress on his book and for the distance he had to go to give it unity and significance. Like the sections of *Miss Lonelyhearts* he had tried out in *Contact*, this was a public experiment. Unlike the novel it became part of, the story has no focus: Tod Hackett, who will give this section of the novel meaning by meditating over it in terms of his painting, does not appear in the story at all. West was beginning from the conclusion he had reached in *Miss Lonelyhearts*, that his narrative must be able to include meditations on events while appearing to be coldly objective. But he had not yet found a center of consciousness in whom the meditations might be played out and on whom the objectivity would—as upon Miss Lonelyhearts—have a striking effect.

During 1937 and early 1938, West wrote and rewrote his book at home, in the evenings. The first draft he wrote in longhand, and he typed and corrected it himself. Jo Conway took over the manuscript for retyping, then it was again revised by hand. This procedure was repeated at least four times.

Encouraged by Saxe Commins, Eugene O'Neill's editor, whom West had known at Liveright, he sent his novel to Random House in April 1938. Commins had gone there after the Liveright debacle to join its founder, Bennett Cerf, who had been a vice president at Liveright until 1927. The book West submitted differed considerably from the one ultimately published. In his second version he had attempted to give the book focus by narrating it entirely in the first-person voice of Claude Estee, who was, like West himself, a former artist-turned-screenwriter. By April 1938, after several revisions, West had generally taken the narration from Estee; yet he still allowed Estee's voice—spouting mock prophecies of doom—to intrude occasionally, even though he otherwise hardly figured in the novel. Estee was eventually split in two, much as Miss Lonelyhearts had been divided from Shrike, and the painter Tod Hackett was created to embody Estee's vulnerable and sensitive side. In the end, all the important characters would be essentially divided. Homer's hands (like Wing Biddlebaum's) hint at an aspect of his personality otherwise unexpressed; Faye's clichéd talk and sensuous gestures seem to have no connection; and Tod himself is split between his artistic vision and lust for Faye. But at this stage of the novel's evolution, Tod remained largely unformed. Moreover, West now included, to a greater extent than he ultimately would, grotesque characters and episodes left over from his earlier ship-of-fools conception. Among these was a glimpse of a "sloppy old nude who drools over her 'cello,' kissing its neck and making it groan in reply," a scene which was used as a preface to the introduction of Abe Kusich. Calling it the "Europa and Bull-fiddle" episode, West attempted, in his next revision, to keep part of the scene simply for the sake of Tod's perception of it as a painter's "subject"—"peppermint towel, deep orange cello, turkey red carpet, peach flesh"— but at last eliminated it altogether. Mrs. Schwartzen, in the April 1938 manuscript, is described as a seven-foot Lesbian who needs to shave every day; in an interlude in Audrey Jenning's call-house, she accosts one of the girls. While she remains mannish in the final version, her original perversions are suppressed. An episode about a bedraggled black hen, finally reduced and made into one of Homer's complaints, originally stood as an image of disgust and horror, a symbol of "what a terrible form [Homer's] torture takes."

Still, except for the fully developed figure of Tod Hackett, the version submitted to Random House, entitled *The Cheated*, contained all the elements which West's further revision was to heighten. On May 17, 1938, he received a telegram from Bennett Cerf: "Definitely accepted *The Cheated* for Random House. Hope you will make few minor changes about which I am writing today. It is a swell book." In the letter in which Cerf expanded on his reservations, he offered an "advance of $500.00 on the signing of the contract against a royalty of 10% of the retail price on the first 2,500 copies, 12½% . . . on the next 2,500 copies, and a straight 15% . . . thereafter, with an option on your next two books." "Here's hoping," Cerf concluded, "that you will be a Random House author for the rest of your natural life."

West was now ready to begin another revision. When he received Cerf's letter on the nineteenth, he radiogramed back: "Yours and Random House enthusiasm extremely gratifying. . . . Agree to Claude Estee change. Taking book to Sierras fishing for week. On return, after careful study, will reply on other changes. On first reading of letter, agree to much you suggest." Anxious to have the book published in October 1938, he proposed, in a letter written when he returned, to do nothing but work on his revisions for the next month.

It was, in fact, not until July 11 that he returned a revised manuscript, one which he felt "shows a great deal of improvement over the previous one—in speed, smoothness and consistency of style." Still, he was beginning to be doubtful about his title and was favoring "The Grass Eaters," a reference to the cultists who infest the novel and make up the Torchbearers. Two weeks later, he had changed his mind again and offered two more: "Cry Wolf" and "The Wrath to Come"—both of which stress the apocalyptic character of the novel's conclusion. Neither title would suffice, though initially he inclined strongly toward the first and in the fall wrote the second on his manuscript. Still, he was not satisfied. "I would like to call it 'Days to Come,'" he wrote to Cerf, "but as you know, Lillie Hellman used that on a play."

In the meantime West began to lay plans, with his usual enthusiasm, for the successful publication and reception of the book. Dashiell Hammett, reading an earlier version, had exclaimed over "the God damnedest set of characters I ever read about," and West counted on him and Dorothy Parker for blurbs. He planned to return to New York in August for the rehearsals of *Good Hunting* and he assured Cerf that there he would give his manuscript another careful revision.

West's powers of revision were never more clear, his deftness and perception more absolute, than in this final draft. More and more, in his meditations on his novel, he had seen Tod Hackett necessarily emerging as its most important character, since he alone could provide an intelligible point of view from which the deformities of Hollywood might be criticized. Even more than Tod's importance as a character, his activities as a painter were to be the book's center; and in his revisions West concentrated almost exclusively on heightening and clarifying the dramatization of Tod's art; for it is his artistic perception alone that stands against the disintegration of his person and the degradation of the society about him. Tod's weakness of will is in some part compensated for by the decisive prophecies of his art; the deformed experiences and incoherent purposelessness of Hollywood life, all of which Tod undergoes, yield to the coherence of the design of "The Burning of Los Angeles," his painting. Tod, we learn in the extremely important first revised passage of the final manuscript, "was a very complicated young man. . . . And 'The Burning of Los Angeles,' a picture he was soon to paint, definitely proved he had talent." Here West made a highly significant dislocation of the time scheme of his novel. In *The Waste Land*, Eliot had created a form in which he could arbitrarily yoke widely separate events and places so that there appeared to be no time- or space-lapse between them. He understood that it was possible, as Bertrand Russell put it, "for the time-interval between two events to be zero: when the one event is the seeing of the other." West, who read Eliot all through the twenties and thirties and heard Russell and C. H. Currier lecture on Einstein's relativity theory at Brown, took the hint. At least in part, he suggests, the time perspective of *The Day of the Locust* is retrospective, narrated after the riot which proves Tod an accurate prophet. The picture, which during the time of the novel he is said to be planning, is really completed. It is a great painting. Society has dissolved into chaos, but art remains.

At the same time, the depiction of the present in the novel holds our attention. The people and events of this moment in Hollywood are absurd, confused, and degraded. There is no hope for them: their future must be apocalyptic. They can achieve no way of ordering reality; Tod's painting exists in the present only as fragments, as uncompleted studies and sketches. His only accomplished art are his costume designs for the movie which ends in catastrophe. Eliot had perceived much the same condition in modern London; only by seeing it against a simultaneous background of the past wisdoms and ritual order which it had lost or destroyed could he give it any sense at all. West kept the form and reversed the implications of Eliot's poem. His more modern Hollywood had no meaning even in the perspective of the past, on which moviemakers preyed for fantasy and romance. Only by implying a future quite different from the past and present, one in which art might be meaningful, could the present have any meaning at all. Eliot gave his poem tragic meaning by pointing to what the present had frivolously destroyed. West's novel, rather, is a satire which shows to the full the rule of chaos over both past and present by hinting at an alternative state of man, with his illusions revealed, returning to what Pope termed his "lawful callings." West refused to turn his vision, romantically and nostalgically, backward; in the best sense his vision was classical, stoical, and reserved; what beliefs he had were held without hope. Only Tod, among the characters, has glimmers of this sort of future in attempting to paint the image of chaos. But in the book's iron present, of course, he is like all the rest of the characters: his dreams or sensibilities cannot be realized in action. For all his own writhings, he too, as a personality, must remain a starer and be engulfed in the final riot. There is no optimism in the book: its city and people are ravaged by the locusts of their fantasies. Only the stony perspective of the future remains.

West saw at the last moment that art must be implicated in the center of normalcy which exists outside the present of his book, where all else is deformed; every important reference to Tod's prophetic painting was put in during the final revision. References to the painters of Decay and Mystery—Salvator Rosa, Francesco Guardi, Monsu Desiderio, and Alessando Magnasco—were almost entirely inserted at the last, when West was supremely conscious of the implications of his book. None of these baroque painters was well known in the thirties. West's "accurate and macabre" reference to them reminds us again of the special character of his taste and knowledge. If his familiarity with their work was a result of his earlier plan to write a book about painters, his study for that book had gone deep. Whatever the source of his knowledge, there is no doubt that he made brilliant symbolic use of it in drawing a parallel between their dream works and the realities of Hollywood that (in another Eliot-like time-compression) they foretell.

Most important of all for his novel, he was able to make Tod's occupation and consciousness as a painter reveal the nature and meaning of the world which, following in their tradition, he is attempting to paint. Josephine Herbst has perceptively likened West's novels to the paintings of James Ensor. Both were interested in the crowd, its violent rhythms and grotesque actions; both took clowns and freaks as representative individuals. Both had imaginations firmly grounded in the daily real, and stressed the ways that reality becomes or appears phantasmagoric. Both returned repeatedly to the Christ figure—suffering and cruelly distorted in Ensor (as in *Ecce Homo, ou, Le Christ et les critiques*), suffering and impotent in West. West may have seen some resemblance between his own and Ensor's imagination as early as *Miss Lonelyhearts*. Certainly, he had him consciously in mind in *The Day of the Locust*, where Ensor's painting *Les Cuirassiers à Waterloo* is the model for West's description of the chaotic (and catastrophic) battle being filmed at National Studios. Tod Hackett's prospective painting, "The Burning of Los Angeles," is reminiscent of several of Ensor's paintings of crowds, most obviously his *L'entrée du Christ à Bruxelles*. *La bataille des Éperons d'or* and *La mort poursuivant le troupeau des humains* contain elements of design which West attributes to Tod's picture.

Through these revisions, West gave his novel two opposing curves of development. The first consists of the story of the "Dancers" and the "Torchbearers," the "super-promisers" and their dupes. Both groups—the collective emigrant to California represented by Homer, and the Hollywood underworld of Faye, Earle, Abe, and Miguel—move from desire to frustration and from discontent to frenzy. The cockfight with its sequels in sexual violence and the riot with its sexual-sadistic terror are essentially duplicates of each other. Not in his person but in his meditation, Tod, the sole character involved in both groups, provides the opposing curve to them, especially in his attempts to arrange them in his painting. He is the one person who can see the subtle ways in which the cheaters and the cheated are always switching roles. If the cheaters sink into the mass (Faye is variously preyed upon), the cheated become performers—Homer most spectacularly, by bringing on the riot at the end of the book. Tod watches the peregrinations and intersections of both arcs. William Dean Howells once told Stephen Crane that the novel is truly a "perspective" for the use of people who cannot use their eyes. West took over or reinvented this painterly conception for *The Day of the Locust* and made his hero a painter in whose prospective painting the proportions might be restored, the balances adjusted. In his personal life, Tod, as Edmund Wilson remarks, "finds himself swirling around in the same aimless eddies as the others." Tod is divided between his sensibility and his actions, his perception and his desires, his art and his materials for art. His painting assumes shape even while his society and his own sanity become so misshapen that they explode sensationally. But his painting takes shape along with the book.

Tod's story, then, mirrors the rest of the novel. On the one hand, he moves from desire to frustration to frenzy and at last personal dissolution; on the other, aesthetically, toward experience, vision, prophecy, and finally art. If his personal life dissolves with the rest of this world, his art remains. West's penultimate version ends as Tod is taken to Claude's house. There he and Estee argue about the possibility of class warfare. The last line of this version reads: "He [Tod] raved on until the doctor came and put him to sleep." West eliminated all of this final chapter, inserting instead Tod's final reflections on his painting. "To forget the agony in his leg, he thought about his picture," West began this revision, shifting the focus from Tod's ravings, his personal agony and dissolution, to his art, and opposing the two.

West made these revisions after returning East in mid-August, at the same time that he was trying to give *Good Hunting* its final shape, rewriting daily under the pressure of Mayer's demands, rehearsals, and world events. His work on the novel and the play blurred together; indeed, there are many resemblances between them. "Everything is O.K. on the novel thank God," he wrote to his secretary on September 19. "It goes into rehearsal (I mean the printers) December tenth and will be out January tenth. The publishers think it will do fine."

There was still the problem of the title. The cover of West's manuscript was by now a palimpsest of titles. But at last, in full possession of the meanings of his work, he set down in dark ink over all his earlier titles "The Days of the Locust" and soon after, by eliminating the plural, focused his title entirely on the climactic riot—the revelation of the raw violence which has all along lain just beneath the romantic surface of American life. The great bonfire of buildings which Tod will paint ranges from "Egyptian" to "Cape Cod colonial." Doubtless, West has in mind a parallel, here as elsewhere, between the prophecies of desolation in the Old Testament and Tod's prophetic painting. Tod "refused to give up the role of Jeremiah." In this sense, the clearest source of the title is a composite reference to the apocalyptic devastations of locusts in the Old Testament. The first of these occurs in Exodus 10:3–6, 13–15: "So Moses and Aaron went to Pharaoh and told him, 'Thus says the Lord, the God of the Hebrews: How long will you refuse to submit to me? Let my people go to worship me. If you refuse to let my people go, I warn you, tomorrow I will bring locusts into your country. They shall cover the ground, so that the ground itself will not be visible. . . . Such a sight your fathers or grandfathers have not seen from the day they first settled on this soil up to the present day. . . . At dawn the east wind brought the locusts. They swarmed over the whole land of Egypt and settled down on every part of it. Never before had there been such a fierce swarm of locusts, nor will there ever be. They covered the surface of the whole land, till it was black with them. They ate up all the vegetation in the land and fruit of whatever trees the hail had spared. Nothing green was left on any tree or plant throughout the land of Egypt." Referring to the first release of the Chosen People into the Promised Land, in his title West also hinted at the apocalypse of that dream, the end of all things foretold in Revelations 9:3–9: "And out of the smoke there came forth locusts upon the earth. . . . And they were told not to hurt the grass of the earth or any green thing or any tree; but only the men. . . . And in those days men will seek death and will not find it; they will long to die and death will flee from them."

Two other sources for West's title are evident. The first is George Seldes's title *Years of the Locust* (1933), and the second a line in Archibald MacLeish's *Land of the Free* (1938), a book combining photographs of underprivileged Americans with poetry described as a "sound track." A few lines near the conclusion are directly relevant to West's book:

> We wonder whether the great American dream
> Was the singing of locusts out of the grass to the West and the West is behind us now:
>
> The West wind's away from us:
>
> We wonder if the liberty is done:
> The dreaming is finished

The Great American Dream, the siren singing of locusts in the West, had been West's subject in *A Cool Million*. MacLeish's lines point to the connection between West's last two novels. Both are concerned with that dream and its corruptions; and both reveal the chaos to which its perversion leads. *A Cool Million* ends with the triumph of the militant middle classes. In West's penultimate version of *The Day of the Locust* he wrote that "the [middle-class] Angelenos would be first, but their brothers all over the country would follow. Only the working classes would resist. There would be civil war." He wisely eliminated this, for his own vision of society was revolutionary but not Marxist. He could never equate ideal society with the triumph of the proletariat. West, as John Howard Lawson has declared, "saw the corruption in society but never treated [it] . . . as something irrevocable." The ideal society, as he made it out, was quite simply that which removed the necessity for illusion and returned society to culture.

Although West adopted a pose of detachment as a mask for his satire, he was hardly indifferent to the dream ravaged by the invading locusts. Tod intends to portray the Torchbearers objectively— "not satirize them as Hogarth or Daumier might, nor . . . pity them. He would paint their fury with respect, appreciating its awful, anarchic power and aware that they had it in them to destroy civilization." If West refuses to imagine the American Dream sentimentally restored at the conclusion of his novel and insists on the power of chaos over it, still chaos might not wholly prevail; and after chaos and old night have had their sway, what "everyone now knows"—as an earlier manuscript puts it—is that Tod, from his immersion in disorder, "made the sketches for one of his most celebrated works, 'The Burning of Los Angeles,' many months before that city was actually put to the torch." Chaos may pass, but aesthetic order can endure. The locusts in Revelations "had power to harm mankind for five months."

West's satire reached to every aspect of society. Perhaps he may be most accurately called, in Kenneth Burke's phrase, "a universal satirist" who, unlike the "satiric propagandist," refuses to make a "clear alignment of friends and foes" and condemns both. West adamantly opposed society's excesses and confusions, its muddy and absurd antics, its compromises and corruptions. But behind his irony lay a sense of the possibilities for good of man and society. This was a faith which his experience could neither support nor entirely destroy. He was as passionate about his hopes in private as he was vehement in depicting his horrors in his fiction. Philip Wylie describes West's innocence and its relation to his satire in a summary of his paradoxical drives: "He had some furious hunger for a different humanity that was hidden by his deep, empathetic, outraged yet somehow, at bottom, loving regard for people." Pope justified his satire of fools in *The Dunciad* by explaining that they became dunces by neglecting their "lawful callings." West, similarly, does not satirize men themselves, only the masks men wear and the illusions they cherish: these are their unlawful callings. Though he lived in and wrote of a world riddled with delusion, he seems to have believed with Freud that the future of illusion could be its disappearance. His satire was designed to return man to himself, to his "lawful callings."

Once he had found his title, and particularly after the failure of his play, West was anxious for his book to appear, and he returned to California early in December to await the arrival of the proofs. Absolutely broke, he began work at Universal almost immediately. After the play, only the latest of many failures, West was increasingly uneasy about the prospects for his novel, and for a time became deeply and almost inconsolably melancholic, though he could still regard ironically the possibility that the novel would fail to sell. "This book means an awful lot to me and probably to American literature," he wrote, "because if it doesn't do at least a little business, I may remain in Hollywood and write no others." But his wit was wearing thin, and the truth was that West was deeply worried. Early in December he brooded to Saxe Commins: "I got back to this sun-drenched desert with everything intact except my spirits, which are lower than ——— of Liveright's Inc. moral standards. During the four months I was away I think that the sand has encroached at least a few feet on this town and if I can get a group of people together to hide the brooms of the Japanese gardeners for a few weeks, maybe the surrounding desert will overwhelm it. That is my present bent." "Don't let California depress you," Commins wrote, advising West that comments had been received from Hammett and Dorothy Parker. Both were good and promised to give the book a boost. "This is the Hollywood that needs telling about," Hammett declared, while Miss Parker wrote: "It's brilliant, savage, and arresting—a truly good novel."

But West was not to be comforted. Never before, even in the darkest period of 1935, had his mood been so unrestrainedly dark; never had his confidence been lower or his fears of failure stronger. He was "disconsolate," Philip Wylie remembers, and convinced that even this novel, his best work, would go unrecognized. A week after Commins's letter, he responded in Dostoevskian tones: "I would be very much obliged to receive a list of worse places at this moment than Hollywood. I suppose you mean Hitler's Munich as one of them. However, if like me and St. Thomas Aquinas, you believe that man is duplex, body and soul being separate entities, then you would also know that there is very little to choose since in Munich they murder your flesh, but here it is the soul which is put under the executioner's axe. With this note I end."

Anxiously awaiting the arrival of proofs, news of the publication date, jacket copy, and so on, West heard almost nothing at all until the middle of January, when he learned that his mail was being rerouted by the post office to a four-year-old address. Then he received all at once what he regarded as unrelieved bad news. The publication date was fixed on May 16, although he had anticipated publication by February. "Life is awfully short," he complained, "and a year between the time of acceptance and that of appearance makes a most terrifying and tremendous stretch." He felt, too, that the copy for the dust jacket and the publisher's catalogue almost wholly misrepresented the nature and audience of this book. If there had ever been any doubt of West's business sense, he proved his shrewdness in his remarks on the copy. It must be improved, he said, "by explaining that the book isn't another, 'Boy Meets Girl,' 'Once in a Lifetime,' or 'Queer People,' but that it has a real and even 'serious' theme, and that its purpose is not to compete with the novels I listed, but others on a much higher plane. One of the mistakes that Liveright made in selling 'Miss Lonelyhearts' (if they ever tried to sell it) was, I feel certain, their attempt to make believe the book was a cheap lending library item and thereby making angry those book salesmen who sold it as such, and failing to immediately bring it to the attention of the people who would have known what it was all about. In other words, a definite attempt, and a successful one, to sit down hard between two stools." West's accurate complaint, however, served no purpose: both publication date and copy remained unchanged. Meanwhile, another problem was on the horizon. "We have engaged a really high-priced artist to work on the jacket design," Cerf advised him. West was afraid he knew what that might mean. The kind of book design he hoped for is suggested by his design for *Contact* 2 and 3: he wanted a book, he reminded Perelman, "with a paper label on the back [to look] like all the old Aldous Huxley English editions used to look. Do you remember how much we once admired them and hoped that we would reach that sober binding with paper label and even possibly a two color ink job on the title page?"

A hopeful bit of news came when George Milburn wrote that he was pressing *The New Republic*, where Malcolm Cowley was literary editor, or the *Herald Tribune* to allow him to review West's book. West counted on an unequivocally good review from him and was delighted. "If you can manage to . . . read it for the *Herald Tribune*," West wrote brightly, "it would count a thousand per cent more in the pocketbook, where I am extremely sensitive these days." Almost in the same mail, the proofs arrived and, revising again, West began to "torment" himself for the next two weeks, "until the words [were] a continuous blur."

After making a few minor alterations and again rewriting the last page of his novel, West sent the proofs to Perelman, who had always been his shrewdest critic, and whom he trusted to "read the thing . . . with that microscopic eye. . . . On punctuation, spelling, etc. I leave it absolutely up to you." With Cerf's reference to the "high-priced" artist sounding more and more ominous to his inner ear, West also asked Perelman to try to get a look at a proof of the jacket.

The uneasiness over the jacket, however, did not keep West's optimism from reviving, now that the book was nearly through production. Milburn's review was certain—he wrote that he had definitely arranged to write it for *The Saturday Review;* Coates would undoubtedly review it in *The New Yorker;* and there were several other critics who had shown interest in West's work in the past. He requested six sets of bound proofs from Random House, and sent the first four to Fitzgerald, Edmund Wilson, Milburn, and Aldous Huxley, "who has mentioned me kindly and who . . . I can get to read it." Later, he sent proofs to Ben Hecht and Erskine Caldwell. Would it be useful to have Steinbeck read the book, he asked. And why not get copies into the hands of the reviewers who had praised his earlier books? He even began to see prospects of revived interest in his earlier work, and inquired about the chances of having *A Cool Million* reprinted in a cheap paperback edition. "A lot of people," he told Commins, "think it is a pretty good [novel] and that the reason it flopped is because it was published much too soon in the race toward Fascism. It came out when no one in this country, except a few Jeremiahs like myself, took seriously the possibility of a Fascist America. . . . I feel that at the present time it might have a very good chance of arousing some interest." In short, he was now fully alive to the possibilities for success and had rebounded so completely from his depression that he could write to an acquaintance that after "the debacle of my little war farce," the "one thing that keeps me from burrowing down in this rut and never coming up is the fact that my new book . . . will be out in the middle of May." Before long he had heard that "Scott Fitzgerald raved . . . about the book," and that Malcolm Cowley thought it "wonderful . . . even better" than *Miss Lonelyhearts.*

West's next disappointment followed shortly after the revival of his spirits. His worst premonitions about the jacket were confirmed. On a scarlet background was a yellow movie camera; the title was printed in white on a black strip of film frames. West was aghast. At once he telegraphed Cerf: "Will pay the cost of removing yellow camera from jacket. Black, red, white is enough for white man's trade. Or is it bait for drunken Mexicans?" The red binding, he declared, "could be used as bait for vampire bats." Now, even before the publication of the novel, he was feeling that Random House "was just as stupid as Covici-Friede or Liveright."

He believed that the jacket and binding proved that his book was not being taken seriously. (Even much later, he was still smarting about the jacket when he jokingly inscribed a copy to Budd Schulberg: "It can be used as a flag when the Day comes.") Still, news was not all bad, and he was willing to find hope in any sign. He was delighted to learn that the novel had an advance sale of 1,100 copies of the first printing of 3,000. With hopes and fears and mingled memories and desires, he waited for the reviews.

About the quality of the first few chapters, where he had retained some of the merely grotesque parts of his earlier "Wanderer" conception, West was uneasy. But the rest, he felt, was the best writing he had done.

The plot is simple, though it allows for episodic variation and improvisation. Tod Hackett, a graduate of the Yale School of Fine Arts, is hired by a scout for National Films to design costumes and sets. A complicated young man, bored with the kind of painting he is trained to do and with the masters—Homer and Ryder—he had learned to admire, Tod is determined to learn something about the nature of Hollywood life and to let his new experiences renew his art. He meets a group of people, each of whom is in some way or other a maker of illusions. It should be remarked, however, that Tod's perception of them is not distorted. A painter, Tod (like West) sees accurately. What shocks him is what shocks in West's fiction in general: the true, pitiable, or horrible image of reality. Not one of the characters in *The Day of the Locust* is imaginatively distorted: the distortion has already taken place in reality. West would even propose to do a photographic study of the background and models for his novel.

A pugnacious dwarf, "Honest Abe" Kusich, not only fascinates Tod, but is a reminder of how intensely the horse-racing fever burned in Hollywood. Leo Rosten has remarked: "A study of Hollywood which neglected to comment on the role of horses, gambling, and race tracks would be derelict in its duty and incomplete in its insights. The offices, commissaries, stages, and dining-rooms of Hollywood echo with knowing tips and detailed genealogies, with debates, wagers, analyses, and grave references to a dozen dope sheets and racing forms. The more devoted votaries of the turf place wagers all year round, on horses they do not know, run-

ning in places they have never visited, in races they never see." But
the horse which Abe touts, Tragopan, is, like Balso's, a Greek
horse, deceptive. Abe is the maker of such dreams of quick wealth,
no less a prophet than the cultists of grass-eating and brain-breathing.

Claude Estee, a friend of Tod's, is a screenwriter whose daily
involvement in the business of romance has infected and distorted
his own imagination until he swims wholly in a world of romantic
promise. He lives in an exact reproduction of the old Dupuy Man-
sion near Biloxi, Mississippi. Although he is "a dried-up little
man," he teetered back and forth on his heels "like a Civil War
Colonel and made believe he had a large belly"; his costume is
absurd. To his Chinese servant, who is serving Scotch and soda, he
shouts, "Here, you black rascal! A mint julep." He takes his guests
to a brothel where there are no girls, and even the movies shown
only hint at passion. Claude keeps not a real horse but a rubber
horse, expensively designed to look drowned, in his pool. His simulated horse, like the horses in *Balso Snell* and *A Cool Million*, is a
symbol of delusion and sham, a crucial sign of his difference from
his creator.

Like the supposedly pornographic movie, Faye Greener, whom
Tod desires, though about equally fascinated and repelled by her,
promises passion but is essentially an amalgam of dreams, automatic, impersonal sensuality, absurd affectations, and bits of gossip
or ambitions drawn from movie magazines. She is a composite of
the aspiring actress, a weak-minded, Westian Emma Bovary set in
a Hollywood where dreams have no counterpart in life. After being
complimented by Claude, "she repaid him . . . by smiling in a
peculiar, secret way and running her tongue over her lips. It was
one of her most characteristic gestures and very effective. It seemed
to promise all sorts of undefined intimacies, yet it was really as
simple and automatic as the word thanks. She used it to reward
anyone for anything, no matter how unimportant." She is, as her
name has it, a "fay," a fairy figure, appealing and elusive because
ultimately illusory. In his earliest description of Faye, in 1936,
West had written: "Her 'platinum' hair was drawn tightly away
from her face and gathered together in back by a narrow baby blue
ribbon. . . . The style . . . had been copied from Tenniel's
drawings of Alice." Her world is one as nightmarish and meaning-

less as Alice's, one where the camera has replaced the looking glass.

Faye's father, Harry Greener, is one of the sad clowns in this Hollywood mirror. His career begins where Lemuel Pitkin's ended, as a "bedraggled harlequin" in a vaudeville act, the humor of which consists in his innocent, bemused dismantlement. After repeated beatings by the Four Lings during this comic acrobatic turn, "he is tattered and bloody, but still sweet." The character and fate of the washed-up vaudeville actor had already been treated in plays like George Manker Walters and Arthur Hopkins's *Burlesque* (1928); but West makes Harry memorable as a terrifying symbol of the way false art can infect life and make it false.

These are the major dream-makers whom Tod meets, but they are mere samples, better developed and more closely seen representatives of the horde of similar promisers, illusion-makers, in the book—from the squat movie director in the opening scene to the funeral director and Earle Shoop, Adore Loomis, and, at last, the radio broadcaster who churns the crowd to frenzy at the première. In *The Day of the Locust*, West is not so much interested in unified characters as he is in the aspects of any personality as it becomes mingled with collective society. He is able to give his novel the appearance of both fullness and rapidity by focusing on the self in dissolution, thus seeing all his dream-makers as mirrors of each other. Like Melville's Confidence Man, they are only one character, who assumes the multiform masquerades of human desire.

Homer, whom Tod soon meets, is the prototype of the crowd. He "seemed an exact model for the kind of person who comes to California to die, perfect in every detail down to fever eyes and unruly hands." He surely is, as Tod describes the people in the crowd, a starer, a consumer of dreams. And while Tod decides at first that Homer is too passive to fit the role, it is the overflow of Homer's suppressed violence that initiates the climactic riot. He becomes the leader of the Torchbearers. Far from being opposed to each other, the dream-makers and starers are intricately related. Harry's clownship, Tod thinks, "was a clue to the people who stared (a painter's clue, that is—a clue in the form of a symbol), just as Faye's dreams were another." The cultists and wave-watchers, those who wait at Glendale airport for a plane to crash, go to funerals of strangers, or follow movie stars about—in each case hoping to find some principle of the value of any life by which to understand the value of their own lives—these Tod sees as more concentrated in California than anywhere else but ultimately expressive of the meaninglessness of modern life for the mass of men. After saving for years, these folks have come to California, following the dream of leisure. But they are the American masses betrayed, not—as the proletariat novels and Party theoreticians were claiming—by capital, but by the dreams they cherish. After a while, "their boredom becomes more and more terrible. They realize they have been tricked and burn with resentment. Every day of their lives they read the newspapers and went to the movies. Both fed them on lynchings, murder, sex crimes, explosions, wrecks, love nests, fires, miracles, revolutions, and war. . . . [Now] nothing can ever be violent enough to make taut their slack minds and bodies. They have been cheated and betrayed. They have slaved and saved for nothing." It is no wonder that the book begins with a scene at "quitting time." This world is exhausted.

From first to last, violence runs through the book. Perhaps, beneath the surface of lives deadened by steady dream-making or dreaming, there is only violence. Only through violence is human excitation possible. And this is true not only for Faye and Earle, for the spectators at the cockfight, and at last for Homer and the Messianic crowd, but also for Tod. He is excited into painting by Abe's pugnacity, by the cultists, and by Faye: and all are subjects for sketches. "Maybe," he thinks, "he could only be galvanized into sensibility." Unwilling to be an artist in the coherent realistic or symbolist traditions of Homer or Ryder, he will be a painter drawing on, by responding to, the archetypal violence of dreams, a painter of mystery and decay, shocked into sensibility. At the very beginning of the book, Tod hears "the tattoo of a thousand hooves." That tattoo beats throughout the novel, not only in the bobbing disorder of the chaotic movie scenes, but in Harry's grotesque act for Homer, in Abe Kusich's barely suppressed hatreds, at Audrey Jenning's and at the cockfight, through the songs of Faye, Miguel, Adore, and the female impersonator, and of course in the final riot of voices at the première.* Like the masqueraders of the book, the siren of violence takes many forms, but all contain the

---

* At one such première, Arturo Toscanini was nearly crushed to death, unrecognized, by a mob in pursuit of Spencer Tracy.

same spasmodic pulsation of terror. Thus, what is at first a tattoo is at last the police siren which Tod imitates hysterically—a scream of pain or a cry for help, and a trumpet announcement of the day of doom.

Josephine Herbst had told West before he went back to the Coast that the end of his book should be revised. The novel, she felt, ended in meaningless chaos. But West had long been convinced that American culture was characterized by violence. He shared the view which William Carlos Williams had expressed in 1924, that America was "the most lawless country in the civilized world." West knew that the root of movie "fan" was "fanatic," and he tried to show the viciousness and fanaticism ready to burst through the apparent adulation which conceals them. He was hardly persuaded by the Marxist conviction that the American masses would become an anarchic Lumpenproletariat. It was civilization, man himself, he felt, which was coming to some kind of violent catharsis on these Western shores. Tod not only wanders through the history of burned-out civilizations in the Hollywood dream-dump; West also put into his novel mock representatives of the sources of Western civilization. In *Balso Snell* he had entered Western history through the symbol of the Trojan horse; in *The Day of the Locust*, Abe (Abraham) and Homer are symbols of the fountainheads of Hebrew and Greek culture which had combined to make Western civilization. Like Squier in Robert Sherwood's *The Petrified Forest* (1935), West was surveying the end of a period of history. "The Petrified Forest," Squier says, "is a graveyard of the civilization that's been shot from under us." Its end would necessarily be violent. Speaking perceptively of West, John Hawkes has suggested that "a writer who maintains a consistent cold detachment toward physical violence is likely to generate the deepest novelistic sympathy of all." The representative novel of the twenties, like Sherwood Anderson's, ended with a young man boarding a train for the city, a place of promise. In the early thirties, the young man was likely, as in *U.S.A.*, to be thumbing his way down that road. But in 1939, at the edge of war, West saw that the mob, unperplexed by destinations, had replaced the individual. History was beginning to turn against itself.

In 1933 West had published a sixteen-line poem in *Contempo*, which Angel Flores called "a splendid tour de force." Actually, this

was only the first part of a three-part poem; the rest is published
here for the first time. Concerned with the apocalyptic reversal of
history, this poem unites the period of *Miss Lonelyhearts* with that
of *The Day of the Locust*:

BURN THE CITIES

I

The Eastern star calls with its hundred knives
Burn the cities
Burn the cities

Burn Jerusalem
It is easy
City of birth a star
A rose in color a daisy in shape
Calls with its hundred knives
Calls three kings
Club diamond heart
Burn Jerusalem and bring
The spade king to the Babe
Nailed to his six-branched tree
Upon the sideboard of a Jew
Marx
Performs the miracle of loaves and fishes

II

Burn the cities
Burn Paris
City of light
Twice-burned city
Warehouse of the arts
The spread hand is a star with points
The fist a torch
Burn the cities
Burn Paris
City of light
Twice-burned city
Warehouse of the arts

The spread hand is a star
The fist a torch
Workers of the World

Unite
Burn Paris

Paris will burn easily
Paris is fat
Only an Eskimo could eat her
Only a Turk could love her
The Seine is her bidet
She will not hold urine
She squats upon the waters and they are oil
A placid slop
Only the sick can walk on it
Fire alone can make it roar
Not like a burning barn but muted
Muted by a derby hat
So also my sorrow
City of my youth
Is muted by a derby hat

The flames of Paris are sure to be well-shaped
Some will be like springs
Some like practiced tongues
Some like gay flags
Others like dressed hair
Many will dance
Only the smells will be without order

The spread hand is a star with points
The fist a torch
Workers of the World
Unite
Burn Paris

III

Burn the cities
Burn London
Slow cold city
Do not despair
London will burn
It will burn
In the heat of tired eyes
In the grease of fish and chips
The English worker will burn it
With coal from Wales

> With oil from Persia
> The Indian will give him fire
> There is sun in Egypt
> The Negro will give him fire
> Africa is the land of fire
> London is cold
> It will nurse the flame
> London is tired
> It will welcome the flame
> London is lecherous
> It will embrace the flame
> London will burn

The central theme of *The Day of the Locust,* like that of Pound's Canto XLV, is *contra naturam;* for the life which issues from such violence, boredom, and hatred can be expressed and truly understood only in inhuman terms. This whole world is so much against nature that it can be described only by ideas, actions, and images which are normally assumed to be contrary to human nature. This provides West's great subject, as it did Pound's. But where Pound sees chiefly satire, West also perceives tragedy. On the most general level, of course, nature itself is disordered. In letters to Cerf, West expressed some concern about his descriptions of nature; for he was trying to show not merely violated nature (as in the scene of the "little park" in *Miss Lonelyhearts*) but nature displaced entirely by artificial substitutes. Around the edge of the hills at dusk, Tod—a painter with accurate perceptions—sees "violet piping, like a Neon tube," and an "enameled sky," later becoming a "blue serge sky [through which] poked a grained moon that looked like an enormous bone button." Another evening is "one of those blue and lavender nights when the luminous color seems to have been blown over the scene with an air brush." In the Sun Gold Market, "colored spotlights played on the showcases and counters, heightening the natural hues of the different foods. The oranges were bathed in red, the lemons in yellow, the fish in pale green, the steaks in rose and the eggs in ivory." In short, nature, in West's world, has become a thing of canvas sets, painted props— wishing itself is so fantastic that unadorned nature cannot begin to satisfy it.

To a large extent, architecture becomes a substitute for nature, not in the sense of the organic architecture that Frank Lloyd Wright was then trying to promulgate, but quite the reverse, as a way of satisfying the extreme cravings for adornment and novelty which grow *contra naturam* from "the need for beauty and romance." The cottages, castles, villas, temples, chalets, and huts which line the streets; the simulated materials of Harry's casket; the sensational architecture of Kahn's Persian (i.e., Grauman's Chinese) Theatre; and the mélange of history in the dream-dump of movie sets have all been created by a civilization dissatisfied with nature.

People themselves have lost understanding of their humanity. Their clothes, their desires, their actions, even their sexual impulses are perverted and fundamentally opposed to their human nature. One of West's plans had been to write a novel built on a series of "double-takes," with people acting in precisely the opposite way from the expectations aroused by their motivations. This would have been low comedy, in a well-established burlesque convention, but West deepened such devices by subsuming them to his large subject, where actions so radically reversing our expectations concerning human behavior cannot remain comic. "It is hard to laugh," West writes. "But it is easy to sigh. Few things are sadder than the truly monstrous."

In common with many satirists, West draws upon the imagery of animal life and of nature-in-chaos to express the character of life *contra naturam*. Tod paints his dream-makers as grotesque dancers who "spin crazily and leap into the air with twisted backs like hooked trout." Spiders, flies, dog-like men, lizards, horses, birds, hunting—these, gathering around the violent image of the cockfight and the horrible image of the sexually abused black hen, point repeatedly to the debased nature of the human life before us.

In a larger sense, of course, Tod's journeys through a scene (as he thinks) "jumbled together" define a cosmos itself wholly lacking in principles of coherence or intelligibility: "There were bridges which bridged nothing, sculpture in trees, palaces that seemed of marble until a whole stone portico began to flap in the breeze. . . . This was the final dumping ground." Here, as elsewhere in Tod's vision, the cosmos is seen in terms not of its genesis but of its possibilities for an "anarchic power" of decreation.

The effect of *The Day of the Locust* is both satiric and tragic. Like Albany in *King Lear*, West understands that humanity may at last "prey on itself / Like monsters of the deep," but not so much from passion as from perversion, from boredom rather than from desire. The guests wandering vaguely about the hotel lobbies, tired men walking the streets or sitting in Hollywood bars, washed-up vaudeville actors and crumby cowboys waiting hopelessly for jobs, hanging around Central Casting and following rodeos—from all he had seen in the last decade, West came to understand that the modern tragedy was the loss of the soul in lonely, desperate people, Desolate, Helpless, and Sick-of-it-all, the modern Everymen.

With the exception of Tod, West's characters are not really people: perhaps each is only a reflex of the others, who are all shattered bundles of mirrors. William Carlos Williams accurately observed that few characters in the novel are really described in physical terms. Faye "hasn't any face that amounts to anything. . . . How would you like to see a woman coming at you with a face such as Picasso gives them? . . . Nathanael West somehow builds Faye Greener out of such deformity before us." Harry, Earle, Adore, and Homer are all faceless or have but two-dimensional sections of faces.

West builds his characters out of the bits and pieces of their machine age, by understanding them as machines. Audrey Jenning, Claude declares, "makes vice attractive by skillful packaging. Her dive's a triumph of industrial design." Tod in reply follows out the mechanistic implications of the metaphor, and Claude sums them up: "Love is like a vending machine, eh? Not bad. You insert a coin and press home the lever. There's some mechanical activity inside the bowels of the device." The book is clogged with such images of human activity made mechanical. Harry's illness is merely the breakdown of a machine. His laugh begins "with a sharp metallic crackle" and rises, beyond animal noises, "to become a machinelike screech." The description of his speeded-up motions is based, of course, on a film run too rapidly, altering human into mechanical rhythms. Earle, the cowboy, "had a two-dimensional face that a talented child might have drawn with a ruler and a compass." Faye and Homer are both automata. At the end, both Tod's initial fear that he is imitating the siren, and then his desire to do so, suggest the division within him. Personally, he has so very nearly lost a self that West does not attempt to show us the process whereby it may be restored.

West was alive to all the implications of his novel while revising his manuscript for the printer. No wonder, then, that as it was about to be published, he was asking himself how far his own art—*The Day of the Locust*, in particular—might survive and even help to bring some kind of moral order to the chaos of an America just barely escaping native Fascism, but about to plunge into world conflagration. Where was his work leading? Who would read him? What was the nature and usefulness of his art and his prospects for an audience?

In a series of remarkable and very similar letters where he discussed the nature of his art, he hinted at how often these questions weighed upon him at this time, the spring of 1939. He first raised the crucial questions with Scott Fitzgerald, on April 5. "Somehow or other," he began, "I seem to have slipped in between all the 'schools.' My books meet no needs except my own, their circulation is practically private and I'm lucky to be published. And yet I only have a desire to remedy all that *before* sitting down to write, once begun I do it my way. I forget the broad sweep, the big canvas, the shot-gun adjectives, the important people, the significant ideas, the lessons to be taught, the epic Thomas Wolfe, the realistic James Farrell—and go on making what one critic called 'private and un-funny jokes.'" That Fitzgerald seemed to understand his intentions, as he showed by mentioning him in his 1934 preface to *The Great Gatsby*, West said, "made me feel they weren't completely private and maybe not entirely jokes."

On the following day, he continued in the same manner to Edmund Wilson: "The radical press . . . doesn't like [my work], and thinks it even Fascist sometimes, and the literature boys, whom I detest, detest me in turn. The highbrow press finds that I avoid the important things and the lending library touts in the daily press think me shocking . . . because there is nothing to root for in my books, and what is even worse, no rooters." By trying out the accusations against his kind of comic writing in letters to Eastern friends, West, in Hollywood, was clearly attempting to re-awaken his own faith in his art, even though it might not prove popular in his own time. West addressed his letters, indeed, only to those writers who had already shown a just appreciation of the nature of his work. Above all, he was announcing, from the core of social and cultural chaos, the publication of his own "Burning of Los Angeles." He was beginning to assert the power of his art—not to be immediately popular, but to endure.

In a letter written to George Milburn on the same day as his letter to Wilson, he picked up where he had left off and began a defense. His novels do have some rooters, he says. "The only people who seem to like them are other writers." And he goes on to begin a shrewd statement of his own solitary artistic way with the novel. "I do consider myself a comic writer, perhaps in an older and a much different tradition than Benchley or Frank Sullivan. Humor is another thing; I am not a humorous writer I must admit and have no desire to be one." Then he struck at the heart of his concern about an audience: "You know how difficult it is to go on making the effort and sacrifices necessary to produce a novel only to find nowhere any just understanding of what the book is about —I mean in the sense of tradition, place in scheme, method, etc., etc."

Apparently, West brooded over these questions, for on May 11, just before the publication of his book, he had them all in mind. He told Malcolm Cowley:

Lately, I have been feeling even more discouraged than usual. The ancient bugaboo of my kind—"why write novels?"—is always before me. I have no particular message for a troubled world (except possibly "beware") and the old standby of "pity and irony" seems like nothing but personal vanity. Why make the continuous sacrifice necessary to produce novels for a non-existent market? The art compulsion of ten years ago is all but vanished.

. . . write out of hope and for a new and better world— But I'm a comic writer and it seems impossible for me to handle any of the "big things" without seeming to laugh or at least smile. Is it possible to contrive a right-about face with one's writing because of a conviction based on a theory? I doubt it. What I mean is that out here we have a strong progressive movement and I devote a great deal of time to it. Yet although this new novel is about Hollywood, I found it impossible to include any of those activities in it. . . . Take the "mother" in Steinbeck's swell novel—I want to believe in her and yet inside myself

I honestly can't. When not writing a novel—say at a meeting of a committee we have out here to help the migratory worker—I do believe it and try to act on that belief. But at the typewriter by myself I can't. I suppose middle-class upbringing, skeptical schooling, etc. are too powerful a burden for me to throw off—certainly not by an act of will alone.

ALAS!

I hope all this doesn't seem too silly to you—to me it is an ever-present worry and what, in a way, is worse—an enormous temptation to forget the bitter, tedious novels and to spend that time on committees which act on hope and faith without a smile. (It was even a struggle this time for me to leave off the quotation marks.)

Later, on June 30, more and more clear about his position and the demands of his art, he told Jack Conroy:

If I put into "Day of the Locust" any of the sincere, honest people who work here and are making such a great, progressive fight, those chapters couldn't be written satirically and the whole fabric of the peculiar half world which I attempted to create would be badly torn by them. I know that the answer to this would be to say that because the reality of honest, admirable, politically-conscious people would tear the book apart, that therefore the book is no good, but I don't quite believe this. What actually would happen would be the mixing of two styles in such a manner that neither set of characters would be any good.

Another thing: I believe that there is a place for the fellow who yells fire and indicates where some of the smoke is coming from without actually dragging the hose to the spot. Remember that famous and much quoted discussion about the comparative merits of Balzac and Eugene Sue which exists, I think, somewhere in Marx's correspondence. As I understand it, Balzac, Marx thought, was the better writer, even revolutionist, than Sue despite the fact that Sue was an active and confirmed radical while Balzac called himself a royalist. Balzac was the better because he kept his eye firmly fixed on the middle class and wrote with great truth and no wish-fulfillment. The superior truth alone in Balzac was sufficient to reveal the structure of middle class society and its defects and even show how it would ultimately be destroyed.

Like Henry James, who had courted popularity for ten years and then, after the failure of *Guy Domville*, abruptly "took up [his] own old pen again" to write novels that satisfied himself, West had understood the conditions of his unpopularity. If, like James, he was doomed to write one shameless masterpiece after the other, each to be ignored, he had nonetheless made himself clearly conscious of the artistic principles of his popular failures and the prospects for his ultimate success. This awareness had a rejuvenating effect. For even as he was brooding over the aesthetics of his possible failure, while undoubtedly still hoping for a success this next time, he was contemplating a further extension of his vision. "If I take a vacation," he wrote to Laura on April 19, ". . . I believe I will go off by myself to some beach where I can lie on the sand in the sun and have a little hotel room in which to pound at a new idea I have for a novel."

"Keep me in touch. . . . Out here we hear nothing," is a lament constantly repeated in West's letters to Cerf and Commins during this time. Whatever confidence and pride West began to feel solely in the accomplishment of his novel, he had not altogether abandoned hope for some measure of commercial success and he wanted all the favorable news he could get. Heywood Broun had hinted that he liked the book, Milburn's and Coates's reviews were (it seemed) fixed, Caldwell had promised a comment, and Stanley Rose had promised to help promote the book. All were good signs.

Caldwell's puff, which arrived too late for use on the jacket, turned out to be useless anyway, a piece of Dada double-talk. Then, on the day of publication, Milburn sent West a copy of his review. On the whole, it was perceptive and highly favorable. Tod's journey through the dream-dump, he wrote, could be compared only to "Stephen Dedalus's vision of hell," and he spoke of the final riot as "a picture of an American Walpurgis Eve." But he also ventured a criticism which stung West: that the structure "follows the choppy, episodical technique of a movie scenario." On the same day that Milburn's review appeared, *The New Yorker* came out with a brief review—by Clifton Fadiman instead of Coates. This review, West said, "burned me up more than any of the others." Fadiman, who had turned down *Miss Lonelyhearts* at Simon and Schuster, not only replaced Coates, one of West's earliest and best supporters; he wrote a review, West felt, that would definitely discourage sales among an important part of his potential audience. Fadiman began: "Nathanael West, who is about the ablest of our surrealist authors, has written a book about Hollywood that has all the fascination of a nice bit of phosphorescent decay." "He is," West moaned, "an extremely intelligent guy and knows what surrealism is and therefore also knows that I am not a surrealist author." Surrealism was popularly imagined to be equivalent to incomprehensibility and West felt that the epithet had sunk the book. "All I hope for," he now lamented, "is to get into the second edition. It would be such a comfort and would help so much in my attempts to write another one."

He still had, in fact, considerable encouragement. *Newsweek* came out with a good notice. Florence Haxton Britten, who had reviewed West's last two novels favorably, proved consistent and intelligent, and helped to balance Fadiman's swipes by writing in the New York *Herald Tribune* that the novel "is superbly written. Less on the surrealist side than . . . 'Miss Lonelyhearts,' it is a more disciplined piece of writing." The reviewer for *The New York Times Book Review* was also enthusiastic. A little too late to help sales, perhaps, but welcome to West, was Edmund Wilson's almost entirely favorable review in *The New Republic.* Unlike all other writers who had gone to Hollywood, Wilson wrote, West has "remained an artist," who "has caught the emptiness of Hollywood; and he is, as far as I know, the first writer to make this emptiness horrible." (Privately, Wilson told West: "Why don't you get out of that ghastly place? You're an artist and really have no business there.") Jack Conroy wrote a long and informed review of all of West's books, calling him "one of America's most brilliant satirists." Published in *Progressive Weekly*, however, this piece attracted little attention.* Coates, who unfortunately did not review the novel, wrote to West that it was "absolutely your best so far."

The most satisfying comment came from Scott Fitzgerald. The novel, he said, "puts Gorky's 'The Lower Depths' in the class with the 'Tale of Benjamin Bunny,' " and has "scenes of extraordinary power." In a remarkably perceptive leap of the historical imagination, Fitzgerald noted that "the book bears an odd lopsided resem-

* Even among radicals, Conroy's review had little effect. He soon sent West a copy of a letter "from a very serious-minded leftist" who objected to the praise. "In a city where the liberal movement is growing faster than any other place in the U.S., West makes no mention of it," this correspondent complained.

blance to Victor Hugo's 'Notre Dame de Paris.'" This praise came too late to be used in advertising. On the other hand, the review in the *Los Angeles Times*, although "a perfect piece of nonsense," West said, was "the best selling review of all, making the book appear as though it were extremely well written pornography . . . [which] resulted, I was informed, in several dozen calls to the lending libraries by sundry lascivious shutins."

In mid-June, West was persuaded by the Universal publicity department to appear at the Broadway Department Store in Hollywood. West, a press release announced, "drawing on his own experiences, will talk on 'Books and Pictures.'" Nervous and obviously embarrassed, he smoked one cigarette after another as he spoke, specifically on one of the themes of *The Day of the Locust*: the conflict between economic or social realities and the desire to daydream. He had spoken, he wrote his mother, to "sixty ladies," and "the comment was very favorable from all the old ladies present." The fact that he gave the speech at all is an extreme indication of West's desire to evoke or promote some response to his book in Hollywood, where there was scarcely a whisper about it. Did not Cerf write to him that "it is women who read most of the novels that are sold today"?

Besides, he could not resist, as he told a correspondent, the chance "to see and possibly meet (I managed to) the kind of person who gets free culture at a department store." He was checking on the accuracy of his novel (advertised on the program as "Bay of the Locust") and adding a new facet to his vision of the starers. Even after their publication, West seems to have continued to brood over the materials of his novels, still driven by the emotions and compulsions which had brought them into being. This had been strikingly true of *Miss Lonelyhearts*. When West arrived in Hollywood in 1933, just after publication of the book, he not only began to notice the loneliness of the starers there (and so to begin collecting, imaginatively, the materials that would go into *The Day of the Locust*); he also met a young woman who had been educated in a convent and questioned her again and again about what convent life was like, trying to get a sense of the special personal appeal of a religious atmosphere and mystique. His involvement, fictively, with politics in *A Cool Million* was probably more the cause of his later political interests than it was the issue of earlier knowledge. What his imagination touched became the more real and fascinating for him. Now, with *The Day of the Locust* done, he continued his researches into the secret lives of the Hollywood starers. Not inappropriately to this investigation, his talk at the Broadway had an interesting sequel. One of the real Hollywood dream-makers, taking West himself for a consumer rather than a collector of dreams, wrote to him that very day suggesting that for a $25 fee he would write a "thousand or so word reaction to [your talk], which would include the reaction of some of my women friends there in the audience." These notes, he declared, would help West perfect his personal appearance "and manner of addressing an audience." This proposal was itself a beautifully ironical confirmation of West's vision. How could the writer know that he was addressing the maker of dream-makers?

Then the blow came. Each day West retreated in his anticipations. On May 29, he told Cerf that he hoped only that the book would "get above the five thousand copy mark." Two days later, he told Perelman (and himself): "I am hoping and praying and unless I am crazy to even think it, a four thousand copy sale in these very bad days wouldn't be bad at all." But sales were to come nowhere near this. Despite the reviews, Cerf wrote, "the total sale from June 1st through June 13th was exactly 22 copies, bringing the total to 1,486. . . . [The] outlook is pretty hopeless." West suggested, in desperation, that the book might be given a lift if Cerf could convince *Look* or *Life* to do a photographic study of its actual background. Not surprisingly, West again turned to visual art for the essential confirmation of the truth of his fiction. As the cartoon was at the heart of *Miss Lonelyhearts*, photography and the film clip provided the basis of the style and structure of *The Day of the Locust*. "It would be very easy to get photographs of the cultists, the bit players, extras, freaks, houses, etc., of this town. I would be glad to collaborate. . . . [It] would be very interesting—the different sects, hermits, prophets are easily photographed, the strange architecture, the old sets on a back lot, like the paintings by Dali, the extra girls, beautiful, hard-pressed, sleeping four in a tiny room and dreaming of stardom, brokendown vaudevillians and ancient comics in their special barrooms, where they work over old routines, the racial types, playing Eskimos one week and Hawaiians the next, etc., etc."

But the book, as he soon admitted, was "a complete financial bust." Although he suggested to Cerf that he would "go half on the expense of an advertising campaign," his only chance "to give sales any sort of impetus," he finally declared, was to assassinate Hitler. By the end of July, the sales had crept to just over 1,500— the total sales for that month being fewer than twenty copies. By the end of August, after Wilson's favorable review, added to the others, had stimulated stores to stock the book, sales seemed to have gone up to 1,700. But when all the figures were finally computed in February 1940, the total after returns stood at 1,464 and made a loss for Random House and a disappointment to West.

Once again, West had tried to find a way of making a living for himself through fiction. But, at last, in delayed response to Wilson's encouragement that he give up Hollywood, he summed up for him the financial aspects of his career: "I once tried to work seriously at my craft but was absolutely unable to make even the beginning of a living. At the end of three years and two books I had made the total of $780.00 gross. So it wasn't a matter of making a sacrifice, which I was willing enough to make and will still be willing, but just a clear cut impossibility." Only by working for the movies could he buy free time to practice his craft, he explained. "Thank God, for the movies," he said to Cerf in final response to the poor sales. Now, surviving another failure—while his advance brought his profits from four novels and a decade of work to a grand total of $1,280—he committed himself to another term at hard labor in the dream factory.

17 / *Ending in the Thirties*

> . . . I sat in a newsreel theatre on Broadway looking at
> lines of tanks and heavy equipment lumbering heavily,
> busily, cheerfully out of the factories like new automobiles,
> and knew that the depression was over. The depression
> ended only with the war, and the war created a new age of
> unique and boundless technical power that was to make the
> lean and angry Thirties seem the end of the old dog-eat-dog
> society and not the beginning of the new.
>
> Alfred Kazin, *Starting Out in the Thirties* (1965)

West returned to Hollywood and resumed screenwriting in January 1939. All during this year, world events seemed to be making for a confirmation, on the largest scale, of the conclusion to *The Day of the Locust*. Everywhere torches were being lighted, while softer lamps, the lamps of peace, were one by one extinguished. Several years earlier the novelist had declared the apocalypse to be at hand; now, in 1939, historians like Harry Elmer Barnes joined him by predicting that "we shall revert to conditions unmatched for mass misery since the early Middle Ages or the era of the Thirty Years' War. . . ." The year 1939 concluded a decade that John Howard Lawson calls a "period of terrible, increasing desperation . . . . [We] regarded a world holocaust as inevitable, [yet] we were fighting to try to find some way out of it."

But the year held hardly a note of hope for the preservation of civilization. In January, the triumphant release of Tom Mooney* after twenty-two years' imprisonment did not compensate liberals for the fall of Barcelona in that same month. The April ceremonies opening the New York World's Fair, held in the Court of Peace and dedicated to "The World of Tomorrow," were bitterly ironical

---

* A friend of West's, who watched him in conversation with Mooney, says that West "looked upon Mooney as some kind of hero."

in light of international conflict, as the hostilities which had outdistanced and doomed West's play now culminated hysterically in
the spread of Hitler's troops, beginning in March, into Czechoslovakia, Poland, Denmark, Norway, Belgium, Holland, and finally
France. It was no wonder that the most memorable American
movies of 1939 and 1940 were concerned with war and Fascism.
But history easily outdistanced even these: *Gone with the Wind*
(1939) could dramatize the healing of war wounds, but the present showed no such promise. Hitler, satirized by Chaplin in *The
Great Dictator* (1940), was no longer a comic figure. For liberals the
most bitter turn of events, however, lay not in Hitler's readiness to
violate his Munich agreements—this had been repeatedly predicted by anti-Fascists everywhere—but in the way the Soviet
Union, as Alfred Kazin puts it, "lighted the fuse in Hitler's hand"
in August by agreeing to a ten-year non-aggression pact. For West,
as for Kazin, the war began in 1939.

At the news of the signing, the idealized, stainless-steel statue of
a workman did not topple from its place above the massive Soviet
exhibit at the World Fair, but in Hollywood the vast edifice of
liberal organizations began to fly apart. "We don't work much
these last few days," West told Perelman a week after the pact
was concluded, "but are continuously discussing the European
situation." When the news first broke, West put up a sign in his
office reading:

RIEN DE POLITIQUE S'IL VOUS PLAIT!
KEINE POLITIK BITTE!
NIENTE POLITICA PREGO!
NADA DE POLITICO GRACIAS!
NO POLITICS PLEASE!

"But," he said, "I keep breaking the rule myself."

West, indeed, had been breaking his rule of the twenties, against
mixing in politics, all during the period between 1935 and 1939.
Life, it seemed to some people at this time, was only politics, since
some political developments seemed to be threatening the continuance of civilized life itself and others seemed to offer its only
hope for survival. Although important intellectuals living in the
East, such as Wilson, Farrell, and Dos Passos, drifted away from

the influence of the Communist Party around 1935, at this very time, when West returned to Hollywood for a long stay, the Party was making impressive gains among those writers living on the West Coast and working for the movies. Virtually the whole of the New York Workers Revolutionary Theatre had followed John Howard Lawson, their spiritual and ideological father, to Hollywood, including Albert Maltz, John Wexley, Clifford Odets, and George Sklar. In the spring of 1935, Party tacticians had announced a shift in emphasis from opposition to Roosevelt as a "social Fascist," to a policy of cooperation in a "united front" with democratic forces everywhere in a fight against Fascism. Associating itself with progressive Americanism and opposition to Fascism, the Party now encouraged liberals to support consistent left-wing policies while not necessarily becoming Party members. Writers professing anti-Nazi, pro-Spanish Loyalist, pro-labor, and anti-Jim Crow sentiments found support in the Party. "Every anti-Fascist is needed in this united front," Mike Gold cried.

West was sympathetic to most of the causes sponsored by the Party, yet he managed at first to resist deep involvement in its activities. He did go in 1936 to at least one lecture and discussion on elementary Communism, half thinking that he might be able to use some of the elements of his "Miss Lonelyhearts and the Communists" sketch in his new novel. And once he suggested to Jo Conway that she take Lawson's course in writing at the League of American Writers School. He frequently talked politics with other screenwriters after four in the afternoon, when a group would gather in his office at Republic. "There [Jo Conway remembers] would be terrific arguments." But his real interests differed in emphasis from the Party's. His sympathies, basically, were with people rather than programs, and what appeared to some of his associates to be a liberal leaning was really a feeling for human tragedy. For West, in contrast to "the professional Communists," as Boris Ingster remarks, "people . . . were never people with a capital P; people . . . were individuals. . . . He became almost sick confronted by an ugly or cruel incident, and would have a tremendous urge to do something about it." In Hollywood, it was clear, he tended far more than in the East to free his emotional inclinations and to conceal his intellectual cynicism. Hovering all during this period between these two impulses, West remained open to the needs and energies of both. He believed, as Henry James remarked, that "morality is hot, but art is icy," and he wished to be an artist. Yet he felt, too, that heat might be necessary if the world were not to perish in ice. He was not at all contemptuous of leftist ideals, only of those people who regarded a fundamental change as easy to accomplish. As events would prove, he knew that while detachment was necessary for art, it might be harmful to society, and he was absorbed both by art and by society. His intellectual inclinations led him to choose detachment in art, but his emotions led him to yearn for fundamental changes in the society whose dead core his art exposed.

West found it all too easy to laugh at the second-rate minds the Party was attracting. In the movie colony, said the writer Frank Nugent, "affluence breeds ennui," and social concern is "a form of entertainment," an up-to-date parlor amusement, "like the rumba, or a new semi-religious cult, like Yoga." West told Gordon Kahn that he regarded Party members as hopelessly confused. Moreover, they were hypocritical, he believed.

"I well remember West's feelings about the current political activity in Hollywood," S. J. Perelman writes. "The noble piety of the Hollywood folks, as they immersed themselves in the plight of the migratory workers and the like, was pretty comical. One couldn't fault them for their social conscience, but when you saw the English country houses they dwelt in, the hundred-thousand-dollar estancias, and the Cadillacs they drove to the protest meetings, it was to laugh." West laughed skeptically, put off by the accomplished opportunists, annoyed by the rigid dogmatism of Communists, and irritated by what Mary McCarthy called their "lack of humor, their fanaticism, and the slow drip of cant that thickened their utterance, like a nasal catarrh." Furthermore, he was bored by the regular routine of their committee meetings. Serious about political issues, in Hollywood West was wary of the people who were discussing them.

These people tended to be worried by West's apparent cynicism and suspicious of the sincerity of his convictions. In the loose organizational setup of the Party among Hollywood writers and actors, decisions tended to be made by a hard core of devotees. From that core West would always be excluded, although he was invited to join the dues-paying periphery. The serious-minded opinion-makers of the Party were troubled by his wisecracks and his sense of the comic; and they were disturbed both that his writing could not be called "proletarian" or "social realist" and that, unlike Donald Ogden Stewart and others, he offered no apologies for not conforming to Party recipes for literary production. They felt, Michael Blankfort remarks, that "there was a kind of bohemianism about West for which the 'serious' Marxist should show contempt." Some Party sympathizers distrusted and resented what they regarded as his failure "to pull his weight in the proletarian show," and at least once he was publicly attacked for this by Lawson. Leftists regarded him—in part, rightly—as a "laughing anarchist" and did not even invite him to speak at the League of American Writers School; indeed, they feared, Blankfort adds, that if invited he would "mock the organizers" of that enterprise. In short, as Lawson now concludes, in Hollywood "the Left underestimated West. They saw his hatred of bourgeois society, but not his talent." West, then, remained outside the Party, though still serious about many of the causes with which Party members were then concerned.

West had gone to Hollywood before the first Writers Congress in New York. This 1935 gathering, however, spawned two Western congresses in 1936, one of artists, and the other, a much larger one, of writers. Among Hollywood writers, West—still interested in both visual and literary art—was almost unique in appearing in both. The American Artists Congress, founded in New York, organized a chapter in California early in 1936, and began to hold meetings late in the summer of 1936. West had already met the painter Fletcher Martin and happily renewed his friendship with Hilaire Hiler, now in San Francisco. With their encouragement and probably at their suggestion, he addressed one of the early open meetings of the congress, a listener recalls, "on the necessity for the creative artist to speak up and to help muster the awareness of the American people to the approaching threat of Fascism and war."

A much larger congress was the Western Writers Congress, held at the Scottish Rite Auditorium in San Francisco on November 13–15, 1936. In the company of other writers, including Lincoln Steffens, Mabel Dodge Luhan, Kenneth Rexroth, William Saroyan, Irwin Shaw, Upton Sinclair, Tess Slesinger, and John

Steinbeck, West signed the call of the congress to "the writers of the West, where the liberty-loving tradition of the pioneer is still fresh." In anticipation of the congress, Carey McWilliams wrote in *Pacific Weekly*: "In retrospect, it will probably be recognized that no more important occurrences broke the darkening circle of post-war reaction than the various national and international congresses of writers, artists, and intellectuals called to protest against the social and cultural decay implicit in Fascism."

The circle around *Pacific Weekly*, founded and edited by Lincoln Steffens, organized the congress. Before its opening, West had become acquainted with Steffens and his wife, Ella Winter. In 1936, the *Weekly* announced twice that in it West was to review books, *Travels in Two Democracies* and Louis Aragon's *The Bells of Basel*. Although he did not review either, far more important, he printed a section of an early version of *The Day of the Locust* in the issue of November 16, 1936. Moreover, his name appeared in Ella Winter's gossip column more than once.* And, finally, he gave a paper in the congress on Sunday afternoon, November 15, on "Makers of Mass Neuroses." West commented on the way in which Hollywood movies mislead and corrupt their public, and took part in a Hollywood round-table series that also included comments by Guy Endore on "Hollywood and Fascism" and by Budd Schulberg on "Motion Pictures and the Left Critics."

West was necessarily drawn too into the agitation over the Screen Writers Guild, which he joined in 1933. His sister Laura and many of West's friends were active members of the guild, several even serving on its executive board, including Laura, Wells Root, Lester Cole, Sy Bartlett, Dashiell Hammett, Lillian Hellman, and Dorothy Parker. The guild became so strong that in April 1936, when its president, John Howard Lawson, branded movie executives responsible for film smut and asked the House Patents Committee for legislation strengthening authors' rights in deciding how their material was to be used, film producers immediately repudiated the guild contract and created a paternalistic organization controlled by Louis B. Mayer and Jack Warner, called

* *Pacific Weekly*, Sept. 7, 1936: "A number of film people are buying farms in Bucks, among them Dorothy Parker, Sid Perelman, and maybe Nathanael West and [Edwin Justus] Mayer. At least the last two were playing with the idea while lunching at Pop Ernst's overlooking the Monterey Bay."—Ella Winter, in the column "They Tell Me."

the Screen Playwrights. Mayer and Warner blacklisted all guild leaders and warned others to resign from the guild or be fired. The writer, both studios and the new guild declared, was an independent creator who could never ally himself with "a man who joins a union."

Crushed by this repudiation, the guild was revived only a year later. When the National Labor Relations Act was declared constitutional, the guild officers demanded a NLRB consent election to determine the legitimate bargaining agent for writers. After hearings which filled more than a thousand pages, the NLRB declared that the producers had conspired to carry out "a plan of interference" with the attempts of the guild to organize writers. Finally, an NLRB election was held on August 8, 1938, with 267 votes cast for the guild and 57 for its rival, certifying the guild the collective bargaining agent for the writers employed in eighteen contested studios.

West himself transferred to active guild membership in April 1936. The fight for recognition of the guild was bitter, and West, urged into it by his friends, worked hard for the organization. But even over this issue, as the labor lawyer Charles Katz observes, West "was not consumed by trade-union problems . . . in the same measure as many of his contemporaries in Hollywood were." He always remained interested in the guild's goals—and intensely committed to the dignity and freedom of the writer—but he was bored by its rhetoric and gesticulations, and one friend who watched him closely saw him slipping out of meetings more and more frequently, to remain in Musso and Frank's bar across the street until he expected a crucial vote to be taken.

Having learned in the guild to organize for political and economic action, writers were soon uniting in numerous other groups to oppose international or local Fascism. All Hollywood was sensitive to international politics, since so much movie revenue came from abroad. Writers, moreover, were fighting against what they considered to be Fascism in the attitudes of movie executives and the Dies Committee investigations, and they saw rising in their midst proto-Fascist organizations like Guy Empey's Hollywood Hussars (founded in 1935, with Gary Cooper as a member), Victor McLaglen's Light Horse Cavalry, and a branch of Pelley's Silver Shirts. Anti-Fascism became for many Hollywood citizens the

Good Cause, imparting, as Eugene Lyons wrote, "an intoxicated state of mind, a glow of inner virtue, and a sort of comradeship in super-charity."

The typical Hollywood intellectual in the thirties passed through several stages. Beginning as the author of novels or plays which did not sell, he came to Hollywood to make money whereby to support his writing. He soon found that he was making money, with prospects of making a good deal more, began to give money to progressive causes, and took pride in his ability to further his social ideals. Subtly his goals changed: the money which he gave to causes replaced the novel which made no money as his ideal of authorship. Finally, movie-writing came to replace creative writing altogether. This was a story repeated in the careers of Samuel Ornitz, Dashiell Hammett, John Howard Lawson, Albert Maltz, Dorothy Parker, and many others.

West never made this mistake, as his preoccupation with *Good Hunting* and his novel prove. Yet his intense involvement with the inner life of the masses, the very engagement out of which his novels came, drew him irresistibly into what he called the "great progressive fight" and its organizations. West took part in activities of social reform not from self-recrimination over being a Hollywood writer, but because he was genuinely compelled by suffering. Though these activities drained time from his work on the novel, ultimately they fed the energy for his fiction. He was able to keep his life simple and whole by turning his yearnings and enthusiasms into subterranean materials for his writing.

West was preoccupied with the fate of the Spanish Republic, whose existence was threatened by the revolt of the army beginning in July 1936. He spoke many times about joining the fight with the Abraham Lincoln Brigade, and of writing a novel about Spain, as Hemingway was apparently intending to do. This was, of course, romance, like the story he told Jo Conway that earlier he had gone to Spain with the money he made from *Miss Lonelyhearts*. But it was even more a cry of distress over the brutal warfare there. In 1937 and 1938 he even overcame his reserve and shyness to collect money personally at Republic Studios. Every month he went from writer to writer there, insisting that the war was "a horrible, brutal thing," soliciting donations for starving and orphaned Spanish children, or working for the Spanish Refugee

Relief Campaign, even though, as a producer at Republic noted, "it was hell for him to go around with his hat in his hand." He collected funds, too, for ambulances and medical aid to Spain, one day coming with Perelman into a radio studio on Hollywood and Vine where Allan Seager and George Milburn were grinding out a radio show. In 1939, he was one of the sponsors for the Hollywood fund-raising exhibition of Picasso's *Guernica*. In the Motion Picture Artists Committee, originally organized for Spanish and Chinese war relief and headed by Dashiell Hammett, West served on the executive board, along with Dudley Nichols, Dorothy Parker, and Donald Ogden Stewart.

There were other causes, there were always causes in Hollywood, and West was more casually involved in many of them. Perhaps under the influence of Lincoln Steffens, who was involved in the strikes of migratory workers in 1936, he attended at least one committee meeting concerned with the plight of migrants, treated brutally in Salinas and the Imperial Valley. With Charles Katz, he went to San Francisco to meet Harry Bridges during the second general dock strike, and to San Pedro to attend a "fish bowl" meeting of the longshoremen. Fascinated by Bridges, West helped his subordinates in Hollywood in their sporadic attempts to organize back-lot workers into the CIO during 1937–8. West, to their surprise, seemed to know a good many back-lot workers and to understand their problems.

As he revealed to Malcolm Cowley, he had attempted to "describe a meeting of the Anti-Nazi League" in *The Day of the Locust*, "but it didn't fit." Founded in June 1936, at a meeting in Donald Ogden Stewart's house, to help bring fellow writers out of Germany and make Americans aware of the menace of Hitlerism, the Hollywood Anti-Nazi League became the most influential and powerful anti-Fascist group in the nation, with a membership of 4,000. West not only belonged to the league but seems to have helped prepare material for its broadcasts on station KFWB and for its newspaper, *Hollywood Now*. Predictably, other organizations called upon him for support. In February, at Ella Winter's request, he joined the Hollywood Committee of the League of American Writers. On May 22, he was appointed studio chairman at Universal for the Screen Writers Guild, as well as secretary of its membership committee. In late September, he was elected to the executive board of the Motion Picture Guild, organized for "the production of liberal and progressive films." Perhaps somewhat to the left of most Hollywood organizations, this listed on its executive board Tess Slesinger, John Wexley, Sidney Buchman, Boris Ingster, Lillian Hellman, Ring Lardner, Jr., Lawson, Samuel Ornitz, Dudley Nichols, Budd Schulberg, and Frank Tuttle, names which appear on one executive board after another. Finally, in November 1939, he was elected to the executive board of the Screen Writers Guild. He joined the Motion Picture Democratic Committee, and even bought stock in the Advance Music Corporation to promote the song, "Mr. Roosevelt, Won't You Please Run Again?" written by Jay Gorney, author of "Brother, Can You Spare a Dime?"

Thus, West had a good chance to observe from the inside the astonishing changes most of these organizations went through immediately upon the announcement of the non-aggression pact. He characterized the bewildering jumps in position in telling S. J. Perelman: ". . . what [Hollywood liberals] really are or think, I certainly don't know. The Hitler-Stalin combination took the sting out of a lot of things out here, and things change so fast that neither the chameleon nor the kaleidoscope could possibly keep up." "Russia's defection from 'peace indivisible,' 'peace front,' 'collective security,' 'Communism and Fascism are mortal enemies, and everyone who says different is a dirty Trotskyite' "—the betrayal of these slogans, West said, "hit here with a cold, icy blast that shook the foundations."

American members of the Party, formerly committed to opposing Hitler, made a rapid shift to a position of neutrality. Party faithfuls at first denounced reports of the pact as lies of the capitalist press, then declared that the pact had been expedient but contained an escape clause. Israel Amter, head of the Communist New York State district committee, assured reporters that if Hitler dared to march, the Soviet would come to Poland's defense. On the first of September, Germany and Russia jointly marched into Poland. The Popular Front was through, capitalist democracy was the enemy of the working class once more, and West—"to my great surprise," he told Perelman—was informed, at a meeting of the Motion Picture Artists Committee, "that Roosevelt was a warmonger." As Hollywood leader of the "writers' faction" in the

Party, Lawson was soon patiently explaining to the wondering faithful that the "pact was a necessity because there was nothing else [for the U.S.S.R.] to do but face destruction." This "imperialist conflict," as he now put it, had, after all, been "brought on because the Allies had failed to stop Hitler."

But these rationalizations failed to convince, and one by one, social-action Hollywood groups exploded or ground to a halt. The Hollywood Anti-Nazi League, with anti-Fascists at once polarized against Communists, split with a spectacular, momentous crack. West, like other members of the league, was perplexed. The problem "as to why against Fascism and why not against Communism," he told Perelman, "often disturbs my sleep." At a climactic meeting which West attended, when resolutions demanding the immediate denunciation of the U.S.S.R. were offered from the floor, the leaders reacted promptly by refusing to allow a vote. Overnight, they turned their organization into the Hollywood League for Democratic Action. Now no longer in favor of "concerted action" against Hitler, they turned to advocating neutrality and denouncing (as their New Year's card for 1940 put it) "the war to lead America to War." But the league's power was ended.

Less spectacularly, but with similar results, the same battle was fought out in other organizations. The truth was, it soon became clear, that liberal organizations in Hollywood, including the flirtation with the Communist Party, had provided fantasy escape, for the majority of their members, from the irksome economics of Hollywood life. Attending the evening lectures at the vegetarian Hollywood Health Cafeteria, taking classes at the League of American Writers School, discussing endlessly in the writers' or actors' "factions"—these were ways of giving screenwork the appearance of having some extra-economic meaning. Rootless and insecure young writers longing for credits and dreaming of power, New York playwrights thinking of Hollywood as (so one put it) "a warm Siberia," established writers vaguely or openly contemptuous of their work and themselves—these all found some special status in liberal activities. They regarded themselves as "cultural technicians" or, as Roy Erwin, a radio writer, put it, as the "commissioned officers" of the revolution. They had found a faith, which, if they could hardly express it on film, they could propagate in life. For the most part, in the early thirties liberals everywhere had felt the appeal of the Party, since it alone had seemed to offer sane programs for reform. But in Hollywood in the late thirties the Party was vaguely regarded as the most interesting of the economic and religious cults flourishing there. Sheridan Gibney, president of the Screen Writers Guild, was asked if he "wanted to be instructed, as you would if you were becoming a Catholic." And Scott Fitzgerald quipped that "Dotty [Parker] had embraced the church and reads her office faithfully every day." His conclusion that, nonetheless, it did not "affect her indifference" was confirmed by Miss Parker herself when she declared that the only "ism" in which Hollywood really believed was plagiarism. She was right. Very soon after the Stalin-Hitler pact, the Party dwindled to a hard core of about two hundred members and its front organizations crumbled.

West, who had taken the life of wishing as his theme and who had devoted at least a decade of study to its evidences, at once saw through to the fantasy thinking and opportunism of most Hollywood liberals. He approved the causes and despised most of the workers. In his early attempt to describe a meeting of the Anti-Nazi League in *The Day of the Locust,* the imagination of the novelist had exposed the pretenses long before the pact did. He had recognized the tragedy of deception from the beginning. Whereas the Marxists emphasized the revolution, John Bright says, "West emphasized its betrayal."

II

After 1936, West's life was sharply divided among his daily stint in studio factories, his private nightly labor on his novel, and his public commitments to organized politics. Hunting, then, became virtually his only means of disengaging himself from the world which suddenly and ominously pressed so hard around him. West's week at the studio was largely absorbed, Jo Conway recalls, by talk of the hunt. All day Friday and Saturday morning would be devoted to preparations for it. On Saturday afternoon the hunters— West, Wells Root, the McGowans, and others—would pile into Root's truck, especially fitted with cots and ice and game compartments, and a chauffeur would drive them two or three hundred miles while they slept, ready to get up on Sunday at 3 a.m. to set out decoys and spend a full day shooting. Monday and Tuesday were occupied by discussions of the weekend, while Wednesday and Thursday alone would (for the most part) be concentrated on scriptwriting.

Hunting, like West's continuing preoccupation with his novel, saved him from Hollywood by returning him to himself. Boris Ingster "used to watch Pep hunt, and it was the romance of the preparation, and the wonderful talks about hunting exploits while you sat in a blind waiting" that really interested West, "and, particularly since I was a Russian, the talk always went to Turgenev. He was living a kind of romantic dream in his hunting." West spoke so vividly to Albert Hackett about "wild doves, ducks, and geese, and of wild swans flying overhead in the early mist," that Hackett, who did not hunt at all, accompanied him on a long, uncomfortable trip. West needed the practical excuse of hunting, perhaps, to allow himself to surrender to his romantic impulses and his love of nature. In *The Day of the Locust,* Tod's one moment of soothing peace comes when he finds himself alone in nature. "He fell prone with his face in a clump of wild mustard that smelled of the rain and sun, clean, fresh and sharp. . . . He felt comfortably relaxed, even happy."

How far hunting satisfied a certain romantic yearning in West— similar to the yearning for escape to the South Seas satirized in *Miss Lonelyhearts*—is suggested even by the kinds of books he purchased and read in Hollywood. A large number were expensively bound and well-printed books about outdoor life, costing upwards of $10: for example, John Gay's *"Rural Sports," together with "The Birth of the Squire" and "The Hound and the Huntsman,"* Foxhall Keene's *Shooting Memories,* and Charles E. Cox's *John Tobias: Sportsman.* Such books combined in West's imagination with Turgenev's *Sportsman's Sketches,* one of the books he most admired, and prompted him to begin speaking of another book which he might do after his Hollywood novel—an American version of the *Sketches,* to be printed privately for the delight of his hunting friends.

One of these friends was William Faulkner. They had become acquainted in New York in the early thirties and met again in 1936 at Stanley Rose's bookstore. Faulkner had read and admired *Miss Lonelyhearts*—and, to West's pleasure, now told him so—while as early as 1933 West had spoken to James T. Farrell of his respect for Faulkner. Together they went hunting on Santa Cruz Island, where after many generations the original Spanish pigs had developed into a fierce strain of wild boar. Crouching in the boars' nests in the brush until the animals returned, then springing up to shoot only at the last moment, West and Faulkner bagged several 200- and 300-pound boars on one such trip. Later, they shot ducks and doves in the Tulare Marshes. "One of the things about Faulkner that impressed [West] very much," George Milburn says, was that "during the entire trip, Faulkner never addressed him in any other way but as 'Mr. West,' which puzzled him." Faulkner's ceremoniousness was merely a part of his hunting etiquette. He and West were close friends while Faulkner was in Hollywood, and West once brought him to a party at Arthur Kober's. Both writers preserved an ultimate social reserve in Hollywood, looking toward a time when novel sales might support them, and it was probably this which makes Budd Schulberg conclude that there were deep similarities between them. It is clear, certainly, that in some details West's Earle Shoop (in *The Day of the Locust*) is a cousin to Popeye in Faulkner's *Sanctuary*; other resemblances between these two novels are obvious. Still, there were crucial differences between the two men. Faulkner could fall back for mental and emotional support upon the habits and traditional structure of belief and action in his South. There is a famous story that Faulkner's producer agreed to let him work "at home," only to find, when he called him for a story conference, that Faulkner had returned to Oxford, Mississippi. Faulkner could go home again, for Hollywood was never his home. West, a wanderer, had no Oxford; Hollywood was as much home as he could claim. His only traditions were those he could make. And whatever reserves of separateness from Hollywood he maintained at last resided in himself alone.

With Faulkner and others, West followed the game and the seasons. During August and September he began with dove shooting around Brawley in the Imperial Valley; or, near Yuma, whitewing dove. Following this came duck hunting in the San Joaquin Valley of south-central California. After the American season ended in December, West and his friends went further south, to Baja. The Mexican season lasted until the middle of February, and here they hunted quail, geese, and ducks at the enormous Los Ojos

Negros ranch situated between Ensenada and Mexicali. Occasionally, they went to a ranch east of Mexicali, sent there by Jimmy
Alvarez, owner of a bar and restaurant called the Leon d'Oro. During this time, of course, few Americans at all ventured into Baja
below Tijuana and Agua Caliente. West, however, seemed to be
able to establish the same kind of immediate contact with the local
folk that he had in Bucks County.* To the remote Ojos Negros
ranch, West brought a bag of gifts for the children and make-up
for the girls each time he came and he was adored by the peons
around the ranch.

By 1939, disillusioned over world politics and disheartened over
the reception of his novels, West turned more and more compulsively to hunting as an escape from the irritations of public and
private life. Throughout the spring and summer and into the fall of
that year, he conducted an interminable and delightful correspondence with a member of the Connecticut legislature who
carved decoys as a hobby. With gifts of books and Audubon prints,
West cajoled from him models of old squaws, Canadian geese, and
other wild fowl. The birds he liked best for appearance, he wrote,
were "Cinnamon Teal, Pintail Sprig, Old Squaw, Golden Eye,
Drake Spoonie, Greenhead, etc., etc. I guess I like them all." West
soon developed a passion for collecting these handmade, ornamental decoys and by the end of the year had ordered from the legisla-
tor pairs of sprig, canvasback, green-winged teal, mallards, spoon-
bills, blue-winged teal, and speckled breasted and lesser snow
geese. This correspondence gave him a wholly non-Hollywood outlet for hunting discussions, reminiscent of his conversations with
the Erwinna farmers. During the summer he wrote about fishing
"in the High Sierras at a place called Red Meadows," where he saw
"literally thousands of Teal"—an auspicious sign for fall shooting;
about large-mouth bass in the Los Angeles and San Diego county
reservoirs (". . . rather dull even on the lightest tackle. There is
something about Southern California that makes even a five-pound

* This was also true with the ranch hands in northern California. Once he
met a cowboy in a bar and through him passed from one person to another
until a 10,000-acre ranch was opened to him. "And," Leonard Fields comments, "it wasn't in a mercenary manner that Nate met these people, because
they would sense that . . . he didn't want to meet people to use them *at all*.
He never used anybody. He met them because he liked them. And in liking
him, they automatically offered him things."

bass rather anxious to get into the boat and have it over with");
and about dove shooting in Arizona, the first hunting of the season
("We begin out here in August, or rather in Arizona, where we
shoot White Wing, a species of large doves. It is pass shooting and
extremely good sport. The birds travel about as fast as a Teal duck
and are even trickier, doing barrel rolls and ground loops. We
shoot them in the desert and this is the drawback, at a place called
Gila Bend where the temperature gets to be about 120 and your
shotgun barrels are red hot before you fire a shot"). At the end of
August he was gleefully and ironically reporting—this time to
Laura—that mixed in with life's "petty failures" is "an occasional
success, like last week when I ran eight straight shooting White
Wing." West's interest in hunting burned so intensely for a while
that one of his closest friends, Lester Cole, was led to conclude that
"he didn't really want to be a writer, he wanted to hunt and fish."

On opening day of the 1939 duck season, early in October, West
received some new decoys from the East and he and Wells Root
traveled 300 miles to shoot at the Standard Gun Club in Los
Banos, California. Root recalls: "N. wasn't feeling very well, but
he never even considered not coming along. We had to walk about
a mile to the blinds, through deep mud and water, carrying probably fifty pounds apiece in guns, shells, decoys, etc. When the shooting began, I noticed that he was not joining in with much enthusiasm. About nine o'clock he climbed out of the blind and lay down
in the brush. He swore it was only a temporary discomfort, stomach upset or something. All day, he absolutely refused to let it interfere with the shooting of the rest of the party. Late that night,
when he got back to Los Angeles, he collapsed. . . . [Until then]
he had endured it, with a stoicism so cheerful that no one suspected that he had anything worse than a bad hangover."

A few days later West's doctor diagnosed his trouble as urethritis
and began to treat him with sulphur drugs. After nearly a week,
when these had no effect, West, suffering a good deal, was admitted to the Cedars of Lebanon Hospital in Los Angeles. There
his condition worsened and he developed complications, a rash and
fever. It was not until two weeks later that he was able to return
home. Even then, he was confined to bed for several days, and he
was cured at last only by a series of five extremely painful treatments inside the urethra, during which he passed out several times.

His obsession with hunting grew so consuming that even his movie work became an aspect of it. One of the few projected films he ever expressed deep interest in was a life of Audubon, for which he did (Wells Root recalls) "a lot of preparatory reading—but no writing." He took great interest in the likelihood that *Flight South*, the original script he and Root and Gordon Kahn had written in 1938, would at last go into production at M.G.M. in the fall of 1939. Despite delays, West was still hoping, at the time he was hospitalized, to "see Clark Gable in the Bureau's uniform shooting them thar market hunters for all he is worth." But neither this jolly scene nor any other part of the story was ever to be shot.

Inevitably, West's hunting became a reservoir for fantasy. One of his most elaborate fantasies, which he declared was fact, was spun out for Boris Ingster, when Ingster accidentally discharged his gun in a blind on the Russian River. Wells Root, West began, had done precisely the same thing. "It seems," as West told the tale, "that [Root] discharged the gun into his hand and they went looking for a doctor. But, it turned out, all the doctors were out hunting too. Finally a farmer advised them to go to a certain veterinarian, who, it appeared, had come from Austria and settled in this area where there were lots of Danes. The veterinarian looked at the wound but declared that he was, after all, forbidden by law to treat a human surgically, although he could give him ordinary first aid. Both Root and West pleaded with him—for the hand was full of shot and powdered batting, and they were dramatically aware of the possibilities of infection and the damage to the nerves, there was such a network of ligaments. Besides, the pain was unbearable and Root was apprehensive that he would lose the hand. Well, at last they persuaded the vet to operate. They talked a little, but he was not giving much. . . . After they got back to Los Angeles, Root went to see his doctor, an eminent German surgeon, and he looked at it and said: 'My, this is a remarkable job— in fact, it was done either by Professor J. or by one of his students —it shows a very special technique.' Well, the next season, they went back and after hunting saw the vet. At last he told them his story, that he had indeed been the right-hand man of this famous surgeon. Forced by the war to flee from Austria, he had come here, only to find that since he knew no English it was difficult for him to be licensed for medical practice. But he found that he could get a vet's license in three months, he had done so, had liked the people, and had settled here." The story had overtones of intrigue and imposture. It was, Ingster says, a "beautifully arranged, romanticized episode" based on the clichés of film and popular fantasy current in 1939–40—the strange encounter, the distinguished disguised person, the exile, the refugee. And it was all inspired merely by an incident in which Root tore his hand on the release lever of his misfiring shotgun and later had it patched up by a doctor who had an accent.

III

Most of West's films during 1939–40 were similarly inspired by his responsiveness to the mass, collective dreams of the age. The first of these films, and in this regard the least interesting, was the remake of an earlier success, *Tom Brown of Culver*, which Burt Kelly was putting into production at Universal when he received West's telegram asking for a job immediately after the debacle of *Good Hunting*. Universal, where West would work for the next ten months, specialized in remakes. Reorganized in 1938 by Nathan J. Blumberg, whose background was in movie selling, distribution, and theater operation,* Universal gave up any hope for art, favorable reviews, or awards, and staked everything on box-office results. The new executives, one historian says, "cut costs mercilessly and fired temperamental talents which could not submit to shooting schedules. They substituted short-term deals for long-term contracts. . . . They scoured the Universal stock of unused scripts, and filmed stories which had been collecting dust in the files. . . . They invented titles which sounded popular and ordered stories written around them. . . . They reissued old successes . . . to raise quick money." Once more, in 1939, box offices were booming—movies accounting for an average, that year, of $25 per family—and the product at Universal catered to this increasing mass audience. After working briefly for one major studio, R.K.O., West was forced again to grind out fantasy for this slightly more grand Republic. For $350 a week, he began work on *The Spirit of Culver* on December 19, 1938, immediately upon returning to Hollywood.

* Only one of the seven voting trustees of Universal Corporation had earlier been associated with film production.

The story of *The Spirit of Culver*, as one reviewer, with supreme understatement, remarked, "develops along routine lines." West, however, gave the picture some initial interest by beginning it not in the shining precincts of the Culver Military Academy, but with shabby scenes of the Depression, against which the virtues of the school would be displayed. It was 1939, engines of war were rolling, like new cars, along assembly lines, and the Depression was already becoming a usable part of history. The thirties seemed like a dream; a film like *The President's Mystery*, decades old. When West's screenplay evokes the Depression, it is the image of a past that is soon to be transcended:

1. MONTAGE establishing depression period. Newspaper inserts of 1932 dates pointing up these conditions will be interspersed with the following shots:
   1. Sign over Bank Entrance:
      CLOSED BY ORDER OF STATE BANK EXAMINER
   2. A workman staring at a bold sign over a locked factory gate:
      NO HIRING
   3. An eviction group huddled under an umbrella in a slanting rain. The father stands out in the rain. Trying to herd his small store of furniture together.
   4. Two bums sitting on a park bench.
   5. An unemployed Parade.
   6. Group of dejected men standing in line at an employment window.
2. EXT. SIDEWALK—MED. SHOT
   We are SHOOTING from the curb into a long line of feet and legs. The shoes are old, cracked, worn. Trouser legs, seen from the knees down, are unpressed, patched, ragged at the cuffs. The legs and feet move with a slow, dragging trudge. . . . Their faces as we DOLLY SLOWLY UP toward head of the line reflect depressed moods, sullenness, abjectness.

For the hero, Tom Brown, however, Culver Academy, the military revitalization of heroic ideals, can bring success. The Depression fades out as rapidly as it faded in, and the story follows "routine lines"; as a reviewer for *Daily Variety* described the plot: "Homeless Jackie Cooper is awarded American Legion Post Scholarship to Culver. Rough, tough, and rebellious at the discipline imposed, he is gradually transformed. Roommate Freddie Bartholomew does much to smooth the way and pair becomes pals. Cooper's father, Henry Hull, reported killed in action during the war and recipient of the Congressional Medal, suddenly turns up in shellshocked condition. Treated at the Veterans' Hospital under an assumed name, he meets his son. Later Jackie discovers his identity, and after pair start for the West, the boy is persuaded to return and finish school while Hull takes a new grip on life."

Contented to plug along quietly at Universal after his despair over the failure of his play, West had as his office a bungalow near the cowboy Western sets. Reading over the proofs for *The Day of the Locust*, he could, like Tod Hackett, walk straight from his office into this fantasy of sets; he could go from the tough actuality of his novel to the fantasies of the *Culver* script, then out to the lot and the sets where those fantasies were made to seem real. It was an absurd circumstance. Still, Universal was "a friendly lot," he and Burt Kelly swapped stories, and he got considerable amusement from eliciting ludicrous remarks about Culver Academy from its commander, at the studio as a technical adviser.

Much to West's gleeful and ironical astonishment, taste was so low among the studio executives that they were delighted with the film. The president sent out a memo declaring that the title did not "immediately indicate the distinction and significance of the picture," and encouraged his writers to "find a short phrase taken either from a patriotic subject, a poem or novel. . . . What I have in mind is something like 'Let Freedom Ring,' 'All the Brothers Were Valiant,' 'Give Me Liberty or Give Me Death.' " Although (as West called them privately) the "dopes in the front office" took to considering the film "the finest picture the still newer Universal ever made," no one was able to think of a more ringing title. After viewing the rough cut, West himself judged that the film was "an over-sweet, over-foolish sob story with here and there a fairly decent moment." For him its success meant only that he would be put on another movie at once.

On January 11, 1939, he was assigned to do a script based on an "original" screen story by Lester Cole. Eventually released under the title *I Stole a Million*, this film gave West his first important solo screen credit. Starring George Raft and Claire Trevor, and directed by Frank Tuttle, who had credits on several successful films, this was the closest to an A-level film that West had yet come.

The major problem with the original material had to do with the moral conventions imposed on films by the Motion Picture Producers and Distributors of America. West had somehow to create sympathy for the hero, a thief, keep alive the excitement of the chase, and yet have the hero brought to justice at the conclusion; moreover, he had to supply suspense to a formula and conclusion familiar to every moviegoer, what one reviewer described as the "familiar double-cross."

West solved the moral problem within the approved limitations. Increasingly skillful at the techniques of turning stories into films, he planned and dictated his screen treatment in a single afternoon and, after executive approval, went directly into a script. A few days later, Joseph I. Breen, the director of the MPPA, declared that his office had handled, during the year, "3,600 stories, scripts, plays, books, novels, etc.," and "it is our unanimous judgment, here in this office, that this new treatment by Mr. West is, by far, the best piece of craftsmanship in screen adaption that we have seen—certainly, in a year." This was another entry for West's scrapbook of ironies, and he joked about it to Perelman. But he was also determined to accumulate some money and out of such letters, West knew, came raises in salary. (He made, accordingly, several copies of the letter, to be passed around.)

His easy beginning on this film did not continue unchecked. For a week or so, it appeared that there might be a legitimate plagiarism suit against the "original" material, and the studio considered shelving the property. Then another writer, Edward Ludwig, was brought in to rewrite West's first-draft script. But in April, when George Raft replaced the actor scheduled for the lead, the studio returned to West's original script and he was allowed to go on to the final draft, which he completed in about three weeks, finishing in haste only the night before shooting was scheduled to begin. All West hoped for the film was that "it may turn out to be a good solo screenplay credit and mean something so far as salary is concerned."

He would get no raise, although this film was reviewed more favorably than any other on which he worked. "Screen play by Nathanael West," one reviewer concluded, "is a concise and conclusive story. . . . Plotting is legitimate and emotions are genuinely built up with suspense and valid character development." *Variety* chimed in: "Script is strongly motivated." "It is a story," the critic for the *Hollywood Reporter* declared, "which will exert pulse-quickening effect on audiences of both sexes. . . . Plot structure and pithy dialogue are all to the play's advantage." Mark Hellinger boosted it in his column. Advertised as a "Thrilling Sensational Gangster Thriller!" the film was a decisive box-office success.

By this time, West was on another assignment. Dick Wallace had recently come to Universal to produce and direct; with a high salary and a good deal of prestige, he was given a free hand at the studio. As soon as West was closed out on *I Stole a Million,* Wallace requested him for work on a studio-owned original by Rufus King called *The Victoria Docks at Eight.* At first West was delighted with the easy way that Wallace went at his work. "He had West on the movie for four months," Burt Kelly says, "with no intention of making it. They would rewrite every day. And the bosses weren't saying to Wallace: 'Get a new writer.' As long as he could get along with Dick, he was in for a long row. Wallace and he would sit around the office and joke about it. Finally, Wallace got called in to the front office. They suggested he get a fresh point of view— Jerry Sackheim said he should have a new writer—and Wallace quipped, 'Who are you going to get, Shakespeare?' "

West stayed on. By the end of July 1939, he produced a sixteen-page treatment in which no part of King's original material remained. By now West was perplexed by Wallace's antics and tried to describe the mad conditions of work to Perelman: "He is a sweet fellow but ever since he fell out of that airplane, I think he's been a little mixed up in the head. He wants the hero to be in love with snakes. I don't know whether he's kidding me or serious. . . . I am having a tough enough time with it because it is a mystery melodrama and that clue stuff gets me down." Like Fitzsimmons's absurd tactics in *Good Hunting,* however, this treatment was taken seriously by the front office. Suddenly, plans were underway to cast it, West wrote his mother, with "Margaret Sullavan, Fredric March, and Adolphe Menjou. If it is, it may mean a great deal in both money and prestige." West rewrote the story almost entirely during the next six weeks and concluded that he had done "a pretty good job," even though he had had to resort to pilfering (he told Perelman) "a few jokes from our script 'Even Stephen,' which I take to be a completely dead noodle so far as both of us are concerned. . . . I promise you that the contribution is under twenty-five per cent, so you won't have to take screen credit." A melodrama-romance, the absurd 138-page script that West turned out before the property was abandoned early in October is best summarized, perhaps, by the clichés of the Universal Story Department: "Love awakens a man who is a failure, and makes a real man out of him."

West's long stint at Universal was ended only by urethritis and his admission into the hospital. All in all, he had put in thirty-six weeks of work and earned $12,600, nearly ten times his earnings from a decade of fiction writing. By the fall of 1939, fully accepting the commercial failure of *The Day of the Locust*, West promised himself that he would work steadily on movies for two years. "Money for Pep," one of his friends during this period says, "was a means to an end. He wanted to have what he called enough 'eating money' in two years to take off a year to do a book." He was convinced that the long span of time over which he had written his last novel had blurred parts of it and was now hoping to alternate long stretches of film work with equally extended periods of far more intense work on fiction. He had accepted servitude in the country of the blind in order to free himself—so he now saw his future—for occasional excursions into the country of the blue. To be sure, there were moments of discouragement. Another of West's dark times came late in October, after his month's illness. Reflecting on the scorn for the serious writer which seemed to be increasing in Hollywood, he advised Perelman: "But whatever happens, don't write an 'A Cool Million,' not even a 'Day of the Locust' because that is really wasting your time. Don't write any books, just pieces for the New Yorker. From that you can probably guess that I am quite depressed today." Yet despite his appearance of bitterness, at this very time, West himself, ever divided, was beginning to plan another novel.

Meanwhile, in an attempt to save enough money by the late spring to take time off to write this book, he was working, in the approved Hollywood fashion, on an original that he hoped to parlay into a screenplay job at a major studio. "I have been keeping myself busy," he told Perelman, "trying to write an original story, a real guzma about aviators, lost cities, jungles, and such guzmarie. Right now, my agent tells me, escape literature is the thing and so the one I am concocting touches the earth nowhere and is spun out of pure, unadulterated bubameiser." Doubtless, the commercial success of *Five Came Bąck*, released by R.K.O. in June, was an ingredient in this airy fancy which West hoped to turn to gold.

Although he did not sell this story, in November he was rehired by R.K.O. For all of West's professed (and real) inability to solve the problems of mystery writing, he had, after all, worked on a mystery at Universal for four months, and according to Hollywood logic he was therefore assigned to develop a treatment for a rather famous studio-owned mystery novel, Frances Isles's *Before the Fact*. This assignment marked a decisive stage in what would be left of West's movie career: if until now he had been involved largely with B- or even C-grade films, from now on, his screen writing would be attended with increasing acceptance. The favorable Eastern reviews of his novels, his circle of influential friends, his special reputation among a smaller group as a really talented, distinguished man—these, John Fante says, provided West with the context for inevitable commercial success in films. And it was beginning to come.

A valuable property, *Before the Fact* had resisted efforts by earlier R.K.O. writers to adapt it for the screen and Boris Ingster had recently been assigned to the project with a chance to direct the film should he be able to complete a satisfactory script. Ingster had come to Hollywood nearly eight years earlier as assistant director on Sergei Eisenstein's abortive *Thunder Over Mexico* and remained when Eisenstein returned. By 1939 he had an established reputation as a plot constructionist and commercial writer. Hesitant in actual scriptwriting, particularly dialogue, though skilled in solving the cinematographic treatment of plot and accustomed to working with another writer, Ingster had read *Miss Lonelyhearts* and *The Day of the Locust* and set out to become friends with West, seeing in him a writer whose talent for the movies lay in dialogue and the invention of special twists of viewpoint as well as surprising or ironic situations. In a period when few Hollywood people read any books at all, Ingster, an admirer of Dickens, broke the ice in his first real conversation with West by discussing the

English novelist's perfect cinematic technique. He talked, enthusiastically too, about adapting *The Day of the Locust* for film, a notion which already glittered in West's mind. "Boris," West was soon telling Laura, "has enough energy to drive a steam shovel. . . . Although he doesn't write English himself, he knows what he wants in that language and aside from the tedium I must say that he really knows a hell of a lot about the business."

Beginning with *Before the Fact*, then, West and Ingster became a "team," a familiar institution in Hollywood in the thirties— Frances Goodrich and Albert Hackett, Hecht and MacArthur, Bright and Tasker were others—when it was believed that film-making demanded a variety of cooperative talents. In this case the expectation proved true. No longer having to worry himself about plot or motivation, West was free to indulge his talent for fantasy and invention. With Ingster setting out a straightforward plot, West would take up the story and characters, elaborating them and giving them uniqueness. Talking, improvising, tossing ideas about, they found that they could turn out commercial screen treatments with ease. It was, as Ingster says, "no sweat."

For a moment, their skill turned chance against them. Delighted with the screenplay, written in seven weeks, the R.K.O. producers offered the part to Laurence Olivier—recently cast as the stormy Heathcliff—and he tentatively accepted. But while Olivier waited for the co-star of his choice to complete a pregnancy, Alfred Hitchcock, also on the lot, became interested in the script, and seeing it as a vehicle for his own way with film, persuaded Cary Grant to star in it. Rewritten by his own staff, directed by Hitchcock, West's script reached the screen as *Suspicion*. In Hitchcock's film, Tony (now Johnnie) is a cad but not a murderer and in the end goes off to join the R.A.F. to prove himself a man. Better conceived, motivated, and dramatized than Isles's novel or *Suspicion*, *Before the Fact* was West's best script: years later, Hitchcock called it an "absolutely beautiful script," which he had altered only because he could not work with material entirely executed by others.

Still, the studio reassigned West to another project. He had been working on an original about aviators? Very well, now he was asked to develop a treatment for an original story by John Twist called

Men Against the Sky. After two months' work, early in April 1940, West turned in a 127-page script to his producer, Lee Marcus. Then, as if he were a staff writer instead of a contract writer, he was now shifted, without a day's break, to a script tentatively called *Malvina Swings It*, which another writer, Charles Roberts, had failed to complete satisfactorily. Marcus said nothing about his aviation screenplay. West, Jo Conway says, "was worried about what had happened to his script—this was his Republic training— he was used to being thrown off movies. Finally he saw Marcus on the lot, and he asked: 'What happened?,' and Marcus answered, 'What do you mean? You made all the changes. It started shooting Monday.' " West was moving up.

Men Against the Sky also gave him another solo credit. *The Hollywood Reporter* pronounced it "a sleeper" and remarked: "Nathaniel West's screenplay is a thoroughly contrived affair, with a sparkling dialogue lifting ordinary situations above the expected mark. With the help of some marvelous trick photography in test dives, West has provided more than the picture's share of thrills." For all its reliance upon well-worn formulas, the picture drew upon the excitement over aviation stirred by the war and was commercially successful. When it opened in August, West even advised his mother to see it.

In the meantime, West was involved in two more R.K.O. projects. After a scattered total of nearly ten weeks' work, he had turned *Malvina* into *Let's Make Music*, a film designed to exploit the popularity of Bob Crosby and his Bobcats. So completely had he rewritten Roberts's script that this too became a solo screen credit for him. His 118-page bit of fluff was accurately summarized by the R.K.O. Story Department: "Malvina, an antiquated schoolmarm, writes a school song which the students turn down, but which Bob Crosby happens across and features in his night club act. He looks up Malvina and offers her a job plugging the song. She comes, with her niece, to New York City and sings her song, 'Fight On for Newtown High,' which Crosby's arranger has made into a hot number. Bob Crosby falls for the niece. Malvina goes back to Newtown High where her classes are filled to overflowing. She has tasted her lost youth." "No doubt worse movies have been made," the reviewer for *The New York Times* commented when the film opened at the Palace, but he wondered what they were. The other reviewers were not so uncompromising. The *Film Daily* critic, for instance, pronounced it "a picture for all situations, ages, and types, although it is conceivable that some inflexible devotees of classical music may be holdouts, and term it esthetically 'gross.' But it's plenty gross for box offices." West would have been glad to forget this film except that during his work on it he at last broke through his "established" salary—unchanged since 1937—and rose to $400 a week, an unmistakable sign that he was in demand.

Certainly, R.K.O. was keeping West busy. Before he made the final changes on *Let's Make Music*, he was shifted, from May 13 to 25, to make the final revisions on a finished script for a Frank Partos movie titled *Stranger on the Third Floor*. Known in Hollywood as a "polish job," this assignment was a further demonstration that the studios had begun to take West seriously. While the scripts of Scott Fitzgerald, working desperately at Twentieth Century to learn film technique, were thoroughly rewritten by hacks, West, indifferent to screen art, was earning a string of solo credits and was increasingly regarded as a skilled craftsman. Fitzgerald had reported to Matthew Josephson that he was interested in making great films, while West confided to Josephson his belief that the Hollywood product was almost always sure to turn out badly. With such ironies both novelists were familiar. But for once, while Fitzgerald's predicament was decidedly tragic, West's was deliciously comic.

Hollywood was, as West had thought, a peculiar half world, with strange turnings. Had not Fitzgerald's books seemed destined for popularity in the twenties while West, in the thirties, saw his own books fall silently into oblivion? Now, for all Scott's thrashings, he seemed helpless in Hollywood, while the same year that West saw another novel sink out of sight, he was beginning to rise out of the ranks of screen hacks. What was success, in either case, and by what curious circuits did it come? And if he could satisfy millions of film viewers, West must have asked himself, why could he reach no more than 1,500 with his novels?

Such were the questions he would have pondered almost exclusively, no doubt, had he not, in the midst of his work on *Let's Make Music*, posed a series of new questions for his present and future. For on April 19 he was married. The international cata-

clysm, the in-fighting of Hollywood liberals, the explosion of their
fantasies, his hunting, and his work on films—these, at least for a
time, dissolved in West's own delight and amazement over this
extraordinary event.

18 / "Une étude de Rousseauisme . . ."

> "Une étude de Rousseauisme tel qu'il se manifeste aux Etats-Unis. *L'homme naturel* dans sa lutte contre les rigidités de la société industrielle. Huckleberry Finn, Soeur Eileen, et Petit Abner, analysés sous l'angle de la tradition américaine du comique-populaire."
>
> —Ruth McKenney, *All About Eileen* (1952)

West and Eileen McKenney had heard about each other long before they met. Eileen, after all, was the model for her sister Ruth's stories in *The New Yorker*, published as the book *My Sister Eileen* in 1938. And several of West's friends in the East knew the sisters, who had lived in New York and in New Milford, Connecticut, near the Josephsons, the Cowleys, and the Coateses. For her part, Eileen had frequently heard conversations about West and his books. Indeed, her sister suggests that Eileen envisioned her husband as a very distinguished man, and that she was initially attracted to West by her "image of him as America's greatest writer." She had in some sense, Ruth McKenney believes, "determined to marry him before she met him."

There is reason to think that West was first attracted to Eileen precisely because he could regard her as a kind of character in fiction, accessible directly to his imagination; he was never as reserved with her as he usually was with women. Even so, when he casually announced, Wells Root remembers, that "he had a girl, very soon after meeting Eileen," it was still shyly, with lingering emotional hesitancy like that of a "little boy." Yet, Root adds, "I was also struck by his strange detachment. He knew that one of the most important things of his life was happening to him, yet one part of his mind was sitting somewhere up high . . . scouting the process."

Perhaps West's 1934 comment about "An attempt to love and the difficulties encountered. The impossibility of experiencing genuine emotion" accurately describes his earlier relations with women. He had, of course, formed more than one serious attachment—in Erwinna, one which had become decidedly too serious. In the winter and spring of 1934 and 1935, he had an intense affair with a married Erwinna neighbor, an attractive and intelligent Jewish woman. When this at last became entirely too serious and embarrassing for him—the woman was possessive toward him and outspoken about their relationship—West moved into the Brevoort Hotel in New York. After a stormy meeting in the city, he conclusively broke off the affair. Within a few hours, the woman attempted suicide; and although she recovered, West still felt responsibility and, in some part, even terror, over the attempt. In 1935, too, Alice Shepard had married. These experiences combined to suggest to him that love brings little but pain. West's departure to Hollywood shortly thereafter was precipitous, something of a flight. No wonder that when Tod Hackett wanders among old sets, he sees "a Greek temple dedicated to Eros. The god himself lay face downward in a pile of old newspapers and bottles."

When the Perelmans were in Hollywood, West dated occasionally under their auspices, but showed little enthusiasm for serious attachments. Nonetheless, he was decidedly an eligible bachelor, and several girls set out to catch him. One, Jo Conway remembers, appeared often at his office, asking to borrow his car; then she would be obliged to pick him up at the studio at night. West enjoyed her gimmick enough to incorporate it into a fantasy, Wells Root recalls, about his "hilarious romance with a girl . . . who made her living posing in gold paint. While walking through a movie set one day he saw her glittering in front of the camera. At first he thought she was a statue but, of course, presently she came to life . . . . Pep was enchanted with this burnished goddess for all of a week or ten days. Then she wanted to marry him, and sternly refused to take no for an answer. She took to waiting in his car every evening in the parking lot outside the studio. . . . He moved the car to a private garage eight blocks away and sneaked in and out the labor gate at the back of the studio. . . . When last heard of, the girl, with a gallon of gold paint under her arm, was still haunting the parking lot."

This was comedy. He was still hesitant in direct personal relations, more able to relate to the distant Spanish orphans than to women at the studio. Yet, with several women who were attracted to him, he had casual affairs, all brief enough that West was never identified in Hollywood with a particular girl. For a time, early in 1939, he carried on an unsuccessful affair with a woman whom he had known well in the East, now separated from her husband. After his urethral infection of the fall, he may have been vaguely uneasy about his potency. When this woman hesitated to make love with him, he became upset and suggested that he would bring a prostitute to her apartment and prove to her that he was potent. Clearly, he was still more at ease with prostitutes than with those girls he regarded as "nice." Like Stephen Crane or Young Marlow in *She Stoops to Conquer*, he had never abandoned a final reserve, and he preferred the casual sexual relation to the serious one which would call for the end of reserve. He delighted in hearing tales of the amorous successes of Boris Ingster and Aben Kandel—though he was indignant when in *Hope of Heaven* John O'Hara exposed the affairs of a young woman they both knew—but he did not speak about his own affairs and was not driven to have them for self-esteem. What he seemed deepest and most intensely to know was that love or marriage was no cure for individual loneliness. He did not believe, as the proletarian writers often insisted, that love is a bourgeois trap; but he could find in it no promise of escape from the trap of self, the last well of true loneliness.

And yet with Eileen he proved to be, as a friend of hers concluded, "the kind of man who could be utterly enslaved." Eileen, a very different woman from the sunny ingénue created by Ruth, called forth the same deep sympathetic response that the Miss Lonelyhearts letters had. From her absolute loneliness, she called for a resolution of his own.

Born in Indiana in 1913, Eileen was largely raised in Ohio by her older sister after her mother died and her father remarried. As she herself puts it—extremely but revealingly—in her sister's book *All About Eileen*, ". . . my origins are obscure, if not horrible." At the least, she and Ruth would always share feelings of estrangement from and abandonment by their parents. For Ruth, these would lead to personal fantasy on the one hand and social rebellion on the other: fictional sketches for *The New Yorker*, as well as *Industrial Valley* (a history of the C.I.O. in Akron) and a series of wooden proletarian novels. Eileen's personality was obviously more vulnerable than Ruth's and it is clear that bobbing in the wake of her sister allowed her to avoid human involvements.

Very early, too, apparently, Eileen became convinced that the world was an affair of masks: she shrewdly attempted to camouflage her insecurities by image-making. In 1935, when the sisters moved from Ohio to Greenwich Village, Ruth recalls, "she was in New York less than a week when she announced that she spoke like a yokel and immediately hired a speech instructor. She made a very quick study, wanting desperately to speak English with an Eastern seaboard accent, and did very soon learn to speak beautiful F.D.R. English." Inclined to be heavy—at a time when slenderness was the feminine ideal—she was at such pains to diet that Ruth often awakened at night to hear her weeping from hunger. Eileen invented the position of "executive secretary" for herself; her chief function, she would say, was to "project an image" of sophistication for her employer. In Hollywood, appropriately, she would work in the Promotion and Story Departments of the Walt Disney Studios, center of the fantasy mecca. Eileen lived by and through her images of herself and those which society, family, and friends offered for imitation. It was no accident that her sister could create so effortlessly a fictive identity for her.

Still, noticeable signs of suffering remained. For all her speech lessons, she stuttered at critical moments. Her humor was entirely without cruelty toward others, but she could be viciously witty toward herself—ironic, self-effacing, self-critical. Eileen "made little of herself, definitely felt inferior," *The New Yorker* editor St. Clair McKelway says. She was a very generous and accepting person who had no ambitions to dominate others. Yet, for all her talent in public human relationships, she was extremely vulnerable and unfortunate with men. Although she appeared to be "sensationally uninhibited," according to Charles Pearce, the Harcourt, Brace editor of *My Sister Eileen*, Malcolm Cowley perceived in her a suppressed reserve which may, he thought, have ended by hurting those who loved her; but it was more true that she herself had been deeply wounded in her attitude toward sex. As an adolescent she had experienced a terrorizing and painful sexual experience which led her to regard love in the light of the suffering it would bring. A close friend says that "she was a woman who invited rejection from men precisely because she expected to be rejected." While she had, compulsively, several affairs—and one very intense one—she wanted to cause her lovers pain, for she clearly suffered from guilt and feelings of rejection. Although she might speak about her sufferings in an offhand way, perhaps as the basis for an anecdote, she was, McKelway says, "sentimental and emotional" and responded deeply only to seriousness in others. Ultimately, she was, he says, "more human than humorous."

In 1935, Eileen had married Morris Jacobs, a New York radio production man, in a desperate attempt to find some kind of personal stability. Not long after the marriage, around the same time she discovered she was pregnant, Eileen decided that she had made a mistake. She had married Jacobs, she now told herself, only because, as she hinted to McKelway, "she felt inferior and believed that she deserved only him." She had her child—a boy, Thomas Patrick—in New York after separating from her husband, and she and Ruth moved with a nurse into a rented "seventeen-room clapboard castle, very neo-Gothic, but with no plumbing, no electric light, no other niceties," in New Milford, Connecticut. "Neither Eileen nor I," Ruth writes in *Love Story* (1950), "had the slightest notion of what to do with a six-months-old baby."

St. Clair McKelway, who had a summer house nearby, "fell for her immediately," he says. By the fall, when the sisters returned to New York, he and Eileen had become lovers and she moved into an apartment rented for her. Now that Ruth's "Eileen" sketches were appearing, she suffered as much as her ego benefited from being a character on public display. Obviously, she was not sufficiently certain of her own identity to have another one imposed upon her. Really in love with McKelway, too, she felt she was merely "his doxy" and was very unhappy over the affair. Concerning her child, she had feelings of both guilt and entrapment. Uneasy over her own early abandonment, she wanted desperately to be a proper mother but felt inadequate for motherhood. Her child represented less a reward than a penalty for her, and she dreamed of her freedom. It was a time when people, as Lionel Trilling has said, "were likely to assume that there was an irreconcilable contradiction between babies and the good life. . . . [The] imagination of parenthood was not easily available, or it worked only to propose an absurdity, an image that was at essential odds with that of the free and intelligent person: what parent known to anyone had ever been free and intelligent?"

Her anxieties and self-doubts led, in the summer of 1939, to a definite break with McKelway, followed by removal to Hollywood to make that break conclusive. She shared a cottage on Fuller Avenue in Hollywood with a family who took care of her child while she worked. To a young woman who met her soon after her arrival, she gave the appearance of being "sentient—alive in every pore. She had antennae out, her reactions were very acute, and the whole effect she gave was of being golden." Yet, she was more and more unhappy. She was dating frequently—John O'Hara, Donald Friede, and Dan James, Charlie Chaplin's assistant, among others. She was hurt again in an affair with a press agent with whom she believed herself to be in love, and was moreover feeling guilty about what she now thought to be her helpless promiscuity. Her two-year-old child was troubled, and clung to her. The child's father, Morris Jacobs, drifted in and out; Eileen merely felt pity for him. She was drinking rather heavily and may even have attempted suicide. "At any rate," Ingster concludes, "it was a very desperate life, a very sad case. And all of Ruth's stories notwithstanding—although all that kind of joy bubbled up—[by 1939] the bubble was hollow—there was nothing gay about it."

She and West met in October 1939 at Lester Cole's house. "I felt—everybody felt—that Pep needed a wife . . . to take care of him," Cole says, and he and his wife "arranged dinner at their house for Eileen and West alone. They hit it off right away." Apparently they arranged a date very soon. Ruth McKenny—doubtless extravagantly—reconstructs Eileen's first response to him: "I met a man named Nathanael West—they call him Pep—last night. I remember you . . . talking about his book *Miss Lonelyhearts.* . . . I'm reading it for homework, before tonight. Tonight is when he's coming to take me to dinner. At first I thought (this was about 3 a.m., in the middle of acute insomnia) I would wear the blue satin—you know, dazzle him with the local glitter, such as it is. But then again . . . I just now called up Dorscher [her housekeeper] and told her to stir up something not out of a can, for two. I mean, that way he could see [Tommy], and I'm not sure if Pep has very much money, or not. . . . Or do you think that he'll mock the homely touch?"

West was enchanted. From the first, he responded to Eileen, and to her child, with an outpouring of a love whose source was compassion. He proposed marriage in December 1939, about two months after they met. This might have been predictable. One of the refrains of West's letters to the Perelmans for the last two years had been queries about their children, Adam and Abby. Tommy, he now told Laura, "is a very nice kid. He behaves well enough and is extremely bright. We get along splendidly until the twenty-seventh hundreth question. I then run him off with a stick." In a letter to a friend he spoke of Tommy as "my child."

Eileen was, as Budd Schulberg (who double-dated with them) says, "an outgoing girl who refused to accept the Pep that we knew" and broke down his social reserve. West surrendered his complexity to her uncomplicated approach to experience. But it was just as secretly true that West refused to accept the inadequate Eileen that even she believed in; he put the same all-comprehending sympathy into raising her out of her bitter sense of personal doom that Miss Lonelyhearts had aspired to give his correspondents. The enormity of her need resolved his loneliness, and he set out to cure hers. The women whom West had admired in the past were invariably serious-minded and independent. His mother was herself a very strong-minded woman; apparently, she had once hoped that he might marry Lillian Hellman. Eileen, however, did not call upon West's sense of admiration. His male friends, indeed, were at first surprised—and some of them disappointed—by the evident outward interest he showed in Eileen, feeling that he should marry someone better.

With them he joked about the problems of getting married. How could he continue—and with a ready-made family!—the helter-skelter life he was accustomed to, he asked. But his deepest responses were to permanent affections and stable situations. How could he, he continued, absolutely broke, hope to support a family? He had earlier associated his poverty with his inability to marry— he spoke of this as crucial in both 1931 and 1933—but in 1939 and 1940 he had money for the first time. What would he do about his hunting, he joked. But hunting had been for him essentially a way of establishing direct human contacts. Besides, Eileen's complaisance had been at the heart of her vulnerability, and he saw at once that she would go along with him on hunting trips. What would he do, in any event, about the dogs, Danny and Julie, who usually slept in bed with him, he asked in a frequent comic routine. But he deeply desired a satisfying sexual relationship. Behind all his jokes was the truth that the very qualities which had made Eileen unhappy would now make her a good wife for him. She had, a friend says, "great compassion and concern, a tenderness for others' egos, and sexual know-how." In her, West found a combination of experience and gentleness to which he could respond, emotionally and sexually, without reserve. Still, it was an enormous step for him to marry and it brought to the surface all his fears about personal entanglements. Less than a week before the wedding, he formed a plan for fleeing to Mexico and arranging to do scripts from there. But this hesitancy lasted only for an afternoon.

Then, on April 19, 1940, West and Eileen were married in Beverly Hills by Judge Charles J. Griffin, with S. J. Perelman as witness and best man. To be married to him was the greatest success of her life, Eileen told her sister. Over the telephone, her stutter came back: "Oh, I'm so *happy*. . . . It's a l-l-lovely day out here, Pep is s-s-sort of nervous, we're both so . . . h-h-happy," Ruth remembers her saying. They ate a wedding dinner at Chassen's in Beverly Hills and received a witty telegram from Ella 'Winter and Donald Ogden Stewart: "Request authority use your name message to President Roosevelt and Bishop Manning Quote Marriage is a Wonderful Institution Unquote and a Big Kiss for Eileen too."

The marriage was appropriately blessed by a joke, for it would be an extraordinarily happy one, "with no frictions or disillusionments," as Boris Ingster says. Very soon Eileen "blossomed out, she began to laugh and do funny things. . . . One night Pep made her tell a story . . . [and] as she was talking there was a great love and admiration in his face. He felt not only personally happy, but happy, also, because he saw a blossoming in her."

There was no immediate honeymoon since West was in the middle of the script for *Let's Make Music*—a piece of work which shows how far from this assignment his attention was. Still, for a year and a half, almost without interruption, he had been creating romantic melodrama for the screen, and he now laid plans to take a summer vacation with Eileen on the McKenzie River in Oregon. Hardly a pioneer type, Eileen gave herself up to this expedition humorously. After they arrived there in July, she wrote to West's mother:

Our usual routine is as follows: Up around 9 or so—mostly or so—breakfast (which takes another three quarters of an hour on account of the stove)—and then Pep starts to work. I do the dishes, sweep up the nest and then off to the store—which is about 4 miles away. . . .

Then the garbage has to be buried—which is a family feud between Pep and Julie to see if Pep can get it in the hole before Julie digs it up. . . .

Gradually we work up to lunch—which I hold out for being cold on account of the blast furnace in the kitchen. . . .

Comes then 5 o'clock and great activity. We start pulling on our fishing costumes—which believe me, is some big pull . . . and we're off.

There are some alleged good wading places close to us here but so far we haven't found many fish waiting for us. Anyway, it's fun and we get plenty of exercise tramping around and wading in the river.

During July and August they followed this routine in a cottage set on a small island connected to the mainland by a pedestrian bridge. Wells Root and Lester Cole flew up for fishing trips on the Deschutes River. And West, who had intended to work on his next novel, found plenty of reason to put off getting down to it. For one thing, a world-famous sportsman named Harry Mack lived nearby and he offered to take West on a fishing expedition. It promised to be the kind of spectacular trip about which West had had fantasies—via *Field and Stream*—since adolescence: Eileen called it "the trip of Master West's dreams. A marvel! Superb! Traveling over miles of uncharted waters, through canyons as deep as the Grand, potting a deer here, a bear there—grouse every night for dinner. Four stout guides, six equally stout boats, trout leaping to and fro over your boat. A savage or two poking around in the bushes—." Then, too, Eileen was a wonderful listener and encouraged West, admiringly, to construct and embroider tales in conversation. (Close friends like Scott Fitzgerald noticed this, Fitzgerald remarking in his notebooks on West's developing "long-windedness in conversation.") To some extent, this new flowing forth of anecdote drained off the source of West's novel-making: he would now more frequently talk out rather than write his fantasies. Instead of giving them form in fiction, he was giving them conversational, anecdotal form. Finally, West felt that his earlier fiction had been marred through "reworking stale stuff by writing a few chapters and then laying off a few months as I have been doing," and he hesitated now to begin at all until he could have enough time to write an entire draft.

Thus, he had done no substantial work on his book—only a dozen pages of notes—by the time they returned to Hollywood in September. The summer had been for him "une étude de Rousseauisme." Essentially, this was true, from the first, of his whole relationship with Eileen. She had been troubled and had seemed fated to personal disaster, but he had found in her *l'homme naturel*. She had given him his own humanity by needing it so desperately. And so they found the way of playing together fresh scenes in *la tradition américaine du comique-populaire*. They were strangely, and gloriously, married.

II

September gave West no time for novel-writing. He had spent almost all the money he had saved. Boris Ingster returned from Europe at about the same time that West came back from Oregon and, according to plan, they began at once to work on original stories for the screen. West left the Feldman-Blum Agency, allowing Ingster's agent to buy up his contract. Within a week, they had worked out a treatment in the genre of *I Stole a Million* in which they used comic elements from *A Cool Million*; they presented it to Columbia Studios as an adaptation of that novel, since treatments of published novels, West said, "got much more money." Ingster understood Hollywood aesthetics and economics, and he agreed with West's rueful declaration that they were safe in this deception since "no one would read the book to check" on their fidelity to the text.

Entitled *A Cool Million: A Screen Story*, the treatment begins, in fact, close to West's novel, as Joe Williams, "a hero out of Horatio Alger," leaves Oatsville, Vermont, for the big city. Everybody he meets there mocks his ambitions and his belief in the gospel of success, until he makes some bookkeeping mistakes and the bank authorities believe that he has embezzled a cool million dollars. Now everyone respects him, even the police; a famous criminal lawyer offers to defend him. Innocent, he was an invisible man. Only as a shrewd thief is he respected: "Joe had been thinking hard all the time. He now realized that no one cared how you got your million as long as you had it. And as long as they thought he had it, okay." He plays the role and opens up a brokerage account on his credit. By the time the insurance examiners discover that the supposed loss of a million dollars was only a bookkeeping miscalculation, he has made eighty thousand dollars in the market. He is, after all, a success.

Now the studios had marked West himself for success. He had a string of solo credits and had recently published a well-reviewed novel. (Fortunately, few Hollywood people had read it.) Five studios bid on this treatment and on September 24 it was sold to Columbia for $10,000. Sidney Buchman, a writer-producer under contract at Columbia, was enthusiastic about turning it into a film with social significance and got the screenplay assignment. This was particularly unfortunate, West and Ingster joked, for since the story was virtually unfilmable, absolutely violating Hays Code morals, they might have managed a long stint trying to do a satisfactory screenplay. Eventually, indeed, Buchman called them in for advice on how to make any kind of movie from the story. He shook his head and asked, over and over, "How do you do it?" Gleefully, they told him that he simply *couldn't* film it. And, as a parting irony, West shot out that if Buchman wanted social significance, "Why don't you go back to the novel?" Eventually, after considering the possibility that it might become either "a vehicle for Eddie Cantor or Bob Hope" or "a book-base for a farce-musical," the studio dropped the property altogether.

Meanwhile, he and Ingster, West wrote to Laura, immediately started upon another original "and it looks even better than the first. We told it to Lubitsch the other day and he was very excited about it. . . . We are writing it now day and night and hope to start peddling it by next week some time."

This treatment, *Bird in Hand,* was snapped up two weeks after the sale of *A Cool Million.* A skeptical reader reviewing holdings for the R.K.O. Story Department in 1945 appropriately summarized the whole tale as "a turkey." Yet the twenty-six-page treatment sold for $25,000. Now, West was delightedly telling Ingster, their efforts were worth about a thousand dollars a page. "Let's take an office on Hollywood and Vine and advertise: 'You need a story? We'll do it'—like custom tailors," he joked. Moreover, R.K.O. hired them to write the screenplay for *Bird in Hand.*

Things were breaking so quickly, however, that by this time they had followed up their sale of *A Cool Million* to Columbia by agreeing to write, on a week-to-week basis, a treatment and screenplay for a Columbia property titled *Amateur Angel.* R.K.O. agreed to hold *Bird in Hand* for them until this assignment was over, guaranteeing twelve to fifteen weeks on the screenplay, at $600 each per week. West's delight was genuine but tinged always with irony. It was clear now that it was his successful image that would make him successful, like Joe Williams in the treatment called *A Cool Million.* He could see that the producers and story editors were nodding to him at parties and that they regarded him as a clever operator. He might not have a cool million, but there was considerable money to be made. He was planning on reaping as great a profit as possible before his image faded. Even movie production itself now became a source of fantasy for him and he and Ingster spun out spectacular plans for a rosy future: "What we dreamed about," Ingster recalls, "was to travel and make pictures. We were confident that we would have film ideas born out of local color that could be produced either in Hollywood or with local backing." However fanciful this plan seemed, it anticipated, of course, the postwar movement toward Hollywood production abroad.

West labored on *Amateur Angel,* an Americanized "Man Who Broke the Bank at Monte Carlo," from late October 1940 until his death. In this screenplay, a professor of geography unwittingly becomes involved with a gangster who owns a gambling boat and then falls in love with the "curvesome blues singer" on it. To rescue her, he goes to the ship, "and, by calculating the effect of the lurching waves on the roulette wheel, breaks the bank." At the end, they leave for the honeymoon-expedition up the Orinoco River he has always dreamed about.

Meanwhile, having returned from their own romantic excursion, West and Eileen were taking a special delight in setting up housekeeping. After 1937, West had generally lived in the Hollywood hills, so vividly a part of the scene of *The Day of the Locust.* He always needed a large house with room for his dogs and had lived in a kind of bohemian grandeur. "He had an artless way of dumping things in [a house] that always made it look very amusing and very warm," a friend remembers. Invariably there was a fireplace, Mexican serapes, shawls, carved ducks, hunting prints, ironware, carved wooden chairs. These and other odd pieces picked up willy-nilly, West scattered in studied carelessness through his rooms. How interested he was in interior decoration as a symbol of the human interior, he showed in everything he wrote.

He gave free rein to this interest in moving from Cahuenga Terrace to 12706 Magnolia Boulevard, North Hollywood, in December 1940. For West, this house was a California reminiscence of Bucks County. Set among groves of walnut and pear trees on two acres of land, surrounded by farms and ranches, it had been built in 1936 by Clyde Cook. Designed in the style of a farmhouse, its brick walls were a foot thick and heavily grouted on the exterior. A beamed entryway led into a living room with three brick walls and one wood-paneled; there was a fireplace and an open-beam ceiling of natural knotty pine. One of the bedrooms had exposed umbrella beaming. The floors were wide, pegged boards.

"They were serious, as all young marrieds are, about furniture and china," Ruth McKenney says. For both, establishing a house was a delightful aspect of being married. By late December the house was only partially furnished, in a suitable colonial style. A blue, green, and lavender flowered chintz couch and matching barrel chair, two wooden rockers, and a Sheraton desk were in the living room, and a Welsh cupboard and trestle table stood in the dining room. Eileen purchased a supply of cooking utensils and an expensive, never unpacked, set of Spode china. Well, it was all a sort of game, like the hunting and the writing of original treatments with Boris. It had little to do with West's serious work as a novelist; but he had years to write novels, he would have said to himself easily, and while he was about this, it was a special, new kind of fun.

West's gaiety was obvious in everything he did in December 1940. One evening he invited Ring Lardner, Jr., Gordon Kahn, Ian Hunter, and their wives to dinner. "Nat," Hunter recalls, "was putting on a newlywed routine and when the maid or cook put a large turkey in front of him to carve, he made quite a ceremony of sharpening the knife. He kept staring at the bird and sharpening the carving tool, and managed to convey to me an air of complete bafflement. I really thought he didn't know how to go about the job. Then he jabbed the fork in, and lined up the knife for a cut in the exact middle of the bird, at right angles to the length of the breastbone. Then he sliced, and the knife went right through. [He] . . . had had the turkey boned and stuffed. He served us with sections from the middle like that, cross sections of breast surrounding a marvelous chestnut stuffing. Later we danced in the garden with each other's wives, and Eileen told me how happy she was."

They were both happy. From the last month of 1938, when West returned to Hollywood, through 1940, the international situation could not have grown worse, as one disaster brought on another; but for West this period was marked by increasing joy. Doubtless it is true that, had he lived, he would not have undergone any fundamental change in his serious point of view. With regard to his recent rise in status as a screenwriter, friends like Budd Schulberg decided, "he would have been as immune to success as he had been immune to failure." And essentially he would have taken his joy with Eileen as stoically as he had taken the frequent disappointment of his hopes. Nonetheless, he was able to surrender to the accidents of joy. Eileen put it well in a letter to West's mother, as, closing, she looked forward to a "really big reunion" with her and the Perelmans in the spring. "At this point I must catch up with Nat and the newspaper—he keeps shouting over dismal cracks or I should say reflections on the European situation which certainly couldn't be worse. And I guess this war makes us all feel a lot closer together and lucky, too, that we have each other and you to love. And believe me, we'll keep it that way."

19 / "The Phantom Hunts That Never Occurred"

I must say, there's something mournful about those letters, isn't there?—the reaching back for the East, and the phantom hunts that never occurred. It makes one feel, I wish, I wish. If I *had* gone out, and had been on that trip, I might have been driving, or Eileen, with Pep and me sitting in back talking, and, well . . . there it is.

—Robert M. Coates to Jay Martin, July 22, 1966

Around 2:30 on the afternoon of December 22, West finished packing his station wagon outside the De Anza Hotel in Calexico and got Julie into it. Then he and Eileen drove down the short street to route 111 and turned right, going north, to return to Los Angeles. He stopped at a service station for gasoline and talked to the owner for several minutes, but said nothing unusual.

West had seldom driven in the last several months. The very night he met Eileen at the Coles' and offered to take her home, she saw that he was a "murderous driver"—this reputation was well established in local legend—and insisted that she drive the rest of the way, just as Wells and Boris and West's other friends invariably did when they went on hunting trips. From then on, she drove. But in the fall of 1940, some people had begun to kid West about this, and though never before sensitive about having his friends drive his car, now West began to take over the wheel a block away from parties. In the last letter that Eileen wrote to Ruth McKenney, she announced that if they went alone to Mexico, Pep would be driving.

Even Eileen had teased him about his careless driving—gently, as most of his friends did, and in a well-established comic patter.

"It was very characteristic—and very terrifying," Wells Root remembers "—that West would get interested in telling a story at the wheel and would spend half the time looking over at you as he talked . . . until you called his attention back. Eileen used to kid him about it. She told a long funny story about him getting involved with the police over something he did that was totally ridiculous; he wound up getting a ticket even though becoming very friendly with the police, and the punchline of the story came when the police said: 'Nice guy, bad driver.' " It was true that he was color-blind, but his vision was accurate. It was also true that he could be somewhat awkward because of poor coordination; but his reflexes worked fast enough for him to shoot well and to set a hook skillfully when trout fishing. Driving, simply, was not an area of interest for him, so his absorption in its skills was very slight.

Now he started up the Calexico road toward El Centro. The few motorists who passed the station wagon on this lazy Sunday later remembered nothing out of the ordinary. He was not driving above the speed limit.

Wells Root had gone East for the holidays, or he would surely have been along. West had called Darrell McGowan, a hunting friend from his years at Republic, and he had at first agreed to go; then he found on Thursday that he would not be able to get away. Boris Ingster, too, had planned to join the expedition. But by the middle of the week he pointed out that neither of them had finished his Christmas shopping. "Let's stay in town and go during Christmas week," he told West. "But Pep said, No, he hated to shop, Eileen would do it."

It had been raining all day Thursday and Burt Kelly and his wife went to the Wests' for dinner that night. "Eileen didn't look too happy," Kelly recalls, when West declared that they were going to Mexico alone. Still, they were enthusiastically planning a Christmas Eve party for Tommy, to which they invited the Kellys.

West's Christmas party would be the hunting trip. Eileen, ostensibly, regarded his passion for hunting as a gentle madness and made it a source of comedy. She spoke as if she didn't know or care anything about it herself; yet, as West had told Laura late in September, Eileen had "developed into quite a shot," and on the opening day of the dove season she beat both Wells and him "in the number of birds, getting nine to our six and seven apiece." In any event, she went along time and again, as few other wives would.

West was particularly anxious to make this trip. At the beginning of the season, he had purchased two matched shotguns. Root recalls that "he heard about an auction of a fancy estate over in Pasadena, where they were selling . . . the deceased squire's hunting stuff. West bought himself a pair of matched Purdy shotguns (worth new . . . around $2,000) for $750." These were the finest guns made. It was a piece of insanity—a defiance of his years of adult poverty—but he was delighted with the shotguns in the same way that he was with Brooks Brothers suits, and he wanted to use them. Then, too, he was a little worried about the weight he had put on and was anxious for the exercise. They left Danny, who had been trained in the East for quail, at Jimmy Lindsay's Kennels. And they made sure that Tommy was properly settled with the maid, Rose Fisher. So, in the end, he and Eileen left late Friday.

Only a week before, on Friday, the thirteenth of December, Scott Fitzgerald and Sheilah Graham had come to the Wests' house for a memorable dinner party. The party had been fine. Elliott Paul, the Hacketts, and Hilaire Hiler were there, and someone mournfully sang "The Last Time I Saw Paris." For all of them, the twenties seemed to hover in the room as an aromatic presence. Fitzgerald had been the incarnation of the twenties and of the Paris now passed away, and West was the last American novelist to be deeply affected by that spirit. Like Fitzgerald, he was a moralist at heart, who really wanted (as Fitzgerald said of himself) "to preach at people in some acceptable form, rather than to entertain them." To be sure, the objects of their compassion and horror had been very different; unlike Fitzgerald, West had never (except in an unpublished satirical tale) attempted to portray the wealthy. Yet they were working along parallel lines even now; West had completed his Hollywood novel, while Fitzgerald had done a first draft of 37,000 words of *The Last Tycoon*. Fitzgerald's characterization of Hollywood—"all gold rushes are essentially negative"—was shared by West.

That dinner at the Wests' was the first party Fitzgerald had gone to in some time. Fitzgerald liked West very much, as well as having, Budd Schulberg remarks, "a really deep professional admiration for him." He took, indeed, almost a "proprietary interest" in the younger man, in some part regarding him as a disciple, and involved himself emotionally in West's progress and future.

Although Fitzgerald seldom went out socially between May and December 1940, he had been to the Wests' for quiet evenings several times, and they had gone to his house in Encino at least twice. He had been seeing West, Sheilah Graham says, more frequently than any other Hollywood friend. Once, when he had the Wests to dinner, he proudly showed them his scrapbooks and the first editions of his novels. Eileen launched into a commonplace attack on Fitzgerald for "pandering" to the rich in his books, but he defended himself, while West remained silent. There was no doubt in Fitzgerald's mind that he had been an analyst of, not an apologist for, the leisure class. Early in his first novel, he had found hope for the future in a kind of vague socialism, and in the last years of his life, Budd Schulberg says, "Fitzgerald was far more interested in paying attention to Marxist critics [of his work] than West was. He would say things like: 'I'll have to re-examine all my characters in terms of their class relationships.' He read a lot of Marx and took it seriously" in a way that West had never done, certainly not in fiction. On another occasion, a Sunday evening in the fall of 1940, Fitzgerald came to West's house and nostalgically watched him put Tommy gently to bed. West, Miss Graham says, was obviously proud of the boy and enjoyed playing at fatherhood.

Fitzgerald had been a kind of literary father to West. Between the two novelists there existed the most sympathetic understanding. They were not only friends but had influenced each other's work. West's description of Miss Lonelyhearts's religious experience ("He was conscious of two rhythms that were slowly becoming one. When they became one his identification with God was complete. His heart was the one heart, the heart of God. And his brain was likewise God's") closely parallels Fitzgerald's description of Gatsby's falling in love with Daisy Fay ("Gatsby saw that the blocks of the sidewalks really formed a ladder and mounted to a secret place above the trees—he could climb to it. . . . At his lips' touch she blossomed for him like a flower and the incarnation was complete"). *Tender is the Night* (1934) seems to have been involved in the genesis of *The Day of the Locust*. Fitzgerald's Rosemary visits a Riviera movie set and sees, as Tod would in the back lot of National Studios, "the bizarre debris of some recent picture, a decayed street scene in India, a great cardboard whale, a monstrous tree bearing cherries large as basketballs." In 1940, Fitzgerald's Hollywood novel was still unfinished, though West's had appeared. Now, West's description of the dream-dump seems to have influenced the older novelist to describe a flooded studio back lot. The locations did not look, he writes, "like African jungles and French châteaux and schooners at anchor and Broadway at night, but . . . like the torn picture books of childhood, like fragments of stories dancing in an open fire." On this flood, the woman who is to be Monroe Stahr's tragic love floats astride an enormous papier-mâché head of the goddess Siva, "stopping sometimes to bump in the shallows with the other debris of the tide." Again, in his description of Stahr's projection room, Fitzgerald followed West's conceptions and images: "Dreams hung in fragments at the far end of the room . . . passed—to be dreamed in crowds, or else discarded." Like Tod, Monroe Stahr is at first capable of perceiving and separating false illusions from true dreams, but is destroyed at the end. Stahr's "plane might fall in a suburb of Los Angeles," Fitzgerald projected in his notes: if so, some of those starers who wait at Glendale airport, in West's novel, hoping for a plane crash, would be soon at hand to pick at the debris. In both novels the heroes are in love with vacuous women who are not interested in them. Fitzgerald's note for a funeral scene, intended to be "an orgy of Hollywood servility and hypocrisy," could as well describe the funeral of Harry Greener. Similarly, Fitzgerald's plan to introduce a *"Hollywood Child.* The hard little face of a successful streetwalker on a jumping jack's body" is anticipated by West's Adore Loomis. Most striking of all, perhaps, is one of Fitzgerald's last notes before his death, which suggests how thoroughly the final riot of West's novel had taken hold of his imagination: "Not one survived the castration." West's novel had become material for Fitzgerald's imaginative projections.

On December 22, 1940, as West started back toward Los Angeles, the older novelist had been dead from a heart attack for nearly a day, and West was riding toward his own death.

So, in a sense, were the 1930's. For West, at least, the climax of his long personal debate over his own relation to politics had not come until this very autumn. Through her sister and her brother-in-law, an editor of *New Masses*, Eileen had strong ties to the Communist Party, and around this time she was encouraging West to move closer to it. West told her that, despite all the prosely-tizing of some of his friends, he had gone to only one Party meet-ing, and then given it up in boredom. Eileen could accept this. She herself could seldom be persuaded to attend unit meetings and listen to long, dull speeches. In Hollywood she amusingly satirized the shoddy quality of the left. She was far more a party girl than a Party girl. Once, in New York, she had invited St. Clair McKel-way to escort her to a Party picnic on the Palisades; he got her a hamper from "21" and rented a Carey Cadillac for the trip. *That* was the kind of Communism to which Eileen was inclined. Still, in this period between the non-aggression pact and Germany's inva-sion of Russia, the few faithful Communists were highly defensive and gathered more closely together, and Eileen's family loyalty drew her closer to the Party. The same kind of loyalty caused West to agree that autumn to take part in a study group conducted by a Party functionary on the elementary principles of Marxism, a pre-liminary to becoming a Party member.

Moreover, West's participation in Hollywood liberal organiza-tions had given him a new sense of the usefulness of action. Jerome Chodorov, who talked politics with West more than once, believes that "he was a skeptic, but a hopeful one. . . . He didn't really believe mankind could save itself . . . by politics or any other thing—but was trying hard to believe it." Now he minimized his knowledge and inclined briefly toward his faiths. Even after liberal action groups had been exploded by the Hitler-Stalin pact, he told George Brounoff, with whom he renewed correspondence: "They consist of sincere, hard-working people whose objectives are be-yond question and whose talents for organization and personal sac-rifice are of the very highest order. The practical results of these organizations . . . have proven themselves in the actual field of progressive politics and aid to labor and other democratic organiza-tions. The number of ambulances provided for Spain and for China, the people actually elected to office here in California, the propaganda put out in every possible field . . . is overwhelming. From a Fascist-minded, anti-labor section of the state, Southern California has become one of the most progressive and pro-labor sections. All these different motion picture organizations, with their quite united front activities, have actually made this concrete change in the past three or four years through an enormous amount of hard work and continuous devotion to the liberal ideal. Until I, myself, participated in these organizations I found it easy to laugh and scoff because of the strange collection of personalities brought together by them. Nevertheless, only a little work showed me how very wrong I was and how easy it is to sit back and scoff and find mistakes in both the people and their program. All this is wrong as hell and makes me very suspicious of the critics who, while giving lip service to a set of ideas, sit back in their armchairs and are perfectionists and comedians, using their own gnawing doubt to eat away other people's affirmative acts. I feel quite bitter about it." West's personality had long been characterized by an inability to respond with action to social ills when he could find his solutions in fantasy. But the nature of the world at this moment forced him to reevaluate the uses of action and to deny himself fantasy.

Beginning in November 1940, then, each Wednesday night West and an influential Hollywood producer sat through a doctrinaire discussion with the functionary. If nothing else, this was a proof of West's continuing seriousness about politics. But he had long ago seen through the political catechism and, along with the producer, soon began to question rather than answer. The Party man was obviously nettled, particularly by their unwillingness to follow without question the Communist line on the Hitler-Stalin pact and to regard the war as imperialist. By December, they had pretty much separated over the anti-Fascist question, and the two men decided to attend no more meetings after the night of December 18. The hope for a faith had once again—this time through Eileen —risen in West, but his disappointment was foreseeable. Only the fact that the pact had rid the Party of most of its fantasy-ridden sympathizers—"it hit them like a dropped option," a local wit quipped—made it at all attractive; for at least its remaining members had the monastic energy of real convictions. But West had come toward the Party through personal sympathy and anti-Fascism; and in the fall of 1940 it was clear how little these were elements of its true constitution.

Now, ironically, as West traveled up the Calexico road, he drove through one of the strongest California centers of native Fascism. Many had been the Hollywood meetings held over the "miseries of the lettuce worker toiling in the Imperial Valley." El Centro, the center of the Valley production, was a byword in Hollywood for Fascist activity. (There was even a Hollywood street named for it, and, coincidentally, Jo Conway had just moved into an apartment on El Centro Street.) One of the most sensational incidents in the futile attempts of the A.F.L. Fruit and Vegetable Workers to unionize the area had come in 1935 when two members of the striking union were shot by deputized strike-breakers. One was brought to the badly staffed and badly managed Imperial County Hospital, where injured field workers received minimal attention. When the man's wife called the hospital to inquire into his condition, a doctor told her: "He'll soon be dead. They ought to . . . kill all those sons-of-bitches." Almost exclusively itinerant farm workers, the hospital's patients were regarded as so inconsequential that no records of their treatment were kept in the thirties.

Before long, this same hospital would receive a call for aid in an automobile accident at the intersection of routes 111 and 80; but the response would be slow.

West might well have asked himself, with the legal limit of game packed in the station wagon, what the hunting would have been like back East. He and Eileen had thought about spending the holidays in Bucks County. Late in November, West had telegraphed Ernest Schaible, who was keeping his coon-hound Lulu, that he would be coming home soon and to have her ready for a hunt. Moreover, Ruth's play, *My Sister Eileen*, was to open on Broadway on December 24 and naturally she wanted them to attend the première. There was talk, too, of West meeting with Earl Browder, who might resolve his doubts about the Party. Certainly, West was uneasy about the publicity over the play, and perhaps about this meeting. Eileen herself was openly ambivalent about being a character on the stage. The character which Ruth had drawn for her had perhaps saved Eileen when her own personality was trembling on the edge of dissolution; but now she somewhat resented the fictive being which was imposed upon her own. And so they had remained in California.

Then, too, West had the contract waiting for him at R.K.O. to work on *Bird in Hand* at a $200-a-week raise above his "established" $400 salary. He would have to begin this immediately after the holidays. With a substantial increase in salary, he would be able sooner to buy the free time needed to take up his new novel in earnest. On Tuesday of the previous week, he had had dinner with Bennett Cerf and his West Coast sales representative, and this had rekindled his enthusiasm for making the long-delayed beginning on his fifth book.

On *Miss Lonelyhearts* and *The Day of the Locust,* West had worked for about four years each, his imagination all the while roving over and over the same essential ground from various points of view, through widely different characters, and in the guise of many fictions. Each element that he took up, even if finally put aside, inevitably left its mark upon the work, which in the end would accumulate a greatness not deriving so much from its separate sources of inspiration as from the prismatic sparkle of its long genesis and history.

By June 1939, after the commercial failure of *The Day of the Locust,* when West made a series of attempts to define his kind of art, he had decided finally that he was now interested in turning to an art with a positive center. He told Perelman then that it was not the subject matter of *The Day of the Locust* but "my particular slant" which caused its failure. "If," he added, "it was written about Martians or even denizens of the deepest canebreak, it would still be shunned like the plague." But he felt that his next novel—"I have got it blocked out in my mind," he declared— would be very different. "One thing I have lately begun to feel (and sales have really nothing to do with it)," he wrote to Bennett Cerf on June 13, 1939, "is that I have come to the end of my interests in a certain kind of writing. I have a new book planned which I intend to keep extremely simple and full of the milk of human kindness, and I am not joking, I really mean it."

One of West's great achievements had been in writing a series of anti-novels in which is summarized the history of the twentieth-century poetic imagination, from symbolism through surrealism and super-realism. He had an imagination with no place for small talk: he had wrung the neck of rhetoric in the novel, as Verlaine intended to do in poetry. He had believed that the writer's role was to represent, as vividly as possible, the chaos, terror, and grotesqueness of this world—simply to tell the truth about it, by refusing to create a novelistic rhetoric which could slip between the truth and his representation of it. West was not, as W. H. Auden observed, "strictly speaking, a novelist; that is to say, he does not attempt an accurate description either of the social scene or of the subjective life of the mind. . . . [He] adopted the convention of the social narrative; his characters need real food, drink, and money, and live in recognizable places like New York or Hollywood, but taken as feigned history, they are absurd." In his books, West was attempting to embody directly that absurdity of the real.

But now he began to feel that all his work had been sketches, "unrealized projects." Precisely because he had been so bent on avoiding the risk of sentiment or melodrama, he had, he now came to feel, lost something of the human drama. Defending *Miss Lonelyhearts* in 1933, he had advised fellow novelists: "Forget the epic. . . . In America, fortunes do not accumulate, the soil does not grow, families have no history. Leave slow growth to the book reviewers, you have only time to explode." But now his sense of the American scene had altered: he was beginning to apprehend the thickness of its civility and the importance of its history. Boris Ingster often insisted, when they talked about this, that *Miss Lonelyhearts* might have been another *Idiot* if West had not committed himself to understatement. During 1939 and 1940, West's earlier imaginative divisions and indecisions over the authority of Dostoevsky or Flaubert, between the sentiment of the Brounoff group and the irony of the Village, came back to him vividly. He told Darrell McGowan that all his books had a message—they dealt with "struggling man's problems"—but he was "strongly interested in writing another book" which would take this theme up more directly. Certainly West's comedy had always been inextricable from his compassion—"the particular kind of compassion," as Norman Podhoretz has said, "that is allied to intelligence and is therefore proof against the assaults of both sentimentality and cynicism." Now he hoped to make these connections abundantly clear.

Although this kind of novel had been much on his mind throughout 1940, he was hesitant about wholeheartedly attempting to write such a book. Clearly this, as much as his movie work, had prevented him from making a start. He told Ingster that to deal truly with "the milk of human kindness" would oblige him "to find new words [whereby] to give expression to the basic things in life——like death, birth, or the confrontation of unfaithfulness—all the basic, dramatic moments of a man's life." But, he concluded, he was really determined "to try a novel . . . in the great tradition of novels, to really probe, to really go all the way, and not to worry about overpopulating the book . . . with characters if they are necessary." To speak any longer of chaos in 1940 would have been a redundancy; to write of the absurd was irrelevant when the world had taken such a decisive turn to manifest absurdity. Now West spoke with intense conviction about his "best work" lying ahead of him, of his ultimate success with this kind of novel; and most of his friends felt (as one put it) that they could see him "growing right in front of your eyes."

Always uncommunicative about the details of his work-in-progress, West nonetheless made frequent references to his hopes for this novel and the imaginative and actual conditions necessary for its completion. Apparently, some of the *Wanderer* tale, which had been in the background of *The Day of the Locust*, remained in West's mind and would also have found its way into this new novel. In the summer of 1939, before meeting Eileen, he had been making definite plans to quit film work "around the first of the year" and he told Cerf that then he would "start to really work on my new book. It is a Joseph Conrad-like story of adventure." At about the same time, he revealed plans to take a three months' vacation in "Mexico or the South Sea Islands." He spelled out his hopes more fully to Laura, saying that he was going to be away "for a long long time": "I am planning to go to the South Sea Islands because my new book is turning out to be (in my mind—nothing on paper so far) a Conradesque piece with maybe even a storm in the middle of it. On second thought, I'll leave out the storm. What I want for a locale is to find a city in the South Seas like I imagine Papeete must be, with skyscrapers and concessions like in Venice or Coney Island, surrounded by jungle. I understand there are several towns like that down there and it will make a perfect setting for my adventure tale." *

Continuous employment at the studios, with the prospect of

---

* West had long been interested in Conrad (by 1933 he had read *Typhoon, Chance, Rescue, Youth, Arrow of Gold, The Shadow-Line,* and *Almayer's Folly*), but Conrad had not seriously influenced him. Now, however, West's changing ideas about fiction returned him to the English novelist and, very likely, also to Herman Melville's South Sea tales, *Typee* and *Omoo*, which he had read in the twenties.

building up capital for a long layoff, and West's courtship of Eileen, prevented him from taking the vacation at all. Moreover, the
South Seas plot began to merge and mingle with other ideas for his
book. Still, when Saxe Commins passed through Hollywood in
February 1940, West outlined a plan for a novel and asked for a
$1,000 advance. "I have the entire story clearly in my mind and
know just what I intend to do with it and am eager to start," he
wrote to Cerf. This was the first in a series of letters in which Cerf
held out strongly against that advance as "utterly unreasonable"
and countered with an offer of $250, which West called a "very
airy pat on the back" but finally accepted, signing the contracts on
April 27.

West's letters throughout the spring repeatedly hinted at his
hopes for the novel. "I have worked out the idea in my mind in
quite a bit of detail and the more I think about it, the more certain
I am it can be a hell of a book," he declared in March. He would
easily do a draft of the book in Oregon; he would, he told Cerf,
"return with a gem of purest ray serene in my satchel."

In Oregon, West took up another plot altogether and actually
made a start on it. Quite consciously, he developed a tale similar in
its outline to *Miss Lonelyhearts,* as if to work out, in new directions, the implications of the earlier book's theme. He described
his hero, Earl Jones, as a "special type of star reporter whose forte
is local color with a comic twist," a Shrike-like writer, in short,
whose subject is the absurdity of the actual. "He is the man who
writes about love affairs in the zoo, the home life of a strip-tease
artist, how it feels to be a peeping tom, the hawk that lives in the
tower of the Empire State Building and hunts pigeons on the steps
of the library, etc. etc. It is a tough job because he has to come up
with a new one every day and can never repeat." He is interested in
human suffering only because it provides, daily, new materials for
his column—West's analogue, as he now saw it, for his own earlier
way with fiction. At present, however, Earl has run out of ideas:
even the grotesque becomes repetitious; even the truly monstrous
at last seems ordinary. He turns to the advertisements in the
"agony column"—always "a fruitful field" for him—and there,
among other good prospects, "he comes to an advertisement soliciting members for the Golden Friendship Club." In a preparatory

outline, West articulated his sense of the meaning of this institution for "the victim on which it lives—the lonely and helpless of the big cities and the farms"—and for himself:

> Sophisticated people are often amused by certain little advertisements tucked away in the personal columns of large newspapers and on the back pages of pulp magazines where they are sandwiched between panaceas for acne endorsements and for miracle-working electric belts. Worded with an optimistic flamboyance which seems comic to those who are in no need of its services, "friendship clubs" offer to find comrades for the lonely and matrimony for the sex-starved. For a small fee they promise to put a prospective member in touch with friends who will make his or her life joyous, turning their dull, drab existence into a full round of dances and parties, where they will probably meet the husband or wife best suited to them. All over the country, thousands of helpless and depressed souls, in dingy hall bedrooms and faraway farms, read those ads and dream of being popular figures in a romantic social whirl surrounded by gallant swains and ravishing girls. It is on these tragic creatures that the friendship clubs prey. . . .

In the first typed draft of the sketches West wrote in Oregon, the newspaperman attempts to investigate the Golden Friendship Club but is recognized and put out by Colonel and Mrs. Burgess, the concrete Dr. Know-All Pierce-Alls of this prospective book. Earl then hires an innocent young female journalism student to join the club and get his material for him. Only later does he see that he has given her up to the moral corruption and real dangers of the club simply for the sake of his story. Then she disappears. Now, for the first time, in attempting to save her, he becomes involved with another human being.

"Pep's book seems to be coming along fine and this makes us both very happy," Eileen wrote in mid-July. But by September, when she and West returned to Hollywood, he had not managed to get his friendship-club sketches beyond the crucial point when Earl enters the world of human tragedy. He talked to Ingster about these preliminary episodes and declared that, though good, they were only a phase in the working out of a novel which would be quite different.

Indeed, with Earl somewhat transmuted, a tale of a friendship club might easily have become one of the episodes in the book which lay closest to West's imagination and inclinations in December 1940. For years he had admired Turgenev's *Sportsman's Sketches,* and had recently been talking of imitating it on native grounds. With Turgenev as his model, he would, as he described his plan, put together a series of loosely-related sketches of the American scene. These would not be anchored in any one spot but strung on a ramble about America. He liked to say that he would have them privately printed for his friends and hunting companions, but now he saw the form's real possibilities for showing a wandering, uninvolved character plunged time after time into experience of all kinds. There had been nothing like this in American literature, he knew; even Hemingway's Nick Adams sketches, *In Our Time,* showed Nick fleeing from intense experience, while West would deal with the flight from indifference.

For this book, S. J. Perelman remarks, "he had some very good anecdotes indeed." Doubtless, a version of his story concerning Wells Root and the exiled surgeon was to be included: his imagination had worked on it and given it a classic form. "The essential incident" of the book, Robert M. Coates remembers, was to be the story of how the hero, following a mountain trail with several companions, slips and falls into a ten-foot snow drift and has to listen as his friends debate about how (or whether) to pull him out. Such a tale, Coates says, accurately expressed "West's metaphysics of the accidentalness of doom."

Not surprisingly, most of the prospective episodes involved a sense of terror, a metaphysics of doom, the condition and nature of human separateness. The simplest might have been a tale of comic terror, like the story West told of being chased by fierce dogs while he was poaching on Hearst's San Simeon estate with Darrell McGowan. Or there might have been wildly romantic stories, like the one which he embroidered about Jimmy Alvarez, the owner of the Leon d'Oro in Mexicali. Alvarez, West maintained, never crossed the border to California because he was wanted for murder in the States, and yet he yearned to stand on American soil once more. Also living in Mexicali, he told Burt Kelly, were some white Russians who had similar secrets in their pasts. Then there were numerous stories about Jesús Fernandez, the Yaqui Indian who always served as West's guide. (As early as April 1939, West had told George Milburn that he might go to Mexico for the scene of his next novel.) No doubt, too, he would incorporate into the book some of the legends about his driving—like the time he had roared down over an erect 4 × 4 post fence into an irrigation ditch, only to be picked up by some hunters a few minutes later and taken to a spot where he had had unrivaled hunting. Perhaps he would make a comedy out of that fall afternoon when, with Leonard Fields, he had looked down into dark water as their car teetered on the edge of a plank bridge, and they had been doomed to live.

On the placid Sunday afternoon of December 22, 1940, West lived out his metaphysic of the accidentalness of doom. When he had been an undergraduate at Brown, not yet twenty-one, he had written a poem called "Death," under the name N. von Wallenstein-Weinstein:

> Cherished inspirer of minor poets,
> How many adolescent wails
> Have reached your fleshless ears!
> Shall I join that inane chorus
> With my poor echo of an old cry?
> Scold you for a thief,
> Cherish you as a friend,
> Beg you for more days,
> Or vainly dare you take me?
> Why must you disturb
> The mediocre mind to thought
> And scare small souls to God?

West had refused to be a minor poet, and in December 1940 his life was filled to overflowing with plans for the future. There was the house to furnish. Some Christmas presents needed to be bought, others were wrapped, and some still waited to be mailed. There were Tommy and Eileen—and he and Eileen were speaking freely to friends of wanting to have children of their own. There were all those "phantom hunts" to make. *Amateur Angel* needed reworking, and there were other, better movies to write and the Hollywood game to play for yet a while. There was an unfinished letter to Sid and Laura in his typewriter, commenting on a draft of their play, *The Night Before Christmas*. And there were books of his own to write and rewrite. Many books; his mind was full of ideas for them.

These were the kinds of thoughts that drew him irresistibly toward the green and dazzling future, when he saw, dreamily, a sign that read *Stop*. But he did not stop.

Appendix/Nathanael West's Film Writing

In the main narrative of this biography I have attempted to give enough information about West's films to suggest their character and quality and to indicate their place in his life. For those who are interested in further details concerning these movies, I have designed this chronology. I have read all of West's scripts, occasionally in more than one draft or state, as well as his original treatments and Story Department reports on his work; and I have thoroughly consulted the business records kept by studios concerning his salaries and the dates of his employment on each project. In describing these movies, I often resort to the press releases or advertisements prepared by studio publicity departments, as providing the only language adequate to indicate the banal plots, situations, and characterizations with which West was obliged to work.

Beauty Parlor. This was West's first Hollywood work and was written at Columbia Studios from July 7 to 14, 1933. The heroine of the story, Carole, is a manicurist in the DuBarry, "a very elaborate and expensive beauty parlor . . . more like a swanky club than a place where women go to have their hands, hair, and faces fixed. Cocktails are served with a tango orchestra." She is "very beautiful" but "hard" toward men; "she knows all the answers." She rejects, among others, Tony Blake, who runs a scandal sheet and blackmails prominent people to suppress their names. Carole's roommate, May, defends Tony and then goes on to argue against Carole's dislike of rich men, saying that, for herself, "she would rather live in sin and sables than in sanctity and stew." Later, she arranges a double date in which two rich men pretend to be chauffeurs. Carole's date is Stephen Ballantyne, who "is fed up with society while his wife is very social." He continues the pretense, though he tells Carole he is married; she insists that they live together until he can get a divorce. Finally she reads the truth in Tony Blake's *Tattler!* Enraged, she lets herself be guided by May and, taking Ballantyne's money, sets herself up in a luxurious apartment, acting "desperately gay." Soon, she discovers that she is going to have a baby, and after some complications, the picture ends with her and her lover embracing in the office of the district attorney.

Return to the Soil. Discussed and summarized in text, pp. 206–7.

Ticket to Paradise, a film released on June 25, 1936, was based on a story by Francis Cockrell, purchased by the studio for $500, that appeared in *Cosmopolitan* magazine in April 1935. This was West's first produced film. His treatment and screenplay were revised by the senior writer on the set, Jack Natteford, and they shared screen credits on it. "Terry Dodd, go-getting young businessman in a hurry to entrain for Pittsburgh, where a million-dollar deal was awaiting his signature," is in a taxi accident and suffers amnesia. "Police, finding him wandering in a daze with $10,000 in his pocket, arrest him" and turn him over to "mental specialists, who find that he reacts to a picture of a taxicab. So they advise him he is a taxi driver—suggesting that he go to work as such, with the hope that someone will identify him." After many adventures, including a romance, his memory returns and he rushes off with his newly found millionairess (Wendy Barrie) to close the deal. The dialogue, *Weekly Variety* said, "is not half bad, most of it being more sparkling than the situations."

On *Follow Your Heart*, West, Lester Cole, and Samuel Ornitz worked between April 28 and June 9, 1936. The film was developed from an "original idea" by Dana Burnet and was a fairly successful attempt—at least financially—to exploit the reputation of a well-known female singer, even though chairs or other supports had to be placed around the set to help the rather inebriated star stand. Marian Forrester, impoverished daughter of a once wealthy Southern family, who has a fine singing voice, refuses to consider a stage career and "prefers to struggle along as a voice teacher. She changes her mind only after the determined efforts of Michael Williams, director and star of a stranded dramatic troupe, to pin her down to a singing contract and a matrimonial one as well."

The President's Mystery. Discussed and summarized in text, pp. 277–9.

After completing his work on *The President's Mystery*, West was briefly assigned to a race-horse story that was never produced. He told a Republic director, Burt Kelly, that "they had a story conference on this movie and he had a piece in the script where the trainer, talking to his horse, cuts an apple in half and gives him a half apple. Nat Levine [the producer] says that he likes that business—couldn't we have some more? So Pep says, 'Well, he keeps talking and in a little while he gives him the other half.' 'That's it,' Levine says," struck by what he regarded as West's inventive mind.

West was assigned to *Gangs of New York* at three different periods (September 21 to October 27, 1936, November 30, 1936, to January 1, 1937, and January 13 to March 13, 1937), although he did not finally receive a screen credit for it in the loose, non-guild method of awarding credits at Republic. Suggested by Herbert Asbury's book, this film, a higher-priced venture than was usual at this studio, starred Charles Bickford and Ann Dvorak, and was completed in March 1938. "Franklin, a police officer bearing a marked resemblance to Rocky Thorpe, an underworld leader of New York, takes Thorpe's place on the day he is to be released from Sing Sing, in order to get the goods on all the gang. The real Thorpe, however, escapes from his guards and, in an effort to get Franklin at all costs, is himself killed. And the gang is cleaned out too. Franklin wins the pretty singer, who was a sister of one of the mobsters."

Jim Hanvey—Detective was loosely based on a short story, "The Woman Pays," published in *Collier's* in 1933. It is a low-budget comedy on which West worked from October 28 to November 28, 1936. "Jim Hanvey [Guy Kibee] may be a hayseed character, but he's a pretty shrewd detective. He's called in by an insurance company to help recover the stolen Frost Emeralds. Young Joan Frost's fiancé, Don Terry, is suspected, not only of the jewel theft, but of the murder as well. Hanvey manages to clear him and wring a confession from Davis, the insurance company investigator."

West worked on *Rhythm in the Clouds*, for which he was credited with an "adaption" of original material by two other authors, from March 16 to April 6, 1937. In this musical comedy, which opens with a shot of a tenement district in New York, "a struggling young songwriter, Judy Walker, takes advantage of a situation in which she uses the name of another, very successful writer, to get her own stuff over to the public on a popular radio show. The complications that flow from this involve a romance she gets into with lyricist Bob McKay which almost goes on the rocks when the hoax is exposed, but is brought to a happy conclusion."

Ladies in Distress, based on a story titled "Meet the Duchess," which appeared in *Liberty* magazine in 1928, as well as on an "original" purchased from Dore Schary, was a comedy prepared for a female team whose earlier Republic movie had been a success. West worked on *Ladies in Distress* from April 7 to April 30, 1937, but his treatment was given to Darrell and Stuart McGowan for rewriting; they earned exclusive screen credit by the time the film was completed, over a year later. "The story . . . revolves around the activities of a lady mayor of a small city who, on learning that her city is infested with gangsters and criminals who are preying on the town's citizens, decides to hire a gangster from a distant city to come and clean up her community. How her theory of thief-catch-thief works out makes what advance reports call 'hilarious yet touching entertainment.' "

West worked on *Bachelor Girl*, a staff "original" by Betty Bubridge, from May 1 to May 3, 1937. He was the last writer on this property before it was put into the dream-factory dump, an almost unique occurrence at Republic, where virtually every studio property was produced. Perhaps West threw up his hands after the three days he worked on it. "Larry Stuart, scion of a department store family, marries, in the midst of a drunken spree, a girl who has vowed to 'frame' a Stuart out of revenge for the dirty deal she got from Larry's half-brother." The elder Stuart declines to pay her off, and Larry, meanwhile, heads for Reno and a divorce, but the two meet up on the way and are brought together by a small boy, Red.

Born to Be Wild was made as a "Jubilee Feature"—Republic's highest budget pictures—costing $150,000. West wrote this 105-page screenplay under contract as an original in about two months, from August 26 to October 23, 1937. "Steve and Bill, a truck driver and his swamper, are instrumental in saving the dam at Indianhead from collapsing. Lives and property will be lost if it does. Spurred on by the thought of a large bonus from their boss, if they deliver a large load of dynamite vitally needed to save the dam, they almost fail, when the timely intervention of a farmer's daughter, Mary, enables them to accomplish their mission." This appears to be the only script which West worked on entirely alone at Republic. "Story and direction," the West Coast Preview Committee told exhibitors, "lack cohesion, but the photography is good and the interpolated songs are appropriate. Family."

It Could Happen to You. Discussed and summarized in text, pp. 279–80.

Orphans of the Street is decidedly a family film. This "original" treatment and script occupied West from October 10, 1937, to January 7, 1938, although his work earned him no screen credit. "Orphaned Tommy Ryan is informed that the money from his father's estate has run out and he will have to leave the Holbrook Military Academy," give up his dog Skippy, and go to the State Home for Boys. The "two pals" escape and begin a series of adventures in which they solve a murder, win prize money, and finally "go proudly back to Military school." West had recently seen this script go into production when Matthew Josephson came to Hollywood, and he had it in mind when he told him ruefully: "I write grade-C scripts only—dog stories and such things for low pay. If the director's wife finds them sloppy enough, then they are accepted."

In the summer of 1937 West had written *Stormy Weather* as an "original treatment," and he returned to it from January 8 to January 12, 1938, to work on a script. "Ma Hooper, keeper of a student boarding house at Somerset College, gets into trouble when caught replacing a copy of examination questions which has been stolen by one of the boys, Dave Tucker. The latter has promised her not to enter the examination in question, but he breaks his promise and does not confess to having stolen the paper. His friend, Fred Allen, discovers the theft and deception, and exposes him just as he is about to play an important intercollege hockey game. Ma Hooper is cleared, and without Dave playing, Somerset loses the game."

Osceola. Discussed and summarized in text, pp. 280–1.

The Squealer. Discussed and summarized in text, pp. 282–3.

Five Came Back. Discussed and summarized in text, pp. 283–4.

Flight South. Discussed and summarized in text, pp. 284–5.

The Spirit of Culver. Discussed and summarized in text, pp. 359–61.

I Stole a Million. See text, pp. 361–3. Lester Cole based his original screen story for this film on a non-fiction article, "Roy Gardner's Own Story," by Roy Gardner, J. Campbell Bruce, and James G. Chestnutt, published in the San Francisco *Call Bulletin* in June and July 1938. The plot was summarized by one reviewer as follows: "Raft's ambitions innocently enmesh him with the law. From that minor infraction, he becomes involved in a bank holdup but tries to go straight when he falls in love with Claire Trevor. Finding the law on his trail and needing a stake for a small town hideaway, he knocks over a post office. With the money, he buys a village garage and settles down happily. . . . With a baby in the offing, the law picks up his trail again. . . . His warped mind sends him through a series of holdups . . . to gain enough plunder to provide for his wife and baby. But even that, he finds, is a mirage, and he prefers death from the guns of pursuing officers rather than face a prison term."

The Victoria Docks at Eight. See text, pp. 363–4.

Before the Fact. Discussed in text, pp. 365–6. After seven weeks, West and Ingster submitted a 133-page screenplay for *Before the Fact.* In it they start with the trial of Ellen McLaidlaw, Lady Aysgarth, for the murder of her husband Tony, and then make the movie Ellen's meditation and testimony on the events, beginning five years before, which led her to shoot her husband. "It may sound strange," she begins, "but it always seems to have started with a dream." She so retells the dream of her terrorization that her voice, meditating on past events, becomes as much a character as the younger Ellen on the screen before us. As the whole past comes back to her, we see what she, in her imagination and memory, sees. In this fashion she relives the nightmare of her marriage to a moral cripple, her feelings of helpless entrapment, even her willing surrender to her own murder. Only at the last, discovering that she is pregnant, does the will to live revive in her; she shoots Tony as he is about to force a poison upon her.

In Isles's novel, the heroine is finally killed. Ingster and West's solution to the problems of transmuting the novel into a film was to make her ultimate dream of life preserve her, while showing her deterioration, through fear, until the very last.

Men Against the Sky. This is the story of a former air "ace" and barnstorming pilot who has been finished as a flyer by drink. However, for his sister's sake he straightens out, and after she designs the world's fastest plane, it is he who risks his life to take it up and locate its weakness. At the end, in a crucial test, he takes another plane aloft to unjam the landing gear, but dies when his parachute is fouled in the plane's tail.

Let's Make Music. Discussed and summarized in text, pp. 367–8.

Stranger on the Third Floor. See text, p. 368.

A Cool Million: A Screen Story. Discussed and summarized in text, pp. 379–80.

Bird in Hand. This original treatment was summarized by the R.K.O. Story Department as follows: "When a young stockbroker wins a turkey in a raffle and then discovers that there is something unusual about this particular bird . . . three different people with three different stories try to get it away from him, and a woman is murdered in his apartment . . . he decides to solve the mystery. Clews take him from New York to Chicago and finally to California; he meets and falls in love with a girl. But in the end he learns the answer to the turkey mystery." The "answer," incredibly, is that the turkey is an army mascot and the secret U.S. bombsight formula is tattooed on its back.

Amateur Angel. Summarized in text, p. 381.

Notes on Sources

CHAPTER ONE

"West may not": Postcard in N.W. file in offices of New Directions, N.Y.C.

Eileen's watch: Hazel E. Livingston, *Reporter's Transcript in the Matter of the Inquisition into the Death of Eileen McKenney West and Nathanael West*, Dec. 22, 1940, El Centro, Calif., p. 12.

"it was a long ways from the highway": *Reporter's Transcript*, p. 8ff.

a photograph of the scene of the accident: *Imperial Valley Press*, El Centro, Calif., Dec. 23, 1940, p. 1.

"tossup between a sentimental gesture": *New York Weekly Variety*, CXLI, Dec. 25, 1940.

Information on effects in West's house is in *Probate of the Estate of Nathanael W. West*, Jan. 27, 1941, County of Los Angeles.

Wilson: "left two books": in a letter to S. J. Perelman of January, 1941.

"Had he gone on": "Day of the Locust," *Tomorrow*, X (Nov. 1950), p. 58.

Hyman: "one of the three finest": "Nathanael West," in *Seven Modern American Novelists*, ed. William Van O'Connor (Minneapolis, 1964), p. 246.

CHAPTER TWO

Ornitz, *Haunch, Paunch and Jowl* (New York, 1923), p. 105.

"less a contemporary of Queen Victoria": Leroy-Beaulieu, quoted in Richard Charques, *The Twilight of Imperial Russia* (Fairlawn, N.J.), p. 47.

loosely confined: Russo-Jewish Committee, *The Persecution of the Jews in Russia* (London, 1890), pp. 4–5; Stuart E. Rosenberg, *The Search for Jewish Identity in America* (Garden City, N.Y., 1965), p. 115.

Tolstoy and Andreyev: Leo Errera, *The Russian Jews: Extermina-*

tion or Emancipation (N.Y. and London, 1894), p. 20; "many Jewish families": *ibid.* p. 118.

Kovno was the district . . . center: John Szlupas, *Lithuania in Retrospect and Prospect* (N.Y., 1915), p. 140.

On Germans in Lithuania, see Constantine R. Jurgela, *Lithuania in a Twin Teutonic Cluth* (N.Y., 1945), pp. 66ff.

the Jewish faith was second: *Persecution of the Jews*, p. 34; E. J. Harrison, *Lithuania, 1928* (London, 1928), p. 5.

"Many Jewish artisans": Moses Rischin, *The Promised City: New York's Jews 1870–1914* (Cambridge, Mass., 1962), pp. 25–6.

Jews "were more competent": Rischin, *Promised City*, p. 27.

The forces that would flow together: Harrison, *Lithuania*, p. 6.

Adam Mickiewicz: *Lithuania, Land of the Nieman* (Moscow, 1959), pp. 140–2.

Zacharias Frankel: Rosenberg, *Jewish Identity*, p. 56.

"actual if not formal de-Judaization": Rischin, *Promised City*, p. 19.

If he failed to appear: M. G. Landsberg, *History of the Persecution of the Jews in Russia* (Boston, 1892), p. 29.

" 'America' was in everybody's mouth": Mary Antin, *From Plotzk to Boston* (Boston, 1899), pp. 11–12.

early immigrants: Mak Wischnitzer, *To Dwell in Safety* (Philadelphia, 1948), p. 332.

Jacob Riis: *How the Other Half Lives: Studies Among the Tenements of New York* (N.Y., 1890), p. 10.

His birth certificate: *State of New York Certificate and Record of Birth of Nathan Weinstein*, #55393.

Matthew Josephson: *Life Among the Surrealists* (N.Y., 1962), p. 17.

Hebrew Standard, quoted in Rischin, *Promised City*, p. 97.

CHAPTER THREE

Abraham Cahan's Yiddish newspaper, Rischin, *The Promised City*, p. 127.

"We pretended": Josephson, *Life Among the Surrealists*, p. 31.

"It is the fellow": *Magpie*, XIX (Oct. 1919), 17.

Like most satirists: see Leonard Feinberg, *The Satirist* (N.Y., 1965), p. 233ff.

A guest speaker at Clinton: *Clinton News*, X, 11 (April 22, 1920).

two million workers: Arthur L. Link, *American Epoch: A History of the United States Since the 1890's* (N.Y., 1955), p. 239; David K. Adams, *America in the Twentieth Century* (Cambridge, Mass., 1967), p. 223.

What the country needs, he said: Edmund Traverso, *The 20's: Rhetoric and Reality* (Boston, 1964), p. 41.

"to . . . bloviate": Marvin Barrett, *The Jazz Age* (N.Y., 1959), p. 28.

McAdoo quoted in Adams, *America in the Twentieth Century*, p. 230.

In this chapter I quote from *The Paradoxian* issues of August 1918, p. 6; November 1920, p. 23; July 1918, p. 6; November 1920, p. 21; November 1919, p. 15; November 1920, pp. 4, 6; August 1920, p. 28.

CHAPTER FOUR

Bliss Perry: *And Gladly Teach,* quoted in Halford E. Luccock, *American Mirror* (N.Y., 1940), p. 239.

College became: Barrett, *Jazz Age,* p. 52; Charles Merz, *The Great American Band-Wagon* (N.Y., 1939), pp. 106–7.

The Brown fraternities: *By Quentin Reynolds* (N.Y., 1963), p. 42.

weekly attendance at movie houses: Robert B. Weaver, *Amusements and Sports in American Life* (Chicago, 1939), pp. 93–4.

CHAPTER FIVE

"a nice touch": Quentin Reynolds, *By Quentin Reynolds,* p. 45–8; "learned and humorous," pp. 58–9.

"My lady's eyes": *The Brown Jug,* Dec. 1922, p. 24.

Perelman, "The Exquisites": *Casements,* 1924, p. 14.

Joseph Freeman: *An American Testament* (N.Y., 1936), p. 285.

"How did you get that name?": William Carlos Williams, *Autobiography* (N.Y., 1951), p. 301.

Rosenberg: *Jewish Identity,* p. 74.

"high degree of intellectualism": Alexander M. Dushkin, *Jewish Education in New York City* (N.Y., 1918), p. 37.

"brought with them": Rischin, *Promised City,* p. 143.

Ford and Rogers quoted in Barrett, *Jazz Age,* p. 132.

T. S. Eliot: *New York Times,* Mar. 30, 1959.

by 1926 the Left Bank: Williams, *Autobiography,* p. 190.

McAlmon told him: Josephson, *Life Among the Surrealists,* p. 88.

Comments by Hilaire Hiler on West are from: Hiler, letter to Kay Boyle, April 7, 1960; and Ms. "Reminiscence of Henry Miller," both in *The Archives of American Art,* Detroit, Mich.; and Hiler, letter to Robert McAlmon, Jan. 30, 1941, in possession of Norman Holmes Pearson.

McAlmon: "fanciful freedom": Robert E. Knoll, *Robert McAlmon: Expatriate Publisher and Writer* (Lincoln, Neb., 1957), pp. 11–12; in a survey conducted in 1928.

Margaret Anderson: *My Thirty Years' War* (N.Y., 1943), p. 3.

CHAPTER SIX

Burke and Chevalier, quoted in Feinberg, *The Satirist*, pp. 42, 147.

Physically, he "moved slowly": Joseph Schrank, "Pep," *New York Times*, Jan. 10, 1957.

This period . . . "was uniquely": Leo Gurko, *The Angry Decade* (N.Y., 1947), pp. 13–14.

Edmund Wilson, quoted in Daniel Aaron, *Writers on the Left* (N.Y., 1961), p. 109.

Mencken, quoted in Feinberg, *Satirist*, p. 286.

Norman Thomas, quoted in Adams, *America in the Twentieth Century*, p. 273.

George Jean Nathan, quoted in Malcolm Cowley, *After the Genteel Tradition* (N.Y., 1937), pp. 218–19.

the International Union of Revolutionary Writers: Deming Brown, *Soviet Attitudes Toward American Writing* (Princeton, 1962), p. 37.

Michael Gold, quoted in Aaron, *Writers on the Left*, pp. 97–8.

Daniel Aaron: *Writers on the Left*, p. 75.

Matthew Josephson: *Life Among the Surrealists*, p. 241.

Roosevelt and Barkley, quoted in William Leuchtenburg, *F.D.R. and the New Deal* (N.Y., 1963), pp. 342–3.

Archibald MacLeish, quoted in Luccock, *American Mirror*, pp. 213–14.

"Nihilism," quoted in Leuchtenburg, *FDR*, p. 342.

W. W. Gibson, quoted in Luccock, *American Mirror*, p. 215.

Murray Kempton: *Part of Our Time* (N.Y., 1955), p. 146.

Hoover, speech accepting the Republican nomination, August 11, 1928, in Palo Alto, California.

Breton, quoted in Josephson, *Surrealists*, p. 226.

"A Barefaced Lie," *Overland Monthly and Out West Magazine*, LXXXVII (July 1929), pp. 210, 219.

Platon Brounoff, quoted in Rischin, *Promised City*, p. 140.

CHAPTER SEVEN

McAlmon: *McAlmon and the Lost Generation*, ed. Robert E. Knoll (Lincoln, Neb., 1962), pp. 185, 305.

"English humor," it announces: "Through the Hole in the Mundane Millstone," pamphlet advertisement for *The Dream Life of Balso Snell.*

Josephson, *Surrealists*, pp. 225, 332–3, 140.

number of people emigrating: Frederick Lewis Allen, *Since Yesterday* (N.Y. and London, 1940), p. 212.

Nicholas Murray Butler, quoted in Charles and Mary Beard, *America in Midpassage* (N.Y., 1939), p. 115.

"look at life from a basement": Halford E. Luccock, *Contemporary American Literature and Religion* (Chicago and N.Y., 1934), pp. 171–2.

Paterson I–IV (N.Y., 1948), pp. 220–1.

"distinctly encouraging features": Edward Angly, *Oh Yeah* (N.Y., 1931), p. 25.

Josephine Herbst, *A Hunter of Doves, Botteghe Oscure*, XIII (1954), p. 330.

CHAPTER EIGHT

one "continuous magazine": Williams, *Autobiography*, p. 266.

"We seek only", Robert E. Knoll, *Robert McAlmon: Expatriate Publisher and Writer*, p. 39.

"I decided": *ibid.*, p. 24.

"it represents": "The Advance Guard Magazine," *Contact*, I, 1 (Feb. 1932), p. 90.

"A New American Writer," *Il Mare*, Rapallo, XI (Jan. 21, 1933); translated by John Erwin.

Josephine Herbst, *Hunter*, p. 321.

CHAPTER NINE

Josephine Herbst, *Hunter*, p. 321.

begging on the streets: Gurko, *Angry Decade*, p. 58.

From three or four million: E. David Cronon, *Twentieth Century America* (Homewood, Ill., 1965), p. 254.

32,000 families: "No One Has Starved," *Fortune*, VI (Sept. 1932), 21ff.

Rexford Tugwell, quoted in Leuchtenburg, *FDR*, p. 19.

Philippe Soupault: "La grande inquiétude des paysans et les calmes des cités industrielles américaines," *L'Europe Nouvelle*, XIV (1931), pp. 1148–51.

Elmer Davis, quoted in Leuchtenburg, *FDR*, pp. 26–7.

MacLeish: *Land of the Free* (N.Y., 1938), p. 88.

W. H. Auden, "Interlude: West's Disease," *The Dyer's Hand and Other Essays* (N.Y., 1962), p. 241.

Theodore Dreiser, quoted in Lloyd R. Morris, *Postscript to Yesterday* (N.Y., 1962), p. 266.

circulation at the free public libraries: Adams, *America in the Twentieth Century*, p. 357.

"lonesome girls were enabled": Simon M. Bessie, *Jazz Journalism* (N.Y., 1938), p. 201.

Heated interests: James D. Horan, *The Desperate Years* (N.Y., 1962), p. 134.

the largest salary: Henry Morton Robinson, *Fantastic Interim* (N.Y., 1943), p. 271.

jigsaw puzzle craze: Horan, *Desperate Years*, p. 166.

secret orders: Merz, *Band-Wagon*, pp. 23–4.

"Go to a motion picture": Quoted in Robert S. Lynd and Helen M. Lynd, *Middletown* (N.Y., 1929), p. 265.

"authentic portrayals of life": Herbert Blumer, *Movies and Conduct* (N.Y., 1933), pp. 198–9.

twenty million people: Merz, *Band-Wagon*, pp. 174–5, 169.

Rosenfeld, "Faulkner and His Contemporaries," *Partisan Review*, XVIII (Jan.–Feb. 1951), 428.

Canby, quoted in Luccock, *American Mirror*, p. 153.

Josephine Herbst, *Hunter*, p. 321.

"Indeed, the public world": Leuchtenburg, *FDR*, p. 342, quoting Archibald MacLeish.

as a historian: Leuchtenburg, *FDR*, p. 342.

CHAPTER TEN

Liveright himself: Louis Kronenberger, "Gambler in Publishing: Horace Liveright," *Atlantic*, CCXV (1965), pp. 94–104.

"success," Lionel Trilling says: "Afterword" to Tess Slesinger, *The Unpossessed* (N.Y., 1966 [1934]), pp. 313–14.

Barton's book sold 726,892 copies.

Henry Ford, Ruth McKenney, and Kenneth Burke, quoted in Luccock, *American Mirror*, pp. 249, 247–8.

increasingly powerful and numerous followers: Morris, *Postscript to Yesterday*, p. 423ff; Robinson, *Fantastic Interim*, p. 203.

"Once inside": Paul Sann, *The Lawless Decade* (N.Y., 1960), p. 191.

"This is Mrs. ———": "Women Threaten to Sue Lovelorn Letters Author," *West Warwick R. I. Times*, May 3, 1933 (INS, May 2, 1933).

"Lonely Heart," copyrighted by the Irving Berlin Music Corp.

"Psychology has nothing to do": "Some Notes on Miss L.," *Contempo*, III, 9 (May 15, 1933), p. 2.

"all rights of the contract": *New York Evening Post*, May 10, 1933.

Only a month before publication: Beard, *America in Midpassage*, pp. 155–6; Roosevelt, quoted p. 210.

Fifteen million persons: Horan, *Desperate Years*, pp. 133–4.

CHAPTER ELEVEN

a critical symposium: in *Contempo*, III, 3 (July 25, 1933): Bob Brown, "Go West, Young Writer," pp. 4–5; Williams, "Sordid? Good God!," pp. 5, 8; Josephine Herbst, "Miss Lonelyhearts: An Allegory," p. 4; Angel Flores, "Miss Lonelyhearts in the Haunted Castle," p. 1; S. J. Perelman, "Nathanael West: A Portrait," p. 2.

A Hollywood gossip columnist: Lee Shippey, "The Lee Side O' L.A.," *Los Angeles Times*, Part II, July 26, 1933, p. 4.

None of this was uncommon: John Paddy Carstairs, *Movie Merry-Go-Round* (London, 1937), p. 56.

membership in the Screen Writers Guild: West's membership card in files of the Writers Guild of America, West.

"men who used to write": Carstairs, *Movie*, pp. 66–7; Leo Rosten, *Hollywood: The Movie Colony, The Movie Makers* (N.Y., 1941), p. 313.

Harrison's Reports: P. S. Harrison, *Harrison's Reports: A Motion Picture Reviewing Service Devoted Chiefly to the Interests of the Exhibitors*, XV, 34 (Aug. 26, 1933), pp. 133, 136.

To appease newspapermen: *New York Times*, Oct. 9, 1933.

One gossip columnist: Jimmy Starr, "Norman Taurog to Direct . . . ," *Los Angeles Herald Express*, Aug. 29, 1933.

"that delightful Disney": *New York Times*, Dec. 19, 1933.

"It is obviously": *New York Times*, Dec. 14, 1933.

". . . by William Shakespeare": Deems Taylor, *Pictorial History of the Movies* (N.Y., 1943), p. 214.

the two most popular movies: Mark Sherwin and Charles Lam Markmann, *One Week in March* (N.Y., 1961), p. 169.

Rouben Mamoulian: Beard, *America in Midpassage*, pp. 594–5.

"marginal and shabby": Rosten, *Hollywood*, p. 67.

"a fantastic maze": Beard, *Midpassage*, p. 589.

"escape, opiate": Sherwin and Markmann, *One Week in March*, p. 167.

regularity . . . fixed charges: Mae D. Huettig, *Economic Control of the Motion Picture Industry* (Philadelphia, 1941), p. 67–9.

The five "major" studios: *ibid.*, pp. 86, 91.

Sinclair Lewis's *It Can't Happen Here*: Ernest Sutherland Bates and Alan Williams, *American Hurly-Burly* (N.Y., 1937), p. 262.

"Winning Another's Love": Edgar Dale, *The Content of Motion Pictures* (N.Y., 1935), pp. 178–85.

Lynds, quoted in George Bluestone, *Novels Into Film* (Baltimore, 1957), pp. 38–9.

Alfred Kazin: *Starting Out in the Thirties* (Boston, 1965), pp. 87–8.

Alvah Bessie: *Inquisition in Eden* (N.Y., 1965), pp. 105–6.

"In this town": Rosten, *Hollywood*, p. 40.

Freeman, quoted in Kempton, *Part of Our Time*, p. 191.

Peter Drucker, quoted in Allen, *Since Yesterday*, pp. 55–6.

"We are Americans": *Americana*, I, 4 (Nov. 1932) [mistakenly marked I, no. 1], p. 2.

"Business Deal," I, 11 (Oct. 1933), pp. 14–15.

"Miss Klingspiel": *Hollywood Reporter*, March 15, 1932, pp. 9, 38.

"Social Viewpoint in Art": Sherwin and Markmann, *One Week in March*, p. 207.

Dos Passos's description: "Introduction" to George Grosz, *Interregnum* (N.Y., 1936), p. 18.

William Z. Foster had polled: Link, *American Epoch*, p. 379.

America, America: *New York Daily Variety*, Sept. 19, 1933.

CHAPTER TWELVE

Coffey, in Aiken's *Conversation*, Bodenheim's *Crazy Man*, Miss Herbst's "A New Break," and Williams's "An Early Martyr."

Aaron: *Writers on the Left*, pp. 270–1.

Gold: "like soldiers": quoted in *ibid.*, pp. 163–4.

Kempton: *Part of Our Time*, p. 1.

Hoover, quoted in Allen, *Since Yesterday*, p. 94.

gross annual income of farmers: Beard, *America in Midpassage*, p. 65.

Humbert Wolfe: quoted in Feinberg, *Satirist*, pp. 175–6.

East European Jews: Rischin, *Promised City*, p. 175.

"Hold fast": *ibid.*, p. 75.

Gold: *Jews Without Money* (N.Y., 1930), pp. 109–10.

Dr. Faunce preach: By Quentin Reynolds, p. 44.

Coolidge, quoted in Adams, *America in the Twentieth Century*, pp. 243–4.

Senate banking and currency investigation: Allen, *Since Yesterday*, p. 168.

"was in reality": Ferdinand Pecora, *Wall Street Under Oath* (N.Y., 1939), p. 263.

"the present system": *Time*, XXIII (April 16, 1933), p. 18.

New York rabbis: Gurko, *Angry Decade*, p. 41.

Berle and Wallace: Leuchtenburg, *FDR*, pp. 33, 347.

"a cooperative commonwealth": *ibid.*, pp. 95–6.

"each individual sub-man": *ibid.*, p. 340.

Roosevelt told reporters: Cronon, *Twentieth Century America*, pp. 218–19.

"the great mass of Americans": Hiram Wesley Evans, "The Imperial Wizard Defends the Klan," *North American Review* (1926), pp. 33–63.

The Klan had spawned: In my account below of semi-Fascist organizations, I refer to Bates and Williams, *American Hurly-Burly*, p. 255; Travis Hoke, *Shirts* (N.Y., 1934), pp. 23–4; Harold Lavine, *Fifth Column in America* (N.Y., 1940), pp. 64–5; Dumas Malone, *War and Troubled Peace* (N.Y., 1965), p. 271; Louis M. Hacker, *United States in the Twentieth Century* (N.Y., 1952), p. 360; Mencken quoted in Leuchtenburg, *FDR*, p. 98; Hoke, pp. 5, 24, 25; Lavine, p. 171–8; 205–8; Hoke, pp. 7–12.

a European visitor: Odette Kahn, quoted in Luccock, *American Mirror*, pp. 20–1.

made his novel out of fragments: I am indebted to the article by Douglas H. Shepard, "Nathanael West Rewrites Horatio Alger, Jr.," *Satire Newsletter*, III, 1 (Fall 1965), pp. 13–28.

CHAPTER THIRTEEN

"Vote Red": motto which Edmund Wilson saw chalked on a West Congress Street, Chicago, wall; see Wilson, *The American Earthquake* (Garden City, 1958), p. 464.

West was not able to be present: New York *World-Telegram*, June 20, 1934.

the Columbia Story Department: Lee Satinson, "Report on *A Cool Million*," June 12, 1934, 6 pp., Columbia Pictures files.

Thomas Hart Benton, quoted in Adams, *America in the Twentieth Century*, p. 355.

"Chapt. I": *Contempo*, III (May 15, 1933), p. 2.

"Jewish writers": "Afterword," *Unpossessed*, pp. 320–1.

Edwin Seaver: "The Proletarian Novel," *American Writers Congress*, ed. Henry Hart (N.Y., 1935), p. 101.

Granville Hicks: *The Great Tradition* (N.Y., 1933), pp. 319, 267.

V. F. Calverton, quoted in Luccock, *American Mirror*, p. 149.

Alfred Kazin: *Starting Out in the Thirties*, p. 73.
"From Shirtsleeves to Shirtsleeves": "Soft Soap for the Barber," *New Republic*, LXXXI (Nov. 14, 1934), p. 23.
This manifesto: *American Writers Congress*, p. 10.
"a young man": Kazin, *Starting Out*, p. 51.

CHAPTER FOURTEEN
signed a contract: Republic Productions files. Details on West's film-writing come from the files in these offices, where his scripts for Republic reside, and where I read them.
a list of the literary works: N. W. West to Mr. Glick, letter dated April 20, 1937; Republic files.
Federal Reserve Board index, Leuchtenburg, *FDR*, p. 256.
monographs and reports: Allen, *Since Yesterday*, p. 210.
Lorentz's films: Bates and Williams, *American Hurly-Burly*, p. 151.
a contemporary observer noted: Wilson, *The American Earthquake*, p. 399.
said "not to be uncommon": Howard T. Lewis, *The Motion Picture Industry* (N.Y., 1933), pp. 132–3.
many prominent writers: Murray Rose, *Stars and Strikes: Unionization of Hollywood* (N.Y., 1941), pp. 62–3, 53, 102, 175.
Madeleine Carroll: Introduction to Carstairs, *Movie*, p. 12.
F. Scott Fitzgerald, quoted in Josephson, *Surrealists*, p. 365.
"Nobody," as Alvah Bessie said: Bessie, *Inquisition*, p. 126.
Daniel Fuchs, quoted in *ibid.*, p. 35.
165 Hollywood writers: Rosten, *Hollywood*, p. 322–3.
he talked, McAlmon says: Robert McAlmon to Norman Holmes Pearson, Aug. 3, 1953; June 10, 1954. Possession of Norman Holmes Pearson.

CHAPTER FIFTEEN
"some three hundred organizations": Robinson, *Fantastic Interim*, p. 190.
"unconditional opposition": quoted in Hicks, *The Great Tradition*, pp. 131–2.
Veterans of Future Wars: Kempton, *Part of Our Time*, p. 302.
a Gallup poll: Link, *American Epoch*, p. 464.
the Nye committee: Leuchtenburg, *FDR*, pp. 217–18.
"the busiest week": *New York Times*, Nov. 21, 1938.
70 percent of Americans: Link, *American Epoch*, p. 469, reporting the results of a Gallup poll.
Roosevelt told: Leuchtenburg, *FDR*, p. 285.

CHAPTER SIXTEEN

suicide rate: Wilson, *The American Earthquake*, p. 418.

In January 1934: on Townsend, see Link, *American Epoch*, p. 401; Allen, *Since Yesterday*, pp. 189–90; Robinson, *Fantastic Interim*, p. 254; Leuchtenburg, *FDR*, pp. 16, 104; Wilson, *American Earthquake*, p. 383, Bates and Williams, *American Hurly-Burly*, p. 185.

The 1930 census revealed: Hacker, *United States*, p. 455.

"Stop! you're speeding": Morris, *Postscript*, pp. 435–6.

"And the Be-Happy": Wilson, *Earthquake*, p. 381.

"Bird and Bottle": *Pacific Weekly*, V (1936), pp. 329–31.

as Bertrand Russell put it: Russell, *The ABC of Relativity* (London, 1925), p. 55.

William Dean Howells: "Howells Fears Realists Must Wait," *New York Times*, Oct. 28, 1894.

as Edmund Wilson remarks: "Hollywood Dance of Death," *New Republic*, LXXXIX (July 26, 1939), pp. 339–40.

Land of the Free, pp. 83–4.

the horse-racing fever: Rosten, *Hollywood*, p. 212.

earliest description of Faye: "Bird and Bottle," 330.

"the most lawless country": quoted in Aaron, *Writers*, p. 111.

John Hawkes: "Fiction Today," *Massachusetts Review*, III (1962), 787.

William Carlos Williams accurately observed: "Day of the Locust," *Tomorrow*, 58.

CHAPTER SEVENTEEN

Harry Elmer Barnes: *Society in Transition* (N.Y., 1939), p. 946.

Alfred Kazin: *Starting*, p. 139.

"Every anti-Fascist": quoted in Aaron, *Writers*, p. 156.

Mary McCarthy, quoted in Leuchtenburg, *FDR*, p. 282.

"affluence breeds ennui": Frank S. Nugent and Douglas Churchill, "Graustark," *We Saw It Happen*, ed. H. W. Baldwin and Shepard Stone (N.Y., 1939), p. 130.

Western Writers Congress: *Congress of Western Writers for Democracy and Creative Freedom*, pamphlet announcement, 4 pp.

Carey McWilliams: "Western Writers Congress," *Pacific Weekly*, V (Oct. 19, 1936), p. 243.

the *Weekly* announced twice: on Sept. 7, 1936, and Nov. 9, 1936.

Hollywood round-table: "Western Writers Congress," *Pacific Weekly*, V (Nov. 9, 1936), p. 309.

the House Patents Committee: John Cogley, *Report on Blacklisting: I: Movies* (N.Y., 1956), p. 57.

"a man who joins a union": *Ibid.*, pp. 58–9.

a NLRB consent election: Rose, *Stars and Strikes*, pp. 183–4, 186; Rosten, *Hollywood*, pp. 318–19.

Eugene Lyons: *The Red Decade*, quoted in Cogley, *Blacklisting*, p. 27.

proto-Fascist organizations: Rosten, *Hollywood*, p. 139; Gurko, *Angry Decade*, p. 105.

New Year's card for 1940: Cogley, *Blacklisting*, pp. 38–9.

"a warm Siberia": Rosten, *Hollywood*, p. 34.

"cultural technicians": Cogley, *Blacklisting*, pp. 24–5; Roy Erwin quoted, p. 29.

Scott Fitzgerald, quoted in Kempton, *Part of Our Time*, p. 194.

Dorothy Parker, quoted in Rosten, *Hollywood*, p. 183.

West's doctor diagnosed: medical records, Cedars of Lebanon Hospital, Los Angeles, Roger Panther administrator. Admitted 10/8/39, discharged 10/20/39.

"cut costs mercilessly": Rosten, *Hollywood*, p. 257.

CHAPTER EIGHTEEN

". . . my origins": Ruth McKenney, *All About Eileen* (N.Y., 1952), p. 237.

"a seventeen-room . . . castle": Ruth McKenney, *Love Story* (N.Y., 1950), p. 9.

Lionel Trilling: "Afterword," *Unpossessed*, pp. 314–15.

"I met a man": *Love Story*, pp. 175–6.

West and Eileen were married: Certificate of Marriage, County of Los Angeles, April 19, 1940.

"Oh, I'm so *happy*": *Love Story*, p. 176.

"long-windedness in conversation": Henry Dan Piper, *F. Scott Fitzgerald* (N.Y., 1965), p. 225.

"a vehicle for Eddie Cantor": Columbia Pictures Story Department Report, Jan. 1, 1941.

CHAPTER NINETEEN

"to preach at people": Morris, *Postscript to Yesterday*, pp. 150–1.

Fitzgerald had been: some details of the mutual literary influence between West and Fitzgerald I take from Robert S. Phillips, "Fitzgerald and *The Day of the Locust*," *Fitzgerald Newsletter*, No. 15 (Fall, 1961), pp. 2–3; David D. Galloway, "Nathanael West's Dream Dump," *Critique*, VI (1963–4), pp. 61–2; and William Bittner, "A la recherche d'un écrivain perdu," *Les Langues Modernes*, LIV (1960), p. 282.

a local wit quipped: William Bledsoe, in *The American Mercury*; quoted in Cogley, *Blacklisting*, p. 25–6.

"miseries of the lettuce worker": James Rorty, *Where Life Is Better* (N.Y., 1936), pp. 294–5.

W. H. Auden: "West's Disease," 238.

Norman Podhoretz, "Nathanael West: A Particular Kind of Joking," *Doings and Undoings: The Fifties and After in American Writing* (N.Y., 1964), p. 75.

admired Turgenev's: S. J. Perelman, "Go West," *New York Times*, March 24, 1957.

"Death": *Casements*, II, 4 (May 1924).

Index

* In this entry, the letter *q* indicates *quoted*.